ISLAM IN THE MODERN NATIONAL STATE

BY THE SAME AUTHOR

Averroes' Commentary on Plato's Republic
(Cambridge, 1956)

Political Thought in Medieval Islam
(Cambridge, 1958)

ISLAM IN THE MODERN NATIONAL STATE

BY

ERWIN I. J. ROSENTHAL

Reader in Oriental Studies in the University of Cambridge and Fellow of Pembroke College

CAMBRIDGE
AT THE UNIVERSITY PRESS
1965

PUBLISHED BY
THE SYNDICS OF THE CAMBRIDGE UNIVERSITY PRESS

Bentley House, 200 Euston Road, London, N.W. 1
American Branch: 32 East 57th Street, New York, N.Y. 10022
West African Office: P.M.B. 5181, Ibadan, Nigeria

Printed in Great Britain at the University Printing House, Cambridge
(Brooke Crutchley, University Printer)

LIBRARY OF CONGRESS CATALOGUE
CARD NUMBER: 66–13638

To

ARTHUR J. ARBERRY

For his sixtieth birthday

CONTENTS

Introduction *page* ix
Acknowledgements xxi
Abbreviations xxii
Note on transliteration xxii

PART I CONTEMPORARY ISLAM IN CRISIS AND TRANSITION

SECTION 1

1 The Human Situation 3
2 Classical Foundations 12

SECTION 2 ISLAMIC OR MODERN NATIONAL STATE?

3 Islam and Turkish Nationalism 28
4 For and against the *Khilāfa* 64
5 Islam and Arab Nationalism 103
6 An Islamic State for Pakistan? 125
7 ʻAllāl al-Fāsī: a Blend of Islam and Arab Nationalism 154

PART II ISLAM IN THE MODERN NATIONAL STATE

SECTION 1 CONSTITUTIONAL ISSUES

8 The Islamic Republic of Pakistan 181
Appendix: Some Reflections on Islam in India today 282
9 Islam in Malaya 287
10 Some observations on Islam in Iran and Turkey 307
11 Islam in Tunisia and Morocco 316

CONTENTS

SECTION 2 CHANGES IN LAW AND THE EMANCIPATION OF WOMEN

12 Changes in Law *page* 332

13 The Emancipation of Women 338

SECTION 3 THE PLACE OF ISLAM IN NATIONAL EDUCATION

14 Islam and Education in Pakistan 344

Appendix: Some Remarks on Religious Education in Malaya 359

15 Islam and National Arabic Education in Tunisia and Morocco 362

Epilogue 373

Notes 376

Select Bibliography 394

Index 404

INTRODUCTION

The study and research on constitutional theory and law, which led to this book, were carried out under a grant from the Rockefeller Foundation, to which I am grateful. The book attempts to relate the findings of my study visits to some Muslim countries to the human situation of our time in general, and in particular in the countries visited during 1960/61 and 1962: Pakistan, India, Malaya, Iran, and Turkey for eight months; and Tunisia and Morocco for three months.

It soon became clear, in the rapidly changing situation, that my personal impressions, received in interviews and discussions on formal and many more informal occasions, would have to be set against each country's historical background and the currents of thought and events leading to its achievement of separate nationhood and independence. To avoid subjective and transitory deductions, fundamental issues had to be clarified. This required time and concentration, both difficult to find in the midst of heavy teaching and administrative duties. An immense and growing literature on the Middle East and South-East Asia had to be studied, and consequently the writing of this book proceeded slowly, with many interruptions. What is offered here is necessarily tentative, for personal as well as objective reasons that must be briefly stated.

Without sympathy and determination to understand the complexities of the situation, of which intellectual uncertainty and uneasy groping for a solution are the most important elements, the Western student of Islam cannot hope to survey and assess the contemporary scene in Muslim or predominantly Muslim modern national states. Moreover, he is acutely conscious that Western civilisation—which Muslims understand largely through the activities and behaviour of their former Western masters—is widely held responsible for the present spiritual crisis and its attendant practical difficulties. He must expect suspicion and resentment, and these are certainly justified to a high degree. The present writer wishes therefore to express his deep appreciation for the friendliness, the warmth, and the generous hospitality with which he was received by many men and women in all walks of life. They willingly answered his questions and discussed with him the spiritual and material problems which they as Muslims have to grapple with in a society whose majority suffers from poverty and illiteracy.

Suspicion, resentment—these personal attitudes do reflect certain objective facts that aggravated, if they did not actually create, the problems at the time of liberation and the attainment of sovereign independence. Conquest or occupation imported alien concepts and institutions and presented challenges which a more or less static Muslim society has been ill-prepared to meet and turn to its own advantage, both spiritually and materially. Colonialism and imperialism are deeply embedded in their consciousness as predominantly evil manifestations of the West, which is moreover different from them in religion and morals, in economic aims and practices, in political and social organisation. It requires time, effort and patience to make the benefits of our civilisation outbalance the acutely felt and bitterly resented disadvantages and hurts.

To gain a fair picture of the existing situation, we must realise that Muslims' attitudes and reactions are well-founded. We cannot discount widely prevalent anti-Westernism as an exaggeration, or as a way of side-stepping, consciously or unconsciously, a great challenge. It is true that self-criticism is not very much in evidence; this is to a large part the result of the legacy we left behind. Let me hasten to add, however, that Western-trained and -educated intellectuals by no means lack this necessary element of self-criticism —in contrast to the rigid traditionalists, whose backward gaze separates them not only from these intellectuals but also from the progressive, though traditionally educated, religious and political leaders like 'Allāl al-Fāsī.

The problem of adjusting a medieval culture and civilisation to the outlook and institutions moulded in the West, which have come to influence and determine contemporary state and society, is aggravated by the deeply felt need of these states to preserve their Islamic identity, both as individuals and as nations. This is the principal subject of this book.

A further complication is the challenge of Communism, understood by the younger generation of Muslims as an alternative ideology to Islam. Hence the stress, especially in Pakistan, on an Islamic *ideology*. Further, it is not realised by Muslims generally that it might be wrong to identify the West as it is today with

Christianity, overlooking the fact that the West itself is caught up in a grave spiritual crisis: one that is challenging not only faith, but also the once universally accepted absolute values of religion and rationalist ethics. Because it is either religion or humanism that must provide modern man with a spiritual centre, the Muslim intellectual believer, as well as the agnostic, must ask the fateful question "What is Islam?" before he can decide what part Islam is to play in his modern national state. For the administration of that state, and its political and economic stability, he must look to the West, which only yesterday was his enemy and today is not only his teacher, but also—to his mind—the cause of his inner conflicts and the source of many difficulties, cultural, social and economic.

My journey was undertaken to study this great human problem: this unparalleled challenge to Islam (and to all religions, but particularly to those based on revelation). Personal contact with heads of state, ministers, civil servants, staff and students in universities and schools, religious leaders, judges, scholars, leading citizens, thinkers and artists, and with the famous "man (and woman)-in-the-street", soon convinced me that the heart of the matter was the question, what is Islam? Is it personal faith, piety, and devotion, or is it a religious and political unity for the community of believers? If the former, then Islam has no role to play in the public life of a modern Muslim state, and it is unnecessary to confirm or refute the views of individuals who think so. Recourse to the classical exposition of the tenets of Islam, or to the history of Islam and its cultural achievements, would be irrelevant. The dangers and pitfalls inherent in the written records—their rationalisation of historical events, of art and literature—would not exist; and the journey could be dismissed as the interesting, enriching, personal experience of a Western student of Islam. But if Islam is both a system of beliefs and practices and a law for the community of believers, then its relevance to the modern Muslim state and society is incontestable.

The crucial question is whether Islam should serve as a guide and inspiring ideal, or as the rule of life—the constitution of the state whose law is to be the *Sharī'a*. With our scholarly urge to classify movements and their adherents, it is hard to label the adherents of either of these two answers. At this introductory stage, let us call the champions of an Islamic "ideology" liberal Muslims, and the others traditionalists of varying degrees of orthodoxy. Both terms are utterly inadequate and imprecise. But "fundamentalists", "orthodox", "modernists" and "secularists", though more differentiating, are also far from precise or correct. Why this should be will become clearer, it is hoped, in the first part of the book, "Contemporary Islam in Crisis and Transition", which deals with the human situation in *some* newly independent Muslim states.

The crisis of modern Islam is similar to, yet also fundamentally different from, the crisis of Christianity (and Judaism) in the West. Inasmuch as faith has become largely problematical, both in individual and in collective life, in men's attitudes and practices, Islam faces the same challenge as Christianity does. The unity of "religion" and "politics", essential in classical Islam down to the threshold of the present century, has now largely disappeared, or breaks down in practice where it is still maintained in theory. That the theory *is* still alive accounts for the difference between Islam and the West from the French Revolution onward.

A second and crucial difference is that Islam has never experienced a Reformation resulting in basic, radical reforms. It has had its reformers, but they aimed rather at the purification and restoration of Islam as practised by Muḥammad, his companions, and first successors.

Therefore we witness today a vulnerable Islam gradually giving way before a secular nationalism. This nationalism reached Muslim lands in the wake of the French Revolution, and it has been felt in two ways: in the realm of ideas, and through foreign domination and influence in the era of imperialism and colonialism. The resulting situation is very complex, yet it is essential to analyse it carefully and dispassionately, the more so since we are at least in part responsible for it. It is not for us to prescribe the remedy. In their scholarly quest for truth, Western students of contemporary Islam can easily be mistaken for "neo-colonialists", especially if they usurp the role of critic and judge. We must try to find the internal and external causes of an existing situation. Even here, not everybody can write such an understanding and penetrating analysis as Sir Hamilton Gibb achieved in his *Modern Trends in Islam*.

By describing from observation a specific, limited problem, it is hoped that a modest contribution can be made to a better understanding of the place of Islam in contemporary national and international life. We therefore take our bearings from the classical political thought in Islam (as set out in my *Political Thought in Medieval Islam*), the better to appreciate the so-called "modernist" movement in modern Islam. We can observe two trends, represented on the Arab side by Rashīd Riḍā and 'Ali 'Abd al-Rāziq. Their writings may serve as patterns for what we would like to call the Islamic and the Muslim states—adopting Ibn Khaldūn's distinction between *khilāfa* (the state based on the *Sharī'a* of Islam) and the "Islamic" *mulk* (the state with a mixed constitution, based on the *Sharī'a and* on the political laws of the ruler). This distinction seems to me to be especially important in the context of the discussion proceeding in Pakistan today between those who want to build up a modern state under the guidance of Islamic ideals, and those who prefer an Islamic state in the strict sense of the term. The conflict is not confined to Pakistan, though for good reasons it is agitating the leaders and intellectuals there more strongly.

Next follows a brief consideration of how the classical medieval position has been corroded by Western philosophy, especially political philosophy, and by Western domination in the nineteenth and first half of the twentieth centuries. The principal result of this twofold challenge is a division of opinion among modern Muslims and a consequent difference in their attitudes and allegiance to Islam. The classical concept of Islam's religious and political unity is now threatened by the notion—arising from the effects of the French Revolution—of the separation of religion and politics.

Despite the inroads this doctrine has made, and despite the spread of nationalist movements, Islam is still to a large extent the one unifying bond amidst ethnic, social, and cultural diversity. Yet I have the distinct impression that secularising or at least laicising tendencies are in the ascendant and are gaining momentum from the political and economic needs and stresses in these newly independent national states. This more than anything else raises the question of the value and efficacy of Islam in our time. For this reason, and insofar as I could obtain accurate information, the views of "traditionalists" of varying shades, of liberals, laicists, and secularists will be discussed in relation to the measures already taken or planned by the governments of the several Muslim states visited. Thus, the first part shows the conflict—in the minds of the intellectuals—between an intellectual orientation towards the West and a strong emotional attachment to Islam, if not as a faith, then as a cultural heritage and a significant historical fact that forms an integral part of a Muslim's being.

The second part, "Islam in the Modern National State", will illustrate this twilight. It is first concerned with constitutional theory and law in contemporary Islam, and here such questions as sovereignty, authority and power will be treated, always from an Islamic angle. Next, the role of society will be discussed; Islamic public law and legislation in modern Muslim states will be touched upon by contrasting the Islamic and the Muslim states. Then the status and position of minorities will be reviewed, followed by a brief report on the position of women in state, society and family. Certain national differences will emerge, depending on whether the newly independent state was formerly under British rule and influence (Pakistan and Malaya) or under French rule or occupation (Tunisia and Morocco). With the point of reference always the Islamic teachings on the subject, changes under foreign influence, as well as internal reforms due to a renewed interest in and revival of Muslim ethics, will be briefly described.

Finally, and perhaps of overriding importance if we take a long-term view, national education will be viewed in terms of Islam and its role in the public life of modern Muslim states. Islam is, if no longer all-embracing, then at least a formative influence in the education of the future good citizen; and as a cultural heritage it may well be or become the spiritual content of what was once *political* nationalism. The question then arises whether the *umma* (the community of believers in Allah) is being merged in, if not replaced by, the *waṭan* (the fatherland, the territorial nation), and thus losing its religious character.

Apart from law, no other sphere than that of education illustrates so well the transitional character of present-day Islam and Muslim states. Not only does the state decide and organise a unified national education system, but the Ministry of National Education is in a special sense the key ministry. For on the success of education largely depends the future of the state and the loyalty and devotion of its citizens. In no other field is there greater need for integration between the old, traditional and traditionalist education and the new scientific training for citizenship; in no other field is the contrast so sharp between the old and the new, nor the gap so wide between ideal intention and actual performance. Instead of criticising, we should rather be mindful of the lack of encouragement and support the colonising powers showed. While their measures differed from country to country, their interest in raising the level of education and literacy for the benefit of all the subject peoples was generally lacking. An enlightened educational policy and a high standard of teaching, modern in approach, method and content, will vitally influence the future of Islam, whether it be the religion of the individual, an integral part of his mental make-up, or the guiding ideal, even the rule, of state and society.

The Muslim countries surveyed here have naturally a number of factors in common, and a certain pattern can be discerned in their reactions to the outside influences to which they were subjected while under foreign domination, as well as in the way they meet the challenge of the times and set about solving their many problems. Most of the modern stirring and revival can be traced back to the French Revolution and its consequences; yet even before that event, Muslim India had produced in Shāh Walī Ullāh a "reformer" or, better, a restorer. He started a movement which is claimed by Pakistanis of all shades of opinion to have had a decisive influence on Islam in the Indian subcontinent, both before and after partition—a significant manifestation of internal religious and political Islamic stirring entirely uninfluenced by outside forces. This has to be taken into consideration—quite apart from the impact of the West in the Middle East and in South-East Asia—when we describe and assess the many tensions causing confusion and contradictions among Muslim intellectuals. The Western observer can only watch with sympathy and understanding, hoping that a workable solution may be found—as it must be found—by the Muslims themselves. Such a solution may well be a compromise: a reasonable give and take without sacrifice of principle or of intellectual honesty.

With Islam it is not so much that modern science and technology have to be harmonised with Revelation and what flows from it as Law. It is, rather, a conflict between belief and unbelief; between the modern, scientific attitude and approach with their warring ideologies (humanism, Marxist materialism), and a philosophy springing from religious faith. Hence adherents of other faiths will watch the course that Islam is taking, not merely as outside observers, but even more as participants in a world-wide confrontation between traditional faith and new ideologies. By seeing the present crisis against the background of classical Islam, we do two things. First we gain fresh insight into the origin and development of classical and modern Islam; and secondly we can also learn not a little about Christianity and Judaism, which have so much in common with Islam despite fundamental differences.

Our main concern in this book—in Part II—is with Islam as a force in the public life of modern Muslim national states. As a by-product, however, our study may corroborate and throw additional light on the findings of critical scholarship concerning the origin and development of classical concepts and institutions, notably Islamic law and jurisprudence, which Joseph Schacht examined in such masterly fashion in *The Origins of Muhammadan Jurisprudence*. Watching this evolution in a living context may help us to understand the writers on constitutional theory, and to realise how they came to grips with the exigencies of their time and sought a workable compromise between political reality and ideal commandment.

The process of constitution-making in Pakistan is instructive as a human problem of great complexity. For here are gathered together a majority of Muslims and a minority of non-Muslims who while under foreign rule were long deprived of responsibility and power over their own state, and who are suddenly forced to make decisions of far-reaching importance. Absolute values have to be translated into practical and enforceable instruments of government and law by men and women of high, but differing, ideals. If the science of politics is not only the means of reaching happiness, but also the art of the possible in extremely difficult circumstances, then compromise is inevitable for doing justice to majority and minority alike.

This book is built round my own observations in friendly contact with living human beings in their own countries and their own homes. I would betray a human trust if I were to quote literally and by name the opinions on live issues freely expressed by those I met. Such evidence can only be provided when I am referring to writings, some of which belong to men I was privileged to meet. I spent a much longer time in Pakistan than in Malaya, and more time in Tunisia and Morocco than in Iran and Turkey. (Of the latter country Bernard Lewis's *The Emergence of Modern Turkey* describes the problem with authority and insight.) Consequently, my description is fuller for those countries in which I had greater opportunities to learn opinions and to see institutions at work. Other countries

I did not visit, especially in the Middle East, will be mentioned only for purposes of comparison or illustration.

In Part II, Pakistan occupies more space than all the other Muslim countries visited taken together. This is due to the importance of the Islamic issue in the evolution of its Constitution, to the fact that constitutional issues have been my principal concern, and to the abundance of material gathered and placed at my disposal after my visit. If I had confined my attention to Pakistan and the issue of an Islamic state there, the subtitle "An Essay in Political Theology" would have been appropriate for much that has been stated in both parts of the book. Political theology, a medieval concept and a medieval approach to political theory and practice, is centred on the sovereignty of God the creator and ruler of the universe and of man within it. Islamic ideology is its modern off-spring; and its adherents believe that it is a more abiding spiritual concept than Communism, superior to its materialism not only in theory, but also because the principles of brotherhood and social justice—the foremost twin postulates of revealed religion—form in it the basis of a modern society and state. But giving political theology a twentieth-century name, Islamic ideology, is not sufficient to transform Islamic law as it evolved in the Middle Ages (when it remained largely ideal theory divorced from political reality) into a twentieth-century constitution that can apply to a modern parliamentary democracy and an egalitarian society. This society, united in one nation, would be guided by one law for men and women, irrespective of ethnic and religious diversity.

In conclusion, the Western reader nurtured by Western political philosophy may be reminded that Rousseau and especially Montesquieu (who seemingly figure so large in contemporary Muslim political thought and practice, and are consequently mentioned in this book in several instances) have, as far as I can see, nowhere been fully accepted—not even by those Muslims who profess a sincere belief in popular sovereignty and the division of powers. The actual extent and range of their influence, particularly that of Montesquieu, deserve a close, long-overdue investigation, which may well show how superficially they have been accommodated. This is bound to be so, considering the vastly different premises of the Enlightenment compared with classical Islam, and of the French compared with Muslim states and societies. (An exception must be made for parts of North Africa, and particularly for Turkey which has proclaimed as a matter of principle and has realised in its public life the complete separation of state and religion. This fact alone would secure a place for Turkey in this book, were it not for another, closely related facet of the emergence of modern Turkey: namely, the gradual crystallisation of a Turkish concept of Islam as a religion in the Western, post-French Revolution sense of the term. In other words, the various phases discernible today in other Muslim countries have already been experienced by Turkey. Whether or not directly influenced by the Turkish break with the traditional concept of Islam—the concept of Islam as a religious way of life as well as a law for state and society and the individual believer—the positions taken up today by the advocates of an Islamic state or of a lay state with Islam as the state religion or as the exclusive concern of the individual citizen were first taken up, developed, and defended in Turkey.

That the other Muslim states discussed in this book have only partially accepted the ideas of Rousseau and Montesquieu may be briefly illustrated by pointing to the decisive elements of their views on religion and state. In his *Du Contrat Social* Rousseau says of law and legislation: "Le peuple soumis aux lois en doit être l'auteur"; and "Chaque citoyen n'est rien, ne peut rien, que par tous les autres et que la force acquise par le tout soit égale ou supérieure à la somme des forces naturelles de tous les individus". He speaks of the danger of religion in that it makes people anti-social: they think of the other world and do not concentrate on victory in war. Naturally he has Christianity in mind, but his criticism applies no less to Islam and is no less unacceptable to a Muslim than to a Christian believer. On the other hand, says Rousseau, civil religion is good, for through its teaching that the laws are holy, that happiness is the reward of the just, and that evil must be punished, the citizens become devoted to the state. We shall see that such a concept of Islam lies at the root of "religious and civic instruction" in many Muslim states today. Rousseau's warning against intolerance is certainly appropriate to modern national Muslim states (and also to Western states): where there is religious intolerance there is also civil intolerance, and as soon as this happens sovereignty, as understood by Rousseau, ends.

Montesquieu, in his *De L'Esprit des Lois*, defined liberty as "le droit de faire tout ce que les lois permettent"; he also believed that liberty depends on moderate governments. Both views are generally accepted today. That there is no liberty where the three powers (executive, legislative and judiciary) are combined in one authority; that there can be no political liberty where one citizen is in fear of another; and that it is the duty of the government to take appropriate measures to remove such a state of affairs—these convictions are relevant today.

His views on religion, however, are bound to meet with opposition from orthodox believers, especially the advocates of an Islamic state based on the effective rule of divine law. For Montesquieu holds that human laws should have the force of precepts, while divine laws should only give counsel. Where both exist they can, he thinks, correct each other. Divine laws are immutable and, he avers, society needs them as guiding principles, whereas human laws are changeable. Religious laws are there to inspire faith and belief: therein consists their force. Human laws are designed to inspire fear.

These are only a few examples of the ideas and opinions that have had considerable influence on modern Western political thought. But they may be sufficient to underline my plea for a comprehensive study of the extent to which this political philosophy has influenced Muslim thought in the era of Western imperialism and colonialism.

If the Western political scientist and constitutional lawyer cannot easily apply their concepts and the terms that express them to things Islamic and Muslim, neither can they expect the contemporary Muslim thinker, statesman, or administrator to deny his spiritual roots in and attachment to Islam and to bid farewell to his inherited concepts by accepting those of the West. Only Turkey, at least as a nation and a parliamentary democracy, has radically and resolutely turned its back on the past and has declared for Western civilisation without reservations. Turkey apart, the Western student of contemporary Islam must try to view Islam and the problems it poses today not with Western eyes and Western philosophical premises, but in the context of Islam's basic tenets and history. This I have tried to do, in the same way that I tried to understand classical Islam in my *Political Thought in Medieval Islam.* Obviously it is much more difficult to lay aside one's own concepts, attitudes and assumptions when dealing with living men and problems than it is with texts of bygone ages. And since these texts form the basis of any attempt to re-activate Islam as a force in public life today, the task of the Western student has not been rendered any easier. This is especially the case when the Muslims themselves read modern ideas and attitudes into their classical texts, in a natural endeavour to prove to themselves and to the outside world that Islam contains in itself the answer to all our present problems. Not only do they hold that Islam has anticipated what is best in Western civilisation today, but they actually equate contemporary political and social ideas and institutions with those of classical Islam. This creates more than simply questions of accurate terminology: in the last analysis it is a problem of clarity of mind and intention in meeting the challenge of modern political and social movements to our inherited values and attitudes.

In the Middle Ages, the extent to which Greek–Hellenistic philosophy was assimilated depended largely on priorities: faith or human reason, the sovereignty of revelation or the sovereignty and self-sufficiency of the human intellect. Today, Islam and the other revealed religions face the same challenge. But here the similarity ends, for the absence or at least the growing weakness of normative faith has created an entirely different and far more dangerous situation, in which the efficacy of the traditional approach and means is seriously questioned. This is largely because industralisation is rapidly turning what was until recently a feudal society into a new economic and social structure. Thus modern Muslims find their inherited roots inadequate to give content and meaning to their lives, and they are seeking new spiritual roots derived only in part from their traditional religion—and this by no means in Turkey alone, but in all the Muslim states.

E. I. J. R.

Pembroke College
Cambridge

October 1964

ACKNOWLEDGEMENTS

My grateful thanks are due to the Rockefeller Foundation for a grant made to Cambridge University on my behalf; to Professor Bernard Lewis for his usual good advice and helpfulness; to Mr J. D. Pearson for placing the facilities of the Library of the School of Oriental and African Studies at my disposal; to Dr Percy Spear for personal introductions; to the Iranian ambassador and to the embassies of Turkey, Morocco and Tunisia in London; to the High Commissioner for Pakistan and his staff and to the High Commission for Malaya in London; to H.M. ambassadors in Tunis and Rabat and their staffs; to the U.K. High Commission in Malaya; to the Ministries of Education in Pakistan, Malaya, Iran, Tunisia and Morocco; to the Ministries of Information and of Law in Tunis; to the Cultural Division of the Ministry of Foreign Affairs in Rabat; to the staff of the British Council in Lahore, Tehran, Isfahan, Shiraz, Istanbul, Ankara, Rabat and Fes; to the Vice-Chancellors, deans of faculties, principals of colleges and many colleagues of the universities of Karachi, Lahore, Peshawar, Dacca, Aligarh, Calcutta, Hyderabad, Malaya, Tehran, Isfahan, Shiraz, Istanbul, Ankara, Tunis and Rabat; of the Qarawīyīn at Fes and the Collège Ben Youssef at Marrakesh; and to many judges, civil servants, scholars, statesmen and politicians with whom I was able to discuss the questions which form the subject of my inquiry.

To the editors of *The Year Book of World Affairs 1962*, I am obliged for their permission to use my article "The Role of Islam in the Modern National State", and to the board of editors of *Islamic Studies*, Karachi, for permission to use my article "Some Reflections on the Separation of Religion and Politics in Modern Islam" (III, 3, 1964).

I received much official help in the preparation of my itinerary and in the arrangement of meetings with heads of state, ministers and their staff, and of lectures, conferences and discussions without which the purpose of my journey could not have been achieved.

To my wife I owe a special debt for her assistance with secretarial help and especially through interviewing Muslim women. Throughout, we experienced splendid hospitality, goodwill and encouragement and received much personal kindness from so many men and women that it would be impossible to make acknowledgement to them individually in this book.

ABBREVIATIONS

BASI	*Beiträge zur Arabistik, Semitistik und Islamwissenschaft*, ed. R. Hartmann and H. Scheel (Leipzig, 1944).
BSOAS	*Bulletin, School of Oriental and African Studies* (London).
EI, *EI*^{2}	*Encyclopaedia of Islam*, 1st and 2nd editions.
EIP	*The Evolution of India and Pakistan 1858–1947*, ed. C. H. Philips, H. L. Singh and B. N. Pandey (London, 1962).
IC	*Islamic Culture.*
MEJ	*The Middle East Journal.*
MW	*The Muslim World.*
PTMI	Erwin I. J. Rosenthal, *Political Thought in Medieval Islam. An Introductory Outline*^{2} (Cambridge, 1962).
REI	*Revue des Études Islamiques.*
WI	*Die Welt des Islams.*

NOTE ON TRANSLITERATION

Discrepancies in transliteration are due to the need to reproduce in quotations the spelling adopted by the authors, e.g. *Shari'ah* or *Shariat* for *Sharīʿa.*

PART I

CONTEMPORARY ISLAM IN CRISIS AND TRANSITION

SECTION 1

CHAPTER I

THE HUMAN SITUATION

The disappearance of the British and French colonial empires from Asia and Africa is not the beginning, nor even the turning point, of ferment and crisis in modern Islam. The gradual renunciation of political control and economic exploitation by Britain and France has enabled the subject peoples of both continents to gain political freedom and sovereign independence within national boundaries. The principle of self-determination enunciated at the end of the First World War led to the emergence of some Turkish provinces into modern Arab nation-states, while the Near and Middle East remained under the influence of European imperialism until the Second World War finally broke its hold. However, the struggle for political freedom had to precede the movement for inner regeneration and liberation, which could only properly come into its own after the attainment of national independence. Statehood, bringing complete mastery over national and international affairs, has now created the conditions necessary for the battle of minds that is to determine the character of the new Muslim society.

The political struggle was won by a nationalism which aimed at liberating the fatherland (*waṭan*) from foreign rule and which had perforce to concentrate all its energies on the achievement of this primary goal. Inevitably, political nationalism diverted and diluted the consciousness of belonging to the *umma*, the universal Islamic community of believers. And the rigidity of the religious leaders with their almost exclusive concern for ritual and a static, traditional religious education, had weakened their link with the *jamāʿat-al-sunna*, the community of orthodox believers the world over, and had thus opened the door wide for foreign influences; as a result, new and revolutionary ideas were propagated with missionary zeal. The abolition of the caliphate by Kemal Atatürk accelerated Westernising tendencies, but by no means initiated them. Such tendencies were preceded by a desire to restore and renew a decaying Islam, a pattern that clearly emerges from the history of Islam in the Indian subcontinent. Apart from the orthodox leaders and their followers, the Muslim intellectuals threw their energies wholeheartedly into the political struggle; even the orthodox elements supported political nationalism in its fight for freedom and independence. (The Muslims in undivided, pre-partition India are, with notable exceptions, in a separate class.)

The political struggle has often been described, and there is no point in going over familiar ground at second hand. The relationship between nationalism and Islam is not always clear, and its ambivalence demands a much more searching treatment than can here be accorded to it. Yet we cannot avoid its consideration by hiding behind the blunt assertion that there were different attitudes taken up by different writers, or by the same person at different times. The real problem only emerged on home ground after the external enemy, against whom both sides combined, had been cleared from the old/new fatherland.

What is important to remember is that the crisis of Islam, as of other faiths, is ultimately a spiritual crisis whose beginnings precede the political struggle; therefore it was bound to re-emerge with increased urgency and gravity once freedom had been born. It goes even deeper than the fundamental, intertwined questions, what is Islam and who and what is a Muslim? Broadly speaking, political nationalism is predominantly concerned with national self-determination. Once this is achieved and a fully independent and sovereign state has been created, then nationalism's other concern—individual self-expression—can and must be pursued to secure the coherence and viability of newly won statehood. Men and women must rediscover their souls and find the means to express their inner being in freedom and responsibility. This self-expression must be preceded by a searching self-examination, especially if the "national spirit", the soul of the people, almost succumbed to the twin evils of internal stagnation and external restraint through conquest and domination.

Therefore we must survey briefly the meaning and significance given to Islam and nationalism by the leading exponents of Turkish and Arab nationalism. Since Arabia was the cradle of Islam, this is justified. For the strength or weakness of Islam among non-Arab Muslims, such as those in Pakistan, India, and Malaya, stands in close relation to the Arab roots of Islam and to the Arabic language in which the classics of Islam, as a faith and a civilisation, are written. Hence another element, Arabism, makes the ambiguous alliance or antagonism between Islam and nationalism even more complex. Again, while this affects in the first place the Arabs, Muslim and Christian, it has repercussions in Turkey, Iran, and South-East Asia—not to mention Central, West and East Africa, which remain outside the scope of our survey.

It is common knowledge that we can distinguish two separate phases of Arab nationalism, each with a quite different emphasis. The first was a revolt against the despotism of the Ottoman Sultan, and the second was primarily directed against foreign domination. The latter struggle was never entirely free from a religious undercurrent, not so much because of memories of the Crusades, but because of Christian attacks on Islam and Christian missionary activity, which led the Muslims to identify "the West" with Christianity. A defence mechanism was set in motion with the usual apologetic and polemic overtones, which necessarily coloured the outlook and activity of nascent nationalism and led to a political movement that drew its inspiration not only from a love of freedom and independence, but also from Islam as a religion and an indigenous culture and civilisation. It may well be that the modern nationalist's identification of the West with Christianity contributes in three ways to the changing attitudes towards Islam. First there is the conservative or even reactionary group advocating and working for an Islamic state on rigidly orthodox lines, in defence of Islam against an allegedly inimical Christian West, completely rejecting everything Western as anti-Islamic. Next there is the middle-of-the-road position, of advocating a coming to positive terms with Western techniques and institutions on the basis of Islamic principles that are to guide state and society. This position contains within itself several shades, ranging from a full synthesis between "East" and "West", through a partial accommodation, to a mere clothing of Western institutions in Islamic words. (This is a very rough classification, for in fact there are shades within shades, and no clear-cut distinctions can be made.) Finally, at the other extreme, we find a complete severance of Islam as faith from the body politic: the separation of religion and politics, as it is—at least in theory and intention—in the Turkish lay state. These appear to be the principal "divisions", since the strictly secularist position can be considered an extension of the principle of separation of state and religion. It is all a matter of interpretation and largely depends on what we understand by Islam.

But it is generally agreed that nationalism is an import from Europe that has wrought great changes in the minds and lives of the Near and Middle Eastern peoples. It has brought benefits, but its secular origin and character have thrown out a dangerous challenge to a largely lethargic society, with consequences for traditional Islam that far exceed those which European nationalism in the wake of the French Revolution caused to Christianity. We are not concerned with the influence of the French Revolution on the political map of the region, but rather with the impact on the Muslim mind of the ideas that underlay and prompted that revolution. Just as Western science and technology cannot be understood and applied without the thought processes that created them and that flow from a specific "modern" attitude of mind, so our political institutions cannot simply be imitated without the political ideas that give birth to them and find their expression in constitutional thinking and governmental organisation.

From Descartes on, philosophy and science in the West have been based on a new attitude toward God and the universe and man's place in it; on a new relationship to authority and a fresh appraisal of the realm within which reason is to rule supreme. Nor must we forget the fundamentally important principle of freedom of conscience, which was first established in the realm of religion by Luther and his Reformation. This new spirit of the Renaissance and Reformation produced the political philosophy of Hobbes and Locke, which in turn left its mark on the Encyclopedists in France whose literary activity can be said to have triggered off the French Revolution—a revolution directed equally against political and ecclesiastical tyranny. There evolved a new concept of state and nation which, like the political philosophy of the ancient Greeks, centred on man as both a rational and a social human being. Natural law, the law of reason, orders the lives of free men: this can easily be reconciled with deism, but not so easily with the God of revelation, the creator and ruler of the universe. Hence Muslims must either choose between the sovereignty of God and the sovereignty of the people, or they must try to reconcile the two in their modern nation-states, as we shall see later.

It goes without saying that the Turks studying in France were bound to be attracted by the concept of the sovereignty of the people; and imbued with the ideas of Montesquieu, Rousseau, Voltaire, and others, they returned determined to obtain political reforms, which meant in the first place consultation and representative government.[1] The foundation for this transformation of the Ottoman state and its legal and administrative system was laid by the *Tanzimat* in the period beginning with the Rescript of Gülhane in 1839.[2] To understand these reforms in themselves and as the first breach in the classical governmental and legal system of Islam, it is necessary to state briefly what Islam is. For modernisation of the Turkish state and of Ottoman society did more than pave the way for nationalism and awaken the desire of the several peoples under the sultan's rule for political liberty and equality. Among the Muslim intellectuals it also raised problems connected with the nature of Islam and its future role in modern Turkey and the whole Middle East.

Islam, the call by the prophet Muḥammad to Allah and to total submission to the divine will, is both a faith and a rule of life for the individual and his society. This society is, to use Western terms, a religious society, *umma*: the community of believers in the unity of Allah and in the messengership of His prophet Muḥammad. The messenger of Allah began with few followers, but as he gained more adherents to Islam when he preached it in the face of strong opposition among his Arab countrymen, he had to assume power over his growing community and to lay down rules of individual and collective conduct. His authority to organise and to rule the original *umma* of Medina derived from his prophetic character as the mouthpiece of Allah. He quelled opposition by force of arms; his campaigns were fought in the name of and for the victory and glory of God (*jihād* = holy war). With political dominion established by a combination of divine authority and power built on persuasion and the sword, the basis was laid for the state and empire of Islam that his successors were to build and develop. It has always been acknowledged—by his helpers and companions and right through the entire history of Islam to the present-day believers—that Muḥammad's authority issues directly from the one and only God, the giver of life and law for all time. But in framing the rules governing his community of believers, their duties to God and to one another, and their relations with those outside the *umma*, Muḥammad had to take account of the existing political and social order, which was that of a tribal organisation. His successors, bearing the title of *khalīfa*, vice-gerent of the prophet, lacked his prophetic gift—he was after all the seal of the prophets—but they were nevertheless spiritual as well as temporal rulers. As military "commanders of the faithful", they extended the realm of Islam by conquest. In setting up government and administration in a far-flung empire they, just as Muḥammad before them, had to take into account existing local customs; and with the growth of Islamic law, these customs had to be "naturalised" in it. The attitude to custom and customary law (*'urf* or *'āda*) has varied throughout the history of Islam, from open acceptance as secondary to the *Sharī'a*, to tacit toleration.

Sharī'a or *Shar'* is the entire corpus of divinely revealed law; it regulates *the path* to Allah, orders the Muslim believer's entire life from birth to death, and ensures his happiness in this world and the hereafter. As the ideal norm its authority and validity have never been challenged, either by orthodox Sunnī Islam or by the majority of sects, especially the *Shī'a*. But while it held unchallenged sway over the minds of many generations of Muslims, and while it, together with the tenets of the faith, has undoubtedly preserved the unity of the universal *umma*, its practical application has been confined largely to the duties to God (*'ibādāt*) and to what we call the personal status law (regarding marriage, divorce, inheritance, etc.) of the *mu'āmalāt*, the social, inter-human laws.

Today, "traditionalists" and "liberals" differ not only in their attitude to the validity of the *Sharī'a* and its place in a modern Muslim state, but also in their understanding of what constitutes the *Sharī'a*. The central position of the *Sharī'a* in state and society as understood in classical Islam cannot be overemphasised. The place it occupies in a modern Muslim state will determine the character of that state: indeed, it will be an *Islamic* state (the aim of traditionalists of all shades) provided the *Sharī'a*—irrespective of its interpretation—is assigned the central place as the authoritative regulative law of state and society today, both in theory and practice.

Among the obstacles to this happening, the principal one, all too often forgotten or overlooked, is the absence of the only admissible basis for an Islamic state: faith in Allah and His will, expressed in this prophetically revealed law, among a body of Muslims whose numerical strength is difficult to assess but whose importance is nevertheless great. For in societies afflicted with large-scale, though fortunately diminishing, illiteracy, the intellectual *élite* has a much greater importance than in societies of a high level of general education and free expression of opinion.

The next important difficulty is the changed and changing faith of believing Muslims. Again this cannot be easily gauged in numbers but is relevant for the same reason as that just given. For in contrast to the faith that prevailed right into the last or even the beginning of the present century—a faith that combined belief in Allah with at least a theoretical acceptance of the obligatory nature of His law—we have today many (undoubtedly Westernised) intellectuals who believe in God and the moral principles of religion which they want to see applied to society, but who insist on formulating new laws appropriate to present needs. For them the *Sharī'a* of classical Islam is time-bound and obsolete, if not in its principles, then certainly in many of its practical rules and enactments. Their faith no longer includes faith in the divine, immutable, all-inclusive and obligatory character of a law, which to them grew over a long period of time and reflects the ideas and the moral, social and political attitudes of bygone ages, out of touch with contemporary reality. In other words, the *Sharī'a* expresses just this religious and political unity of Islam as a faith and a path of life that has been challenged as a result of the French Revolution. Itself the result of a rationalism based on a world-view different from that of its precursor in the faith-secure Middle Ages, the French Revolution found its political expression in the lay state. Such a state is characterised by the separation of religion and politics, and it insists on the exclusion of the Church (in Christendom) from public life. Its citizens, equal and free, are bound in brotherhood to the fatherland and held together by a number of cohesive elements, such as language, history, culture and civilisation, and national boundaries. Ideally they have the same ethnic composition, and national unity is enhanced by the absence of ethnic, religious, and cultural minorities; nationalism is often sparked off by foreign domination and/or minority status within the state. We can say with hindsight that representative government is less essential than equality before the law, whose justice must be visible to all citizens. For our inquiry the form of government is immaterial, as long as the rule of just law is firmly established and in operation irrespective of colour and creed, among majority and minority alike.

Here is common ground between classical Islam and a modern state, but also a source of conflict as far as the origin and nature of the law are concerned. This conflict lies at the root of the clash of minds in Muslim states today.

The heart of the crisis of Islam, as of religion everywhere, lies in the absence of faith or in a weakened faith due to the challenge of modern, predominantly political, ideologies. The security of total medieval faith has gone, and the unquestioning allegiance to religion, as to a master demanding and receiving wholehearted obedience, has given way to doubt and uncertainty. This is obvious in the West, but less serious because the law under which its peoples live has long been "secularised" or, better, emancipated from the divine source by having its authority derive from the sovereignty of the people.

God's will is immutable; the will of the people changes, and with it the law. Thus the crisis of Islam is more serious and acute—quite apart from the practical problems that face newly independent states—precisely because law is the core of the faith, the terrestrial expression of its divine message to and demand upon society. Even if we assumed that the theoretical validity, the sovereign rule and control of the *Sharīʿa*, was largely hypothetical, not to say a legal fiction, throughout the history of the caliphate and its successor states, nevertheless this legal fiction was an inner reality much more persistent and vital than the transient political existence of the Islamic empire. For this law held the *umma* together and provided through its universality a bond much stronger and more enduring than any other loyalty. A more sophisticated world, beset by doubt and cynicism, today believes in the power of reason, in self-sufficiency and limitless human striving. It is a matter of opinion whether materialism is to blame for our unwillingness to submit to a power outside and above our sovereign reason, or whether it is intellectual honesty that hinders us from maintaining a legal fiction which saved our forebears from the same fissiparous tendencies that competing ideologies threaten us with today.

It may be objected that our age is faced with the same challenge as was the Middle Ages; it only takes a different form. For did not the battle rage between revelation and reason then as now? Superficially this may well be so. But the emancipation of modern man from ecclesiastical authority, which occurred in the Reformation in Europe, was but the prelude to a changed relationship between man and God: unfettered by supernatural command and law, man has asserted and increasingly exercised his freedom to arrange his mundane affairs. The development of the concept of Natural Law, from its identity with Divine Law (in the view of the Stoa) to its autonomy as the Law of Reason independent of a divine source (in the concept of modern man), clearly illustrates this change, which is tantamount to a revolution. And yet man is not happy, in the West or East. In his search for self-identification he must examine all the "isms" that the market-place offers him in exchange for the security he once possessed in his traditional faith. Hence religion—be it Judaism, Christianity, or Islam—is being examined as to its essence and its relevance to self-identification and group affiliation. As an integral part of this re-orientation, nationalism is undergoing a significant change.

This means that Islam has somehow to be built into self- and group-identity. Some accommodation will have to be made if the emotional attachment to traditional Islam and the intellectual orientation towards the West are to be integrated into a whole personality: one that is conscious of its heritage and at the same time determined to belong to this age and to build a future world which is one economically, yet differentiated politically, socially, and culturally. To achieve a balanced personality, both on the individual and the collective level, we must preserve historical continuity.

CHAPTER 2

CLASSICAL FOUNDATIONS

A brief consideration of the classical concept of the state in Islam and its relevance for contemporary thought and action may be useful. Oversimplified, historical continuity can be preserved and reactivated as a positive force in a Muslim polity in one of two ways: either by the renewal of Islam as a faith and way of life with or without the *Sharīʿa* or a part of it; or by a secularised Islam, that is, part of a Muslim's mental being: an historical memory of value and meaning; an indispensable cultural heritage to be integrated with contemporary philosophical and scientific trends.

THE CONCEPT OF THE "KHILĀFA" OR "IMĀMA"

If *umma* designates the community of believers as a religious society, its political organisation is contained and its protection of life and property guaranteed in the *khilāfa* or *imāma*. Under the sovereignty of God and the authority of His law, the *Sharīʿa* of Islam, the caliph is the temporal ruler of the state and the defender of the faith. As such he is charged with implementing the *Sharīʿa*, for its application in the everyday life of individual and society secures wellbeing in this world and bliss in the hereafter.

How and when did the *Sharīʿa* arise and achieve its dominant position as the constitution and the law of the Islamic state? Jurisprudence (*ʿilm al-fiqh*), the science of law, is "the knowledge of the rights and duties whereby man is enabled to observe right conduct in this life, and to prepare himself for the world to come". Thus runs a Ḥanafī definition of *Fiqh*, often used as a synonym for the *Sharīʿa*. Traditionally, jurisprudence is divided into *uṣūl* (principles) and *furūʿ* (branches, derivations, i.e. the law in force). We are at present concerned only with the principles, of which there are four: *Qur'an* (the revealed word of God) and *Sunna* (the example and sayings of the prophet Muḥammad) are the fundamental sources, to which have been added *ijmāʿ* (the consensus of the community represented by the *ʿulamā* of the age)[1] and *qiyās* (legal deduction by analogy). It is significant that modern adherents of the Islamic state equate *Sharīʿa* with *Qur'an* and *Sunna* or with the *Qur'an* alone.

Western scholarship, notably the work of I. Goldziher and Joseph Schacht,[2] has shown that Islamic law did not begin to crystallise until the advent of the Abbasid dynasty, from 750 on. Yet Muslim tradition associates the full flowering of Islamic law with the golden age of the true *khilāfa* of the prophet's first four successors, the *khulafā rāshidūn*, the ideal rulers who guided the *umma* on the right path (*sharīʿa*).

The classical formulation of the *khilāfa* or *imāma* was propounded by Al-Māwardī in the first third of the tenth century of the common era, and it remained authoritative until Ibn Taymīya (d. 1328) shifted the centre of interest and importance from the *khilāfa* to the *Sharīʿa* itself. A direct line leads from him to the Wahhābī movement in the late eighteenth century; to Rashīd Riḍā, the disciple and continuator of Muḥammad ʿAbduh, and to those contemporary *ʿulamā* and thinkers who want to restore the rule of the *Sharīʿa* in an Islamic state.

It is therefore essential to bear in mind the intention and method of the medieval jurists who left us treatises on constitutional theory and law as part of *Fiqh*. They wrote in defence of the Abbasid caliphate, whose authority was threatened by effective political rulers, amirs or sultans. Their principal aim was to maintain the unity of the *umma* in face of the growing disintegration due to the effective power having slipped from the hands of the caliph, who was the symbol of Islam's religious and political unity and the protector of the *Sharīʿa* throughout the Islamic empire. In this process the *Sharīʿa* became less and less of a reality, hence the greater need to preserve it as the ideal constitution and law of the *umma*. The reforming zeal of Ibn Taymīya, long after the fall of the Abbasid caliphate in 1258, was aimed at full restoration of the *Sharīʿa* to secure the survival of Islam in its pristine purity in conformity with the *sunna* of the prophet.[3]

These constitutional treatises were not merely academic exercises. On the contrary, they were caused by a political situation fraught with grave danger to the survival of the *umma*, and they represent a significant blend of ideal theory and ugly political reality, often only achieved by far-reaching concessions to expediency. In this lies their importance for their own time and for ours. It is true that they were composed centuries after the birth of the institution which they set out to justify. In fact, the caliphate had already begun to decline. But this only enhances their importance, especially when seen in conjunction with a no less significant factor that helps us to understand what Islam was in its classical period, what it is today, and what it might be tomorrow. This concerns their theory of the Islamic state.

They were guided by the biography of the prophet (*sīra*) and by the historians of the early caliphate of Muḥammad's first four successors and of the Umayyad and Abbasid dynasties. Precedent supplied the material for their theory about the origin, purpose, and function of the *khilāfa* or *imāma*. They did not study their sources critically, nor did the jurists adopt a detached, critical attitude toward what the historians related about the election or designation of the prophet's successors and about their conduct of the affairs of state and society. They accepted and shared the historians' bias against Mu'āwiya and the Umayyad dynasty he founded, as well as their bias in favour of the "pious" Abbasids who ousted the Umayyads from power. They related what they read in these histories to Qur'an and Sunna and made deductions from the views of the *salaf*, the first generation of Muslims; they also used their own judgement in the light of contemporary events and the developments of the Abbasid caliphate. Somehow they had to harmonise an existing historical-political situation with the principles and practice of the *Sharī'a*; at the same time, a realistic assessment of the situation and a sober approach to the question of authority and power were demanded. As already stated, the power of the amir or sultan was weakening the Abbasid caliphate at its centre, and the jurists had to find a plausible way to secure and maintain the spiritual and temporal authority of the institution and its head. For, to repeat, the caliphate was the symbol of the unity of the *umma*, whose preservation was an ineluctable necessity—in fact, the foremost duty of the theologian-jurists. The constitutional treatises were without exception the response to a crisis in the relations between the *khalīfa* and *amīr* (or *sulṭān*).

The theory itself is simple: sovereignty belongs to God; authority is vested in the *khalīfa* as the vice-gerent of the prophet, the messenger of Allah. It is the duty of the caliph to implement the *Sharī'a*, to defend the faith against heresy, and the faithful against attack, and to ensure their ability to live by the prescriptions of the *Sharī'a* and thus to attain happiness in this world and in the hereafter. Thus we find Al-Māwardī defining the *imāma* as the institution "replacing prophecy in the defence of the faith and the administration of the world". It is "demanded by the *shar'*, not by reason". This is no doubt directed against the philosophical justification based on the Aristotelian dictum that "man is a social [or political] being".

A close study of the defence of the *khilāfa* or *imāma* from Al-Māwardī through Al-Ghazālī to Ibn Jamā'a clearly shows how these champions of the unity of the *umma* bowed to political necessity and tried to justify pre-Islamic Arab tribal, and Sassanian, and Byzantine governmental practice in order to preserve the ideal Islamic norm and the all-embracing religious nature of state and society. In this, their overriding concern, they went to practically any length. The more remote and indistinct the ideal became, the greater and more far-reaching their concessions to expediency.

Yet their political realism undoubtedly saved Islam as a spiritual force capable of sustaining a distinctive culture and civilisation. Fear of anarchy made Ibn Jamā'a, following Al-Ghazālī, condone usurpation of the *khalīfa*'s office. Ibn Taymīya even went so far as to deny the necessity of the *imāma* by concentrating on the rule of the divine law. By going back to the Sunna and also by administrative reform, he tried to restore the *Sharī'a* to its full authority and efficacy. He stressed the importance of *ijmā'*, the voice of the *umma* through its *'ulamā*, and he insisted that the welfare of the community (*maṣlaḥa*, common weal) depended on a Muslim's obedience to God and His *Sharī'a*; he pleaded for just government based on Qur'an, Sunna, and *ijmā'*. Together with his disciple Ibn Qayyim al-Jawzīya, Ibn Taymīya is the source for all modern "reformers" like Muḥammad 'Abduh, Rashīd Riḍā, and their successors to this day. Advocates of an Islamic state in our time appeal to the full exercise of *ijtihād*, a searching, independent, personal judgement based on Qur'an and Sunna; and at least in theory they want to re-activate the original *Sharī'a*, purged of later accretions in *Fiqh*, in the light of *maṣlaḥa*.

We must not anticipate a later and fuller treatment of this delicate question. It is sufficient to say here that *maṣlaḥa* is an elastic term open to many possible interpretations in a given situation, and that *ijtihād* is a fine, sound principle, but its application is by no means simple. It depends on whether anybody can go to Qur'an and Sunna and extract from them a fresh interpretation that suits the exigencies of the times, or whether the exercise of *ijtihād* is reserved to the experts in Islamic law and lore, the *'ulamā*; if the latter, would they be bound by the decisions of their predecessors or not? Here the principle of historical continuity is at stake.

Earlier on, we briefly touched upon the relationship between the *Sharī'a* as divinely revealed law and customary law (*'urf* or *'āda*)—a matter of great importance since both exist side by side in the body politic. The distinction between the *Sharī'a* and *Qānūn* is of no less importance, especially in view of the legal practice of the Ottoman empire and the attempt of the Ottoman sultans to extend the realm of the *Sharī'a* of Sunnī Islam. *Qānūn* (or its plural form *qawānīn*) represent legal injunctions issued by the ruler and endowed with binding force. But how can the legislative activity of the ruler be justified if the highest and exclusive authority is vested in the *Sharī'a*? God is the sole legislator; the prophet announced His law and his successors are to administer it. Does this not mean that, with divine law revealed for all times, all that is left to the *umma* is its *interpretation* by the experts, the *'ulamā*? This is, indeed, the accepted orthodox view. But there is another view, held by the equally orthodox advocates of a modern Islamic state: the prophet has left a wide field open for human legislation outside the Qur'an, provided that such laws conform to Islamic principles.

For the jurists concerned with constitutional theory and law, *khilāfa* in the strict sense of the term was confined to the four *khulafā rāshidūn*, that is, God-centred rule in accordance with the *Sharī'a*. Mu'āwiya established a *mulk*, or a temporal rule within his family, which became the ruling dynasty of an absolute monarchy. Although some of the Abbasid caliphs came close to the ideal standard, thus blurring the rigid distinction between *khilāfa* and *mulk*, they were in fact nothing but absolute monarchs. But insofar as their absolutism was, at least in theory, limited by the veto of the *'ulamā*, it can be maintained that the jurists recognised only the *khilāfa* as the truly Islamic state while ignoring the *mulk* in their ideal constitutional pattern. In other words, their political realism stopped short at the point where Ibn Khaldūn began his searching analysis of the state as it was. They started from the ideal theory but compromised it in order to keep unsullied the image of the ideal *khilāfa*. Ibn Khaldūn started from the state built on power as he found it in existence, but he then opposed it with the *khilāfa*, which, for him also, was the ideal norm based on religion as understood by a Muslim.

IBN KHALDŪN: "KHILĀFA" AND "MULK"

The constitutional problem posed by an Islamic state can, I believe, be better understood through an appreciation of Ibn Khaldūn's fruitful distinction between *khilāfa* and two kinds of *mulk*—a distinction that may usefully be applied to the present situation. For it not only helps to clarify the issues, but may also serve as a pointer to possible solutions. A constitutional tangle with Islam as a major issue—in Pakistan, for example—reveals the crisis of Islam more clearly than does anything else, especially if it is considered together with the vital question of the kind of law that should regulate the life of the state. Further, Muḥammad 'Abduh was a keen student of Ibn Khaldūn's *Muqaddima*, as was Rashīd Riḍā, who violently disagreed with Ibn Khaldūn (as did 'Ali 'Abd al-Rāziq, though for the opposite reasons). Nor should we forget that Ṭaha Ḥusain, one of the foremost contemporary Egyptian thinkers, devoted a penetrating study to Ibn Khaldūn's social philosophy, and that Arab nationalist writers often discuss his ideas with approval or disapproval.[4]

A further reason for reviewing Ibn Khaldūn's ideas in our present context is the exceptional nature of his thought, especially in matters of political theory. For here is a statesman and a judge steeped in Mālikī *Fiqh* who has applied his original mind to an empirical study of political reality unhindered by his profound attachment to Islam and its ideal state, the *khilāfa*. Moreover, he rejected as hypothetical the ideal state of the philosophers (*falāsifa*), thus lending added weight to the only states he recognised: the *siyāsa dīnīya*, identical with the *khilāfa* or *imāma* of the jurists, and the *siyāsa 'aqlīya*, the power-state founded upon human reason. The last-named demands our attention.

Ibn Khaldūn deals with the state in the larger context of his novel study of civilisation, his "new science". Settled urban life is the precondition for a proper political organisation in the state under one-man rule. He recognised the will to power and domination as man's principal driving force; and to prevent mutual destruction, man's evil inclination must be held in check either by religion, which provides a natural restraining authority based on the divinely revealed law, or by a governor whose authority derives from a law devised by human reason.

Ibn Khaldūn was exclusively interested in the power-state, whose nature and organisation he describes with rare insight. *Mulk*, government by authority based on power, is natural to man. Though convinced of the superiority of the state built on the prophetically revealed law, Ibn Khaldūn insists—against the philosophers—that prophecy is neither natural nor necessary for political organisation in a state. The usual form of such organisation, the power-state, is the natural response to man's natural needs as a rational, social being. After all, the majority of mankind exists without prophets.[5] Their rulers exercise authority by power and/or *'aṣabīya*, which unites their supporters. *'Aṣabīya* is a concept of Ibn Khaldūn's that has aroused the opposition of modern orthodox Muslim thinkers, who regard it as contrary to Islam. In fact, he stresses its significance, saying it is needed for the success of prophecy and of *du'wa*, the call to religion. But just as it serves to reinforce religious zeal—and as religious enthusiasm gives it increased force—it can also grow weaker when enthusiasm and the original will to power flag and religion becomes a science sapping man's courage and drive. Its foremost role, however, he assigns to the power-state, for *'aṣabīya* is a corporate feeling; a common bond, due in the first place to ties of blood and family tradition, creating a sense of solidarity; it inspires common action and is an indispensable driving force in the formation of states and dynasties; its aim is *mulk*, dominion.

'Aṣabīya gives teeth to the necessary restraining force. At first it sustains the tribal chief, who is *primus inter pares*, and maintains his authority through the *'aṣabīya* that animates his family and clan. Later he aims at sovereign power and uses this powerful feeling of solidarity for his own ends. Yet urban life under the restraining laws of the *mulk*, into which the *khilāfa* of the *khulafā rāshidūn* was transformed, led to the gradual loss of courage and self-reliance. This is because the restraining force inherent in the *Shar'* was replaced by that of the sovereign ruler whose state was built on power and conquest.

While Ibn Khaldūn thus subscribes to the traditional hostility to

Mu'āwiya, he does not blame this founder of the Umayyad dynasty, but sees his rise as an inevitable result of the decline of religion in the reign of 'Ali, the fourth caliph. He draws the further conclusion that *qawānīn siyāsīya* (political statutes), that is, the sovereign's own legal enactments, are necessary in the *mulk*: thus he qualifies the exclusive authority of the *Shar'*. Consequently, he defines the governmental system of the Muslim *malik* or *sulṭān* as *siyāsa 'aqlīya*, in contrast to the *siyāsa dīnīya* or *shar'īya*, and he does so even though the primary laws by which this Muslim king rules his subjects are those of the *Sharī'a*. He says:

Politics based on reason can take two forms. In the first, care is taken of welfare in general, and of the advantage of the *sulṭān* in respect of the maintenance of his rule in particular....Allah has dispensed with it for us in [our] religious community (*milla*) and for the time of the *khilāfa* [that is, of the first four caliphs], because the statutes of the *Sharī'a* dispense with it in respect of the general and the particular welfare. The statutes of the *mulk* are included in it (the *Sharī'a*).

In the second form care is taken of the advantage of the ruler and that the *mulk* should be firmly established for him by force and superior power. The general welfare of the subjects takes second place. Such a government (*siyāsa*) is that of [all] the other kings in the world, Muslim and non-Muslim, except that the Muslim kings act in accordance with the requirements of the Islamic *Sharī'a, as far as they can*. Hence, their laws are composed of statutes of the *Sharī'a*, of rules of right conduct, of regulations which are natural for [political] association, and necessary things concerning power and *'aṣabīya*. The requirements of the *Shar'* come first, then the rules of conduct of the philosophers and the way of life of kings.[6]

This mixed constitution, though falling short of the Islamic ideal, is still representative of a basically Islamic state. It is clear from Ibn Khaldūn's definitions and exposition that the golden age of Islam was blessed with the unchallenged rule of the *Sharī'a* under whose authority the *khalīfa* stood in the same way as all the other members of the *umma*. There were no sovereign masters and subjects: all were servants of Allah alike. But it is equally clear that he observed early Islam and the transformation of the *khilāfa* into the *mulk* with the eyes of the political scientist—naturally a Muslim political scientist. For, as we saw, the decline of the original *khilāfa* as a political entity was attributed to the decline in religion, and he saw altogether a close connection between religion and politics.

Next, he determined the character of the state by the law in force. Here again it is the Muslim political thinker who discerns the fundamental difference between the *siyāsa dīnīya* under the rule of the religious law, and the *siyāsa 'aqlīya* under the authority of the human sovereign who simultaneously adopts laws of differing origin, import, and purpose. In view of the distinction that Muslim philosophers made between divine and human law, and in view of Ibn Khaldūn's rejection of the *siyāsa madanīya* (by which he means Plato's *Republic* adapted to Islam), it is necessary to clarify precisely what Ibn Khaldūn means by *siyāsa 'aqlīya*—quite apart from his dividing it up into a Muslim *mulk* with a mixed constitution and another *mulk*, the power-state pure and simple, which is outside and independent of Islam. *'Aqlīya*, rational, must mean a law devised by the political, practical reason of the ruler, and not by the speculative reason of the philosopher, whose governmental organisation Ibn Khaldūn calls *madanīya*, the ideal city-state of the Greek *polis*.

But why should the Muslim *mulk* have any significance beyond Ibn Khaldūn's own time? Is it anything more than the empirical recognition, based on his living Islamic faith and his historical consciousness, of the Muslim states of his own time? Why should his correct diagnosis have any relevance for the Muslims' modern nation-states? The answer lies in the fact that Ibn Khaldūn was deeply rooted in, and in his political analysis attached great importance to, the traditional Muslim values, in particular the twofold aspect of the ideal Islamic polity which comprises *dīn wa-dunya*, "religion" and "politics" (literally: worldly affairs). For he defines the *khilāfa* exactly as Al-Māwardī did, as the vice-gerency of the lawgiver to guard religion and administer the world. He devoted a separate chapter to the *khilāfa* and another one to the "religious concerns of the *khilāfa*". From both it is clear that during the transformation of the *khilāfa* into the *mulk*, the specific qualities of the former were not entirely lost, but in part preserved in the Muslim *mulk*. Further, though religion is the sole determining factor in the former, it is still a formative element in the latter.

He applies his own experience in Islam to society and civilisation in general. He thus combines a primarily theological with a power-political concept of the state, without in any way abandoning the accepted Muslim position, since the spiritual and the temporal power are united in the caliph or *imām*...he would not be a Muslim if he did not stress the support, often decisive, which religion lends to the *'aṣabīya*, transforming a driving force originally based on descent or common material interests into an irresistible spiritual influence reinforced by the energy and striking power of a closely knit group of activists....Ibn Khaldūn has correctly deduced that a weakening of the religious *élan* must strengthen the temporal component of the *khilāfa* and inevitably lead to its transformation into absolute monarchy in the form of the *mulk*. On the other hand, religion...is the source from which great empires spring. For where otherwise rivalry and discord might threaten to disrupt the *'aṣabīya*, religion unites all hearts, replaces the desire for the vanity of the world with its rejection and turns men to God, seeking right and truth in unison.[7]

It must be said that Ibn Khaldūn was more concerned with the political relevance of religion than with its moral and civilising aspects, though he does not neglect these by any means.

Although the *mulk* is capable of looking after the welfare of man in this world, even this is achieved more perfectly with the aid of the laws of the *Sharī'a*, since the prophetic lawgiver knows best what is to man's advantage in both mundane and religious matters. "Therefore, if the *mulk* is Islamic it comes second in rank after the *khilāfa*, and they are linked together. But the *mulk* is isolated if it is outside the religious community (*milla*)."[8]

Ibn Khaldūn surveys the history of the Umayyad and Abbasid caliphates from the standpoint of the *khilāfa*'s inevitable transformation into the *mulk*. Once religion ceased to be the innate restraining force its place was taken by the *'aṣabīya* and the sword; out of the mixed Islamic *mulk*, and with the disappearance of the *'aṣabīya* among the Arabs, there finally emerged a mere royal power-state. "It is, therefore, evident that the *khilāfa* at first existed without *mulk*, then their character became intermixed and finally the *mulk* alone remained, isolated at the moment when its *'aṣabīya* became separated from that of the *khilāfa*."[9] In this context, religion (*dīn*) clearly means *Sharī'a*, and it cannot be repeated too often that what matters for a Muslim is the character and intention of the law of the state.

It is a common view of mankind today that the rule of law is the indispensable condition for the welfare of the individual and of his society and state. Ibn Khaldūn expressed this long ago, from his own experience in the Maghrib (North-west Africa). Discussing the need for *qawānīn siyāsīya*, that is, laws regulating the administration of the *mulk* and the relations between the ruler, whose authority rests on power of conquest and force, and his subjects, he says: "If the state is without such a *siyāsa*—government on the basis of legally binding rules and regulations—its affairs are not in good order, and its authority is not complete."[10]

Since these "political" laws are, as we have seen, also part of the *Sharī'a*, the religious and political unity of the *khilāfa* is obvious. The Islamic *mulk* as a mixed constitution still seeks to promote the wellbeing of the *malik*'s subjects in this world and their happiness in the next, but the strictly religious concerns are *subordinated* to the political and social needs of the state and its ruler, even if the *malik* assumes the title of *khalīfa* or *imām*.

Ibn Khaldūn makes it quite clear that if the political laws are promulgated by God through a prophet, they are superior to those issued by the king as rational laws in the public interest, because the divine lawgiver aims at the higher purpose of the citizen as a religious creature. Hence the *qawānīn siyāsīya* included in the *Sharī'a* of Islam are designed to fulfil, through the good order of state and society, the main purpose of the religious law: to prepare the believer for the hereafter. Again, *mulk*, or dominion exercised in a political organisation, is something natural and necessary for human association, and it is provided for in the *Sharī'a* alongside rules of trade and commerce, personal and family affairs, and strictly religious duties such as worship, fasting, almsgiving, and pilgrimage. And yet, conversely, since political authority is necessary, purely political laws are required. But they are legitimate only insofar as they do not serve merely the interests and whims of the temporal ruler. If they do, it is reprehensible on the grounds of both religion and political wisdom, since the ruler cannot expect the support needed to maintain his rule if his laws are dictated by his will to power and by human passion, without due regard for the needs of his subjects. Where, as Ibn Khaldūn puts it, "the light of God" is absent, as in laws dictated exclusively by political considerations, the true interests of man are neglected. Only the divine lawgiver knows these needs, which culminate in man's happiness in the world to come. Hence the *khilāfa* has to see that the people live by the injunctions of the *Sharī'a* and act accordingly in all their affairs, that is in their relations with God and with their fellowmen.[11]

To repeat, Ibn Khaldūn is fully aware of the fact that he is contrasting the realities of political life with the ideal *norm* of the *khilāfa*, which ended with Mu'āwiya's conquest of power. Yet, the *khilāfa* is not only the ideal, it is also the fountainhead of political power in the Islamic state and empire. Its effective directing power has decreased with the passage of time; the Umayyad and Abbasid dynasties declined as *da'wa* and *'aṣabīya* ceased to reinforce each other and the combination of religious zeal and power/political motives became weaker.

But since the state—whether religious, mixed, or "secular"—is subject to a natural law of growth, peak, decline and fall, a dynasty runs its natural course to be replaced by another vigorous one whose founder, if he is a Muslim, combines religious zeal with the *'aṣabīya* of his supporters. This means that religion as a power in the land is bound up with the life-cycle of a dynasty: the Almoravids and Almohads in the Maghrib are examples chosen by Ibn Khaldūn to illustrate this point. Similarly with the early Umayyads and Abbasids, in whom religious zeal and the desire to follow in the footsteps of the first four caliphs were strong whereas they declined among the later caliphs of both dynasties. Because of his insight into the nature of man and the interplay of political, social, economic, and cultural forces, Ibn Khaldūn considers this decline inevitable. He does not pass value-judgements as a moralist; he observes and makes empirical deductions.

Thus, if the political significance and social value of religion are obvious, the danger of institutionalised religion is equally clear to Ibn Khaldūn. The activity of the prophet had something spontaneous and elemental about it which fired his companions with zeal and enthusiasm. Obedience to his commands and to the exhortations and warnings contained in the Qur'an in no way diminished their prowess, courage and energy. Only when the example of the prophet and the *Salaf* gave way to the performance of religious duties out of fear of punishment and to the study under Sheikhs and *imāms* of the religious sciences, only then was the restraining force within man replaced by that of political and legal authority. This coincided with the transition from rural to urban settlement, which latter is as harmful to manly courage and determination as is submissiveness to law.[12]

Convinced that the religious law is superior to the man-made political laws, Ibn Khaldūn clearly sees the danger in obeying out of fear a static law, which has become a science to be taught and learned, as opposed to the spontaneous fulfilment of the divine commandments. This affects not only the individual believer, but also—and this is why Ibn Khaldūn discusses it—his state and society. It is the problem of primary and secondary authority. Applied to the state in Islam—the *Sharī'a*-controlled *khilāfa* and the constitutionally mixed *mulk*—it can be understood through the analogy of *ijtihād* as opposed to *taqlīd*: the creative, independent legal decision in contrast to the acceptance of legal authority established by earlier jurists. *Ijtihād* is only possible on the basis of deep faith, insight and wisdom when, to use Ibn Khaldūn's terms, *dīn*, religion, is strong; on the other hand, *taqlīd* is the outcome of "the *Shar'* having become a science and a craft which one acquires by instruction and education", with the result that the urban population "submits to *aḥkām* (statutes)",[13] issued by the government.

It must again be stressed that this process is inevitable—as inevitable as the transition from nomadic to settled life is necessary for *'umrān*, human civilisation. Just as settled, urban life is the prerequisite of the state, so political organisation is the indispensable condition for civilisation. Ibn Khaldūn actually uses both terms, *tamaddun* and *'umrān*, interchangeably. Just as ease and luxury can only arise in city-life, and do so in the nature of things, so their effect on state and society is both good and bad. On the credit side, there is greater production of goods needed for civilised living, enhancing the arts and crafts, and greater wealth with a larger circulation of money. On the debit side, character traits arise that are harmful to manliness, independence and public spiritedness, and that breed submissiveness to authority. Thus Ibn Khaldūn's contrast between *dīn* and *aḥkām* makes itself felt more and more, and the more the ruler has recourse to *aḥkām*, that is, *qawānīn siyāsīya*, the smaller the realm and the influence of the *Sharī'a* become.

One of Ibn Khaldūn's more important insights is precisely his recognition of the interconnectedness of the factors that make up political and social life.

Following Al-Māwardī's exposition in his treatise on constitutional law, Ibn Khaldūn traces the growing importance of the office of judge, whose duties have multiplied in proportion to the growing preoccupation of the rulers with state policy. The judge (*qāḍī*) together with the *mufti*, who is qualified to issue legal decisions (*fatwā*), hold their office under the *Sharī'a*, but they also have to decide cases for which the religious law has not made provision (*maẓālim*). Ibn Khaldūn is careful to distinguish between executive and judicial functions, which he keeps strictly separate; and he believes that the tradition ascribed to the prophet—"the *'ulamā* are the heirs of the prophets": a Jewish view that found its way into Islam—should not be adduced in support for giving the *'ulamā* a share in politics. Though he stresses the fact that these scholars were largely non-Arabs and hence not highly esteemed by the ruling Arabs, we are more concerned with another observation of his: that the *'ulamā* occupied with problems of the mind, discovering general principles from which they make deductions and the like, are therefore liable to make errors when dealing with questions of practical politics.[14] The politician, averse to speculation, applies his practical mind to the day-to-day tasks; he is concerned with questions of policy, with concrete situations that require workable decisions. Ibn Khaldūn reserves executive functions for those who have power to enforce their authority by *'aṣabīya* and/or force of arms. Consequently he holds that the scholars, even those who are among the ruler's advisers for "political" reasons (as a mark of respect for religion and its representatives), have only a limited, judicial, function: to issue *fatwās* and to administer the law in which they are expert.[15]

This opinion is highly significant, as is clear from Ibn Khaldūn's interpretation of its supporting tradition. To begin with, he again distinguishes the *dīn* that was in full force during the formative period of the *Sharī'a*, from the time of the prophet, through the first four caliphs and the *Salaf*, to the founders of the four orthodox rites or lawschools. During this period the *'ulamā*, by the depth and breadth of their knowledge, which covered the whole range of theology and of the all-embracing law were, indeed, the heirs of the prophet. In other words, in the time when the *Sharī'a* held unchallenged sway its interpreters were the natural advisers of those in power. Later, however, when the predominance of *dīn* gave way to *dunya* or *sulṭān*,[16] slipping gradually from a state of balance to one of inferiority in the *mulk*, the power-state reserved executive authority to those in control of *'aṣabīya* and force. It is interesting to find Ibn Khaldūn applying his distinction between the *khilāfa* and the *mulk* to the *'ulamā* and their authority in each state. It is obvious that they should wield a dominant influence in the *khilāfa*, where government and the entire administration were regulated by the *Sharī'a*, and the religious scholars had to possess comprehensive theoretical as well as practical knowledge; to Ibn Khaldūn's mind they were in fact of that stature and consequently enjoyed the status of judicial authorities and advisers to the executive. By contrast, the *mulk* came into being through *'aṣabīya* and brute force as a requirement of human civilisation, and the *Sharī'a* must now share authority with the *qawānīn siyāsīya* of the ruler; thus the *'ulamā*'s sphere of influence is naturally restricted to matters in which the religious law is applied, that is, to issuing *fatwās* when asked to do so. In a power-state built on a feeling of solidarity and concerned with the worldly welfare of the subjects and the interests of ruler and dynasty,[17] political advice is outside their competence.

This division of authority and functions is characteristic of the Muslim state in contradistinction to the strictly Islamic state. In the former, religion plays an important part—how important depends on the ruler and his respect for Islam—but it is not the sole determining factor behind all aspects of personal and collective life. Its law is a mixed law, hence the *'ulamā* are restricted in the range of their authority and function. Religion and politics no longer form an indissoluble unity: they are separate realms concerned with different issues and functions, decided and performed by different experts. Religion's influence over the minds and lives of citizens must be shared with other forces, represented in Ibn Khaldūn's world by the *'aṣabīya* and the will to power.

If we turn to our own time, we have no need to cast round for determining factors, for religion is at bay, and nationalism is foremost among several "isms" competing for the allegiance of modern man.

Ibn Khaldūn lived at the end of an epoch to which he was firmly rooted through his traditionalism; but he also foreshadowed the new era through his detached attitude and empirical method. He looked political reality fearlessly in the face and avoided the capital mistake of utopianism and romanticism: to mistake what is for what should be. The ideal Islamic state is the pattern that belongs to the past, though history lives on and the pattern remains the shining ideal—

suitably adapted to new circumstances. He experienced the present and tried by acute observation to understand it as it was and in relation to the past. His new science of civilisation bridged the gap by applying the law of cause and effect to the past and the present; it enabled him to explain why the *khilāfa* had to be followed by the *mulk* and how the two could and did exist together in the *Islamic mulk*, that mixture of divine and human law.

SECTION 2

ISLAMIC OR MODERN NATIONAL STATE?

CHAPTER 3

ISLAM AND TURKISH NATIONALISM

In retrospect we might say that modern developments, culminating in the predominance of the human element and the separation of religion and politics, are adumbrated in Ibn Khaldūn's crucial distinction between the divine and the human in politics. For him there is no nostalgia for the golden age of the past; his is the recognition of historical continuity and change. His political realism is born of psychological insight into the working of political institutions, created by man for man.

His thoughts were far in advance of his time, and centuries passed before an interest was taken in his *summa* of civilisation. While he may have influenced modern thinkers of the Muslim world, he did not father their ideas about Islam in an age of rationalism and nationalism, nor their ideas about state and society. But his ideas are relevant for present-day Muslims who have to determine what part Islam is to play in the public life of their modern states. At least this is my opinion, especially in the field of legislation. This will emerge when we now briefly survey the constitutional and legal problems that Muslim states have to face in our time.

RELIGIOUS CONSERVATISM AND POLITICAL LIBERALISM

We begin with the Young Ottomans and their reactions to the *Tanzimat* from the point of view of the *Sharīʿa* of Islam, and we then proceed to the Young Turks. Our central point of reference is the character of the state: Islamic or national Muslim.[1]

The strict Sunnism of the Ottoman Turks made itself felt in that sphere of Islam most characteristic and sensitive: the law of the state. *Qānūn*, the legal enactment of the sultan, approximated much more closely to the *Sharī'a* than did Ibn Khaldūn's *qawānīn siyāsīya* of the *malik*. The break-up of the old order was caused and accelerated by the growing influence and assertiveness of the European powers, and by the internal rumblings of Arab Muslim and Christian subjects of the Ottoman empire. To meet this threat the *Tanzimat* were promulgated, yet they satisfied nobody: neither the Turks under Western influence through education in France in the ideas of the Enlightenment and the French Revolution; nor the traditionalists; nor the non-Muslims. The measures, largely forced on the government by foreign pressure, did not achieve a balance between Islamic ideas and forms of Ottoman statecraft and administration, and the new European ideas of truly representative government and the equality of all citizens before the law and in opportunities of government service and economic enterprise.

We confine ourselves to the criticism levelled by the Young Ottomans, notably by Nāmik Kemāl and Ziya Paşa, on grounds of traditional Islam. Their attitude was conditioned both by religious conservatism and nineteenth-century European political liberalism. They hoped to combine the two by accepting European methods of government, administration, social organisation, and economic activity without the underlying Western philosophy and by simultaneously implementing Islamic ideals and ideas. Or, alternatively, if Western political ideas were to be adopted, it would be assumed they were nothing more than Islamic ideas. The contents were to be Islamic, and it was sufficient to clothe them in European forms in order to modernise Ottoman state and society. Such modernisation would actually lead to a revival of Islamic concepts of justice and equality. This attitude has become typical of conservatives throughout the Muslim world, but it does not resolve the dichotomy between the old Islamic ideal and contemporary reality. The Qur'anic commandment addressed to the prophet to consult with his followers (*shūrā*)[2] is interpreted to mean representative, parliamentary, or popular government; it is immaterial what constitutional and legal form this consultation takes, since what matters is the idea, the substance. Nāmik Kemāl, who was deeply influenced by Rousseau and especially Montesquieu,[3] adopted the principal concepts of European political thought but was at pains to find them all in Islamic law. Thus he equated the concept of popular sovereignty with the *bay'a*, the oath of obedience the *umma* swears to the newly elected caliph, as laid down in the treatises of the jurists on constitutional law as part of *Fiqh*.

His criticism of the *Tanzimat* is moderate and judicious; he is animated by respect for the *Sharī'a* (*şeriat*), the absolute Islamic norm, and by patriotism (he introduced the word *waṭan*, fatherland, and also *hürriyet*, freedom);[4] and he judges reforms by these standards. Defending their architect, Reşīd Paşa, against the accusation that he placed them under the guarantee of the European powers, Nāmik Kemāl asks who else could have been chosen as guarantor.

> "It could not have been the *Şeriat*," he answers, "for had it been in force the *Tanzimat* would not have been necessary. Neither could the *'ulamā* guarantee it, for had they preserved the *Şeriat* there would have been no need for a document, issued under the protection of Europe, to guarantee human life, that temple of God, against *fatwās* of execution issued without due trial."[5]

This is significant, for the decline of the Ottoman state is exemplified in the disregard for the *Sharī'a*, which Nāmik Kemāl considers the surest guarantee of justice and fairness.

Ziya Paşa was at one with Nāmik Kemāl in applying the standard of the *Sharī'a* to public life, which included the measures of reform adopted by the Ottoman government of the day. Concerning the equality decreed by the *Tanzimat*, Ziya says: "...The rights of Christian subjects were placed under triple or fourfold guarantees, and the Ottoman Empire in allowing this has even transgressed its Islamic duties." While Christians are protected by foreign embassies, the Patriarchate, and their national assemblies, the Muslim who is unjustly treated has no means of redress. While upholding the rights and privileges of the Christian subjects of the Sublime Porte as fully justified, he pleads for equal treatment for the Muslims.

Similarly, Cevdet Paşa sums up the effect of the Decree of 1856 thus: "Today we lost our sacred national rights which our ancestors gained with their blood. While the Islamic nation used to be the ruling nation, it is now bereft of this sacred right. This is a day of tears and mourning for the Moslem brethren."[6] The terms "Islamic nation" and "national rights" indicate not only Turkish nationalism in the face of the national aspirations of non-Turkish citizens in a liberalising, modernising Ottoman state, but also the Islamic character of this Ottoman Turkish nationalism as essential.

Notable is Ziya Paşa's criticism of the inequality inherent in granting equality to non-Muslims:

> ...the Sublime Porte did not deny that the Decree of Reforms was incompatible to a large extent with our national customs and ethic. At the same time it mentions the efforts made in order to modify these national customs, and says that inequality is illegal, as if it had never seen a book of the Islamic Canon Law or studied a history of the Islamic state, saying that the illegality of inequality has become the basis of the polity of the Ottoman Empire....

Nāmik Kemāl and Ziya Paşa were much concerned over the attempt by the *Tanzimat* statesmen to make laws contrary to the *Şeriat*, as the following quotation from an article by Ziya Paşa shows:

> Until the time of the *Tanzimat* the Ottoman Empire applied only one set of laws, the Islamic *Şeriat*. It is true that since the close of the age of *ijtihād*, i.e. for the last 800 years, the recorded judgements of Canon Law have not proved adequate in dealing with problems of the present age and that, therefore, there was a great need for establishing and postulating rules required by contemporary problems. Nevertheless, although it was possible to meet this need by making use of the unlimited resources of the *Şeriat*, recourse was not had to this means and the great mistake was made of issuing laws outside the *Şeriat*.

This criticism goes to the root of the problem, namely, the *'ulamā*'s inability to bring the principles of the *Sharī'a* to bear upon current exigencies. This would be possible by a fresh interpretation that could lead to necessary modifications without issuing new laws unconnected with the traditional religious law, which has been left behind and has lost its adaptability. The traditionalists deplore this state of affairs but believe that the remedy has to be sought in a revivification of the *Sharī'a*. The liberals hope that by saving the principles of Islam and applying them in new legislation, Islam's much-needed modernisation can be effected to meet the need of the hour.

The article just quoted goes on to deny the European claim—seemingly admitted by the extraneous laws issued by the *Tanzimat* statesmen—that progress was incompatible with the out-of-date provisions of the *Şeriat*, and it deplores the fact that "the opening of commercial, provincial, administrative and appeal courts..., the decision to deprive *Şeriat* courts of many legal functions, leaving them to deal only with matrimonial disputes, weddings and divorces and other religious affairs, can only be interpreted as an attempt to abrogate the whole of the *Şeriat* and, in so doing, to cut a fine figure in European eyes".[7] This attitude is born of a profound respect for tradition but shows little appreciation of modern needs, which have to be met if liberty and equality, justice, and fair play are to prevail. Meeting these needs cannot be dismissed as a pandering to European prejudices.

Writing on the same theme, Nāmik Kemāl starts from theological and philosophical premises, contrasting the divine origin of Islamic law and justice with the philosophical and human motivation of Western law:

Two sets of laws cannot be applied side by side in this state....They do not know that the essential provisions of justice are always and everywhere the same. The wise men of Europe have derived the principles of the present regulations from the characteristics of wisdom and the general rules of Nature....Similarly, the learned men of Islam codified their Canon Law in the same way, but because natural laws are contained in divine commandments and prophetic traditions, they derived their principles from these....If a collection of religious decisions is examined it will be seen that its political aspects can be applied to the laws of the best-ordered state....At the same time, it will be seen that Islamic Law is preferable to European legislative practice, considering that men do not want to follow the rules laid down by their fellow beings and that it is, therefore, easier to ensure general obedience to laws that are divinely determined. Although we have got in our hands a heavenly gift, such as the *Şeriat*, which is capable of meeting all the requirements of civilisation, the thoughts and imaginings of some eight or ten unjust and ignorant men have been considered the basis of law in our country.

Belittling the patchy nature of the *Tanzimat*, which are partly translated from the French, he stresses the superior character of the laws of the *Şeriat*, which

derives its principles from the provisions of Natural Law contained in Qur'anic verses and prophetic traditions, extended...by the extraordinary efforts of all the learned men...during the last 1,250 years among a people numbering 200 millions, men who not only tried to determine the truth and to attain to knowledge but also to earn themselves a reward in the next world. There is no doubt that a law based on this foundation is bound to be more just and conform more to the requirements of the age than even all the laws in force in civilised states.[7]

In his view, Qur'an and Sunna are identical with Natural Law, that is, he offers a contemporary philosophical justification of divine law reminiscent of medieval religious philosophy. Moreover, he underscores the excellence of this law by citing the *'ulamā*'s search for truth and their otherworldly interest throughout Islamic history! In addition, he appeals to the third principle of Islamic jurisprudence, *ijmā'*, and claims that the main principles of law are based on natural rights.

In our case these natural rights are contained in the laws of divine justice, as determined by the Qur'an. Being under divine protection, the *Şeriat* can only be suspended, but never amended even by the greatest conquerors. We should seek our survival in the observation of this basic law.... Various courts have been founded and laws introduced... the only result has been to break the power of the *Şeriat*.

Kemal Atatürk and the Grand National Assembly have, indeed, "suspended" the *Sharī'a*; Nāmik Kemāl could hardly have foreseen that his prophetic cry would be fulfilled. Is he right that amendment is impossible? The history of legislation in modern Muslim states from his time to our day seems to prove that Nāmik Kemāl, whom N. Berkes called a "utopian Islamist", was right.[8] His conviction that the *Sharī'a* is perfect and suitable for any state anywhere was undoubtedly firm and lasting; it is an often-recurring theme in his articles. He is opposed to the adoption of French law, saying it is contrary to "the ideas and the conduct of the Eastern population", which are "generally derived from the rules of Islam". While admitting that the *Mecelle* or Civil Code of 1869 did not contain any laws that ran counter to the *Şeriat*, he objected to its promulgation as a civil code "without making a whole set of laws based on the *Şeriat*".[9] "The provisions of Canon Law in our possession are superior to all the legislative rules in the world from the points of view of justice, discipline, comprehensiveness and regularity." Besides, foreign law was not only inferior to the divine law of Islam, it was inadmissible because it was foreign. He advocates an extension of the *Mecelle* to replace the *Dustūr*, the legal enactments of the *Tanzimat*.

There can be no doubt that he wanted Islamic law because he wanted Turkey to be an Islamic state, with popular consultation as the expression of political liberty. To the question, how could non-Muslims be expected to obey the *Şeriat*, Nāmik Kemāl replied:

> There is no problem simpler than this in the whole world. The political rules of the Islamic religion are, we think, in conformity with justice, civilisation and progress. Why should we expect others to hesitate to accept this logical proposition? Christianity does not interfere with politics and should not, therefore, be afraid of any offensive by an Islamic policy. Whatever is logical, is also useful. Why should followers of other religions refuse to accept things that are licit in Islam?

If a constitution were granted, he thought it only right that the *Şeyh-ül-Islam* and the *'ulamā* should consider all constitutional proposals and should issue a *fatwā* provided the proposals accorded with the *Şeriat* and the demands of the time. So certain was he of the justice of his view that he wrote:

> I believe that the Ottoman nation to which I belong wants freedom. But if it were to forget that that jewel is a divine gift, and seek to obtain it by the favours of this or that person, it will both destroy its honour and harm its interests. I was born free; why should I then accept to be manumitted? Why should I accept the legality of the actions which have enslaved me and, therefore, implicitly agree to their return? Considering that the *Şeriat* is unchangeable, why should I base my rights on human actions which are essentially changeable?

The only concession he apparently made was that an Assembly could debate all the questions arising from the granting of a constitution. The actual constitution was to be promulgated on the basis of a *fatwā*. Divine protection and sanction were needed to secure the legality of the constitution, which was to be clearly an Islamic Constitution.

If we apply the criteria of Ibn Khaldūn, we see that Nāmik Kemāl was for the *khilāfa* and against the *mulk* with "two sets of laws". Events have shown that "the demands of the time" offer only the choice between a Muslim state (Ibn Khaldūn's mixed-constitution *mulk*) and a lay state (pure power-state); we shall see this when we discuss the long drawn-out struggle for a constitution in Pakistan. There is no change in position and argument from

1867, when Nāmik Kemāl raised this issue in his articles, to the present day. It is no less significant that Nāmik Kemāl was convinced that his equation between natural law and divine law, and between natural rights and divine rights, was the legitimate expression of his "Islamism" and his "modernism", for this defender of the *Sharī'a*'s unchangeability and eternal validity was also the disciple of the Enlightenment, of Montesquieu and Rousseau. Claiming that the Imperial Rescript of Gülhane was based on the *Şeriat*, though Sultan Abdülaziz did not even mention the word, he explains this omission as follows:

The truth of the matter is that the Ottomans were until that day the slaves of the Sultan. The impression which they tried to create was that the Sultan out of his kindness decided to grant freedom to his subjects. We cannot accept this idea since we believe that the rights of the people are eternal like divine justice. The Sultan can rule us but not own us. We have got in our hands an indestructible basis for justice. It would be regrettable to let it go and to base ourselves on a single person against whose change of mind we have no guarantee.

One can hardly deny the logic of his argument, even though action, especially political action, does not spring from logical reasoning alone.

Or, in reply to the view expressed in Europe that Islam is responsible for the backwardness of the Ottoman state, he says that non-observance of the *Şeriat* "is the foundation and the origin of our administration". He concludes: "Briefly, if one wants our state to remain in existence, one must not fail to honour the *Şeriat* or seek to deprive the state of its Islamic character. This is because the *Şeriat* is both the soul and the substance of our state. It is also the most effective remedy." His defence of religion as the guiding principle and rule of individual, social, and political life is coupled with a plea for progress and a rejection of ethics in place of religion. He was a deeply religious man who distrusted the human basis of civilisation and the power of man to secure liberty and justice unaided by divine command and divinely revealed law. Since they based their case on religion (which Europeans identified with backwardness and fanaticism), the Young Ottomans were accused by them of being against progress. Nāmik Kemāl's reply is polemical in tone and designed to dispel Christian apprehensions of an Islamic state:

Are you afraid that we might oppress Christians? You should know that our religion provides a general equality of rights...if we follow the provisions of our religion, this would constitute the greatest possible safeguard for you, since it does not allow not only injustice, but even trickery. What we want is constitutional government in our country. We want a National Consultative Assembly. This would include representatives of every religion and its job would be to supervise the Government. The whole people will then attain to political freedom. We base this case on the requirements of our religion. After all this, you dare claim that our religion is an obstacle to progress? Would progress be ensured if authority remained in the tyrannical hands of a few men?

He goes on to remind the Young Ottomans' critics of the past glory of Islam, saying it was the teacher of Europe in the Middle Ages and it "widened and revived the boundaries of knowledge and wisdom". This has remained the stock argument ever since, as has the Muslims' identification of Western civilisation with what they consider its bad features: "If you think that civilisation consists in women being allowed to walk about freely in the streets or dancing at parties, these things are contrary to our customs and we refuse to have them." Opposing the science of morals, which leaves to man the decision of what is just and unjust, good and evil, he asserts:

Only the Qur'an and the tradition of the prophet can provide for the Muslim nation, a nation which is in possession of the *Şeriat*, the necessary provisions and rules which would establish the laws of liberty in the name of reason govern human conduct, order social morals, clarify what is necessary for our life, teach us our duties and our rights and tell us what is good and what is evil, which are the virtues and which are the vices....If man were able to learn what is just and what is unjust from a science of morals, what need would there have been of a divine revelation?

He claims that Plato and Aristotle were incapable of creating a "civilisation approaching that of the Abbasid caliphate".

Therefore, a return to the *mores* of the *Şeriat* would save the Ottoman state and society and serve them better than a slavish imitation of Europe, especially of French manners. Both Nāmik Kemāl and Ziya Paşa are agreed on this, and they attribute the decline of Ottoman power to their neglect of the provisions of the *Şeriat*. Apart from their nostalgia for a truly Islamic state, they criticised frankly and courageously the policy of the government and the parlous state of its finances and economic practices. This must, however, remain outside the scope of our study. Suffice it to repeat that the Young Ottomans, notably Nāmik Kemāl and Ziya Paşa, appreciated the necessity for reform but approved only those *Tanzimat* measures that were in conformity with the *Şeriat*. They deplored the import of foreign laws, because they were convinced that all that was needed to cure "the sick man" was an all-out revival of the indigenous religious law. For this law, they believed, provides for all the institutions and measures which the European powers pride themselves on and take credit for: such as popular consultation (meaning an Assembly that controls the government and ensures liberty and justice for the subjects of the sultan, who himself is bound by the religious law) and the separation of the legislature from the executive.

Whether their religious zeal could have been translated into action and have led to the recuperation of state and society in the Ottoman empire through the exclusive application of the *Şeriat*—this question is largely hypothetical since Nāmik Kemāl and Ziya Paşa were not given the opportunity to put their ideas into practice. What matters more, however, especially in view of later developments in Turkey and in other Muslim lands, is the fact that their patriotism and their desire for constitutional and administrative changes in the spirit of European liberalism were closely linked with their love for Islam and their belief that all that was best in Europe, politically and socially, was contained in Islam. In their view, Islam possessed moral teachings which were not only superior to those of European rationalism, but were, because of their divine source, capable of achieving far-reaching reforms more lasting and effective than anything the human mind could devise and attempt. The full restoration of the *Şeriat* would spell progress not only for Ottoman Turkey but for all Muslims.

Nāmik Kemāl's "nationalism" is a blend of Ottoman patriotism and Islamic fervour; both elements are united in his concept of *waṭan*, fatherland. The Ottoman fatherland contains diverse religious and ethnic groups, held together by the absolutist rule of the sultan-caliph. The more oppressive this centralised control was, the more pronounced became the fissiparous tendencies among the different "nationalities", Muslim and Christian; this was partly due to the influence of liberal-national ideas from Europe, fanned by the policy of the Great Powers. In their struggle for liberty and equality, and against the absolutism of the sultan, men like Nāmik Kemāl and Ziya Paşa had to preserve a balance, at all times precarious, with their loyalty to the institution of the caliphate, if not to the person of its holder as the symbol of the *umma*. Their problem was how to reconcile the claims of a universal Muslim brotherhood (*umma*) with the demands of a territorial fatherland (*waṭan*).

This problem has been with Muslims ever since, and it seems that its solution is more easily attainable through a separation of religion and politics in a lay state like modern Turkey. This is no doubt an oversimplification of a very complex problem, in which emotional and religious factors often pull in a different direction from rational and political considerations. These in turn are aggravated by historical memories and ethnic and religious antagonisms, all within the often arbitrary boundaries of a multi-national and multi-religious state. The result is an uncertainty of minds and confusion of issues. While Nāmik Kemāl's concept of Islam is clear and straightforward in its classical formulation, and while it aims at restoration of Islam's original purity, his idea of the fatherland is more complicated perhaps precisely because it is so closely linked with his love and concern for Islam. What the two have in common derives from his recognition that restoration of the *Sharī'a* is the ineluctable condition for restoring the Ottoman state under the sultan-caliph. In reality, only the Islamic component was even theoretically feasible, though its strong appeal to history led straight into pan-Islamism. A strong but politically liberal and progressive caliphate would secure Ottoman leadership of the Muslim world and would thus reinforce political independence and stability, which the patriotic Young Ottomans hoped would result from constitutional reforms. But in practice even this seemingly realisable ideal had to face great difficulties on the political as well as religious plane. That the Young Ottomans were fully aware of the religious difficulties is clear from their reassurances in reply to Christian fears. But they did not reckon with the growing desire of the Arabs and Balkan peoples for political independence: even a liberalised central government with the promise of equality would not satisfy them. By highlighting the semantic development of the terms *vatan* (*waṭan*) = *patrie*, and *millet* (*milla*) = nation, and by his comment on Nāmik Kemāl's patriotic, Islamic Ottomanism, Bernard Lewis traces the twilight surrounding this inner conflict.[10] In his view, Ottomanism was bound to fail and leave the field to nationalism.[11]

But the ideas of Nāmik Kemāl, Ziya Paşa, and Ḥayreddin Paşa, as well as those of the more radical Ali Suavi, lived on in their generation and the following, until they were ousted by the nationalism of the Young Turks that culminated in the Republic under Atatürk. The Islamist movement is typical of earlier Islamic Ottomanism after the revolution of 1908. The Constitution of 1876, modelled partly upon the Belgian Constitution of 1831, was short lived. Its revival as a result of the Young Turk revolution had far-reaching constitutional consequences that greatly influenced the position and influence of Islam in Turkey and beyond. The constitutional separation of the legislature and judiciary from the executive, in the sense of Montesquieu's threefold division of power, laid the foundations of a modern national state; but it also paved the way for Atatürk's sweeping reforms which culminated in the expulsion of Islam as a force in the public life of the lay republic. This was, naturally enough, achieved by predominantly political means. But the political struggle was accompanied by a fierce, open battle of the minds between Westernisers and Islamists. To label these two groups liberal-progressive and conservative-reactionary would be taking too narrow and extreme a view, and would also be too one-sidedly political in the Western sense of the term. However, there is some truth in the labels inasmuch as the Islamists, at least in their pan-Islamic tendencies, had the support of the deposed Sultan 'Abdülhamid, whose absolutist rule had favoured Muslim fanaticism.[12] Though in some respects the successor to the enlightened Islamism of Nāmik Kemāl and his colleagues, the Islamist movement gained political influence because its adherents included religious dignitaries of every rank and ministers of the old regime.[13] Helped by preachers in many mosques, their ideas resonated among the population at large. This was supplemented by a large output of literature for the educated reading public.

T. Tunaya credits the movement with having a hand in the genesis of events that led to a coup within a year of the proclamation of the constitution. According to him, the Islamists share with the Young Ottomans this conviction: that the Ottoman empire declined because the *Şeriat* was no longer observed as the embodiment of the doctrines and principles of Islam at home, and because Christian hostility threatened to destroy Islam abroad. The Islamists likewise deplore Ottoman imitation of the West: Islam cannot be saved by copying an alien political and social system. They fight the ignorance and apathy of the masses and try to rouse them by an appeal to the values of Islam, for the moral decline—evident in the widespread departure from those values—can be halted only by a return to them. Their appeal is addressed to all Muslims the world over and not merely to those living within the Ottoman empire; the condition of the empire, however, affects all Muslims, hence its present economic backwardness is equally destructive of Islam.

What do the Islamists mean by Islamic Renaissance or Islamisation? Says Prince Muḥammad Sa'īd Ḥalīm:

> If it is accepted that Islam is a religion with social implications, applicable to both religious and worldly matters, to material and to moral things, to become Islamized means to interpret the Islamic system of doctrine, morals, social thought and politics in accordance with the needs of the time and place and to abide by the rules of that system.

That this means Islamic exclusiveness and xenophobia is clear from another statement by this leading exponent of the Islamists:

> A Muslim who believes in the moral systems of Kant or of Spencer, who adopts the social conceptions of the French and the political conceptions of the English, may be a very learned person, but he still does not know what he is doing. How can a man have anything concrete in his mind and in his conscience, when his mind is full of so many contradictory and incompatible things?

The question is, do contradictions arise from the European mixture or from its incompatibility with the Islamic system as understood by Sa'īd Ḥalīm? How are we to understand "the rules of that system"? Are they the rules fixed by the jurists of the past or by the *'ulamā* of the present time? If the former, we can hardly expect an interpretation "in accordance with the needs of the time and place" to fit the rules laid down in totally different circumstances. If the latter, the modern *'ulamā* would not only have to be competent *mujtahids* (independent legal experts and decisors), but must also possess deep understanding of and insight into the political, economic, and social needs of the day. On the other hand, the Islamists favoured progress. They claimed that Islam as a dynamic social religion "did not constitute an obstacle to progress" and they admitted that it contained the seeds of reform in its dynamism. Centuries ago, they held, Islam had possessed a society and a state based on principles that the West only now adopted, thinking them to be new. Consequently, Islam has the innate ability and power to create a modern Islamic civilisation of a standard at least as high as that of twentieth-century Europe. The West has completely misunderstood Islam and misconstrued the reasons for its present parlous state, particularly in the Ottoman empire. For their part, the Islamists attributed the decline to tyrannous administrations, such as the one Turkey had just freed itself from. Not Islam but the deviation from its principles must be blamed. Nor are its rules obsolete and their practice harmful to civilisation. On the contrary, it is Islam that has brought civilisation to every people and country it conquered. Islam can therefore provide salvation even for Europe, which practises exploitation.[14]

The Islamists were rightly critical of Europe; they acknowledged its excellence in technology and science but rejected its moral and social practices and resented its attempt to conquer and convert the East to Christianity. Since Islam was afflicted with lethargy and superstition, the danger of its falling a prey to the predatory West was real. Salvation consisted not in imitating the West, but in making the Ottoman state strong through an Islamic revival. Basing themselves on certain assumptions, the Islamists advocated a modern state founded on the political principles of Islam. Their assumptions were: first (and this was their basic theme), Islam was not against progress; hence the scientific and technological achievements of the West had to be rapidly adopted and used for the strengthening of the Ottoman empire; next, Islam had not been affected by the moral and social crisis of Europe—it had only to shake off its lethargy; and last (though this was actually their fundamental assumption), Islam alone was capable of saving the Ottoman empire and, through it, all the Muslims and the world.

The Islamic renaissance should begin in the administration and in public law. What are the political principles of Islam, in their opinion? They are enshrined in the *Şeriat*, which reflects Islam as a social religion that provides adequate guidance for man in this world through good government. The political principles of the

Şeriat go back to the Qur'an. Thanks to them, Islam can lead mankind to happiness: in fact Islamic society has already progressed along this road. They claim that a people that adopts Islam enjoys a moral and social evolution, and this evolution is a condition of survival. Since Christianity obviously cannot satisfy Europe, she has adopted materialism and keeps religion separate from state and civilisation. On the one hand, they claim that the *Şeriat* lays down precise rules for ensuring man's welfare in state and society, and that it reserves the right to modify them in accordance with the needs of the age. But, on the other hand, they declare that the religion and rules of Islam are eternal and take precedence over state and society. Islam establishes final and compulsory rules for the government of a civilised society; "it has been revealed as a particular law ensuring happiness in this world and in the next".

"From the point of view of public law and administration", states T. Tunaya, the conclusion can be drawn from the Islamists' views that "the Islamic state rests on religion, is subject to the *Şeriat* and a separation of religion from the state is impossible.... The ideas of religion, humanity and civilisation are joined like links in a chain, and if one is broken, the others fall away." It seems to me difficult to reconcile the eternal character of the rules of the *Sharī'a* with the postulate of modification and even less with the concept of evolution; nor is their distinction between the *kullīyāt* and the *juz'īyāt* unequivocal. God has established the former as general principles, things in outline; but, to quote T. Tunaya again, "can one say... that the shape of the constituent parts, of current laws (*qānūn*) and regulations (*niẓām*), is also directly linked to God?". He reports a sermon on this question. The preacher holds that competent people can decide on the good order (*tanẓīm*) of particular things; but being only the instruments through which the *Şeriat* is carried out, these people must act upon its instructions.

The Islamists adhere to the classical theory of the *khilāfa*, the unity of religion and politics in Islam. This is clear from the answer one of them gave to the question: is the establishment of government a rational obligation, or is it demanded by the *Şeriat*? "Although government is essentially a rational obligation," he said, "the Islamic religion teaches that it is also an obligation under the *Şeriat*." Al-Māwardī declared that the *khilāfa* is demanded by the *Shar'*, not by reason, and in fact the reply just quoted adds that the caliphate should be considered a divine injunction. It is perhaps natural that such views should have been held by the Islamists, for a number of them were learned jurists and holders of the office of *Şeyh-ül-Islam*; for example, we would expect Musa Kāzim Effendi to advocate a strict Islamic theocracy with God as sovereign and His *Şeriat* as supreme authority. Politics, in their view, is linked with Ethics, but the two do not form part of practical philosophy as taught by the Muslim philosophers following their Greek masters Plato and Aristotle. Both stem from the divinely revealed law, the fountainhead of every human institution and activity. Hence the *Şeriat* guarantees the perfect just society, and he who wants to achieve true justice must live in an Islamic society. Since the Islamists by and large propound the classical theory of the *khilāfa*, with God as the sovereign, the prophet as the herald of His Law, and the caliph as the prophet's vice-gerent charged with the defence of religion and the administration of the world, a further elaboration would be tiresome. Suffice it to say that in their exposition a certain polemical tendency against Christianity, identified with Europe, is not unexpected. This serves not only to bring to the attention of their countrymen the supreme excellence of Islam, but also to stress their view that Christianity is irrelevant since it is not interested in the social order. From this stems the separation of state and religion in Europe, which accounts for the unjust treatment the Great Powers mete out to the Ottoman empire, the foremost Islamic state. By definition, no state and no society can be just unless justice is based on Ethics that derive from God. From their concept of divine justice they deduce the Muslims' right and duty to depose an unjust caliph and his government.

Next to justice, the principle of consultation (*shūrā* or *mashwara* in Arabic, *mesveret* in Turkish) is adduced as a precondition of just government and invoked in support of the demand for a National Consultative Assembly. It is curious, in view of the foregoing, that the Islamists should treat the caliph as sovereign when they say his responsibility is bounded by the two principles of justice and consultation. Strictly speaking, he cannot be given the highest executive *and* legislative authority (for the latter rests with God and His Law) unless we apply the distinction, mentioned a little earlier, between *kullīyāt* and *juz'īyāt*, reserving the former to God and allowing the latter to the caliph. That his neglect of both justice and consultation entitles his subjects to revolt has nothing to do with that, however. The right to revolt, with the consequent deposition of the sultan-caliph, had at least a practical significance, since the *Şeyh-ül-Islam* had to issue a *fatwā* to make the deposition of 'Abdülhamid and other sultans legal and effective. The Islamists' other considerations remained in the realm of ideal Islamic political theory—with the exception of the concept of the unity of all Muslims, the *umma* of Islam. This concept made the Islamists advocates of pan-Islamism, just as Jamāl al-Dīn al-Afghānī saw in the unity of the Muslims of the world which he strenuously propagated, the surest guarantee of Islamic survival in face of the challenge of Christianity and Western imperialism which were largely considered one and the same evil thing. Pan-Islamism is at least logical from the point of view of the religious and political unity of Islam. It has a strong basis in theory and in history, unlike pan-Arabism, the child of modern nationalism with little if any basis in theory or history.

But unity of all Muslims in the *umma* or *jamā'a* (community) is understood not only on the international, universal level, but also within the Muslim Turkish *millet* on a national level. In this, we undoubtedly see the influence of the prevailing political situation. Yet the Islamists who understood this twofold love, of religion and of "nation", as a divine gift opposed nationalism (*qavmiyyet*) and tribalism (*'aṣabiyyet*). This was directed against the Turkists, advocates of Turkish as opposed to Ottoman nationalism.[15] The Islamists only recognised one unity, that of all Muslims under the *Şeriat*.

In accordance with their belief that all the achievements of which European civilisation boasts are already contained in pure Islam, the Islamists stress the democratic virtues of equality and liberty in Islam (including freedom of worship and conscience granted to non-Muslim citizens); they oppose aristocracy as a claim to privilege, and they deny the existence of a clergy in Islam. In like manner they claim that human rights were present in Islam fourteen centuries earlier than their proclamation in modern democracies: liberty, equality, and fraternity are time-honoured Islamic virtues.

While Marxism is incompatible with Islam, it is their considered opinion that if man were to live by the dictates of the Qur'an, the social conflicts of the West would "...disappear radically. In accordance with the principles of Islam, capitalists who are proud of their worldly riches and contemptuous of the poor are not acceptable people". Islam lays stress on human duties rather than on human rights; or as we might say, the rights follow from a willing fulfilment of the duties that are all enjoined by religion.

Although firmly rooted in traditional Islam, the Islamists were also children of their time, as shown by their participation in the wider Young Turk movement. They were, therefore, as much concerned with political liberty and independence as were the Westernisers and the Turkists, but with this decisive difference: they considered these modern demands not the concomitants of Western philosophy adapted to the political struggle of European nations, but rather the religious postulates of Islam as a unitary religious and political system. How we in the West evaluate this tendency is quite irrelevant. What matters is not which way the mutual approximation and adaptation moved: whether from Europe to Muslim Turks, or from Islam to its Turkish adherents exposed to the winds blowing from the West. No, the characteristic feature of this symbiosis is the fact that the Islamists took their bearings from classical Islam, which they claimed to interpret in the spirit of the age; and they understood modern European political philosophy as only a *replica* of the original teachings of their glorious Islam and its *Şeriat*. Thus they aver that the Islamic state, guided by the *Şeriat*, which contains the political principles of justice, consultation and human rights, must be an independent entity. It cannot tolerate foreign domination, but must establish and maintain its independence. It is against imperialism.

Here we do well to remind ourselves that classical Islamic doctrine divides the world into the *dār-al-islām* and the *dār-al-ḥarb*, and the latter must be brought within the realm of Islam, if necessary by *jihād* (holy war)—despite the modern tendency to restrict *jihād* to defensive wars. The Islamists assign to the Islamic state a civilising mission, which, on the strength of its social principles, will first establish peace and prosperity within its own confines and then bring prosperity, progress, and above all a higher morality to those countries to which it expands. This is undiluted pan-Islamism, militant and reformist. The ideal Islamic state they want to realise will save destitute nations and promote a new, just social order in the world. The necessary civilising energy can come only from an

Islamic Renaissance that will restore original Islam, the Islam of Qur'an and Sunna with the *Şeriat* as its constitution.

T. Tunaya also examines the Islamists' attitudes to the Ottoman Constitution of 1908, and he cites the opinion of an Indian Muslim, Seyyid 'Abdul Mejīd, who had given a lecture in London in 1910 in which he compared Islam with the British Constitution: "The form of constitutional rule in force in the Ottoman Empire and in Persia is in conformity with Islamic principles of government." In Turkey itself, the office of the *Şeyh-ül-Islam* issued a proclamation that contained the sentence: "The *Şeriat* is the basic law of the Ottoman Empire, and the forces of the Government come from a combination of the wisdom of the *Şeriat* and of logic."

Yet others, influenced by the political and military disasters that rapidly followed the proclamation of the constitution, took a negative view. They criticised the framers of the constitution for having stopped short at political reforms whereas Islamisation demanded social and religious reforms in the spirit of Islam. They missed the principle of unity and deplored the danger of nationalism due to disunity. The imitation of Western institutions, they said, prevented the emergence of Islamic social values. The Balkan disaster was interpreted as a divine punishment for preferring European to Islamic institutions. Prince Sa'īd Ḥalīm Paşa, although several times Grand Vizier before and after the Young Turk Revolution, blamed the constitution for causing a social crisis that prevented the success of the reforms. He deplored its Latin character and imitation of France as well as its hostility to religion, which was, in the view of the constitution's architects, an obstacle to progress. The upper classes came in for sharp attack, for as the ruling circles they had wrecked the reforms. His shafts are directed especially against the wholesale import of and experimentation with foreign ideas without regard to the historical and social conditions prevailing in the Ottoman empire; this has caused only confusion in the social life of a people hopelessly divided between West and East. One can detect in his strictures a deep anxiety lest the traditional character of the Ottoman nation be corrupted by foreign ideas and institutions, which he considered alien to Turkish religious and social traditions. This was bound, he held, to sap the strength of society and prevent it from bringing about its salvation in its own way. Instead, salvation was expected to come from French ideas.

This dilemma has remained with the Muslims to the present day.

The principal controversy raged round the Basic Law. Those who favoured it maintained that it confirmed the political rules of Islam as laid down in the Qur'an even though some of these rules were codified in European form. Besides, it was not the highest law of the Ottoman state: this was, is, and must remain the *Şeriat* based on the Qur'an. Against it, Sa'īd Ḥalīm Paşa expressed the view that its political laws were far in advance of the rights and liberties granted to the most advanced civilised nations of the West, and moreover they bore no relation to the social conditions in Turkey. He carped at its foreign character, which ignored the political reality of the Ottoman empire with its many nationalities differing in language and religion. Proclaimed to destroy tyranny once and for all, it could not solve the political problems by the introduction of an alien parliamentary system. He cited as proof the many amendments chasing each other.

Utopian, romantic, reactionary, or idealistic; animated by religious zeal and a strong consciousness of belonging to an old civilisation that is fighting for its life against foreign aggression and influence—whatever label we attach to the Islamists' views, we cannot deny their missionary fervour and lively sense of historical continuity, linked to a desire to restore pure Islam. These are the expressions of a love for traditional Islam as a religious and political unity, and they stand opposed to Westernisation and secular nationalism. In Turkey the Islamist movement was the last overt defiance of new, outside forces and a last determined stand on behalf of an old/new Islamic order. In the face of Europe's powerful and dangerous challenge, their reading of contemporary world history was tinged with a nostalgic chauvinism: this is the natural corollary of a traditionalism that must glorify the past and stake exaggerated claims in order to find energy and hope for building a better future in spite of the weakness and backwardness of the present. Events have moved fast and overtaken the Islamists in Turkey, as a political force and as an organised body of opinion. But their ideas live on in other Muslim lands, not only in the *Ikhwān al-Muslimūn* (Muslim Brotherhood), but in other movements and among individual Muslims.

ISLAMIC OR WESTERN CIVILISATION?

Another nationalist and more forward-looking movement, attracted by the new ideas Europe had to offer, has won the day.[16] Though it falls into two separate groups, we shall treat it as one movement whose cure for all the ills of the Ottoman empire is the integration of Turkey within Western civilisation. What about Islam and Islamic civilisation? As with the Islamists, civilisation is the touchstone of contemporary life; to be civilised is the duty of man. The question is only to which civilisation a modern Turk has to belong and what and how he has to contribute to it. Is a choice to be made between Western or Islamic civilisation; is Islam by a renaissance to become the dominant civilisation for Muslims and the others; or is modern man to effect a symbiosis between the two, if not a harmony or even complete integration?

Integration must be ruled out at once, since it is not possible between two civilisations so differently orientated and constituted. This might appear strange, since the Hebraic element and the Greek component to a lesser degree are common to both Islamic and Western civilisations. But the fundamental difference remains that Islam as a political and religious unity cannot, at least in its classical medieval form, merge with Western civilisation as it is today, since to the latter the separation of state and Church is basic. Islam has never been a Church, and even if it should undergo a radical reformation (of which there is no sign and which is not even being considered by any Muslim who thinks in terms of authentic Islam), it would have to change its traditional character completely. This it may do without a reformation, though with considerable reforms. The result may well be a new and different Islam. For, if a Western student of Islam may venture an opinion, it is not a question of modifying the *Sharī'a*, of adapting it to conditions that are the result of foundations and concepts quite different from its own. Is Nāmik Kemāl right after all in his view that the *Sharī'a* can only be suspended but not amended? There have been reformers in Islam—it awaits a *mujaddid*, a restorer, in every century—but they set out to restore the pure, original Islam purged from alien accretions; they leave basic principles and substantive law untouched. The so-called "modernists", from Jamāl al-Dīn al-Afghānī, Muḥammad 'Abduh and Rashīd Riḍā, down to their present-day continuators, have not touched the basic provisions or the structure and range of the *Sharīʿa*. This may well be because a faith and way of life based on a divinely revealed law stands and falls with that law.

Is there, then, no fresh interpretation possible? Is this law so rigid that no detail can be modified? It seems to me that *ijtihād*, which is on every "modernist's" lips, can only operate within very narrow, closely defined limits. Analogies are dangerous and at their best approximations, never establishing a real and complete identity. But if we take the Qaraites for an example, we see that, though they ostensibly recognised only the written *Torah* (i.e. the Hebrew Scriptures) as their guide, their rejection of Rabbinic law, the *Halakhah*—which corresponds to the *Sharīʿa*—forced them to evolve their own *Halakhah*, or way leading to God. It is the discipline of the so-called law, and not the profession of universal ideas, that gives the religious community its character and preserves its identity. Islam without a *Sharīʿa* (not necessarily the classical, medieval *Sharīʿa*) is not historical Islam any longer. The dilemma is very real; every religion based on a law is faced with the danger—and the reality at one stage or another—of stagnation or petrification, reached when the courage and creativity of the "lawyers" run dry and they shelter behind the authority of their predecessors: in Islam, *taqlīd*. Opening the gate of *ijtihād*, as our "modernists" demand, is one thing; ignoring the historical growth and continuity of divinely revealed law through many generations of experts who honestly tried to bring law and life together is something quite different. At best it is a perilous undertaking endangering the structure and fabric of historical Islam; at worst it produces a new *Sharīʿa* in a transformed Islam, both of which share with their prototypes little more than the name. We have seen that the Islamists would have nothing of it; they talked and wrote much about reforms to meet the demands of time and place but, unless I am entirely mistaken, they made no such changes. However, this point will receive our attention in greater detail later. Let me stress here the inherent difficulty, if not impossibility, of radical change. Add to this the further dilemmas of the onslaught on faith and the challenge of social and political ideologies with their claim on the total allegiance of man—just as total as that of Islam on those who profess it—and we must realise that we cannot expect quick, clear-cut decisions. This makes it increasingly difficult for the Western student to come to a valid and fair assessment of contemporary Islam. But it is the modern Muslims' concern, not his. Much of the groping in the dark, the uncertainty and the apparent inconsistency and contrariness is inevitable. The crisis of Islam has been in progress for some considerable time; it has worsened under the appalling difficulties of the fight for political liberty, for economic improvement and cultural advance. The pace has been set by the West's unprecedented advance in technical skill and scientific discovery. Political institutions that had time to grow gradually in the West, where they were created and developed by a strong middle class, cannot be transplanted to men and places that lack the conditions for their working.

And yet the problems of the mind cannot be shelved indefinitely. A look at the Turkish scene in the years following the Young Turk Revolution of 1908, through the Great War to the establishment of the Kemalist Republic, convinces us that the question "Islamism or Westernism", a religious ordering of life or a lay state within Western civilisation, agitated many intellectuals and still does in other Muslim lands. Faced with political disintegration due to the national aspirations of the non-Turkish and non-Muslim minorities within the Ottoman empire, these men passionately debated the question of the character of their state and society. To them it was not an academic problem, but a matter of life and death. We are concerned only with the part Islam played in this great debate. Having ruled out the choice "either-or", we will have to consider the other possibility: "the one and the other", that is, the side-by-side existence of both Islam and Western civilisation.

If we refer once more to Ibn Khaldūn, it would appear that Islam has always been able to absorb within its realm several cultural streams that flowed side by side most of the time. Sporadic attempts at integration, at harmonisation, were made, notably by the *falāsifa*, the Muslim philosophers, who tried to resolve the dichotomy of faith and reason. Though such attempts never affected the mainstream of Islam as a faith and a way of life, they greatly enriched Islamic civilisation, and their echo can be heard today among certain Muslim intellectuals. There was some interaction between the two sovereign traditions of the West and Islam; but more often the two streams never merged. Turkey apart, which decided on one way and rejected the other, other Muslim states may well opt for "two sets of laws" in a lay state. Composed of representatives of all classes and groups of citizens, including *'ulamā*, but not dominated by them, its legislature would promulgate laws that serve the needs of a contemporary society. In the process, it would take account of the customs and traditions worth preserving and worth building, together with Western ideas and institutions, into a new pattern of Muslim, if not Islamic, civilisation.

As already mentioned, Turkey has decided on a lay state with separation of state and religion. This is the outcome, perhaps inevitably, of Turkish nationalism culminating in a modern national state within Western civilisation. Its theoretical basis was formulated and a number of practical measures for its implementation were suggested by Ziya Gökalp.[17] His attitude to Islam, though not uniform and not entirely consistent throughout his literary activity as a Turk and a Muslim, is highly significant, for it represents, at least in its principal features, a valuable contribution to the solution of the problems of the meaning of Islam and its role in a modern national state. Gökalp approached the problem both from the inside, because he was bound by strong ties to the teachings and the history of Islam, and from the outside. That the two approaches should not always be in harmony, or lead in a straight line to one unequivocal position, is only natural in the existing dilemma.

RELIGION, STATE AND NATION

Ziya Gökalp's outside approach and method are sociological. U. Heyd has shown that Durkheim was his principal teacher, but that his distinction between culture and civilisation probably stems from Tönnies. This distinction lies at the root of Gökalp's theory of nationalism, and it largely determined his view of Islam and its role in society. The central idea of his social philosophy is evolution, both of society and of the factors, including religion, that determine it. In particular, he distinguishes two types of society, primitive and organic.[18] Religion is the sole authority in the former; whereas in the latter, religious *mores* are followed by political and cultural *mores*, with the result that three different kinds of authority exist in it at the same time, producing three different social units. The unit bound by religion is an *ümmet* (*umma*); the one under political authority is a state; and cultural *mores* produce a nation.

Evolution presupposes differentiation with mutual interaction. "All institutions of primitive societies...necessarily spring from religion and acquire their power and value from this source of sacredness."[19] But in organic societies, religion as a social force should be confined to "institutions which are relatively spiritual and represent the collective conscience of society....It becomes harmful when it is extended to worldly or secular [temporal], and especially to material, institutions because it prevents these institutions from adapting themselves to the expediences of life". Having established this differentiation and the consequently differing functions of the three elements, he applies his sociological method to the religious *mores*—an unprecedented procedure in Islam. For him, "religion is the most important factor in the creation of national consciousness as it unites men through common sentiments and beliefs. It is because of this that genuinely religious men are those who have national fervour, and genuine nationalists are those who believe in the eternity of faith".[20]

How does he apply this positive evaluation of faith to Islam? He accepts the religious sanction for morals, and, in a rather ingenious way, distinguishes between *naṣṣ* (the Qur'anic textual command and prohibition) and *'urf*, which he defines as "the conscience of the society expressed in the actual conduct and living of the community". Accommodating the usual Islamic classification of actions under these two sources, he claims that the social conscience (*'urf*, custom and the law based on it) sometimes has precedence over *naṣṣ* ("under necessity *'urf* may take the place of *naṣṣ*"). This is only a little more surprising than his assertion that *'urf* is one of the generally accepted principles of Islamic jurisprudence (*uṣūl al-fiqh*). While some jurists recognise *'urf* as a fifth principle, this is not the accepted orthodox Sunnī view.[21] *'Urf* is tolerated if it does not go against Qur'an or Sunna. But in Malaya today *'ādat*-law exists alongside *Sharī'a*-law.[22]

Ziya Gökalp's emphasis on *'urf* no doubt arises from his desire for change in accordance with the needs of society in an evolutionary process. If acceptable, this could indeed lead to far-reaching reforms of Islamic law, though Atatürk's action closed the door in Turkey to an experiment with Gökalp's ideas and intentions. His distinction between traditional and social *Sharī'a* led him to suggest parallel studies of *'urf* and *naṣṣ*, a joint venture of sociologists and *fuqahā* (experts in *fiqh*). He says:

But the social *Sharīʿa* is in a continuous process of "becoming", like all social phenomena. It follows, then, that that part of *fiqh* is not only liable to evolution in accordance with social evolution, but also [that it] *has* to change. The fundamentals of *fiqh* related to *naṣṣ* are eternally constant and unchangeable, whereas the social applications of these fundamentals which are based on the *ʿurf* of the public and on the *ijmāʿ* of the scholars of *fiqh* have to adapt themselves in accordance with the necessities of life.[23]

Elsewhere he says that *fiqh* is based on revelation and on society, which is only another way of combining *naṣṣ* and *ʿurf* as the two basic sources of law.

The divine part of the *Sharīʿa*, being a divine act, is in a state of absolute perfection; hence, it is exempt from any evolution or progress. The fundamentals of the faith cannot be subject to the law of evolution like social institutions....The social principles of *fiqh*...are subject to the transformations taking place in the forms and structures of society, and hence are subject to changes along with society. Every *ʿurf* is invariably the *ʿurf* of a certain social type.[24]

But how can he then maintain that *ʿurf* sometimes has precedence over *naṣṣ*?

What is essential in this argumentation is Gökalp's attempt to explain the social element in Islamic law as inconstant, subject to change and to the "law of determinism in social life": this view conforms with the findings of sociologists who compared institutions of different societies under "similar social conditions" and found that like produces like. Linking this sociological law with the observation of "certain of our *ʿulamā*...[that] the natural laws...observable in natural phenomena (are nothing else but) the *sunna* of God", he is convinced that it is legitimate to apply this to "the natural determinism observable in the natural laws of society". Hence, he concludes, *ʿurf* has at least by implication a divine nature as well; and basing himself on an alleged saying of the famous jurist Abu Yūsuf ("If *naṣṣ* is derived from *ʿurf*, then *ʿurf* is preferable"), he deduces that "the *naṣṣ* relative to temporal affairs and social life is a derivative of the *ʿurf*. When we accept social determinism and the uniformity of social phenomena as the expression of the way of God, it becomes natural to regard this divine *sunna* as the basis of the *naṣṣ* relating to the social life". In other words, by claiming a divine nature for the social conscience of the community, Gökalp assigns it first place as a source of law, and in his opinion this primary legislative force has greater significance for society than the immutable other source, the revealed *naṣṣ*. If such an interpretation were permissible, based on this somewhat daring argumentation, the way would lie open for radical reform of the *Sharī'a*.[25]

In Gökalp's view, *'urf* reflects the moral, social, and political aspects of the conscience of the community; and once this is considered, if not superior to the *naṣṣ*, then at least of equal or even primary importance, the step is not far to freeing the *Sharī'a* of its revelatory character and taking legislation altogether out of the hands of the experts in *Fiqh*. This is of great practical import since, with the inroads nationalism has made into Muslim society, the *umma* has come to mean a predominantly religious association. Once it has to share its claim to allegiance with other group loyalties, like those of the nation (*millet* for Ziya Gökalp), the secularisation of legislation becomes likely, if not certain.

And it becomes inevitable if in political thought the sovereignty of the nation takes the place of the sovereignty of God and His absolute authority. As far as the *Sharī'a* is concerned there can be no fresh legislation in Islam, but only application of the immutable law by the use of definite canons of interpretation that allow a certain degree of flexibility through such concepts as *maṣlaḥa*. Only in the realm of *qānūn*, Ibn Khaldūn's "political laws", is legislation freed of the principles of *Fiqh*, but even there it must not run counter to the *Sharī'a*. Gökalp's division into traditional and social *Sharī'a*, directly revealed and implied divine Islamic law, leads logically to the separation of the two streams and can lead to the suspension of the traditional part.

We know from the Kemalist revolution that Atatürk abolished the *Sharī'a* and substituted a secular law for it, going right out of the Islamic world and radically into Western civilisation by having the Swiss Civil Code adapted to Turkish requirements. That he went further than Gökalp probably intended does not alter the fact that Gökalp's sociological approach was a decisive breach in the traditional concept of law and paved the way for radical reform and departure. His plea for a strict separation of the offices of *mufti* and *qāḍī* (one issues and the other applies decisions) points in the same direction and has had similar, if not equally radical, results. Here—and this is important—he is following early classical practice, since the two offices were always separated. But he wants to keep separate the two *realms* they represent, that of piety and of jurisprudence.[26] Citing an example, he says that according to piety the taking of interest is forbidden, but it is permissible "by a fictitious transfer". He could not have expressed more clearly the gulf between ideal and reality, between religious norm and economic necessity. Here again the step is not far from the consciousness of a dichotomy to its removal as a practical necessity. Yet this does not mean that he underrated religion as a great social force; on the contrary, he proposed positive measures designed to spread its influence as a character-building element of great value for individual and society. He wanted to centralise in a "Ministry of Pious Affairs" all the strictly religious matters that have always been entrusted to *mufti*, teacher, *shaykh*, *imām*, and *khatīb* (preacher). He attributed the decline of religion to the confusion of the perfect principles with "the backwardness of our judicial methods and practices". A separation of functions would benefit both fields and thus religion.

The separation of what he calls religious and judicial functions is, however, only part of a wider problem, that of the relation between state and religion in all fields of activity. In another of his statements he says: "People can neither entirely drop the religion they hold sacred, nor can they dispense with the necessities of contemporary civilisation. Reason demands, not that one be sacrified at the expense of the other, but that an attempt be made to reconcile the two."[27]

The occasion for this pronouncement was the annual convention of the Party (or Committee) of *Union and Progress*, of whose central council Gökalp was a member. At this convention two views were expressed: one maintained that Islam can be reconciled with modern civilisation, the other that this was impossible. The latter was represented by two factions which drew extreme and fundamentally contrary conclusions: one faction, which Gökalp calls "the zealots of Europeanism", wanted to give up Islamic principles in favour of European civilisation in its material and spiritual aspects; whereas the other, "the zealots of scholasticism", rejected modern civilisation completely and wanted to uphold traditional Islam. In this context, Gökalp severely criticises the reforms of the *Tanzimat*, showing, on the basis of Al-Māwardī's exposition, that they completely misunderstood the nature of the *khilāfa*. For they held that the caliphate and the sultanate were two different functions united in one person, which therefore gave him two different judicial functions. The disastrous consequence of their mistaken notion was that the office of *Şeyh-ül-Islam* was given authority over both *muftis* and *qāḍīs*. In reality, only *muftis* are under his authority, whereas *qāḍīs* enjoy the caliph's delegated authority under the Grand Vizier. Hence all judicial matters are under the authority of the state and all matters of piety under that of the Grand *Mufti* or *Şeyh-ül-Islam*, whose ratification—by *fatwā*—of judicial decrees is contrary to Islam and harmful to both religion and state.

It is difficult to see how Gökalp could reconcile the separation of religious and judicial powers with the unitary character of Islam, except on the basis of his already quoted differentiation between the two parts of the *Sharī'a*, and, in the same context, between piety and law: "Islam has manifested its moral sublimity in its injunctions of piety. Judicial injunctions are nothing but acts of tolerance on behalf of religion in accordance with the necessities of [the] time." This shows his awareness of the dilemma facing a modern Muslim who is determined to uphold religion and build a modern national state. A solution seems possible only by assigning piety to the private world of the believer and keeping all worldly affairs firmly under the political authority and social control of the lay state under popular sovereignty.

This is a new interpretation of the meaning and place of Islam, for it treats it like other religions. Atatürk's abolition of the offices of caliph and of *Şeyh-ül-Islam* have made it such. Religious affairs now come under a government department. At the same time, Gökalp insists on the sacred character of the state in Islam as

> a merit, for if it had seen government and law as profane and secular institutions, it would have invented a spiritual government such as we find in Christianity....Islam did not establish institutions contrary to the laws of nature and life such as a priesthood. It was because Islam had brought state, law, and court into the realm of the sacred that those traits, such as loyalty to the secular ruler, a genuine fraternity and solidarity among the believers, sacrifice of interests and life for the sake of *jihād*, tolerance and respect towards the opinions of others, which are the very basis of a permanent order in society, were cultivated among all Muslims as common virtues.[28]

We might legitimately ask how this appreciation of classical Islam can be reconciled with such a strict delimitation of its scope and functions in the setting of a modern state within European civilisation. This question becomes particularly acute since he maintains that Christianity "is irreconcilable with a modern state", which is why France laicised the state, and religion became unofficial. Did he recoil from the logical consequences of his own thought—consequences that led Atatürk to do exactly the same as the revolutionary régime had done in France? For he is quite explicit in his claim that only Islam is compatible with a modern state. In support he points to Protestantism in Europe as an approximation to Islam (he actually calls it an imitation) as the result of the Crusades, and he claims that the modern state first came into existence in Protestant countries.[29]

Or has he in fact entertained two different views of Islam? For he deals at length with Islam as an *ümmet*, a religious group, in contradistinction to a "grouping called 'nation'" in which

> language, morals, law, and political institutions, fine arts, economic organization, science, philosophy, and technology are all common unifying elements, in addition to religion...and the totality of these we call "culture". Culture is an all-inclusive term, comprising all social institutions. Therefore, we may define the nation simply as the "sum total of men who belong to the same culture".[30]

No doubt this concept has come from outside Islam and probably explains the two different views of Islam he entertains without being conscious of their incompatibility. Applying the thought-categories of contemporary Europe to Islam, he advocates a separation of Islam from Oriental civilisation in order to be able to combine Islam with Western civilisation. He associates internationalism with the *ümmet*, since it comprises "in most cases a collection of several societies or nations". The break-up of the Ottoman empire has taught him that the head of such an *ümmet* cannot be the political head of only one of these nations. "The function of the head of an *ümmet* is to serve the religious life of the Muslims. The function of the state...is to serve national life." He adds that the recently proclaimed principle of popular sovereignty "obviated the claims of single persons to be the sole possessors of sovereignty".

It is characteristic of Gökalp that at every turn he illustrates his thought with examples taken from the history of the caliphate in Islam. The caliph is the symbol of the unity of the *ümmet*. "How could it be permissible to defame such an office...through the politics of a particular nation, and inevitably to disfigure it through the unavoidable and human faults of politics?" He mentions the Seljuks and Mameluks as examples of different headships, as well as of the separation of religion and state; and he goes on: "These were the greatest periods in the history of Islam, both politically and religiously. It was only when Selim I had again unified these two offices that the decline of the Ottoman Empire ensued; its religious as well as its political life began to deteriorate."[31]

He hails the election of a new caliph by the Grand National Assembly as a red-letter day in the history of Islam: "Although Turkey and the Turkish nation is its main support, all Muslim states and nations will support it materially and spiritually. But its real and most powerful source will be the greatness of Islam which has today [1922] forced the European world to respect it." Before, he maintains, the Ottoman caliph-sultan exercised religious authority only over those Muslims who were his political subjects; but now he exercises it over all Muslims throughout the world. Again Gökalp refers to Islamic history, this time to the period of the prophet himself, in order to prove that the political organisation of the neighbouring nations was completely independent even when they heeded the prophet's call to embrace Islam as their religion. He justifies the institution of *jihād* by the refusal of these nations to accept Islam: they had therefore to be incorporated into the *dār-al-islām* by force of arms. He envisages an "independent Islamic organisation" such as was not even possible in the time of the prophet in response to his letters he addressed to the neighbouring states, because now for the first time the caliphate is independent: Turkish action has separated it from the sultanate.

Surveying the history of the caliphate, he distinguishes four types: first, the caliph-ruler type of the four *khulafā rāshidūn*; their primary function was to be caliphs, and they assumed political authority only because a state organisation did not exist. Next we find the ruler-caliphs of the Umayyad, Abbasid, and Ottoman dynasties, whose primary function was political rulership. Under the Seljuks and Mameluks there existed a "Caliphacy without organisation": deprived of their political function, they could not exercise their religious function either, because an organisation comprising *muftis* and *mujtahids* did not exist, and they themselves were not competent to decide matters of piety and law. The fourth type has been created only now, with the establishment of an "independent and organized Caliphacy".

Recalling that he said the period of Seljuk and Mameluk effective political control was the heyday of Islam, we can see that there is in Gökalp—inevitably—some inconsistency and even contradiction. The latest form of caliphate had little chance to come into its stride, for it was abolished sixteen months after its establishment, when he was still alive. The religious and political functions of the Islamic state were no longer exercised separately by caliph and sultan: indeed, both had disappeared, and with them an *ümmet* of Islam that had been visibly organised and felt as a unifying bond—a religious unity amidst national diversity—for all professing Muslims.

The effect of this startling event can be studied in the views that the "modernists" hold on the caliphate, and in particular in the special treatises of 'Ali 'Abd al-Rāziq and Muḥammad Rashīd Riḍā. But before we examine their views, we must briefly discuss one more of Gökalp's important contributions to the genesis of contemporary Islam: his views on the place of Islam in national education. That "Islam is one of our ideals in education" is clear from the curriculum, which comprises Turkish language and literature; the Qur'an and the history of Islam and Islamic languages; and modern foreign languages, mathematics, and natural sciences. "This shows that the aims we pursue in our education are three: Turkism, Islamism, and Modernism."[32]

Surveying the three branches from the time of the *Tanzimat* to his own day, Gökalp deplores the decline in Islamic education: "Religious education lost its vitality." Two ideals fought for supremacy: Turkish nationalism and Islamic internationalism (pan-Islamism). Neither provided a good education, let alone a modern one; yet, he avers, "These three aspects of education must aid and complement each other" and must be clearly defined and mutually delimited. "When secular education transgresses its own material realm and reaches into the spiritual realm, it clashes with the education of [*sic*] Turkish and Islamic ideals."[33]

We note that secularism is equated with materialism but forms a legitimate component in an all-round, integrated education, which must be national education. Nationalism for Gökalp is a spiritual value, just as cultural nationalism, on a par with religion, is another spiritual value. He is conscious of the difficulty to delimit national against religious education, since Islamic traditions belong to Islam as a religion and also to the nations that contributed to it: the Arabs, Persians, and Turks. He defines (national) culture as "the sum total of the value-judgements that constitute the ethos of a people", that is, in terms of the regnant sociological theory and education "simply means inculcating this culture in the habitual attitudes of the individual members of that people. We call the sum total of all reality judgements current among a people its techniques". Under the influence of religion,

> national culture becomes overshadowed by the traditions of international civilization. Civilization is the product of all reality judgments of the peoples who belong to the same *ümmet*.... Within a civilization-group, education tends to be of an international rather than a national character. It tends to inculcate the international civilization rather than the national culture. The modern nations who regain their political independence and cultural freedom from international civilization-groups immediately set out to re-discover their national cultures....It is then that national education reigns over everything.[34]

He then applies this general rule to the Turks who adopted Islam and with it a civilisation, but preserved their national culture side by side with this international civilisation without integrating one with the other. With the *Tanzimat* a second civilisation, that of Europe, was superimposed upon the existing dichotomy with the result that the national culture disappeared, leaving the two civilisations in conflict with each other. This was aggravated by the rise of Turkism, which created the imperative need for an objective study of the affinities and especially the divergencies of the several civilisations in order to discover the true national culture, "by the scientific methods of sociology".

U. Heyd has described the shifts in emphasis during different periods of Gökalp's life, first before the Great War, then during and finally after it. He shows how Turkish culture became the object of his striving and how he tried to fit Islam—as a religion, no longer as an (international) civilisation—into Turkish nationalism so that Islam could be combined with European civilisation just as it had once been united with Oriental civilisation.[35]

This Gökalp held to be possible because a community of religion is no longer the criterion of civilisation; instead, modern civilisation is the result of the rise and application of the positive sciences. This means that religion, though still a social factor, is no longer as decisive as the other values, the political and cultural *mores*. He wanted to exclude foreign, i.e. Arab and Persian, elements from Islam, pleading for the use of Turkish in worship. But, apart from the call to prayer in Turkish instead of Arabic, this plan was not adopted, not even after a committee appointed by the Theological Faculty of Istanbul University in 1928 had suggested it as an important means of improving religious services.[36]

Though Islam has been eliminated from public life, which is firmly based on the theory and practice of the lay state, it is still deeply rooted in the minds and hearts of the people. The state is ever watchful lest the former religious leaders, their successors and the religious functionaries of the mosque should regain something of their influence in public life. Kemal Atatürk set his face against the old traditional education and would no longer allow it to run parallel with the secular education which for a considerable time had been modelled on Western education. No separate religious education could be tolerated, but allowance had to be made for the religious education of children whose parents wanted it, provided this was given within the one, undivided national education. This subject will engage our attention later, together with the national education in other Muslim countries, at all levels. Suffice it to quote Atatürk's programmatic declaration which echoes the spirit of Ziya Gökalp: "The nation has finally decided to achieve, in essence and in form, exactly and completely, the life and means that contemporary civilization assures to all nations."[37]

This was spoken in 1924 after Islam had been officially disestablished and ousted from political life. This clear declaration that Turkey was irrevocably committed to Western civilisation and was to achieve national unity and greatness as a full and equal member of it, set the tone for the life of the Republic once and for all. No concessions made since Atatürk's death and the emergence of a legally recognised opposition were allowed to remove or even undermine the lay character of state and society. Islam is strong in present-day Turkey, but without overt influence on politics, law and economics.

The recently amended constitution of the Turkish Republic is explicit about the character of the new Turkey as a nationalist, democratic, lay state. And yet the visitor to Turkey is soon aware that Islam has cast more than a shadow on politics. Here is an unsolved problem demanding a solution, or at least an accommodation which does not, however, appear to be in sight, despite the length of time the movement towards Western civilisation and Turkish identification with it has been in full swing. Turkey, which of all Muslim countries has broken most radically and systematically with Islam in its classical theory and practice, has so far not been able to establish a natural, harmonious equilibrium setting the whole nation free to pursue its national life unhampered by this internal irritant. It is not simply a question of old versus new, of a bygone past trying to stage a comeback and put the clock back. If it were nothing more, the firmly based popular democracy would long ago have succeeded in eliminating in practice what it abolished by legislative action backed by the strong arm of the executive.

Religion still means a great deal to a large part of the people, and in the form of traditional Islam it obviously fulfils a deeply felt need. For these reasons it will have to be given sufficient living space to develop within society and state without in any way endangering their lay character. Since legislation has been completely secularised, Islam can no longer give its ideas and concepts legal form and force; hence its character will inevitably undergo radical changes and come closer to the character and status of religion in the West. It is, no doubt, paradoxical that without a clergy and all that it involved in the West (before the Reformation but especially since the French Revolution), there should be "anti-clericalism" in Muslim countries today. This in itself is a sure sign that the attitude of the educated groups—the administrators of government and law, the professional classes, the industrialists and merchants, and the teachers, especially those in higher education—has changed in respect to religion. It has moved nearer to, and in many cases has become identical with, that of their corresponding groups in the West.

The real influence of the West can be seen, not in science and technology, but in this new attitude to religion, with its stress in Islam on principles rather than on strict observance of the legal provisions. Therefore, the often-repeated assertion that Islam is not against learning and science, but that on the contrary it recommends the pursuit of knowledge and praises the exercise and use of man's intellect in the service of God and his fellow-men, does not touch or effectively meet the real and much deeper problem of faith in our time. Seen as the apparent conflict between religion as a set of principles and as a set of immutable rules, laid down by divine command and obligatory on the believer for all time, it is obvious that if Islam is both—principals and law—we cannot expect the agnostic or even atheist Muslim to recognise the binding nature of a law given by a God whom he does not acknowledge in his life and thought.

For a time—and it may be quite a long time yet—he may accept it as a convention to which he will conform from habit or from a sense of cultural affinity and history. But eventually everybody, apart from the thinking minority, will need guidance, a central reference, or whatever we may call the stabilising norm which gives cohesion to a group, a sense of belonging, security to its members, and even in this materialistic age an ideal to live for. Without it man cannot live meaningfully, achieve the inner peace he craves, or possess a set of values that he voluntarily recognises and without which his contribution as a citizen cannot be expected or made.

CHAPTER 4

FOR AND AGAINST THE "KHILĀFA"

It is obvious that modernity and modernisation affect in the first place political thinking and institutions, economic affairs, and such social questions as the position of women in contemporary society. If this society is Muslim, the legal status of woman and her participation in political and economic life are also involved. However we look at Islam, nobody can deny the central position of law in its structure and the important place it has in the divine plan as the guide to God and to man's happiness in the hereafter, but also—and this is significantly stressed in our time—his wellbeing in this world: in state and society.

ISLAM AND THE "MODERNIST" MOVEMENT IN EGYPT

The whole Muslim world watches with interest and anxiety the developments in Turkey, for what happens in one Muslim country is bound to have repercussions in most, if not all, of the others. Whether the reactions to movements and events in another part of the Muslim world are positive or negative, they reveal a natural concern of fellow Muslims even if the struggle for independent nation- and statehood demands their foremost attention.

This is especially true of Egypt, the cradle of the "modernist" movement under Muḥammad 'Abduh and his disciple Rashīd Riḍā, and the scene of a prolonged fight for political independence from British occupation and for constitutional reform. For in Egypt, national and nationalist aspirations, represented by political organisations such as the *Wafd*, went hand in hand with the movement for religious reform and regeneration. As long as the desire to rid the country of British rule united all Egyptians, differences about the role of Islam in a united independent Egyptian nation and state had to be shelved. This does not mean that deviation from strict orthodoxy did not arouse the hostility and retaliatory action of the guardians of tradition, especially the *'ulamā* of Al-Azhar.[1] Nor did the national struggle interrupt the discussion of law reform in respect to personal status, the equality of women, *waqf* (religious endowments), *Sharī'a*-courts, and similar questions involving Muslim institutions. It was inevitable that religion should be drawn into the political struggle, since constitutional and legal reform affected the principles and substance of Islamic law. This is clear from the 1923 Constitution. But the patriotic duty to secure independence and a constitutional monarchy united all.

It is important, however, to distinguish between patriotism and nationalism, since the former—love of country—is fully compatible with Islam, while the latter cannot be accommodated so easily within classical medieval Islam, yet does seem to fit with an Islam that is a largely secularised, yet none the less important, cultural heritage and historical memory. In the minds and hearts of traditionalists (both "conservative" and "orthodox", to use Western terms), the *umma*, the community of all Muslim believers, can exist as an ideal side by side with the *waṭan*, the Turkish, Egyptian, Syrian, or Iraqī fatherland. But the *qawm* (in Turkey, *millet*), the national community of citizens, comprises members of all religions on an equal footing, at least in theory, and it does not grant Islam any prerogatives and privileges, even in those Muslim countries where Islam is the religion of the state. This levelling down of Islam is difficult to reconcile with the twin claim of universalism and finality seeing that the prophet Muḥammad was the seal of the prophets. Islam is no longer the all-pervading spiritual force and dominant factor in state and society.

That patriotism can be strongly influenced and reinforced by pan-Islamism is clear from Jamāl al-Dīn al-Afghānī, who links the union of all Muslims with the prior achievement of political independence. This is his reaction to European encroachment on the Orient. It is equally significant that pan-Islamism as a tendency, not as an organisation,[2] has engendered Muḥammad 'Abduh's movement for reform on the basis of the original Islam of Qur'an and Sunna, as it was practised by the *Salaf*, in response to the challenge of Christianity. Then, undoubtedly under the impact of events in Republican Turkey, Rashīd Riḍā and 'Ali 'Abd al-Rāziq have grappled with the fundamental problem of what Islam is and what it is to be in the twentieth century. But before we can discuss their important contributions, we must touch briefly on an earlier Egyptian thinker, Rifa'a Badawi Rafi' al-Tahtawi.[3]

Five years' stay in Paris made a deep impression on this Egyptian.

He translated Montesquieu, whose praise of patriotism strongly appealed to him, just as Silvestre de Sacy awakened in him an interest in ancient Egypt. Both interests prompted al-Tahtawi to encourage the publication of Arabic classics, among them the works of Ibn Khaldūn. His political thought is in accord with the classical Islamic theory of the authority of the *Sharī'a* which the absolute ruler must respect. He divided society "into four 'estates': the ruler, the men of religion and law, soldiers and those engaged in economic production".[4] (Incidentally, we find the same four classes already in Al-Dawwānī.)[5] The influence of the French Enlightenment is evident in al-Tahtawi's view that the principles of Islamic law are not very different from Natural Law which forms the basis of modern Europe. It seems that what Plato is for Al-Dawwānī, Montesquieu and Rousseau are for al-Tahtawi. His equation enabled him to legitimise recourse to modern law codes for an interpretation that would bring about a modernisation of Islamic law to meet the exigencies of the time. According to A. Hourani, this Egyptian held education to be the key to *ḥubb al-waṭan*, the love of the fatherland, which has the same significance as Ibn Khaldūn's *'aṣabīya*. An interesting development has occurred in al-Tahtawi's widening the circle of important builders of state and society by including doctors, engineers, and other scientists, with the *'ulamā* coming next in importance after the ruler. The fatherland is Muslim Egypt.

RASHĪD RIḌĀ'S ADVOCACY OF THE CALIPHATE

Al-Tahtawi died in 1873, a year after the meeting between Muḥammad 'Abduh and Al-Afghānī which was to have such decisive results. In 1923 Rashīd Riḍā published his programmatic treatise *Al-khilāfa aw al-imāma al-'uẓmā* (*the Caliphate or the Supreme Imamate*);[6] this had first appeared in his periodical *Al-Manār*—itself the successor to the joint venture of Al-Afghānī and Muḥammad 'Abduh's *Al-'urwa al-wuṯqa*, but as the mouthpiece of Muḥammad 'Abduh and not of Al-Afghānī who was much more radical and favoured political action. As a writer and a teacher, imbued with religious zeal and patriotic fervour, Muḥammad 'Abduh worked for reform and regeneration.

Like "modernism", the term "reform" should be used with caution, since neither he, nor Rashīd Riḍā, nor any of their successors in Egypt, in North Africa, or in India and Pakistan ever touched the basic structure and main body of the provisions of the *Sharī'a.* They remained loyal to the preceptive side of Islam and to its traditional observance. Their aim was purification rather than easement or reforms on a large scale, and by denouncing *taqlīd* and extolling *ijtihād* they endeavoured to revive and reactivate the fundamental tenets of Muslim piety, devotion and social ethics. They were convinced that Islam was perfect and fully equal to the finest achievements of the West which they identified not only with Christianity—the traditional enemy of Islam and determined, so they averred, to destroy Islam—but also with materialism and all the oppression, injustice, and humiliation that go with imperialism and colonialism. Because of the latter, their love for and pride in the pure Islam of the *Salaf* which they worked devotedly to restore, could be combined with an equally strong and sincere love of freedom and of country. They held fast to the traditional concept of the *umma* and firmly believed that the *Sharī'a*—and only the *Sharī'a*—could provide the bond uniting all Muslims, especially in the face of a growing nationalism that stressed national rather than religious identity.

The above-mentioned treatise of Rashīd Riḍā offers us the best opportunity to acquaint ourselves with the "modernist" movement's ideas on the future of Islam as a religious and political unity, as faith and law for state and society.[7] Rashīd Riḍā's is the classical formulation of what an Islamic state is and should be in the twentieth century and beyond. The treatise has lost nothing of its topical character, utopian and romantic though it may be. The significant fact is that, apart from a few details and perhaps a slightly different emphasis here and there, no contemporary advocate of an Islamic *Sharī'a*-state has gone beyond Rashīd Riḍā. This is not surprising, since Rashīd Riḍā is a rigid adherent of the classical theory of the *khilāfa* and firmly believes in the need to re-establish the caliphate in the best interests of Islam and the *umma* of believers: the *ahl al-sunna wa-l-jamā'a,* who are governed by the *siyāsa shar'īya* as expounded by his great examples, Ibn Taymīya and the latter's disciple Ibn al-Qayyim al-Jawzīya.[8]

Rashīd Riḍā's treatise on the Islamic state was no academic exercise intended to be read only by *'ulamā*; it was written with much traditional learning as a battle-cry for action, and it expresses the views of a writer who is also the founder and leader of a movement. The *Salafīya* is at the same time a political party whose programme is contained in the treatise and whose aims *Al-Manār* is to further. For *Al-Manār* contains not only Muḥammad 'Abduh's commentary on the Qur'an (continued and completed by Rashīd Riḍā),[9] but also the several parts of the treatise in question, as well as articles on many other topics connected with Islam and its desired revival. In addition, it published valuable reports on world affairs insofar as they concerned Islam and Muslims, such as the Kemalist revolution in Turkey, the reactions of the Indian Muslims in the *Khilafāt* movement, polemics against Lord Cromer and rejoinders to his book on modern Egypt, and East–West relations in general.

The high purpose of Rashīd Riḍā is always the spirited defence of Islam against Christianity and Europe, and of Muslims against European expansionism, immorality and materialism. Much of it a Westerner may consider ill-judged or naïve, but we cannot doubt its sincerely held conviction, nor its effect on his fellow-countrymen as well as Muslims outside Egypt who read *Al-Manār*. Rashīd Riḍā had a group of patriotic and traditionally learned contributors to support his movement, to propagate its views and further its intentions. Although nobody today would seriously think of re-establishing the caliphate, Rashīd Riḍā's plea for just this does not in any way invalidate his main thesis, which is still that of present-day advocates of an Islamic state: the rule of the *Sharī'a*, suitably attuned to our needs. The term "attuned" is used advisedly because there is no intention of really coming to terms with the modern world, especially in such matters as *ribā* (interest or usury?), inheritance of widow and female heirs, or mitigating the rigour of some *ḥudūd* (penalties). The difficulty is that one can hardly demand this of men who are convinced of the *Sharī'a*'s divine origin and thus of its perfection and suitability at all times in all climes and circumstances. Moreover, this leaves out of consideration the very limited area within which *ijtihād* can be exercised. It would perhaps be different if the *Sharī'a* were restricted to Qur'an and Sunna, as is claimed, for example, by Sa'id Ramaḍān;[10] or if a radical departure from the established canons of Qur'anic interpretation were contemplated and applied; or if the *naṣṣ* or text of the Qur'an were confined to very few passages, such as Muhammad Asad[11] advocates. The case of Maulana Abul A'lā Maudūdī[12] is somewhat different. Squarely facing "the modern world", he advocates *ijtihād* and stresses the permissibility of human legislation in fields left free by Qur'an and Sunna. Yet, not unlike Rashīd Riḍā, he seems very reluctant to resort to radical reforms to bring the *Sharī'a* and through it Islam in line with contemporary ideas on such issues as the legal and social equality of women and their full share in political and economic life.[13] To the extensive literature on this question we must add the widespread, active discussion by earnest Muslims today who try to preserve normative and practical Islam and at the same time want to be citizens of a modern state and participate fully as equals in the affairs of the contemporary world.

Rashīd Riḍā's traditionalism is matched by his Arabism, since the Hijāz was "the geographical cradle of Islam" and Arabic the language of the Holy Qur'an and the Sunna of the prophet. He thus retained the condition that the caliph must be of the Quraish, in accordance with the classical theory of the *khilāfa*. That is to say, he reserved this condition for the ideal *khalīfa* of the future, the effective head of the *imāma 'uẓmā*; for the time being, until the atmosphere has been created for a canonical caliphal government, he would content himself with what he terms the *imāma* of necessity.[14] His intention was to prepare the ground for the establishment of the true caliphate by training, in a special college, the *'ulamā* needed for implementing the *Sharī'a*. He called them by the traditional technical term the *ahl al-'aqd wa-l-ḥāll* (literally: the people with power to bind and to loosen) and demanded that they be *mujtahids* with the ability to interpret and apply the *Sharī'a* in the spirit of early, pure Islam and in conformity with the requirements of the age.

His moderate reformist party must provide this education, he said. He was convinced that it alone was independent-minded and resolute enough to understand the importance of the *Sharī'a*, its character and function, and at the same time the spirit of modern civilisation. This would enable them to terminate the divisions in the Muslim community, between Turks and Arabs and among the Arabs themselves, and to restore the *imāma*. He appealed to the Indian Muslims to give moral and financial support to bring about the restoration of pure Islam. He appealed to the Turks to re-establish the legitimate caliphate with a true caliph at the helm, either in Turkey or in Mossul where he could restore unity among Arabs, Turks, and Kurds.

Muslim disunity contributed to the break-up of the Ottoman

empire, and Muslim rivalry to the seizure by foreign powers of Arab lands. But this, according to Rashīd Riḍā, is not the only cause of the weakness of Islam and its caliphate. Of equal seriousness and even greater danger, to his mind, is the lack of independence of the *'ulamā*, who are venal and therefore an easy prey to the powers that be, whether Muslim or foreign. Society is full of people who are estranged from Islam because they consider it inferior to Western civilisation; and blindly imitating the West, they forget that what is good in European government is all to be found, in its purity and to the utmost perfection, in true Islam. He refers in particular to the institution of *shūrā* (consultation) and to the *ahl al-'aqd wa-l-ḥāll*.

For him, Westernisation and Europe are identical with France and the French, hence he calls the Westernisers *mutafarnij* and what they do and think *tafarnuj*. They try "to efface the last vestiges of Muslim law" by introducing French law into Egyptian legislation, a measure denounced some ten years later by Sheikh Abbās al-Jamāl, who blamed the *'ulamā* of Al-Azhar for not opposing the Khedive Isma'īl when he applied "to Muslims and Egyptians French jurisprudence which did not answer their requirements in that it did not safeguard their religious ethics, did not appreciate their praiseworthy customs and did not sanction their noble traditions".[15] Rashīd Riḍā blames European education for the opinion that religion is not suited to modern politics, science and civilisation, and he accuses the majority of Westernisers of wanting to set up a lay state, suppress the caliphate, and weaken religion in the nation.[16] This is in the first place directed against the Turks, who moreover try to exchange Islamic solidarity for a national ethnic consciousness.

In his view, *jihād* for the glory of God and obedience to the sultan-caliph have been replaced by love for the Turkish fatherland and pride in the glory of the Turks. Little if any help can be expected from those who have discarded Islam as "a spiritual principle and a social and political ideal".[17] Nor do the conservative *'ulamā* fare any better, for they are servile imitators of the four law schools. Therefore, he models himself and his moderate reformist party on such Muslims as Al-Afghānī, Muḥammad 'Abduh, the Indian Muslim Abu-l-Kalām Āzād, and the Egyptian nationalist and leader of the *Wafd*, Zaghlūl Pasha.

Reintroduce—he demands—the institution of *shūrā* and entrust your affairs to the experts in the *Sharī'a*, and Islam will rise again in its pristine glory. It is remarkable to see Rashīd Riḍā in one passage blame the Turks for having forsaken religion—when in fact they have only eliminated Islam from public life and relegated it to the individual conscience—and in other passages praise them for having achieved freedom by prowess in war. He considers liberty a prerequisite for effecting the muchneeded reform of Islam through the determined application of what he terms "absolute *ijtihād*". Nothing less can save Islam and restore its purity.

He even goes so far as to equate the deputies of the Grand National Assembly in Ankara with the *'ulamā* as the *ahl al-'aqd wa-l-ḥāll*.[17] Yet he must have been aware that this Assembly combined executive with legislative power and counted among its members only a minority of experts in Islamic law and jurisprudence. Nor can his critical statements about Kemal Atatürk be reconciled with such a positive appraisal of the Turkish parliament. He takes him to task for taking a decision about the right of women to do the work of men, although he is expert neither in the theory nor in the practice of law, but is guided solely by his personal opinion. His military prowess and political power persuade the masses to follow him. The jurists (*'ulamā*) preserve silence; and the only way to establish the *juste milieu* (*wasaṭ*)—by *ijtihād* which finds a middle road between conservatism and daring innovation—is ignored by the Turkish government.[18]

Now if *ijtihād* meant that anybody, through a fresh interpretation of the primary sources of Islamic law, the Qur'an, and the Sunna, could arrive at new laws that preserve this balance which Ibn Taymīya calls *wasaṭ*, then a workable accommodation between the old and the new, even something quite new, might emerge. The form would be observed, we would still be within the confines of the *Sharī'a*. In the formative years of Islamic jurisprudence, such flexibility no doubt saved and maintained the continuity of authority in the hands of jurists who were expert in interpretation and alive to the social and economic needs of their generation. But is it possible to discard the whole corpus of *Fiqh* and to bring a fresh mind, unencumbered by the knowledge of generations of *mujtahids* of the four schools, to bear on a new situation for which the divine message of the Qur'an and the prophet's exemplary life and practice (Sunna) have made no provision? From the eighteenth century on voices grew until they became a chorus in our time demanding the radical exercise of *ijtihād*. Apart from Muḥammad 'Abduh's ruling on *ribā*, the *fatwās* published in *Al-Manār* do not seem very relevant to contemporary social and economic needs. And this is nothing new. To allow music and figurative representation in art in certain circumstances is no doubt a reform and must be considered a concession to the spirit of our age. As such it marks a definite advance. Yet it may legitimately be asked whether such reforms are not rather ephemeral; they do not touch any of the more vital aspects of a modern state and society, such as the position of women. On this matter, so important for the economy and the political wellbeing of a less developed society, Rashīd Riḍā and all who think like him today are not prepared to grant women complete equality. It does not accord with his claim that Islam grants legislative power in administrative, political, military and financial matters, i.e. in everything outside the cult in the widest sense of the term. This legislative power is entrusted to the community and is to be exercised through consultation (*shūrā*) by all those who possess knowledge and judgement, presumably the *ahl al-'aqd wa-l-ḥāll*.[19] Their complete accord, as the representatives of the community to which in reality all power belongs, provided they are all *mujtahids*, is called *ijmā'*, the third principle or source of law.[20] In fact, it is this law which forms the cornerstone of his thought, for he starts from its supreme excellence (which is due to its divine origin) and he is convinced that it is "the richest and most perfect of all the laws". For this reason he considers it all-inclusive (clearly in conflict with his view that legislation is allowed in all matters not connected with the cult); and by stressing the religious character of many social concerns and virtues, he severely limits the field of free legislation. It is possible that this explains his attitude towards the equality of women in Muslim state and society. For he claims that "the legal position of woman in Islam is certainly much the most elevated, just and best"[21] and insists on the equality of the sexes in Islam.

Yet he points to two verses in the Qur'an that qualify this claim considerably. Sura II, 228, grants women the same rights as men, but "the men have a degree above them". This has always been interpreted, and is so interpreted by the traditionalists today, as giving man superiority over woman. Sura IV, 38, says: "Men are the managers of the affairs of women for that God has preferred in bounty one of them over another, and for that they have expended of their property."[22] Rashīd Riḍā justifies male superiority, implied in this verse, by the particular qualities God bestowed on men and the financial duties laid upon them. He is convinced that women would never want nor need to earn their living if men had taken their duties as enjoined by the Qur'an seriously. He stresses that women can satisfy their own requirements, such as clothing, ornaments and cosmetics, out of the household expenses, and he adds: "If there is here trickery, it is, indeed, the husband who is the victim."[23]

Deeply rooted in classical Islam, which was born into and shaped a medieval society, Rashīd Riḍā cannot be expected to deny the clear implications of the verses quoted. Emancipated modern men and women may smile at his naïve belief that woman's lot could nowhere be happier than in Islam properly applied. For is not woman's natural sphere the home, to be wife and mother? This is his considered opinion, shared by most conservative religious leaders in Islam to this day.

Too often we Westerners do not realise that our standards and habits, though they may suit us perfectly, are not approved or even understood by others outside European civilisation; they often run counter to the standards and habits prevailing in other societies. Nor should we forget that even we "enlightened" and "progressive" people needed a suffragettes' movement and a long social and legal battle before women's emancipation was accepted. Even now nobody can say that women's emancipation and status of equality have been completely realised in practice, as is clear from the different scales of pay that exist for the same jobs, and from other facts. Do not we, too, talk about physiological differences justifying different interpretations, to avoid the ugly word discrimination?

Yet all this does not go to the root of the problem. Naturally there must be a definitive standard by which state and society are regulated and guided. This standard, so the modernists no less than the traditionalist-orthodox maintain, is set by the teachings of the Qur'an vouchsafed to Muḥammad through the angel Gabriel from God by revelation and by the teachings of the Sunna, the exemplary life and work of the prophet as we find it in the authentic body of traditions (*Ḥadīth*). Now a Jew might deny that the

Torah, as we have it today handed down by long-established tradition, is the infallible word of God; but as long as he is a believer he will still acknowledge that it is divine revelation, even though filtered through an inspired but all the same fallible human mind. The Christian will adopt the same attitude towards the Bible. Barring the fundamentalist, both apply literary and historical criticism to the text of Scripture. This is rarely if ever done by a Muslim; at most he adopts such a critical attitude to the Sunna and thus goes beyond traditional criticism which is confined to the "chain of tradition", that is, the unbroken going back to the prophet or one of his companions, with all traditionists considered genuine. The modern student applies criticism to the contents as well, and he will accept as authentic only what agrees with the Qur'an and what we know of the intellectual currents and social and economic circumstances of the formative period of Islam. Only what passes this test is considered Sunna in the strict sense, and as such it is an authoritative guide for new legislation. This is, for example, the view of Gh. Parwez in Pakistan.

On the face of it, there is nothing to prevent a re-interpretation of the verses about women quoted above to bring the sense into line with present-day attitudes towards women and views on their place in the public life of a modern state. Such a reinterpretation would result from the vigorous application of *ijtihād*. This is Rashīd Riḍā's principal means of reviving Islam and of re-establishing an Islamic government, in the form of the caliphate, that has the authority to enforce the *Sharī'a*. He never tires of repeating this demand.

The college he wanted to establish would have the task of teaching the appropriate method and supplying the necessary tools for the training of the future *ahl al-'aqd wa-l-ḥāll* who must be *mujtahids*. These tools include an expert knowledge of Arabic and all the other traditional Muslim sciences, such as *tafsīr* (Qur'an exegesis), *kalām* (theology, comprising doctrine, religious duties, etc.), and *tasawwuf* (mysticism). Alongside these Muslim sciences, the students—from whom the future caliph is to be elected by an electoral college drawn from the entire *umma* of Islam—must also study international law, universal history, heresiography, sociology, and the organisation of religious institutions, such as the papacy and the patriarchates.[24]

He believes that *ijtihād* alone can bridge the gulf between the *Sharī'a*, reflecting the high moral principles of the Qur'an, and the requirements of the age which for him are scientific and technical knowledge and application.[25] From Muslim history, especially during the Umayyad and Abbasid caliphates, he set out to prove that failures and disasters were due to the neglect of the government to implement the *Sharī'a* on the advice of *'ulamā* who were free to issue their decisions through the exercise of *ijtihād* in the way the *Salaf* did. He based his own activity of issuing *fatwās* on the teachings of these *Salaf*; hence the modernist movement called itself *Salafīya*.

He claimed that Islam would never have fallen behind if Muslims had upheld their religion as prescribed in the *Sharī'a.* They were in the vanguard of civilisation, and nobody could surpass them even today if they had remained loyal to Islam. The renaissance in progress is not genuine, since it is secular and nationalist and does not spring from the spirit of pure Islam. Europeanisation, heresy, atheism, and a relapse into bedouinism would never have occurred if *ijtihād* had been practised instead of power politics and imitation of Europe.[26] This is where the Young Turks went wrong, when they assumed that Islam (or, as he says, religion) was incompatible with progress and modern civilisation. We mentioned earlier his ambivalent attitude to the Kemalist Revolution, and would supplement this by some further details to show how he judged Turkish actions, remembering that he wrote his treatise before the abolition of the newly set up spiritual caliphate.

His lack of enthusiasm for both Arabs and Turks as incapable of implementing his dream of the restoration of a central caliphate that had power and authority did not hinder him from placing great hopes in the free Turks. For he believed they could overcome the two principal obstacles to restoration of a supreme *imāma*: Europeanisation and disunity. For the Turks, he holds, are midway between blind attachment to tradition and the narrow spirit of the Arabs and Arabia; they are of the opinion that religion, though an obstacle to the development of the sciences and the arts, is none the less indispensable for civilisation and the prosperity of a nation; and they advocate the "madness" of Westernisation, through which they want to deprive the community of all the institutions which it owes to religion and history and which constitute its originality. But, he insists, Muslim civilisation, like the caliphal government, finds itself in a "middle road", an equilibrium (*wasaṭ*) between the spirit of conservative immobility and the materialism of Western civilisation

...for this civilisation is in our time doomed to ruin...the supreme qualities of leadership (decision, tenacity, courage, daring) manifested by the new Turkish government are the surest guarantee of success, if the Turkish government wants to promote a Muslim reform. It is an Islamic government *par excellence* which has shown the most brilliant gifts in the modern art of war; hence it is capable of maintaining its territorial and political integrity and thus can serve its neighbours as an example and a master.[27]

His enthusiasm for the political and military successes of the Turks led him no doubt into wishful thinking. For nothing could have been further from the minds of the *Committee for Union and Progress* than to promote pan-Islamic aspirations. What attracted him was the freedom of the Turks in contrast to the bondage of the Muslims of Egypt and of India. For he was convinced that only free people could bring about the desired restoration of the caliphate as the rallying point of the *umma* and the guarantor of the *Sharī'a* of a renewed Islam.

This may also be the reason for his faith in Turkish ability to overcome Europeanisation and disunity—a faith he held despite his criticism of their Westernisation and their hostility towards religion. But it still leaves unexplained how he could combine this, on balance positive, judgement with his "Arabism", his conviction that the Arab nation was the vital principle of Islam without which there could be no unity of purpose and action among the Muslims.[28] For he appeals to the Arab princes to unite after setting their house in order through efficient government based on scientific and technical knowledge. This faith in the Arabs is understandable since Rashīd Riḍā is a Syrian Arab, and it is quite possible that his ambivalent attitude to both Arabs and Turks—due to his romantic, but not political, nationalism and to his realistic evaluation of the existing situation among both—was somehow harmonised in his pan-Islamism. For his overriding concern was the restoration of the authority of the *Sharī'a*-state under a strong caliphal government. Yet he does not seem to realise that rationalisation of government, administration and economy—his demands addressed to the Arab princes—is not possible without adopting the philosophical principles underlying Western science and technology and, most likely, the separation of politics from religion as well.

He reproaches Western civilisation for its strict separation of the spiritual from the temporal, as contrary to the religious and political unity of Islam. Yet he himself is, at least in practice, advocating such a division. If this were not so we could not understand his inconsistent and contradictory views on the nature and function of the caliphate he wants to see established. On the one hand, the caliph is a purely temporal ruler charged with the defence of Islam under the *Sharī'a*, a constitutional monarch, since Muḥammad was only a transmitter of revelation, not a tyrant.[29] On the other hand, he demands a caliph who is the fountainhead of power and authority capable of exercising *ijtihād* in promoting legislation.[30]

In complete agreement with the classical theory of the *khilāfa* or *imāma*, Rashīd Riḍā accepts and defends, as demanded by the *Shar'*, the twofold task of the holder of the office who is at the same time *amīr al-mu'minīn*, Commander of the Faithful: to direct both the temporal and the spiritual affairs of the *umma*. He stresses, however, the need for consultation (*shūrā* or *mashwara*) to prevent the head of the *umma* from having absolute power. This is a principle attributed to the *khulafā rāshidūn* and practised in their exemplary *imāma 'uẓmā*. He also stresses *maṣlaḥa*, public interest, common weal, following Al-Ghazālī and especially Ibn Taymīya, to whose *siyāsa shar'īya* Rashīd Riḍā is greatly indebted, especially in his insistence on the power and authority of the *'ulamā* as *mujtahids*. They are really the ruling class in an Islamic state as he envisages it, even if he emphasises their consultative status in respect of the caliph.[31] Rashīd Riḍā claims that the Muslim conception of the state is much superior to any other doctrine, "for it permits...to avoid evil, to guarantee the material interests, cause law and justice to be respected and to propagate the virtues which perfect the dignity of man".[32] Hence the need is imperative for a strong Islamic government, determined and able to implement the *Sharī'a*, reinterpreted by *ijtihād* in agreement with *maṣlaḥa*, the welfare of the community in contemporary conditions.

As stated before, *maṣlaḥa* is an elastic term and permits adjustment over a wide field of political and social action. We must not forget that the jurists who formulated it did so to justify their compromise with expediency in order to preserve the unity of the *umma*: they condoned even the usurpation of effective power by amirs and sultans as long as these recognised the authority of the caliph by mentioning his name in the *khutbah*, the Friday sermon, and by having it inscribed on the coins they minted (*sikka*).[33] Since Rashīd Riḍā is primarily concerned with the rule of the *Sharī'a* in a re-established caliphate, we do not need to take too seriously his astonishing inconsistencies relating to this office. However, it is surprising to find him denying the caliph any spiritual authority in his capacity as chief of a constitutional government, though he is right that he has "neither authority nor control over the souls and hearts".[34] For, as we have seen, he demands the ability of *ijtihād* in the caliph, thus giving him legislative authority that he otherwise reserves to the community represented by the *'ulamā* as *ahl al-'aqd wa-l-ḥāll.* Comparing the caliph's position to that of the Pope, Rashīd Riḍā makes a distinction between the spiritual guidance of the caliph and the spiritual authority of the Pope, a somewhat specious argument due, most likely, to his polemical attitude towards Christianity. How can he say that "every legitimate *imāma* rests on *ijtihād*"[35] and deny the caliph authority other than that over religious education and matters of personal status? Is this not tantamount to a separation of religion from politics? But even if he assigns the activity of *ishtirā'* to the *'ulamā*, it is the caliph on whose authority they exercise this function "to establish laws which a government needs in order to ensure justice, protect its territory, assure the interests of the nation and arrest the propagation of evil".[36] The laws vary with time and place and with the temporal and religious situation. As repeatedly stated, he claims religious significance for matters that are obviously political and social, such as respect for life and property, abstaining from violence, deceit and iniquity. Whether the caliph is a temporal ruler or a spiritual guide, his duties as head of the *umma*, which is identical with the Islamic state of universal dimensions, comprise religion *and* law, which, according to Rashīd Riḍā, together make up Islam. He asserts that the caliph-sultan alone has the power of coercion to secure law and order. How can he then maintain that the community has supreme authority over him?[37] That obedience is due only to the law, not to the caliph's person,[38] may be taken as justifying this claim. For he also states that "true obedience is only due to God, and coercive power has been entrusted to the social body of the community. The head of state is only the personification of social unity".[39]

This sounds very much like "the sovereignty of the people", and we have here obviously the parallel existence of two sets of values stemming from two different traditions based on different principles: one is classical Islam, the other modern European political thought in the wake of the Enlightenment and the French Revolution—the same Western civilisation that Rashīd Riḍā condemns and sees already in ruins. Islam is the normative world in which he lives, though he feels obliged to explain its political principles in European terms thereby causing confusion and contradiction. And yet the caliph is the vice-gerent of the prophet to whom alone the Muslim owes obedience, for he was the herald and transmitter of the divine message in the form of the law that he applies, but not in temporal matters.[40] In this view Rashīd Riḍā is close to 'Ali 'Abd al-Rāziq, who, however, draws the opposite conclusion, for he denies the necessity of the caliphate and insists on the separation of religion and politics.

It is possible that his religious fervour led Rashīd Riḍā to play down the dual role of the caliph in recognition of the dichotomy in the modern world between the spiritual and the temporal. This may, perhaps, account for his distinction between the caliph as the vice-gerent of the prophet, and as the chief *amīr* of the *ūlu-l-'amr* (those in [effective political] command). Of these men he says: "The authority of those in command is only established by God in the general interest in order to assure the application of the *Sharī'a*",[41] with the unifying factor of the law as the important element.

Two reasons may be adduced for this distinction: one is his desire to resolve the apparent dichotomy by concentrating on the *Sharī'a*; the other may be a desire to disarm Western criticism of and opposition to the re-establishment of the caliphate as an Islamic state under Islamic law. Since Islam possesses general laws covering state and society, with justice as the principal virtue, he fails to understand why non-Muslims should oppose such a re-establishment.[42] Rashīd Riḍā is so convinced of the superiority of

Islam that he sees no conflict between his ideal Islamic state and a modern state such as the heretical Westernisers have in mind. They do not realise that they play into the hands of the imperialists, the European Christians, when they want to reduce Islam to a cultural and national bond denying it any religious significance and obligation. For internal as well as external reasons, then, an Islamic state based on the *Sharīʿa* is essential, and he sees one of the tasks of his party in winning back these heretics to a purified, ideal Islam which is practicable in the twentieth century. To this end the caliphate should organise Muslim propaganda—despite the disclaimer that the caliph has any spiritual authority—and should apply legal sanctions yet assure complete religious liberty.[43]

How can the imposition of penalties (*ḥudūd*) be reconciled with complete religious liberty? Liberty for whom? For non-Muslims or also for Muslims—notwithstanding the difficulty of being a Muslim without observing the *Sharīʿa* at least from Rashīd Riḍā's point of view? It is likewise not clear how he can demand of the caliph to organise religious propaganda and at the same time ask the state to entrust all religious matters to free religious societies and to properly trained persons. Rashīd Riḍā recommends the establishment of an institute of propaganda and direction of conscience, free from all political influence and authority.[44]

It may be assumed that he upholds in theory the religious and political unity of Islam, yet in practice he is advocating a separation of religious and political functions when he takes religious matters out of the province of the caliph, understood as a temporal ruler, and wants them to be exercised by independent, strictly private religious societies. On the other hand, the total claim of "religion" is asserted by the advocacy of an institute of propaganda and direction of conscience. This agrees neither with religious liberty nor with the separation of religion and politics as understood in the West.

That his approach is religious in the all-embracing sense of the term is not only clear from what has been said about the *Sharīʿa* and *ishtirāʿ* which must accord with its principles. It is also clear from his uncompromising rejection of Ibn Khaldūn's concept of *ʿaṣabīya*.[45] The solidarity of the tribe is incompatible with Islamic teaching, since it challenges the overriding loyalty to religion, by which he means, naturally, Islam. He admits that *ʿaṣabīya* is a legitimate force in monarchies, but it cannot be attributed and applied to prophets and their vice-gerents (*khulafā*). It substitutes force for the law of Islam. Ibn Khaldūn "wrongly applied it...to the apostolate of the prophet which he subordinated to the social prestige of their families and to the authority of their clans". Misunderstanding Ibn Khaldūn, he charges him with constructing his theory of the caliphate on this wrong theory of prophecy. As we saw, Ibn Khaldūn (*a*) reports correctly the orthodox theory of the *khilāfa* and (*b*) consequently draws a line between the *khulafā rāshidūn* and Mu'āwiya and his founding of a dynasty. Moreover, he stresses that *da'wa* and *'aṣabīya* are necessarily complementary and interdependent. On the other hand, Rashīd Riḍā quotes with approval much of Ibn Khaldūn's criticism of Umayyad and Abbasid caliphs who acted as hereditary monarchs and allowed non-Arabs, such as Persians and Turks, to corrupt Islam. That is, incidentally, another example of Rashīd Riḍā's Arabism and of his conviction of the importance of the Arabs for pure Islamic government and law.[46] Rashīd Riḍā blames on neglectful caliphs the decline of Islamic law and of *ishtirā'*, carefully excluding the first Umayyads and Abbasids.[47]

But his inevitable inconsistencies and even contradictions are less important than his repeated insistence on the rule of law in the form of the *Sharī'a*, which he considered his foremost sacred task to restore.

It is precisely because law requires political authority—the state—for its enforcement that the application of this law depends on an *Islamic* state....His ideas are fundamental to all subsequent thinking and writing to the present day....Moreover, they illustrate—to my mind—the basic problem as one of incompatibility between a law based on revelation and its application in an age of doubt and unbelief. Rashīd Riḍā forcefully demonstrates the conflict between an Islamic and a Muslim state, a religious law governing a community of believers and a political law securing individual freedom, life and property irrespective of belief and religious conviction. In this lies his importance, even today....[48]

In the course of his discussion (in the form of a letter) with Lord Cromer, Rashīd Riḍā insists that the Muslim law was based on Qur'an and Sunna and was not a corpus of doctrines elaborated by the jurists, "an essentially human work". Therefore, "the majority of the judicial and political laws of religion constitute general principles that correspond to the interests of man at all times and in every place, for their aim is to hinder evil and to promote good, through a consultative council. All prescriptions of detail... derive from these principles." Lord Cromer warned Turkey not to imitate Europe but to implement the law of Islam. Rashīd Riḍā took exception to the implication that European laws were not suited to Muslims, saying: "For all that is true and just in these (European) laws has been established for a long time by our *Sharī'a*."[49] "In Islam alone", he claimed, "did justice ever exist."[50] Islam "is a religion of freedom and independence, man obeys God alone, the prophets are only messengers, they have no control over men's consciences and cannot wield any power over their thoughts".[51]

This is not the same as his assertion that "only God and the prophet have the right to exercise authority over the faith and beliefs of any Muslim".[52]

Ch. Adams[53] quotes from *Al-Manār* Rashīd Riḍā's claim on behalf of his party of "moderate reformers", which affirms "that Islam, if interpreted according to their principles, will be found to provide the only adequate solution for modern social, political and religious problems", but justly says, "In any question of choice between the Conservative or the Liberal attitude, the position of *Al-Manār* amounts practically to that of the orthodox party". With Muḥammad 'Abduh, Rashīd Riḍā called for a return to the early simplicity of Islam and claimed that "the Divine law-giver delegated detailed legislation in all matters not covered by the Qur'an to the learned men and the rulers, who are required by the Divine Law to be men of learning and justice, that they may take counsel together and prescribe what is of most advantage to the Community, according to the requirements of the time".[54]

Rashīd Riḍā was sure that only a fresh interpretation of the Qur'an would yield that *absolute ijtihād*—in contrast to the *ijtihād* within a *madhab* (rite)—necessary to achieve this aim. In theory this is unassailable, but in practice it is only possible in an Islamic state composed of believers who willingly recognise the authority of the learned, the *'ulamā*, and entrust their affairs to them. Would Rashīd Riḍā's suggestion that scholars of all Muslim lands should meet and compose a book of laws culled from the four schools which would meet the needs of the times,[55] have the desired effect? Are not these decisions time-bound and, therefore, not necessarily applicable to our age? There is a discrepancy between his plea for a new exegetical attempt and the conservative selection of existing decisions. But it does show that *ijtihād* in practice is not absolute as a rule, that is, it is not quite new and independent and based solely on a fresh interpretation of Qur'an and Sunna. "Absolute *ijtihād*" might well, and perhaps necessarily would, lead to an Islam vastly different in its everyday life from classical Islam.

Islam, properly understood, has anticipated what is best in Western laws, and, if applied with a fresh mind, it could avoid the failures and shortcomings of European civilisation: these two claims will have to be put to the test. To my mind—judging from my experiences in the Muslim countries I visited—it is unlikely, though not impossible, that a *mujaddid*, a restorer, will arise somewhere in the Muslim world. In the present crisis of faith and the devaluation of values once considered absolute, it is equally unlikely that Islam will rise phoenix-like and re-establish its *Sharī'a* so completely and perfectly that it can solve all problems and answer all needs.

In conclusion, I would say that we can detect in his writings the parallel existence of conflicting premises even though they are held together, or rather at bay, by his passionate plea for *ijtihād* and for a return to the practice of the ideal *khilāfa* of the first four caliphs. We may be forgiven if we consider this basic position utopian and romantic, principally for the reason that Western-educated intellectuals cannot easily submit to the acceptance of a religiously orientated and based law unless they believe in a divine lawgiver and His eternally valid and binding law.

Without faith such a law and such a state cannot exist, let alone operate. What does Rashīd Riḍā mean when he says that social relations and civil and commercial transactions should be separated from religion, and that their regulation was not sacrosanct for all time in accordance with the rulings of the four rites?[56] What guidance do Qur'an and Sunna, the immutable basic principles of the reformers, give in these matters?

Perhaps more important is the difficulty of implementing religious liberty and freedom. Does he who maintains the imposition of *ḥudūd* grant freedom of conscience to Muslims who are citizens of an Islamic state? Does freedom of conscience imply the freedom to contract out of Islam, to be an agnostic or atheist? "There is no compulsion in religion" is a Qur'anic statement. So is "Fight an unbeliever where you find him". Does the latter abrogate the former?

Rashīd Riḍā's Islamic state is a positive demand culminating in the full authority of the *Sharī'a.* There is today another Islamic attitude, less demanding, but still concerned with the norm contained in the *Sharī'a.* Its representatives insist that no law should go against the principles of Islam. In between we find a demand that no law in force or to be promulgated should be incompatible with Qur'an and Sunna, thus expressing almost negatively and defensively the positive demand that the law of the land must be the *Sharī'a,* based on Qur'an and Sunna. Surely there is a fundamental difference between the positive and the defensive approach and attitude which is bound to show itself in the political, social and economic life of state and society.[57]

Nobody could deny that the principles of Islam in the field of social ethics are, like those of Judaism and Christianity, the common possession and profession of the whole civilised world today. But adherence to principles does not make the state law based on them the religious, all-comprehensive law of classical Islam, no matter how much its substantive part is reformulated to meet the changed conditions of the twentieth century.

Why is it that we find so many devout and observant Muslims who are convinced that in the present situation a strictly Islamic state is not feasible, and who, therefore, are in favour of a lay state which treats religion as the concern of the individual's conscience and guarantees the unhindered practice, within the limits of the public good, of Islam and other religions? There are many shades of opinion and distinctions within the various groups. It is clear, however, that the crucial question is their attitude to the *Sharī'a* and to its place in the public life of state and society. The "lay" element wants legislation decided upon by a legislature—be it elected, under whatsoever franchise, or appointed—in the form of modern law-codes embodying modern legal principles and concepts. At the other end of the scale, only experts in Qur'an and Sunna and *Fiqh* can, strictly speaking, frame laws that could legitimately be called *Sharī'a.* Here, too, opinions differ concerning the scope and range of religious legislation. Yet all Muslim believers are agreed that no law must run counter to Islamic ideals and ideas.

The effect of Rashīd Riḍā's efforts to revitalise Islam was more emotional than intellectually convincing, in the view of M. Colombe. He considers him "more a propagandist of faith than a theologian" and looks upon him as the apostle of a nationalist (Egyptian-Arab) interpretation of Islam.[58]

'ALI 'ABD AL-RĀZIQ AND THE SEPARATION OF RELIGION AND POLITICS

But before we follow this line in Egyptian writers and in such movements as the Muslim Brethren (or Brotherhood), we must consider in some detail the views of a bold and consistent advocate of Islam as faith alone, and consequently of the complete separation of religion and politics, 'Ali 'Abd al-Rāziq. His treatise *Al-Islām wa-'uṣūl al-ḥukm* (*Islam and the principles of government*) aroused the fierce opposition of orthodoxy; and the Grand Council of al-Azhar condemned his thesis as contrary to accepted orthodox doctrine, deposed him and expelled him from this foremost seat of learning in Islam. The treatise, published in 1925,[59] is a reply to Rashīd Riḍā's thesis and in a sense a defence and justification of the Turkish Revolution and its divorce of religion from politics. Any similarity with the thought of Ziya Gökalp is superficial; there is no affinity between the two thinkers in their basic approach and assumptions, religious or philosophical. In fact their differences are fundamental, and they strikingly illustrate the contrast between an '*ālim* (Sheikh 'Ali 'Abd al-Rāziq) and a sociologist (the thoroughly Westernised Ziya Gökalp). It is important to realise that the '*ālim*'s argumentation is scholastic, medieval, the result of a critique of the religious and historical sources of Islam by means of the rational, empirical method employed by Ibn Khaldūn, who deeply influenced him even where he disagreed with this North African Muslim thinker of the fourteenth century. Not only in his method but in his whole approach Gökalp was Western inspired and outward looking, in spite of his attachment to traditional Islam, which, however, becomes less and less pronounced in his evolution towards Turkish nationalism and integration in European civilisation.

It is quite different with Rashīd Riḍā whose basic concepts and outlook can be paralleled in the Islamist movement without being directly influenced by it. There is, rather, a common ground in Islamic tradition and perhaps the influence of Jamāl al-Dīn al-Afghānī on both. ʻAli ʻAbd al-Rāziq's reading of Islamic doctrine and history appears to be influenced by the course of the Young Turk Revolution, which culminated first in the separation of caliphate and sultanate and finally in the abolition of the sultanate and the setting up of a (short-lived) spiritual caliphate. But his novel, unorthodox thesis owes nothing to the theory of Gökalp, logically leading to the Turkish lay republic. That his inquiry into the nature of Islam and of the caliphate should result in a justification of the complete separation of state and religion does not entitle us to exchange the roles of cause and effect. It is my contention, therefore, that we meet in his treatise, for the first time, a consistent, unequivocal theoretical assertion of the purely and exclusively religious character of Islam.[60]

He asks and answers the basic question "what is Islam?" in order to define and decide the place of Islam in our time as a universal religion, a religious call (*daʻwa*), announced by an Arab in Arabic, but addressed to all mankind. Pre-eminence in Islam is due to piety, not to any race or language, any nation or ethnic group. The religious community (*umma*) is the creation of Muḥammad. The *khilāfa* or *imāma* is not demanded in Qur'an and Sunna and is unnecessary; indeed, its institution and function are contrary to true Islam.

The theory of the *khilāfa* or *imāma* is the work of theologians and jurists and is strictly separated from the history of the *khilāfa*. While he rejects the theory altogether, he subjects the history of the caliphate to a searching criticism, guided by reason and experience. Implementing Muḥammad's religious message has, he avers, nothing to do with politics, which is left to man and his reason exclusively. Even the *khulafā rāshidūn*—accepted as we know, as exemplary pious and just rulers—have betrayed the pure *daʻwa* that is Islam. Abu Bakr was the first *malik* (king) or temporal ruler; his imitation of the prophet in private and public life has given him a religious *nimbus* which must not be confused with a purely religious rule. For ʻAli ʻAbd al-Rāziq religion and rule are incompatible. Since Islam has nothing to do with politics, there can be nothing specifically religious in the caliphate, for him. The jurists and Ibn Khaldūn are wrong when they claim the religious and political unity of Islam. He categorically denies this claim as unproven and as a misreading of the message of the prophet Muḥammad. Uncompromisingly, therefore, he demands the complete separation of religion and politics as the indispensable basis of a modern state and in the interests of the permanence of Islam as a universal faith.

The consequences of his views are far-reaching: it is unheard of to apply historical criticism to the golden age of the *khilāfa* under the first four successors of the prophet, instead of beginning with Mu'āwiya and his *mulk*. But it means also that pure Islam, for him, is limited to the prophet as the apostle of Allah. Muḥammad is the undisputed religious leader and example, his "political" activity is merely accidental to his *da'wa* and has nothing in common with political rule except its name. The religious mission in its creative, normative phase came to an end with the prophet's death; it was not transferred to his vice-gerent, the *khalīfa*. The unity of the Arab nation is religious, not political, since it is exclusively based on and centred in the message transmitted from God through the prophet.

Whatever the merits or faults of 'Ali 'Abd al-Rāziq's remarkable interpretation, his position is definite. Free from any ambiguity and doubt, he is able to assign Islam a momentous role in the life of the Muslim believer in our age: it becomes a clarion call to God without even the most tenuous connection with politics or with the rights and duties of the state. The strength of this attitude lies in the recognition that unless we decide what Islam is, it is impossible to define its role in contemporary society: he has the courage of his convictions and takes Islam as a religious *da'wa* right out of national and nationalist politics. Whether his premise is right or wrong, he appears to safeguard that purity and relevance of Islam as universal faith which Rashīd Riḍā strove so assiduously to recover and then preserve.

Nowhere does the gulf between the two men show more clearly than in their diametrically opposed concepts of the *imāma 'uẓmā* of the *khulafā rāshidūn*. Rashīd Riḍā wanted to restore it in the twentieth century because for him it was the purest form of Islam. But 'Ali 'Abd al-Rāziq denied its canonical necessity and rejected it as contrary to the nature and intention of the original Islam of the prophet Muḥammad. It may be assumed that he approved of the Turkish "solution": a lay state that guarantees freedom of religion to all its citizens but excludes Islam from public life altogether, depriving it of all influence on government and administration, in legislation and jurisdiction.

It is only natural that 'Ali 'Abd al-Rāziq's interpretation should have aroused the violent opposition of the guardians of the traditional interpretation of classical Islam and should have led to his public disgrace. That his ideas fly in the face of a very old tradition does not automatically rule them out as untenable, however. They may be dangerous to the orthodox establishment, but they may well contain the seeds of a solution to a grave problem and provide the basis for a reorientation and fresh thinking about the meaning of Islam in our time. They may even have a better chance of bringing about that renewal so fervently desired by all believers than the setting up of an Islamic state, as advocated by Rashīd Riḍā and those who think like him (in Pakistan today, for example). His interpretation rests on the sound distinction between the political actions of the prophet that accompanied and consolidated the prophet's *da'wa*—"political" only in name—and the political actions of the caliphs, who were, in his view, temporal rulers of a state.[61]

If he is right, then the whole theory of the *khilāfa* falls to the ground and with it the Muslims' traditional view that the first four vice-gerents of the *rasūlu-l-Llah* (the apostle of God) represented the golden age: the shining example of the ideal ruler under God. He substitutes for it the concept of power and personal rule and authority, as formulated by Ibn Khaldūn. More than that, the concept of the *siyāsa shar'īya*, formulated by Ibn Taymīya and his modern disciple Rashīd Riḍā, becomes untenable. This means that the commanding position of the *Sharī'a* is in jeopardy, being thoroughly undermined by 'Ali 'Abd al-Rāziq's exclusion of religion from law in the state: the *Sharī'a* cannot become the law of an Islamic state if Islam is unpolitical, and religious law is a contradiction in itself. It appears that the lay state is inescapable, and no conflict need arise between the demands of Islam upon the believer and the exigencies of a modern national state, or of any state. The legislative function of the state must be based on political considerations; necessity dictates the laws, tempered with right and justice, yet without religious sanction and without regard for either the historical *Sharīʿa* or a new one that would result from a fresh interpretation and application of Qur'an and Sunna. These two primary sources and root principles of Islamic law have, according to his reading of them, absolutely nothing to do with politics and state law.

It is therefore not surprising, but highly significant, that the *Sharīʿa* is hardly mentioned in his treatise as a factor of consequence; it is irrelevant even though the avowed purpose of the treatise is an inquiry into the nature of Islam and the theory of government, its origin and the source of its authority.

By a critical examination of the theory and practice of the *khilāfa*, the author sets out to disprove and reject the orthodox claim that the *khilāfa* is the foundation of all authority in Islam. And yet *imāma* or *khilāfa* is incomprehensible and meaningless without recognising the place and function of law in it. The student of Islam from the time of the caliphate to the modern age is aware that the question of a religious or a lay state depends on the role of the *Sharīʿa* in a state created by and for Muslims. The source—divine or human—and the extent of the law of such a state determine its character. By definition, a state whose criminal and civil law are not based on the *Sharīʿa* is not an Islamic state, even if Islam is the official religion and personal status law is *Sharīʿa*-law. It is immaterial whether this personal status law is the time-hallowed orthodox law or has been modernised in varying degrees; whether the jurisdiction is in the hands of religious judges or is, as in Tunisia today, exercised by judges appointed by the government and coming under the authority of the Ministry of Justice.

ʿAli ʿAbd al-Rāziq's thesis might be the basis for a Muslim as distinct from an Islamic state, on the model of Ibn Khaldūn's mixed *mulk*. In any case, his views deserve attention since they are, to my mind, an important contribution to the current debate on the role of Islam in a twentieth-century sovereign independent nation-state.

Al-Māwardī insists on the necessity of the *khilāfa* or *imāma* in the light of the Qur'an, Sura IV, 62; not reason but the *Sharʿ* demands it; it "is established to take the place of prophecy in the defence of the faith and the administration of the world".[62] 'Ali 'Abd al-Rāziq quotes in addition Ibn Khaldūn's definition,[63] and considers, as already stated, that neither the jurists nor Ibn Khaldūn proved the necessity of an *Imām* from the Qur'an, which merely lays down that some Muslims are responsible for public affairs.[64] The institution of the caliphate can therefore be justified only by *ijmā'*, which is, according to the jurists, necessary to make the contract between the *umma* and the *Imām* binding. But in his view, supported by a quotation from *Al-Mawāqif* (II, 464),[65] *ijmā'* has no authority in tradition. Nor does the Sunna justify the *imāma*, and the *ḥadīth* of Huḏaifa was wrongly adduced by Rashīd Riḍā, who was moreover anticipated by Ibn Ḥazm who quoted Qur'an IV, 62 and numerous *aḥādīth* in support of its necessity. While he does not doubt the authenticity of these traditions, they do not prove that the *imāma* is a religious obligation, for they merely speak of *imāma*, *bay'a* (oath of allegiance), and *jamā'at al-muslimīn* existing, not as divinely ordained or necessary. For 'Ali 'Abd al-Rāziq, these traditions are on the same level as Jesus's saying, "Render unto Caesar...". His argument is cogent: we must obey rebels who rule us by force, yet we do not recognise rebellion nor authorise revolt against effective authority any more than we hold that the injunction of the *Shar'* to respect and care for the poor implies the command that we have to create them. The same applies to slavery.[66]

Ibn Khaldūn had taught him that personal power, based on *'aṣabīya* in the form of solid support of family, clan or tribe, and military force are essential for gaining political power and authority and for maintaining both. While he admits that the historical caliphate rests in theory on the authoritative decision of the *ahl al-'aqd wa-l-ḥāll*, he is convinced that in practice it is based on force, for he says: "We do not at all doubt that brute force has always been the support of the institution of the *khilāfa*."[67] The history of the Umayyads, Abbasids, Mameluks, and other dynasties proves this conclusively to him, and he quotes many supporting examples from historians who have shown that there was always opposition to the caliphs since Muslims voluntarily obey Allah alone. Even Abu Bakr had encountered opposition. He agrees with Ibn Khaldūn that the *khilāfa* disappears when the *'aṣabīya* grows weaker and ceases altogether.[68] Power is the motive force of the caliph, as Yazīd b. Mu'āwiya's murder of Ḥusain clearly proves.[69]

God does not want His religion to be subjected to a specific form of government nor to a particular group of rulers.[70] Religious observance is independent of the caliphate, as is the wellbeing of the Muslims in this life.[71] Political power and authority are thus unnecessary for the realm of faith. On the other hand, he does not deny that Islam has formulated laws to be practised by its adherents: laws founded on brotherhood and equality.[72] By implication, political laws are founded on power and force. He says nothing about enforcing the religious laws which must have some social significance and application since they are the practical expression of brotherhood and equality—precisely the two qualities that form the basis of Islamic social ethics and are claimed today as the content of Islamic socialism.

In fact, Rashīd Riḍā went so far as to claim that European socialists would be converted to Islam if they only knew that true socialism was taught in Islam alone and should be practised by every Muslim.[73] For this reason, he was convinced that the Islamic state is the best, not only for Muslims, but for all mankind. *Zakāt* (alms tax to support the poor and needy) is Islam's answer to the social scourges inherent in materialist and atheistic governments.

'Ali 'Abd al-Rāziq never makes any claims of this kind; he concentrates on Islam as a religion and on its application in everyday life, without any apologetic or polemical anti-Christian and anti-European tendencies. He realises that a religious community, like any other human group, cannot thrive or even exist without organisation, but he insists that this has nothing in common with politics and political organisation. He draws a definite line between the supreme leadership of the prophet and the political government of the caliph and "those in authority" comprising all dignitaries and functionaries of state, between a religious authority and political power based on force.[74]

The religious authority inherent in his divine mission died with Muḥammad and his prophecy. What followed was political rule, which 'Ali 'Abd al-Rāziq calls *za'āma lādīnīya*, lay authority (non-religious, not anti-religious), "which is neither less nor more than civic, political authority (leadership) (*madanīya aw siyāsīya*), governmental rule (*ḥukūmīya wa-l-sulṭān*) but not religious leadership (*lā za'āmat al-dīn*)".[75] He is at pains to show the fundamental difference between the prophet as the apostle of God (*rasūlu-l-Llah*) and a governor (*ḥākim*), be he a *malik* (king) or a *sulṭān*. He analyses all the political terms in use, for since the prophet's death the Arabs have instituted a *mamlaka* (state), a *dawla* (dynasty), and a *ḥukūma* (political government). Islam is the *dīn al-sharī'ati kullihah* (religion of the whole *Sharī'a*, that is, Qur'an and Sunna). Even though it was built by Abu Bakr on the foundations of a religious call (*da'wa*), the state of the Arabs is *ḥukūma madanīya dunyawīya*, a political worldly government, that has nothing to do with religion.[76] "The prophet was the eminent leader of the Arabs and the centre of their (religious) unity. Abu Bakr after him was a *malik* over the Arabs and the rallying point for their unity in the present-day political sense."[77] Since the prophet's authority is spiritual, any application of these temporal and political terms is imprecise, a manner of speech that is in fact on a higher level than when used of a temporal ruler whose authority and power are founded on and maintained by force. The prophet's authority extends to the hearts and minds of the community of believers.

Yet he must admit that the prophet's *risāla* or apostleship—so different from the *mulk* of his successors—demands a certain *quwwa* (force) so that he can fulfil the divine command (*qawl*) and see that men follow his call (*da'wa*). Here 'Ali 'Abd al-Rāziq follows Ibn Khaldūn. The *rasūl* must have an authority (*sulṭāna*) higher than that of a governor over the governed, and of a father over his sons. "Higher" means also "more", "wider", since the prophetic authority includes everything implied in temporal authority as well. But above and beyond that, it includes an additional function which the prophet shares with no one: his is "the rule over the affairs of body and spirit...the administration of this world and of the hereafter".[78]

This comes very close to the traditional definition of the *khilāfa* by Al-Māwardī and the other jurists. No doubt, 'Ali 'Abd al-Rāziq is fully aware of this, for he stresses that the prophet has a general as well as a comprehensive authority over all men whom he is commanded to lead to God, an authority different from and exceeding that of the kings or sultans. They rule over subjects (*ra'āya*); he leads his people (*za'āma qawmihi*). Hence his *quwwa* must be different from the brute force of temporal rulers: it is a *quwwa qudsīya*, a holy power, transcending and dissimilar to the power of kings and the authority of sultans. In short, the prophetic government (*ḥukm al-nubuwwati*) is fundamentally different from the *ḥukm al-salāṭīn*, the government of the sultans. This is because the former has a religious sanction and purpose—to lead man in voluntary submission to his eternal happiness (*sa'āda abadīya*)—whereas the latter is concerned only with man's material interests in this life.[79] Therefore, he calls the prophet's authority spiritual (*wilāya rūḥīya*) and the king's *w. mādīya* (material). The prophetic government, he insists, was not a *dawla siyāsīya*, a political government,[80] and he demonstrates the purely religious mission of Muḥammad by quoting from the Qur'an and Sunna. For example, Sura XXXIII, 40, clearly shows that he was the apostle of Allah and not a king: Islam is a *da'wa* to God, a call for the religious unity of all mankind (*waḥda dīnīya*), but not for one world government, a political unity. In order to further religion and to support his preaching, Muḥammad made use of means which in other men we would call political actions.

After Qur'an and Sunna, 'Ali 'Abd al-Rāziq turns to the history of Islam to prove that Islam was addressed to all mankind; it is not an Arab religion even though an Arab preached it first to the Arabs; it aims at and achieves a unity of faith, not of a state; an Arab nation united in faith. All rules established by Islam have absolutely nothing in common with the methods of political government and the civil organisation of the state. The prophet did not designate a successor; he died after completing his mission as the apostle of God.

'Ali 'Abd al-Rāziq knows that his views are diametrically opposed to those held by the majority of Muslims, and he illustrates this with a quotation from Ibn Khaldūn. He labours the point that if the prophet did combine prophetic with royal dignity, this was more apparent than real, and he tries to reinforce this argument by qualifying Muḥammad's power as holy and his authority as spiritual. Words legitimately have different meanings in different contexts, but it may be questioned whether 'Ali 'Abd al-Rāziq's interpretation is justified.

He is on surer ground in his historical critique, which shows not only sound political realism, perhaps learned from Ibn Khaldūn, but also a modern critical method that is the more remarkable since it is in such striking contrast to his otherwise medieval scholastic argumentation and interpretation of the basic sources of Islam. It is likewise characteristic of him that he uses the argument from silence to prove that the prophet's rule or government was unpolitical. In his view, laws and deductions must be based on verifiable factual knowledge; if this is absent, we can conclude that everything connected with the prophet's mission must have been different in essence and in degree from ordinary government and rulers.

In one important respect this assumption appears to be disproved by known facts: the prophet engaged in *jihād*, holy war, in order to make his preaching prevail in the face of Arab and Jewish opposition. How, then, can 'Ali 'Abd al-Rāziq state that "religious propaganda is incompatible with the application of force"?[81] Not a single prophet, he asserts, had recourse to the sword in order to win people over to faith in God, yet it is undeniable that Muḥammad waged wars. Is this justified even if establishing the rule of Islam by force was something quite different from his prophetic mission? For did it not mean that he was at the same time the apostle of God and a political "king" (*malik siyāsī*)?[82] By linking Muḥammad's prophetic call with his other activities, through his being under the constant influence of divine revelation (*waḥy*), 'Ali 'Abd al-Rāziq tried to resolve this obvious contradiction, claiming that the prophetic mission cannot be separated from the political and military measures in its support. And yet he strenuously denies the view of Muslims who hold that the prophet's political administration is part of his apostolate; and while he gives credit to Ibn Khaldūn for having been the only Muslim writer to conclude from this that Islam is the only religion in which religious and political authority are united, he rejects this view as well. For if they were united we would know much more about the political organisation and administration of the state founded by Muḥammad, the divinely inspired prophet.[83]

Surely he must have known of the "Statute of Medina" upon which the theory of the *khilāfa* is modelled? How can he, then, say that since the historical sources are silent on the prophet's government, he cannot account for our lack of knowledge? He insists that there is no clear proof in Qur'an and Sunna of the political character of Islam, and that the claim put forward by jurists and historians that it is a religious and political unity is mere conjecture. "But conjecture (*zann*) cannot replace anything of the truth":[84] this is a sound principle, yet without rejecting the religious and historical sources as tendentious, 'Ali 'Abd al-Rāziq's allegation of "non proven" does not appear to be convincing.

More weight can be attached to another of his assumptions, however. Treating Abu Bakr as a monarch, he maintains that his religious behaviour was designed to foster the belief that the caliphal office was a religious office which was of advantage to the successive caliphs in preserving and enhancing their power.[85] This, read together with his warning not to trust the historians without applying to their reports the criteria of reason and experience, shows something of our modern scientific approach and method. He claims and exercises the right of interpretation of Qur'an and Sunna, and in doing this arrives at conclusions that are the very opposite of accepted traditional exegesis. His critical approach to history, on the basis of Ibn Khaldūn's realistic reading of Muslim history, convinced him that political motives are dominant and religion is used to serve political ends. We have in his opinion no detailed knowledge of the organisation and administration in the prophet's time in contrast to that of the caliphate. This confirms him in his view, which amounts to religious conviction, that the prophet's mission was purely religious: a call to Allah. He states that by his own reason, unaided by divine help, he cannot establish the reasons why we do not know more about the prophet's government. Moreover there is strong opposition to a rational inquiry into religious matters. He therefore offers several possible explanations, guarding himself against objections by asserting that since the prophet's government was based on divine revelation and wisdom, it was perfect in every respect though inaccessible to human reason.[86] No successor-state is or can be like it. This is what makes it so difficult to establish rationally that the prophetic government is, contrary to appearances, not a temporal political government.

We must accept that 'Ali 'Abd al-Rāziq is in a dilemma. By a sincere, devout faith in the divine truth enshrined in Qur'an and Sunna, he accepts perfection in everything the prophet said and did; by rational inquiry into history, he discovers the gulf that separates the rule of religion, represented by Muḥammad, from the power-state of the caliphs. He would like to probe into the nature of Muḥammad's religious rule, but, torn between faith and reason, he hides behind the scarcity of verifiable factual knowledge. Yet he is compelled to lift the veil of uncertainty. Hence we find statements that may be understood as an attempt—not entirely successful or satisfactory, it is true—to furnish proof for his thesis of the separation of religion and politics and his resulting advocacy of a lay state.

This can best be appreciated by starting from his principal contention that the prophet's "state" differs from the usual connotations of a state as we know it. Abu Bakr's is a political state, which is something quite new. The fact that he tried to imitate the prophet as much as possible, taking the place of the *rasūlu-l-Llah* as indicated in his title "vicegerent of the apostle of Allah", misled the Muslims into thinking that his was a religious office. 'Ali 'Abd al-Rāziq denies that the wars of Abu Bakr were religious wars; no, they were purely political wars, as is clear from the fact that Abu Bakr began his reign (*dawla*) with a war, called the "war of apostates (*murtadīn*)" regardless of whether they were religious rebels (i.e. apostates) or political rebels. For political reasons the fiction was maintained that obedience to the *Imām* was equivalent to obedience to Allah, hence rebellion against the rulers was rebellion against Allah. He considers this a crime of the caliphs against the Muslims. Similarly, the conflict between Malik and Abu Bakr was exclusively political, not religious, since the argument between Khālid and Malik was about the royal dignity of the king, not about the principles of religion (*dīn*).[87]

The laws the prophet promulgated, 'Ali 'Abd al-Rāziq claims, were simple and natural in a simple state (*dawlat al-basāṭa*) with a natural government (*ḥukūmat al-fiṭra*). They concern prayer and fasting. Simplicity was the keynote of the prophet's life (*yuḥibbu-l-basāṭata*), hence his government lacked those appearances which political scientists today consider foundations (*arkān*) of political government (*ḥukūma madanīya*). The prophet was *ummi*, unlettered, and the apostle to unlettered people; therefore it is possible that the political organisation in his time was based on natural simplicity. What we today consider essential for government is in fact artificial; vague and confused as the prophetic government may appear, it is on the contrary nothing but true simplicity and the pure state of nature. Hence, according to some, political organisation and government are accidental conventions (*istilāḥāt ʿāriḍa*) based on human decisions; they are artificially created institutions (*awḍāʿ maṣnūʿa*) that are not necessary for a simple state.[88] Yet our author does not agree with this view although it accords most with religion; it is unsound (*lā ṣaḥīḥ*) and another explanation must be found. This leads him to the fundamental distinction between prophetic and temporal authority, which we have already discussed.[89]

The introduction of other views seems to be nothing more than a scholastic device of dialectic enabling him to arrive at conclusions that are in agreement with his thesis. We are led to this opinion by the contradictions in which the author involves himself, two of which we will mention here. In the first place, he admits that the prophet engaged in *jihād* in order to further his purely religious mission, and that *jihād* is one of the five pillars of religion. All the same, he declares without hesitation that *jihād* is a war of aggression incompatible with religious propaganda, although it may promote civilisation (*ʿumrān*, a favourite term of Ibn Khaldūn's). He goes on to say that this is "a brutal means, but who knows, perhaps evil is at times necessary for good to arise, and sometimes destruction is necessary so that civilisation may be perfected".[90]

The other inconsistency reveals the difficulties which a scholar steeped in traditional law and lore must have encountered in his struggle to proclaim a new concept of Islam, based on a new, personal interpretation of its religious texts in the face of a solid orthodox opposition that could claim the support of tradition. I refer to his assertion that the prophet's laws were simple, concerned with prayer and fasting. Yet elsewhere in his treatise he explicitly states that the principles, social relations, ethical rules and legal punishments Islam established are all contained in a *sharʿ dīnī*, a purely religious law directed to Allah and to man's religious welfare (*maṣlaḥa*).[91] Obviously the *Sharīʿa* here contains much more than simple regulations about prayer and fasting, and he seems to be in complete agreement with the orthodox view.

But since he wants to separate political from religious concerns, he distinguishes—quite legitimately—between the religious law and the administration of justice, that is, its application, which is a purely political function like finance and military affairs which all fall under *maṣlaḥa madanīya*, the political or civic welfare of man. Since he states that neither the prophet nor the religious law is interested in civic welfare, we may ask how this division follows from the all-inclusive character of the *Sharī'a*, which, in conformity with the rule of the prophet, has provisions for the temporal welfare of man in preparation for his spiritual welfare in the hereafter.

The separation of the legislature and the judiciary is a modern principle, and we saw earlier how in Turkey Ziya Gökalp advocated separating the offices of *mufti* and *qāḍī* on the basis of the same distinction between the religious responsibility of the *Şeyh-ül-Islam* and the political responsibility of the sultan who appoints the *qāḍī*. It may be that 'Ali 'Abd al-Rāziq did not want to abandon the universal claim and range of religion, but at the same time wanted its purity not to be sullied by its being dragged into politics. Hence his stress on the religious unity of the Arabs, due to religion in the form of the *Shar' dīnī*, and on their political, social and economic diversity. Religion minimised Arab dissension and differences, but with the death of the prophet their unity vanished, as is attested by Abu-l-Fidā.[92]

This necessarily leads us to ask what law is in force in the temporal state as which he designates the *khilāfa*. If none of the rules of Islam have any connection with political government and administration, is there room for the *Sharī'a*? We find no direct answer in the treatise except the statement that

> Islam has nothing to do with the *khilāfa* as the Muslims understand it; it is not a religious function any more than the judiciary and other essential functions of the state (*dawla*). All political functions are left to us, our reason, its judgements and political principles. Religion has nothing to do with them; it neither commands nor forbids them, it simply leaves them to us so that in respect of them we have recourse to the laws of reason (*aḥkām al-'aql*), the experience of the nations and the rules (*qawā'id*) of politics. There is nothing in religion which hinders the Muslims to compete with other nations in all the social and political sciences, to destroy the old order (*niẓām*) before which they bowed and to which they submitted. Let them build up the bases of their *mulk* (lay state) and the organisation (*niẓām*) of their government (*ḥukūma*) in accordance with the most recent (rules) the human intellect has devised and with the best principles of government (*ḥukm*) in the experience of the nations.[93]

Again and again he dissociates religion from politics. Islam is a call to God; the prophet issued a call to religious unity by faith in Allah. Universality belongs to Islam as a *waḥda dīnīya*, a religious unity, and a *waḥdat al-imān wa-l-maḏhab dīnī*, a unity of faith and a religious way (and direction), but not as a *waḥdat dawlatin wa-maḏāhib al-mulk*,[94] a political unity and temporal-royal institutions (and directions). Islam is a *da'wa dīnīya*.

One religion for mankind is reasonable, says 'Ali 'Abd al-Rāziq, but to subject the whole universe to one government and to the authority of a common political unity is not the divine will and may not even accord with human nature. God has left this entirely for man to decide in freedom and in accordance with his reason, knowledge and interests. God wills that civilisation be perfected, but he leaves this to man's impulse.[95] The Qur'an is cited as proof that the prophet never referred to an Islamic or an Arab state (*dawla islāmīya, d. 'arabīya*).[96] He never mixed in political affairs, never deposed a governor, nominated a *qāḍī*, nor regulated economic affairs such as agriculture and industry.[97]

From all these passages it is clear that 'Ali 'Abd al-Rāziq, contrary to the accepted orthodox opinion and intention, goes back beyond the *khulafā rāshidūn* to the prophet himself as the apostle of God who brought His message and lived an exemplary life. His only reservation concerned *jihād*. He rejected the *khilāfa* or *imāma* as a temporal state based on power and brute force, in the sense of Ibn Khaldūn's *mulk* (both in its mixed and sheer power-state form). In his attack on the caliphs he showed himself the apt disciple of Ibn Khaldūn and his theory of the power-state. We have seen that he charged the caliphs with having, in the name of religion, deliberately misled the people for their own personal ends of power and prestige; in this they did great harm to Islam as a universal faith. And they also harmed their own state by denying their subjects that freedom of science and learning (*ḥurriyat al-'ilm*) which is both the prerogative of man as a rational human being and the necessary condition for rational government and efficient, benevolent administration. The caliphs "forbade them [the Muslims] research in the science of politics in the name of religion....All this ended with the death of the power of research (inquiry) and of intellectual activity among the Muslims. They were stricken with paralysis in political thinking and in the investigation of anything connected with the *khilāfa* and the *khulafā*".[98]

As early as the beginning of his treatise, 'Ali 'Abd al-Rāziq deplores the neglect of political science among the Muslims and declares that he knows of no author who has devoted himself to the study of politics. Therefore, there is no research carried out into the organisation of power and the principles of politics (*siyāsa*). He asks why the Arabs have neglected the study of Plato's *Republic* (*jumhūrīya*) and Aristotle's *Politics* (*siyāsa*). Why did Muslim scholars absorb Greek philosophy but neglect politics when they were so enthusiastic about Aristotle, to whom they gave the surname of "the first teacher"?[99] He supplies his own answer by pointing to the fact that political science constitutes one of the gravest dangers to royal power,

> because it reveals different kinds of governmental power (*ḥukm*), their peculiarities and constitutions compared with others....It is therefore necessary for the ruler to combat these sciences and to forbid access to them...for fear it might assail the very foundations of his rule...hence the royal oppression of freedom of learning and science. The king monopolises the institutions of teaching....[100]

This provides him with a further reason for considering the caliphate to be a bad institution. To the Western student, his claim that the political writings of Plato and Aristotle were neglected is a little surprising, the more so since 'Ali 'Abd al-Rāziq quotes Hobbes on the divine right of kings and John Locke on popular sovereignty when he complains that the Muslims did not tell us where the power of the caliph comes from. But he was obviously unaware of the political treatises of Al-Fārābī, Ibn Sīnā, and Ibn Rushd in particular, and of others among the *Falāsifa*, the Muslim philosophers. Nor does it appear that he was aware of the similarity between his exemption of Muḥammad from the range and character of temporal rulers, and Ibn Sīnā's and especially Ibn Rushd's distinction between Muḥammad's prophecy and the prophetic character of all other prophets.[101] This shows how little effect these political treatises of the *Falāsifa* had on the constitutional thinking of the jurists and theologians of Islam.

In conclusion, it may be suggested that 'Ali 'Abd al-Rāziq's primary aim in writing was to establish that Islam and politics, *dīn* and *siyāsa*, are worlds apart.[102] He did this by demonstrating that the *khilāfa* is a betrayal of the mission and message of Muḥammad, and that the Muslims should follow the prophet in their faith but build a modern polity on modern principles. It can hardly be claimed that he succeeded in demolishing the traditional orthodox theory of the *khilāfa* or *imāma*. The real difficulty does not seem to lie in his giving constitutional terms a different meaning when applied to Muḥammad, as distinct from their current connotation when applied to his successors. (We need only think of the new contemporary meaning of such terms as *ijtihād* or *shūrā*.) It lies, rather, in the fact that he seems to abandon Islamic law, the *Sharī'a*, as the central instrument of the prophet's religious call (*da'wa*). It may be assumed that this was his primary purpose in demolishing the orthodox theory, since the *khilāfa* is practically synonymous with the *Sharī'a*, and that for this reason he had to pay the penalty for his unorthodoxy. Does he mean that because the prophet's state was not a state in the usual sense of the term, his political ordinances and actions embodied in the *Sharī'a* —which in Muḥammad's time did not yet exist!—need not be considered binding today? This seems to me the only possible interpretation; it implies a revolutionary departure from the orthodox position. Why, then, does he in one place speak of the *Shar' dīnī* as a set of simple rules limited to purely religious matters of cult and worship, yet in another include within it regulations governing social relations, legal punishments and ethical rules? Are we justified in making a distinction between *shar' dīnī*, the creation of Muḥammad under divine command, and the later *Sharī'a* of the *khilāfa*? The confusion, if there is any, may be traced to his traditional learning. In fact, he also mentions the term *Sharī'a* in connection with Abu Bakr, when he says: "The error could spread among the Muslims that the *khilāfa* was a religious dignity and the vicegerency of the *ṣāhib al-sharī'ati*."[103]

Whatever the verdict[104] on the consistency, coherence, and logical cogency of the treatise, it can certainly provide the theoretical basis for a radical separation of Islam as religion, undimmed and capable of peaceful expansion, from the affairs of state which are the exclusive concern of man. His justification of a lay state for Muslims, inspired by the events in Turkey, cut at the root of traditional thought about the *khilāfa* as represented by Rashīd

Riḍā, and transferred the struggle which Islam had lost in Turkey to the Arab world. No doubt the new Egyptian Constitution of 1923 points in this direction and must have brought this struggle into the open just in Egypt. It marked the end of a constitutional and modernising development that had begun with the Khedive Isma'īl, and the beginning of further secularisation that culminated in the Egyptian Revolution of 1952 and the Constitution of 1956.

CHAPTER 5

ISLAM AND ARAB NATIONALISM

MUḤAMMAD AL-GHAZĀLĪ AND KHĀLID MUḤAMMAD KHĀLID

Rashīd Riḍā and 'Ali 'Abd al-Rāziq are the protagonists of the two principal Islamic attitudes and tendencies in the age of nationalism, which came after the Muḥammad 'Abduh phase of "modernism". They set the tone and provided the framework for the continuing debate on the character of the sovereign independent states whose establishment marks the achievement of the first goal the national movement set itself against foreign domination and influence (colonialism and imperialism): this goal was self-determination. The debate is an essential part of the second phase whose goals are self-expression and self-fulfilment. For this reason it is not simply a theoretical exercise about the place of the *Sharī'a* in the state in relation to its constitution, economic and social structure and culture. It is also of vital, practical importance, both internally and externally, in the battle of the mind that is to decide the place of these states in modern civilisation. The fate of the *Sharī'a* will decide not only what Islam is to be today and tomorrow, but also what part it is to play in the confrontation between Europe and the East, between Islamic and Western civilisation.

This J. Schacht clearly recognised in 1932[1] when he discussed the problem of *Sharī'a and Qānūn in modern Egypt*. He wrote then that the mixture of *Sharī'a* and *Qānūn* was a phenomenon of transition. Nor must we forget in following the debate about an Islamic versus a lay state—for this is what the debate is actually about—that it only echoes the constitutional debate in which the political and social forces of the country are engaged. The decision is, indeed, a political one insofar as it is made by the politicians, but it profoundly affects the mind and soul of the nation.

The '*ulamā*, as H. A. R. Gibb[2] says, expected the purification of religion from superstitions to lead to an Islamic revival, whereas the Westernised intellectuals, who formed the cadres of civil servants and officers, aimed at a reform of Islam "in terms of Western thought" and in imitation of Western political organisation and legal codes and courts.

Rashīd Riḍā and 'Ali 'Abd al-Rāziq wrote their respective treatises a year before and two years after the promulgation of the new Egyptian Constitution which established a constitutional monarchy with representative government. It also adopted modern law codes, with the exception of personal status law which remained *Sharī'a*-law. The *'ulamā* did not protest.[3] In fact, French laws had already been adopted under the Khedive Isma'īl condoned by Al-Azhar, which, as stated earlier, was attacked by Sheikh Abbas al-Jamāl in 1936 for this betrayal of Islamic ethics and traditions.[4]

The trend towards secularisation of law and court procedure continues unabated, to the accompaniment of the debate between "Islamists" and Westernisers about what kind of state with what laws Muslims should develop.

In Muḥammad al-Ghazālī we meet a follower of Rashīd Riḍā who, like him, stresses the imperative duty of Muslims to apply the teachings of Islam to political and social life. His views are those of the Muslim Brotherhood (*Ikhwānu-l-Muslimūn*), strongly coloured by the nationalists' uncompromising stand against Western "colonialism" and "imperialism", which he holds responsible for the mistaken separation of religion and politics. Nationalism is no less deadly an enemy of Islam.

He wrote his treatise *Min hunā na'lam*[5] in refutation of Khālid Muḥammad Khālid's *Min hunā nabda'*,[6] which constitutes a radical application of 'Ali 'Abd al-Rāziq's thesis. Muḥammad al-Ghazālī opposes not only the separation of state and religion in practice, but also its acceptance in the minds of Muslims today who distinguish between temporal power and spiritual forces. This, he claims, is the result of Western imperialist influence: by isolating Islam from legislation and government they hope to destroy religion.[7]

He takes the offensive by declaring that Islam must gain political power to be successful, just as the French and Russian people did in their revolutions. For, "this happened in the case of the great prophet, the master of this *Sharī'a*: he began as a preacher, announcer and warner, but he ended as a judge and a ruler (*ḥākim*)....His apostleship turned from *da'wa* to *dawla*...".[8] Like the prophet, the *khulafā rāshidūn* were religious rulers guided by God and His book, not by their own desire for power. They used their power and authority "to maintain Islamic government and apply its *Sharī'a*".

Obviously this is his answer to 'Ali 'Abd al-Rāziq. He blames the traditional enmity of Europe for her "considering Islam a religion (*dīn*) set apart from the state (*dawla*)" (pp. 24 f.), and this enmity he traces back to the Crusaders whose spirit is still abroad today. Israel with Judaism as both religion and state is another of Europe's devices to crush Islam. Yet, he holds, political power not only protects the territory of Islam, it also preserves its truth through education. For him, Islam is a government of free men dedicated to the cause of their religion and nation (*umma*; pp. 27 f.). Creed (*'aqīda*) and law (*sharī'a*) form a unity in Islam, and it consists of *mu'āmalāt*, including *ḥudūd* (social duties, with penalties for crimes) and *'ibādāt* (duties to God, such as prayer, fasting, alms-giving and pilgrimage). The social duties and the religious duty of *jihād* require an organisation such as only the state can provide (pp. 55 f.).

He thinks it is significant that the cry "Islam is a religion, not a state" should be raised just at a time when the traditional quarrel between the Islamic East and the Christian (*ṣālibī* = crusader) West is stirred up again. The only possible explanation is that the West, acting under the influence of a crusading Church, is trying to occupy the lands of Islam and destroy its laws and traditions (p. 39).

While one must make due allowance for justified suspicion of Western intentions, in view of the past record of the European powers' colonising and missionary activities, it is a little difficult to understand why in our day a largely secularised West of lay national states should want to destroy Islam. Organised religion is just as much threatened in the West as it is in the East. It is true that the separation of state and Church in the West is one of the results of the French Revolution and of the ideas that prompted it. Because of these ideas Christianity is challenged no less than Islam, though in a different way, since Christianity and Islam are unlike in their theology, structure, organisation and practice. Their differences are particularly great if we think of the classical theory of the religious and political unity of Islam, as represented by Muḥammad al-Ghazālī but not by his opponent Khālid Muḥammad Khālid, whose crime must appear the more heinous since al-Ghazāli brackets him with the hostile Christian West. For why should Muḥammad al-Ghazālī emphasise that the demand for a separation of Islam from politics coincides with an alleged recrudescence of the "traditional quarrel" between East and West—why should he emphasise this timing if not to discredit Khālid Muḥammad Khālid, whose arguments he does not adequately answer by sustained factual criticism?

Does not the threat to classical Islam come from a secular attitude and from a political philosophy whose roots lie in the Greek and Roman rather than in the Judeo-Christian tradition? For this reason it is so dangerous, and to meet this challenge Muslims naturally ask the fundamental question, "What is Islam?". To repeat, the answer is, broadly speaking, that of either Al-Afghānī, Muḥammad 'Abduh, Rashīd Riḍā, Muḥammad al-Ghazālī and others who demand an Islamic state based on the *Sharī'a* (of Qur'an and Sunna with or without historical *Fiqh*); or that of 'Ali 'Abd al-Rāziq, Khālid Muḥammad Khālid and like-minded advocates of a lay state in which Islam is either the official religion of the state or the private concern of the individual Muslim citizen. To use Muḥammad al-Ghāzāli's terms, Islam is understood either as *'aqīda* and *sharī'a*, fundamental tenets and principles embodied in a religious state law, or as *'aqīda* alone with a state law that is modern, independent of religious origin and sanction, but in conformity with the *'aqīda*. This grouping ignores the out and out secularists who want to build up a modern state within modern civilisation without any conscious reference to Islam.

Muḥammad al-Ghazālī's first chapter is headed *ḥukm islāmī lā qawmī*, "Islamic, not nationalist government", and sums up his attitude and his programme well. It also focuses attention on the central problem in Islam today: the validity of the *Sharī'a*, with all that this implies in an age of doubt and unbelief.

In the Middle Ages, Islam could face the challenge of Greek-Hellenistic philosophy and science because its adherents were united in faith and willing to submit to a religious law that regulated their entire lives. There were heretics, naturally; but the overwhelming majority of Muslims, whether Sunnī or sectarian, accepted the obligations imposed by Islam. The unity of faith in Allah and the acknowledgement of Muḥammad as His apostle made it possible for the Sunnī majority to allow limited deviation in legal practice through four orthodox rites (*maḏāhib*). I think it is a fallacy to assume that all will be well if *'ulamā* get together and draw up an agreed law-code out of the existing four rites. For today the crucial problem is not so much submission to a law considered to be of divine origin and sanction; it is, rather, nothing less than faith in God. For if we believe in God, we can, by an act of will born of faith, also accept His law adapted from the eternal sources interpreted by our reason, which is controlled by our faith.

The first consideration must therefore be faith as the necessary basis of an Islamic state. The next question is what is to be done about those—and they are not an insignificant minority, but even if they were it would not materially affect the justice of their case—who honestly cannot believe in God and consequently cannot acknowledge the validity of religious law, to which they would have to submit as citizens of an Islamic state. "Non-believers" here means Muslim agnostics and atheists as well as non-Muslims. It is clear that we have several different minorities, a Muslim minority and one or more of different religions, who are all ideally of one and the same nation, or at least of the same nationality as citizens of one state. This applies to an Islamic state only. A lay state must by definition grant complete religious liberty to all its citizens irrespective of their particular faith; it must also grant the freedom to have no religion. A modern state cannot have, at least not in theory, equal and less equal second-class citizens like the *ḏimmīs* of classical Islam, protected "possessors of a revelation" (*ahl al-kitāb*).

Within this digression (necessary in view of the intention of those who want to establish an Islamic state as an ideological state, as we shall see later) a further point must be made. It arises from the status of a *ḏimmī*, as defined in Islamic law. While he is adequately safeguarded by what we today call human rights—and it must be freely acknowledged that Islam has treated Jews and Christians very well indeed—his inequality concerns, perhaps paradoxically, his duties. He is not entitled to bear arms in defence of his state and nation; in return for his protection he pays a poll-tax, *jizya*. Muslim apologists point out rightly that this poll-tax is lower than the alms (*zakāt*) a Muslim is obliged voluntarily to pay, but this does not alter the fact that *zakāt* is a religious command enjoined upon Muslim believers, whereas *jizya* is imposed by the state on non-Muslims who have no choice in the matter. They cannot render military service to escape it since they are excluded from taking up arms. Admittedly this is a complicated matter because "religion" and "state" in the classical Islamic state are inseparable, and modern advocates of an Islamic state intend them to remain so. Since *jizya* is a Qur'anic legal stipulation, it could only be reinterpreted, that is, interpreted away, for no Qur'anic injunction can be ignored in an Islamic state based on Qur'an and Sunna as the two primary root-principles of the *Sharī'a* (and, as already stated, considered the only constituents of it by some modern advocates of an Islamic state).[9] Or, if *d̲immīs* were permitted to serve in the national army, payment of *jizya* would not be exacted. Examples of Jews and Christians doing military service and being exempted from payment of *jizya* have been recorded.

In connection with *jihād* another problem arises, in the sphere of international law and international relations, which is of great relevance to an Islamic state in the modern world. Modern Muslims are agreed in the interpretation that *jihād* is purely defensive; it is to protect Islam and its adherents against attack from without and against rebellion and heresy. This presupposes a state, at least in the case of rebellion, since rebellion implies authority and this authority is both religious and political. Even if we bear in mind what 'Ali 'Abd al-Rāziq said about the wars of Abu Bakr and what Muḥammad al-Ghazālī said about the wars of the prophet, who went into battle as he first led in prayer only after the kings had refused to accept his invitation to join the Muslim community, a war of religion is still war. Today war is ruled out, theoretically at least, as a means of settling conflicts between nations.

According to the classical theory of Islam, the world is divided into that part in which Islam is established, the *dār al-Islām*, and the other part in which it is not yet established, the *dār al-ḥarb*, realm of war, which must be conquered and incorporated in the

Islamic state to make Islam prevail in the whole world: a world religion in a world state. (The intermediate area does not concern us here.)[10]

Rashīd Riḍā and Muḥammad al-Ghazālī and all who think like them believe in the universality of Islam and also in the regenerative and healing power of its beliefs and principles. Islam alone, in their sincerely held view, can cure the ills of the world, restore the true faith, and thus bring peace and prosperity to the whole world. For the West is doomed, is bankrupt, sunk in materialism and vice. Leaving aside the somewhat naïve and unrealistic assessment of the West and the optimistic estimate of Islam and its influence on our age, there remains the division of the world into Islamic and Islamic-to-become. If the latter does not voluntarily embrace Islam, will the Islamic government—provided it has the necessary force at its disposal—embark on a war of conversion by conquest?

This question is not intended to belittle the excellence of Islam as a faith and a way of life. It is intended to show as a fact that, apart from the internal difficulties of setting up one or more Islamic states (and this is certainly the internal concern of those Muslims who desire a strictly Islamic state), there are also external complications which Islamic states as members of the comity of nations have to consider in the light of the United Nations Charter and the Bill of Human Rights. The simple answer may be that conversion by force, both within and without the boundaries of Islamic national states, is ruled out. This is only one of many examples which show that modification and adaptation to modern concepts are inevitable.

To return to Muḥammad al-Ghazālī, it is worth noting that he regards the separation of religion from the state as *bid'a*, heretical innovation. On the other hand, he is convinced that not only the Muslims but the world needs Islamic government, for it guarantees the protection of revelation. Religion without power—and this means the power and authority of the state—would be useless. This is also the view of Ibn Khaldūn.[11]

Muḥammad al-Ghazālī points to all the texts that speak of the combination of spiritual and temporal authority and power (*sulṭata rūḥīya wa-zamanīya*) in the person of the ruler who is at once military commander, judge and *imām*. It is only Christian domination and cultural imperialism, he repeats, that separated them in our minds and in reality.[12]

Could Islam flourish in a nationalist state? He does not answer his question directly, but states that Islamic ideals and teachings must be realised in and by the state; if a nationalist government were to disregard them, it would be an irreligious government which no Muslim ought to obey. Every Muslim must fight such a government and replace it by another government that acts in accordance with Islamic teachings. He adds that the present constitution of Egypt provides for the rule of a wise Islamic government (p. 64).

He calls nationalism "a return to the first *jāhilīya*" (pre-Islamic tribalism) and blames it for the loss of Muslim unity, just as he makes the separation of state and religion responsible for the loss of the Turkish empire. "The nationalist attitude was the most important thing we copied from the West and it formed the cornerstone in building the modern state."[13] "How could we abandon the Islamic for the nationalist government?" he asks. The bond of Islam is stronger than kinship based on common blood (p. 70).

Nothing less than a determined return to the purity of Islam can save the world, he says, for Islam is universal and Allah is the sole ruler, lawgiver and judge. Islam's internationalism and religious and political unity stem from its pure monotheism. Truth, brotherliness and justice as taught by Islam form the solid basis of world order (pp. 73 f.). In his political and social actions the prophet was guided by God, not by circumstances. His wars were not wars of conquest, but of liberation of subject peoples. Khālid Muḥammad Khālid is as wrong in attributing to the prophet base motives of power as he is in claiming that prophethood is superior to ruler- and governorship, for prophecy as religious government uses power only for the good of all, not for its own sake: this is true Islam (p. 81). He pleads for repentance and a return to God and His book and for the application of His *Sharī'a* (p. 90).

He launches a spirited attack on the colonial powers and their aggression in India, China, America, North Africa, and Syria, and he quotes G. B. Shaw and Gustave Lebon (whose views are often adduced by Turkish, Egyptian and other Arab writers) in his support. In contrast to France's suppression of liberty in her colonies, Islam spread beyond Arabia, liberated Egypt, Syria and

Persia, and brought virtue and prosperity to a large part of the world. For Islam and its state are based on Qur'an and Sunna, and as in its glorious past so today it is our only salvation (p. 112).

In this claim he is at one with many religious writers who support nationalism as long as it has its source and driving force in Islam. They take their stand on Qur'an and Sunna and eschew Western authorities, saying there is no need for them—despite the claim put forward by Khālid Muḥammad Khālid, who quotes Rousseau's *Contrat social.* Rousseau criticises the religious scholars of the past for their support of unjust rulers and draws the conclusion that the separation of religion and state will prevent collusion between religion and politics, and is the only way to rid the people of unjust government. Muḥammad al-Ghazālī has recourse to the *Ḥadīth* in order to prove that Islam opposes injustice and tyranny, but he only confirms Khālid's opinion. In his polemics he passes over in silence Khālid's insistence that religion (*dīn*) without being *dawla* or *ḥukm* has an important moral role to play in the life of the people. "The mission of religion is prophecy, not royal authority; guidance, not government."[14]

On the other hand, he agrees with Khālid's strictures on certain religious leaders—called by Khālid "priests"!—yet declares that people's misconduct and faults cannot be blamed on the faith they profess. If the authority of Qur'an and Sunna were upheld and if they were acted upon virtue would prevail. He asserts: "we accept whatever agrees with Qur'an and Sunna and reject whatever contradicts them" (p. 134), and exempts Islam as the only universal religion from the nationalists' opposition to all religions, without drawing any distinction between Judaism, Christianity and Islam. He claims—although this is not borne out by facts—that there is no minority-problem in Islam since it gives to adherents of other religions the same rights and duties as to Muslims. To say otherwise is sheer imperialism; nationalism means ruin for Islam, "for inasmuch as Islam is a general nationality (*jinsīya 'āmma*) among its followers throughout the five continents, it has grown weaker in proportion to the growing strength of the particular nationalisms (*al-qawmīyāt al-khāṣṣa*)" (p. 138).

It is more than an insignificant detail that he should accuse Salāma Musa of serving the British through his sectarian publications, as "everybody knows", when in fact this Copt went on record as saying "Islam is the religion of my fatherland, it is my duty to defend it".[15] This bears out that the religious leaders make common cause with the nationalists against the common enemy, the foreign occupying power, but they distrust their non-Muslim compatriots.

He admonishes the *'ulamā* to bring the people back to God and to oppose the government if its measures offend against Islamic principles (p. 142). Islam is the basis of the state and the religion of the majority of Egyptians; political government must, therefore, be founded on Islam. He again attacks Salāma Musa's attempt to unite all Egyptians, Muslims and Copts on a non-religious basis, neither Muslim nor Christian, when in reality—so Muḥammad al-Ghazālī maintains—he is plotting against Islam and wants to bring the Copt minority to power (pp. 153 f.). He condemns Communism for severing religion completely from public life, but charges imperialism with separating the state from religion only in the case of Islam (p. 161).

In his views on socialism he is in full agreement with Rashīd Riḍā. Russian socialism is irreligious and must be rejected in favour of Islamic socialism, based on monotheism and the brotherhood of all men. First, fundamental principles derived from Qur'an and Sunna must be formulated, and then Muslims can legislate for their realisation. An Islamic constitution is essential, everything else must follow from it (pp. 224 ff.). He mentions Abul A'lā Maudūdī in Pakistan and others, e.g. Sayyid Quṭb in Syria, whose views resemble those of himself and his associates in Egypt: for all, Islamic socialism offers the best remedy to the crisis of Islam on the basis of Qur'an and Sunna. These views are typical of the Muslim Brotherhood. Muḥammad al-Ghazālī offers little guidance as to how he would meet the crisis by detailed measures beyond the generalities just quoted.

Yet on another question, he shares the views of Rashīd Riḍā: on the position of women in modern Islam. He wants educated women, but would not let them "take over the reins of government", since men, not women, have always taken the great decisions and shouldered the heavy burdens of mankind. Where is a woman of the calibre of a Stalin or a Molotov even in Soviet Russia, he asks? (pp. 172 f.). (One wonders what he would say to the Russian woman cosmonaut who was the first woman in space?)

Neither Oriental nor Western customs do justice to woman's part in society. The happy mean is only to be found in Islam. But he frankly deplores the completely negative attitude of the *'ulamā* of Al-Azhar and of Islamic organisations to Western traditions, and attacks the silence of responsible religious leaders on this question. In his opinion, Islam is neither bound to Oriental nor to Western traditions. It accords equality to moral excellence of both sexes: 'A'isha surpassed men in excellence. The male superiority quoted earlier from the Qur'an refers to man's worldly efficiency which is why he occupies the leadership of the family by divine command. Woman's intellectual inferiority is indicated through the fact that two female witnesses are required to one male witness. He pronounces against segregation and the veil as Oriental and against complete freedom as Western, but advocates a return to Islam and the performance of the duties imposed by it. A woman cannot be a judge since she is not even competent as a witness by herself. Hence, both at home and in public, man carries a heavier burden. When he says: "It is not by accident that God has never sent a woman prophet"[16] he forgets those of the Old Testament. He deplores the state of affairs prevailing in Oriental countries today and compares the ignorance of the women with "the heroic fighting qualities of Israeli women whom our men meet on the battlefield" in Palestine (p. 206). He, therefore, pleads for women's education, but not so that they become secretaries, section heads or ministers in the government (p. 207). Education should be to their benefit in making a home and bringing up a family. This is the general opinion among orthodox Muslims. Muḥammad al-Ghazālī is also against birth-control: he wants more births, not fewer (p. 235).

The topics he discussed were in part suggested by Khālid Muḥammad Khālid's treatise which Muḥammad al-Ghazālī wanted to refute. For this reason, we reported his views in some detail. Khālid's socialism is Western, not Islamic, and this is also criticised by Sayyid Quṭb in his book *Social Justice in Islam*[17] from the standpoint of Islam which comprises this world and the hereafter and regulates economic affairs in its own way. Sayyid Quṭb is, therefore, opposed to the secular organisation Khālid prefers.

Muḥammad al-Ghazālī shows little if any understanding, even awareness, of the social and economic problems of the contemporary world, although he has devoted a special treatise to them. Religious fervour, stemming from the basic texts of Islam as pure monotheism with a high ethic preaching justice, equality and brotherhood, is not enough to grapple with a complex economic and social situation amidst poverty and lack of adequate education. It is no accident that he cannot convincingly and in detail answer Khālid Muḥammad Khālid's attack. This is because he lives in the ideal world of Islamic precept to which he appeals; he shuts his eyes to the need for practical measures in a changed world which has not only a different approach to faith in God, but starts from a modern concept of man and his place in the universe with or without God.

Against these negative features—negative in the eyes of the Western observer—there must be set considerable assets which may well outweigh them. Muḥammad al-Ghazālī wrote his treatise for his Muslim countrymen as a member of a group, the Muslim Brotherhood, from a sense of vocation. The emotional appeal should not be underrated, since he addresses ordinary men and women who are unaffected or, perhaps we should say, uncorrupted by Western ideas. In a bewildering situation of great social and economic stresses, he offers them something positive which could give meaning to their lives: the true and pure Islam of the prophet with its message of justice, equality and brotherhood. By contrasting Islam with the "corrupt" West he diverts their sense of frustration outwards so that on psychological grounds alone his revivalist fervour cannot fail to produce a feeling of superiority and a social cohesion which can have a stabilising effect, if contained by disciplined obedience to authority: the spiritual authority of the leadership of the Brotherhood and the temporal authority of the government. To dismiss him and those who think, speak and write like him as utopian demagogues would be not only too easy, but definitely wrong.

That he gives expression to widespread popular attitudes and represents the predominant Islamic attitude to state and society cannot be doubted. An Islamic revival could perhaps more likely come from this quarter than from the Western-educated and orientated intellectuals.

ISLAM: RELIGION *AND* STATE

Muḥammad ʻAbdullah As-Sammān's *Usūs al-ḥukm fī-l-Islām* (*Principles of Government in Islam*)[18] starts from the same basic principles of the excellence of Islam and concentrates on its political aspect. Curiously enough, it is to the people who are sovereign and not to God that Islamic government is responsible. But if we expect a clear definition of popular sovereignty and a practical blue-print for representative government which implements Islamic principles and law we will not find it in his exposition.

"Islam considers rule a vital factor in the formation of the state...[it] is not a devotional religion only, nor is it just a human message, but also and above all a state with its own being, its own principles and its own organisation....The prophet was the head of the state and the source of legislation." He claims that all other states are based on the absolute sovereignty of the state, following Plato and Aristotle. But "Islam takes into consideration only the sovereignty of the people and looks upon the state as the servant of the people...". He is against absolute rule as it was introduced by Muʻāwiya and is practised in most Muslim states, because he sees a "natural alliance between these absolutist families and Western imperialism". He extols the virtues of the ruler in early Islam whose primary concern was the welfare of the people.

He wants a simple education for a free people of Muslims whose most precious gift from God is Islam, "a religion full of dignity". "We wish the Muslim people to understand that their fatherland is a part of their creed, that they are its guardian and responsible for its freedom, independence and honour, that they have to expend blood and treasure in order to preserve its freedom, independence and honour...."[19]

Instead of the useless Arab League he wants to see founded an Islamic League, but he is careful to stress the co-existence of nation and world-wide Islamic brotherhood, as is clear from his statement:

> The Muslim has a smaller fatherland which is the state where he was born and bred. Islam requires him to defend it and glorify it. But the Muslim has also a greater fatherland: this is the Muslim state towards which he is attracted by a creed anchored in the depths of his soul.... Muslim rule...will not come into being, unless the Muslim peoples

have a union to preserve their existence. And the Muslim peoples will not have a corporate existence unless they are ruled in the true Muslim way and thereby attain internal stability and unless they have an Islamic union strong enough to provide them with power and a voice which counts in the world....[20]

He is not an Egyptian nationalist, but a patriot. Otherwise he could not be a citizen of two states even though Islam is common to both of them. His foremost concern is the political realisation of Islam for the good of the people.

In Ḥasan al-Bannā we find the "ideology" of the Muslim Brotherhood most forcefully and authoritatively expressed with a remarkable transformation of what we generally understand by nationalism through a religiously motivated interpenetration of religious fervour, patriotism and anti-Westernism. To begin with, this is already evident in his definition of Islam as "creed and worship, fatherland and nationality, law and culture, tolerance and strength....For the *Ikhwān* Islam is religion and state; and Qur'an and sword".[21] He conceived of his movement as the spearhead of the Muslim nation capable of understanding and applying the lofty principles of Islam which is "superior and sufficient for all purposes" and can, therefore, dispense with Western inspiration and methods. It is significant that anything Western is excluded from the self-contained and self-sufficient Muslim mind which cannot fail to have a possibly adverse effect in the midst of wholesale adoption of Western education and technology.

His attitude to nationalism may be defined as an attempt to neutralise it by declaring the whole Islamic fatherland to be one fatherland, transcending geographical and ethnic boundaries, and dedicated to high principles and pure and right beliefs "and the truths which God has made a source of light and guidance for the world at large".[22] This spiritual nationalism is, however, not free from political undertones as when he speaks of

aggression against one part of the Islamic fatherland is an aggression against the whole....We want the integration of all parts of our Islamic fatherland which have been cut off from one another due to the machinations of the Western powers and their imperialistic greed and avarice.... We also do not recognize these international treaties and agreements which have rendered Muslim states weak enough to be devoured by aggressors.

He advocates not *one* Islamic state, but a *hay'at al-umam al-islāmīya*, an organisation of Muslim nations, along the lines of the Arab League, but not confined to Arab Muslims. It is worth noting in this connection that when in 1951 Iran and Pakistan wanted to be admitted to the Arab League as Muslim states they were refused membership.

Ḥasan al-Bannā is not a nationalist in the accepted sense of the word. While Muslims are in duty bound to assist in the struggle of emancipation from foreign domination and oppression, they owe allegiance to both, Egypt and Islam, and combine a double loyalty —*al-qawmīya al-khāṣṣa* [particular (Egyptian) nationality] with a general Islamic one. "The *Ikhwān* respect their particular nationality on the consideration that it is the first foundation of their cherished (Islamic) renaissance.... After this the *Ikhwān* support Arab unity as the next step towards this renaissance. Then they strive for pan-Islamism as a fence of protection for the general Islamic fatherland."[23] In their programme, they speak of *waṭanīya* and *qawmīya*. The former obviously refers to their Egyptian fatherland and the latter to the Muslim nation as a whole.

It is understandable that pan-Islamism and pan-Arabism are closely related aspirations, since the Arabs have given their language to Islam—and its Holy Book—and carried it victoriously over a large part of the globe. Yet, in the minds of those whose overriding loyalty for religious reasons is to Islam as a religious and political unity, Ḥasan al-Bannā's "particular nationality" is on closer inspection also strongly coloured by the religious component, as is the case with all conservative Muslims. For, he is not prepared to include non-Muslim Egyptians in a common nationality. As Z. I. Ansari rightly says: "they would grant them more or less equal statutory rights. Yet the idea that those non-Muslims who share with them their fatherland are also genuinely a part of their *umma*, that they are an integral part of their cultural society and share their aspirations has not become a part of the Islamic attitude."[24] Ḥasan al-Bannā, as quoted by him, said: "We shall remain in peace with them as long as they are peaceful towards us: and we shall remain their well-wishers as long as they desist from committing any aggression against us. We believe that the tie between us and them is that of *da'wa*.... It is our duty to invite them towards our creed, for it is a blessing for all mankind."

Benevolent neutrality is not enough, it seems to me, to establish real national unity which can only be forged on the basis of complete equality and mutual acceptance without reservations. Missionary zeal is not conducive to real equality before conversion.

Z. I. Ansari is right when he holds that only the secular nationalists are prepared to regard non-Muslims as part and parcel of the national community. Nationalism is after all Western in conception, and orthodox Muslims are understandably at pains to resist Western ideas and their application in matters of political institutions and legislation, and wish to limit borrowings from the West to science and technology.

RELIGION, PATRIOTISM AND NATIONALISM

The frontiers between political and spiritual "nation" and "nationalism" and, in the international field, between pan-Islamism and pan-Arabism are extremely fluid as is clear from the almost indiscriminate use of terminology: *sha'ab* (people), *qawm* (nation), *umma* (religious "nation", community) are sometimes used separately in the narrow meaning of the term, but more often interchangeably.[25] The imprecise meanings indicate that the movements built round the terms (or the terms used to express the movements!) can easily be interchanged by their adherents at one time or another; or that, as we have seen in Ḥasan al-Bannā, they can actually be combined as succeeding stages in a gradual evolution towards the realisation of a classical ideal: the *umma* of Islam of world-wide dimensions.

On the other hand, it would be a mistake to see in pan-Arabism simply pan-Islamism turned secular and nationalistic. For Islam, even though "secularised" as a historical and cultural bond with a linguistic base, is much more than a convenient means to further political aims. Of this there are many examples. Thus, earlier than the *Ikhwān*, Mustafa Kāmil[26] links religion, i.e. Islam, with patriotism. Fatherland and nation, people and nation are complementary. Though concerned with Egypt as his fatherland and nation in the first place, he demands that Islam should be made the basis of national education. Religion teaches love of country as "one of the first and most sacred duties". He warns against the

West which, he claims, intends to draw the Egyptians away from their religious principles.

Yet he is interested in Islam and pan-Islamism, following Al-Afghānī, largely as a means to hasten Egypt's liberation. He stands aloof from Muḥammad 'Abduh's "modernist" movement and is, in turn, attacked by *Al-Manār*. It is possible that he emphasises "the true principles of Islam" and not the "modernist" reform movement because his primarily political nationalism made him insist on an Egyptian nation (*umma*) which comprised Christian Copts and Jews whom he welcomed to the ranks of his National Party. F. Steppat remarks that his nationalism threatened, in the eyes of Muḥammad 'Abduh and his movement, "to split the unity of the Islamic *milla*".[27]

Mustafa Kāmil's views on Western civilisation are strongly influenced by his political opposition to British occupation. He distinguishes between a national civilisation, centred in Islam, and a supranational, "humanitarian" civilisation of wider appeal. Both are complementary. There is, no doubt, some similarity with Ziya Gökalp, as Steppat quoting Heyd remarks. It is equally significant, to my mind, that Mustafa Kāmil's terminology should be modelled on Ibn Khaldūn's (*madanī*, *tamaddun*, *ḥaḍāra*, *'umrān*).

Himself free from religious fanaticism, Mustafa Kāmil became convinced after Fashoda that Christian fanaticism inspired European politics. This made him sceptical towards the West and the advantages of Western civilisation, but, true to his motto *ḥubb al-waṭan min al-imān* (love of fatherland based on faith), he advocated, for the sake of national unity, loyalty to Islam for the Muslim Egyptians and to Christianity for the Copts. His tolerance of other faiths goes hand in hand with his conviction that religion is an essential factor in national life and assures, together with love of fatherland, the greatness of a nation. Islam is for him in the East what Christianity is for the West, hence he wants to see the principles of Islam followed.

For him there was no conflict between Islam and nationalism. His state was to be based on Islamic principles, but not on Islamic law. It is obvious that the latter would have meant excluding Christians and Jews from the national movement on equal terms. For him the concept of the sovereignty of the people as the guiding idea of his political philosophy is, therefore, logical and natural, while it is not so in the case of As-Sammān whose ideas we discussed earlier on.

That he should see in Islamic law the pattern of the separation of powers, and in Islamic government a constitutional monarchy, enabled him to combine the Western concept of popular sovereignty with its twin: popular representation. The latter in the form of Western parliamentarianism became important after his visit to France. He looked upon parliamentary institutions largely as a means to withstand a foreign oppressor and, internally, as "the only guarantee...of the inviolability of the laws and of personal and general liberty and freedom".[28]

F. Steppat is, no doubt, right in interpreting his thought as that of a "Muslim nationalist" and not of a "nationalist Muslim", since he did not separate politics and religion. Yet, judged by my distinction between an Islamic and a Muslim state—provided this is a valid distinction—some qualification seems to be called for. Mustafa Kāmil demands a parliament like the European parliaments to which the government is responsible. Presumably such a parliament is elected and its members represent all classes and groups of the national citizenry, irrespective of religion. The legislation which it debates and decides—while in accordance with Islamic principles—is definitely not *Sharī'a*-law. Hence the state is a lay state, as distinct from a secular state. Perhaps F. Steppat means "secularism" when he says "laicism" to which Mustafa Kāmil was opposed. Whether he integrated Islam into his nationalism, as Steppat holds, or rather set one side by side with the other, it may be doubted whether "the non-recognition of the totalitarian claim of religion" can be construed as "its subordination to the nation" with the result that "...the way is free to fulfil the totalitarian claim of nationalism. Nationalism can take the place of religion".

Neither Mustafa Kāmil nor other nationalists view this intricate, delicate problem of the relationship between religion and nationalism as the ineluctable choice between the one or the other. They do so not solely under the influence of the West with its separation of state and Church, but also in the wake of Ibn Khaldūn whom they have studied. From him they have learnt to distinguish between *khilāfa* and *mulk*, either the *mulk* of *Sharī'a* and *Qānūn*, the Muslim power-state, or the naked power-state, the *siyāsa* '*aqlīya* with political laws based on human reason. Religion is the central all-pervading factor in the *khilāfa*, one of several equally important factors in the *mulk*.

NATIONALISM ABSORBS ISLAM

'Abd al-Raḥmān al-Kawākibi's pan-Islamism was, however, replaced by pan-Arabism through his concentration on the *umma* as founded by the Arabs. Just like Al-Afghānī, he wanted as an orthodox Muslim a thorough reform of Islam to make it impregnable against Western imperialism. The *umma* contracted, so to speak, through its exclusive concentration, in his mind, on the Arabs. Miss Haim[29] quotes this definition he gave of *umma*: "...the sum of the individuals with a common ancestry or *waṭan*, language or religion...." He links the Arabs with the foundation and expansion of Islam to such an extent that he arrives at a complete identification of the Arab Islamic state with Islam. Once he applies the Western concept of "nation" to the Arabs as the spearhead of Islam, it does not require much to connect the reform of Islam with the Arab nation of his day.[30]

'Abdu-l-Raḥmān al-Bazzāz starts from the same premise. He extends the role of the Arabs as the founders of Islam to that of being the saviours of the world from oppression and ignorance—an interesting application of the term *jāhilīya*, originally confined to the Arabian peninsula—and eagerly appropriates the statement of Gustave Lebon, that the Arabs were the most merciful conquerors that the world has known. He stresses that the national government he wants to see established does not conflict with Islam, and calls for a pan-Arab organisation in Asia and Africa. Islamism and Arabism are like two circles. He does not say whether this is intended as an integration or a parallel existence.

He reassures the non-Muslims in the words of a leading Christian Arab nationalist scholar, Qustantin Zuraiq: "True nationalism can, on no account, contradict true religion." Islam is the concern of every Arab; "he must...study Islam and understand its true nature, and sanctify the memory of the great prophet to whom Islam was revealed".[31] Q. Zuraiq opposes both Sufism and a petrified "clergy", hence his emphasis on the prophet and early Islam. He insists that both religion and nationalism stem from the same source and says: "If nationalism is opposed to anything it is not to religious spirituality, but to the disruptive partisanship which places communal solidarity above the bonds of nationality and which refuses to be assimilated within the framework of the nation. The upholders of this partisanship are the enemies of Arab nationalism and the destroyers of its unity."[32]

It is clear that an accommodation with nationalism, a marching hand in hand of Muslim and Christian Arabs, the *avant garde* of Arab nationalism, is only possible if Islam is understood as faith, not as the classical expression of that faith in law. In other words, Islam and Christianity are put on a par as tenants living in harmony on the basis of genuine toleration in the same house. This is only possible if Islam renounces its claim—which it made and has maintained throughout history to the present day—to regulate not only the entire life of the individual believer, but also and foremost the life of the body politic of the community of believers.

That Christian Arabs—whose Westernisation preceded that of their Muslim compatriots—should favour such a transformation is natural. It is not so automatic for the Muslims steeped in Muslim traditional law and lore, for it is not the same as the disestablishment of the Church even though that was the result of modern Western political and social philosophy. It stands to reason that the conservative element in Islam should resist Western penetration, hence the dilemma in which contemporary Muslims, who have achieved political independence and freedom from Western domination and have to build a modern state, inevitably find themselves.

There are few voices which speak with such force of conviction and sureness of intention among those who defend Islam as a total, comprehensive religious way of life as the *Ikhwān al-Muslimūn* and the advocates of an Islamic state in the direct line of succession of Rashīd Riḍā. Few nationalists are so outspoken as Sami Shawkat who said: "We have to be firm in our belief that our age is the age of nationalities (*al-qawmīyāt*), not the age of religions."[33] This statement obviously implies that Islam is a religion like other religions; it has to vacate its dominant position and make room for the national movement.

Already in 1913, Aḥmad Lutfi al-Sayyid wrote:

The *salaf* used to say that the land of Islam is the *waṭan* of all the Muslims. This is an imperialistic rule the application of which serves every nation desiring to enlarge its possessions and to increase its influence every day over neighbouring countries...now, this rule is not compatible with the actual situation of the Muslim nations and their ambitions. There is no other alternative but to replace it by the one faith consonant with the ambition of every Eastern nation that has a defined *waṭan*. And that faith is the faith of nationalism (*waṭanīya*).[34]

This quotation shows both a lack of historical sense and political realism. The latter results in giving up the *umma* of world-wide Islam in favour of territorial national aspirations of which Islam does not seem to form any important part, perhaps none at all, in face of the threat of foreign domination. The former understands *umma* as nation in the modern sense, placing religious "imperialism", pan-Islamism, on the same level as the political imperialism of modern history.

THE CLASSICAL ATTITUDE IS REASSERTED

Yet the present orthodox attitude is best reflected by the *Ikhwān* who stress the religious and political unity of classical Islam. Thus Sayyid Quṭb formulated in his already-mentioned *Social Justice in Islam* the essence of Islam as a religious way of life applicable to contemporary Muslim society in these words, replete with traditional concepts and terms of the *Sharī'a*:

Islam is a religion (*dīn*) which represents the unity (*waḥda*) of worship and social relations (*al-'ibāda wa-l-mu'āmala*), of faith and conduct (*al-'aqīda wa-l-sulūk*), of spiritual and material values, of this world and the hereafter, of heaven and earth. From this grand (all-embracing) unity stem its laws and obligations, its directives and penalties, its views on the administration of government and finance, on the distribution of booty and tribute (*al-maghānim wa-l-maghārim*), and on rights and duties. In this great principle are included the other parts and details [of the *Sharī'a*].[35]

Sa'id Ramaḍān likewise sees in pan-Islamism the true unity which only Islam but not narrow nationalism can provide. Aḥmad Amīn is opposed to nationalism, but not to patriotism: "The love of the *waṭan* is inherent in man...to work for the wellbeing of the *waṭan* is natural...."[36] But there is also the lofty universalism of Islam which is not contradicted by love of the fatherland, but is incompatible with nationalism and its narrow morals serving nationalistic ends which are likely to conflict with justice and equity in contrast with religious moral values.[37]

When Ḥasan al-Bannā stresses the need for Arab unity as the essential condition of "the restoration of the glory of Islam, of the establishment of the Islamic state and of the consolidation of the dominance of Islam", two prominent leaders of the *Ikhwān* after his assassination plead for the Qur'an to "be made the programme for the whole of our life" and wish the Islamic state to "judge in accordance with what Allah has revealed" (Al-Ḥuḍaybī) and complain that "the suspension of the *Sharī'a* is the suspension of Islam itself" ('Abd al-Qādir 'Udah).[38]

Utopian the ideas of the *Ikhwān al-Muslimūn* may be, but they are for all that not without force and considerable effect. Backward looking to the great past glory of Islam and dreaming of a glorious future through the restoration of the true Islam of the prophet (by the application of the injunctions of the Qur'an), their adherents in other Muslim countries, such as Indonesia, Malaya and Pakistan, try to implement their teaching in the present time in a struggle for power and influence, with such modifications as local circumstances demand.

For the concept of an Islamic state attracts a following determined to realise it now or as soon as practicable. They bend their energies to the achievement of this goal. That they pursue concrete political aims is clear from their use of the word "ideology" which has no rightful place in a religious context as religion is understood in the West. But it may be justified if Islam is understood in its traditional sense—despite 'Ali 'Abd al-Rāziq's challenge to it—as a faith and a way of life for man in society and state.

CHAPTER 6

AN ISLAMIC STATE FOR PAKISTAN?

Naturally, not all advocates of an Islamic state in our time are followers of the *Ikhwān* and their tactics. Nor do the same generalities and the same vagueness of detail characterise all efforts resulting in blue-prints. Two treatises devoted to the constitutional framework and to the government and administration of an Islamic state deserve special attention. This is because they supply the theory underlying the attempt to set up an Islamic state in Pakistan, and thus their discussion will naturally lead to the second part of this book illustrating the various aspects of the practical measures to build a modern national state in countries with Muslim majorities where Islam is a problem. In our context it does not matter whether Islam is a central or a mere peripheral problem in the state as long as we preserve a sense of proportion. But as long as Islam is a factor in such a state it is important to know how those determined that Islam should play a role in public life envisage this role in practice. These treatises are not theoretical speculations; they are conditioned by the practical needs of a state and constitute a programme for political action.

MUHAMMAD ASAD'S PLAN

Muhammad Asad elaborates in his recent book *The Principles of State and Government in Islam*[1] the ideas he propounded not long after the emergence of the state of Pakistan in his essay *Islamic Constitution-Making*. We are here only concerned with the theory of Muhammad Asad, which he formulated in the concrete political situation of a struggling state whose *raison d'être* was Islam and the desire of the majority of Indian Muslims to have their own state where they could live as Muslims. This may explain the use of the term "ideology" by religious and lay leaders and politicians in connection with Islam and state in Pakistan.

The author starts from the thesis that the *Sharī'a* is formed by what Qur'an and Sunna have commanded, and excludes *Fiqh*, the traditional Islamic law. "Thus, it is the *nuṣūṣ* [clear textual injunctions] of Qur'an and Sunna—and only these—that collectively constitute the real, eternal *sharī'ah* of Islam."[2] This means that Muhammad Asad only considers as valid and obligatory what is explicitly commanded and forbidden in clear, authoritative, unambiguous terms in the Qur'an. The Sunna in the form of authentic *Ḥadīth* elaborates and supplements these texts; it is equally authoritative and binding on Muslims, "whereas the far larger area of things and activities which the Law-Giver has left unspecified...must be regarded as allowable (*mubāḥ*) from the *shar'ī* point of view".[2]

He justifies his opinion by claiming the support of the Companions of the prophet and of outstanding jurists, in particular Ibn Ḥazm. Through the exercise of *ijtihād*, necessary, additional legislation can and must be provided "in consonance with the spirit of Islam". He would *occasionally* refer to legislation of the past, arrived at by *ijtihād*, and stresses the temporary character of all such legislation since it must be bound to the special circumstances of time and place. Yet, it is always "subject to the authority of the irrevocable, unchangeable *sharī'ah*". He claims that the ordinances of the Divine Law conform to "the real nature of man and the genuine requirements of human society at any time". It follows from this that the *nuṣūṣ* are

> in the first instance general principles...and, in the second instance, provide for detailed legislation in such matters as are not affected by changes due to man's social development,...whenever changes are indispensable for human progress (for example, in matters of government, technology, economic legislation...), the *sharī'ah* does not stipulate any detailed laws, but either lays down general principles only or refrains from making any legal enactment. And this is where *ijtihādī* legislation rightfully comes in. To be more precise, the legitimate field of the community's law-making activity comprises (*a*) details in cases and situations where the *sharī'ah* provides a general principle but no detailed ruling, and (*b*) principles *and* details with regard to matters which are *mubāḥ*... [pp. 14 f.].

He adduces Sura v, 48, "For every one of you We have ordained a Divine Law and an open road" in support of his contention that "the Law-Giver has conceded to us, within this area, an 'open road' (*minhāj*) for temporal legislation which would cover the contingencies deliberately left untouched by the *nuṣūṣ* of Qur'an and Sunnah". He pleads for "a return to the realities of Qur'an and Sunnah" as a creative movement in order to find an Islamic solution to the cultural crisis of Islam, and rejects as a destructive movement "the present drift of Muslim society toward Western concepts and institutions" which would spell the ruin of Islam.

He thus rejects the West completely, forgetting that despite its failings and weaknesses its political, social and economic structure are based on precisely those high moral principles which he attributes—exclusively, it seems—to Qur'an and Sunna. That the West does not live up to its principles surely does not mean that they do not exist or are bad, just as is the case in the Muslim East. Necessary temporal legislation by *ijtihād*—arrived at by going back to what the author terms "the socio-political program of Islam"—takes account, in the light of his just quoted definition, of the prevailing conditions. It would, therefore, be surprising if such legislation were very different from Western efforts at promoting economic wellbeing, social justice and creative leisure for free individuals in the good society.

He is, as we saw, not the only modern Muslim thinker to demand "back to Qur'an and Sunna" in order to achieve a renewal of Islam in an Islamic state, but he has the merit of attacking the crucial question of the place and scope of Islamic law with clarity and simplicity. He rightly stresses the need to get back and down to fundamentals by cutting through the "many layers of conventional and frequently arbitrary interpretation". He does not stand in awe of tradition as is clear from his claim that

> the outward forms and functions of an Islamic state need not necessarily correspond to any "historical precedent". All that is required of a state in order that it might deservedly be described as "Islamic" is the embodiment in its constitution and practice of those clear-cut, unambiguous ordinances of Islam which have a direct bearing on the community's social, political, and economic life. As it happens, those ordinances are very few and very precisely formulated; and they are invariably of such a nature as to allow the widest possible latitude to the needs of any particular time and social condition.[3]

It would not be fair to hold against this simple programme that it brushes aside too lightly what we called earlier on the concept of historical continuity. It may well be that the application of this "ideological" plan will result in an Islamic state, but it may seriously be questioned whether it shares with the historical Islamic state—as formulated by the jurists determined to create an ideal pattern in opposition to a quite different political and historical reality—anything but the name. We could only judge if Muhammad Asad's plan had been or would be realised in Pakistan. But in view of his critical examination of Western terminology in itself and when applied (or as he rightly says, misapplied to Islam) it is justified to question the practicability of the programme. For the author is evidently aware that the simplicity of the Islam of the prophet is not unconnected with the economic, social and cultural situation of seventh-century Arabia. Can we establish in the vastly different twentieth century a much more complicated state and society on the basis of an "ideology" formulated then? Assuming this to be possible—and the author's answer to our question would certainly point to the divine character of the *Sharī'a*, the explicit statements of which in general principles and detailed injunctions are eternally valid—can we ignore the development of this Islamic "ideology" through the ages?

Reference, by way of analogy, was made earlier to the Qaraites and their rejection of Rabbinic law and how circumstances forced them to create their own *Halakhah* (corresponding to the *Sharī'a*). This doubt—criticism would be unwarranted—does, however, not impugn the sound principle and bold grasp, unhampered by traditional legal thinking, that characterise Muhammad Asad's programmatic formulations. This is even more true since he acknowledges historical evolution even in the time of the *khulafā rāshidūn* some of whose legal enactments and administrative measures are unconnected with Qur'an and Sunna, but, he claims, are in conformity with the spirit of Islam.

No doubt it is no accident that the author speaks of community, not of society. Therefore, he sees in the state only a means of promoting the "growth of a community of people who stand up for equity and justice, for right and against wrong—or, to put it more precisely—a community of people who work for the creation and maintenance of such social conditions as would enable the greatest possible number of human beings to live, morally as well as physically, in accordance with the natural Law of God, Islam."[4]

This is indistinguishable from the goal of any political philosophy of our time and is not any more Islamic than it is Jewish or Christian. Islam as the natural law of God is not new either.

He condemns nationalism as opposed to the "fundamental Islamic principle of the equality of all men" and states that Muslim unity must "be of an ideological nature, transcending all considerations of race and origin: a brotherhood of people bound together by nothing but their consciousness of a common faith and a common moral outlook" (p. 32). The tasks he sets an Islamic state are to be met with in every writer; he only expresses them in modern, attractive terms. If the state acts according to all the principles attributed to Islam it "can rightly be described as 'God's vice-gerent on earth'; its foremost duty...consists in enforcing the ordinances of the *sharī'ah* in the territories under its jurisdiction" (p. 34). He demands that "the constitution must explicitly lay down that no temporal legislation or administrative ruling, be it mandatory or permissive, shall be valid if it is found to contravene any stipulation of the *sharī'ah*" (p. 35). Obedience to legally constituted authority is a religious duty and must be rendered as long as the government acts within the *Sharī'a.* The community must supervise the actions of the government which is, thus, "subject to the people's consent". This popular consent depends on the free choice of the government by the people. This deduction does not seem to be cogent.

He examines the question of where the sovereignty of the state resides and attributes the assertion that it resides in "the people" to Western political theories. He considers this "unrestricted sovereignty on the part of the community as a whole" as un-Islamic as the autocracy Muslims suffered in the past. The reason he gives is that the people's consent in an Islamic state "is but the result of their having accepted Islam as a Divine Ordinance, [therefore] there can be no question of their being endowed with sovereignty *in their own right*".[5] He is here interpreting Islam correctly, in contrast to the advocates of popular sovereignty we discussed before, for example, As-Sammān.

In another place he defines the purpose of the Islamic state as "the establishment of Islamic Law as a practical proposition in man's affairs" (pp. 39 f.). While the non-Muslim citizen is to enjoy full religious, cultural and social freedom, he admits that "without a certain amount of differentiation between Muslim and non-Muslim there can be no question of our ever having an Islamic state or states in the sense envisaged in Qur'an and Sunnah". In practice, this means that "they may not be entrusted with the key position of leadership". A non-Muslim could not "work wholeheartedly for the ideological objectives of Islam; nor in fairness could such a demand be made of him" (pp. 40 f.). It is difficult to reconcile this with the lofty, universal objectives of the Islamic state as defined above (pp. 30, 33). Moreover, Qur'an and Sunna envisage a community of believers, not necessarily a state.

By mistaking Islam for an ideology like Communism or Fascism, Muhammad Asad introduces a foreign, alien concept which results in qualifying and restricting the equality of non-Muslim citizens as well as the universal application of Islamic principles. Since, however, he includes in these principles the duty to "propagate the teachings of Islam to the world at large" (p. 33), he possibly makes their general application contingent on conversion to Islam. This seems to be borne out by his assertion—in connection with the restriction of authority and policy-making in an Islamic state:

> if we are resolved to make Islam the dominant factor in our lives, we must have the moral courage to declare openly that we are not prepared to endanger our future by falling into line with the demands of that spurious "liberalism" which refuses to attribute any importance to men's religious convictions; and that, on the contrary, the beliefs a man holds are far more important to us than the mere accident of his having been born or naturalized in our country [p. 41].

Even if "religious convictions" are understood in the context of the religious and political unity of Islam, "ideology" seems to be a misnomer since it is a strictly political term without any connection with religion.

That the head of state should be a Muslim is a matter of course; but who should have authority to enact the necessary *ijtihādī* legislation? The Qur'an decides this by the principle of consultation (*shūrā*), as stated in Sura XLII, 38, *amruhum shūrā baynahum*, which the author translates by "Their [the believers'] communal business (*amr*) is to be [transacted in] consultation among themselves". He interprets this to mean that all temporal legislation has been entrusted to the community by *ijtihād*, the "exercise of independent reasoning in consonance with the spirit of Islamic Law and the best interests of the nation" (pp. 43 f.).

It is to be noted that, whereas the author before demanded *ijtihād* to be "in consonance with the spirit of Islam",[6] he now simultaneously seems to widen and to restrict its scope by adding a further most important principle which was emphasised by Rashīd Riḍā—with whom Muhammad Asad has much in common. This is the principle of *maṣlaḥa*, "the best interests of the nation", but at the same time "Islam" in the phrase "the spirit of Islam" has now become "Islamic Law", unless the two are coterminous? The Qur'anic verse about *shūrā* is to be understood "as the fundamental, operative clause of all Islamic thought relating to statecraft" (p. 44). It means "that the legislative powers of the state must be vested in an assembly chosen by the community specifically for this purpose". By "community" is meant the whole community, and the Legislative Assembly to which he gives the traditional Muslim name of *majlis ash-shūrā* "must be truly representative of the entire community, both men and women" (p. 45). Such an assembly must, in his view, be elected "by means of the widest possible suffrage, including both men and women". This is demanded by present circumstances which can and must legitimately be taken into account for all legislation outside of and additional to the *Sharī'a*.

Muhammad Asad speaks throughout of the community which, no doubt, means the community of believers. Does this imply that he excludes non-Muslims both from voting for and sitting in the Legislative Assembly? This would appear to be a logical deduction, especially in view of the qualifications he stipulates for the members of the *majlis ash-shūrā* whose work only relates

> to matters of public concern, and more particularly to matters which have not been regulated in terms of law by the *nuṣūṣ* of Qur'an and Sunnah. Whenever the interests of the community call for a legislative enactment, the *majlis* must first look into the context of the *sharī'ah* for a guiding general principle of law bearing on the problem under consideration. If such a general principle is forthcoming, it falls within the scope of the legislature to draw up an enactment in consonance with the established *shar'ī* principle. But very often the *majlis* will be confronted with problems on which the *sharī'ah* is entirely silent....In such

instances it is for the *majlis* to devise the requisite legislation, taking only the spirit of Islam and the community's welfare into consideration. All this presupposes...that the members of the *majlis* are not only possessed of a good working knowledge of the *nuṣūṣ*..., but are also people of understanding and insight...alive to the sociological requirements of the community and worldly affairs in general: in other words, education and maturity are indispensable qualifications for election to the *majlis ash-shūrā* [pp. 47 f.].

It may be argued that, since the Muslims are in a majority in the state, this is reasonable. But it is not only contrary to the author's insistence on "the fundamental Islamic principle of the equality of all men"—after all he equates Islam with "the natural Law of God", and we are all God's children, irrespective of creed and colour—but it is also incompatible with such a state's membership of the United Nations which requires adherence to the Bill of Human Rights. The author's restriction of voting for and membership of the *majlis* to the Muslim community is not only differentiation which he admits as inevitable in his "ideological" state, it is discrimination. For, the minorities are as much, if not more, affected by decisions concerning public matters as the majority.

This clearly shows the ineluctable choice a modern Muslim nation-state must make between Islamic principles, determining its structure and policy, and Islamic law regulating the public life of the state which includes non-Muslims in addition to laicist and secularist Muslims. For, there can be no different standards and laws for different sections of the citizenry of a unitary state in matters of public concern. The blessings of Western political and social democracy are apparently reserved in Muhammad Asad's Islamic state to the Muslim majority.

In the matter of the relations between the Executive and the Legislature he insists on their interdependence, since independent existence and functioning would be against Islam. The head of state (*amīr*)

by virtue of being the focal point of all *amr* cannot be merely an ordinary member of the *majlis*, but must be its leader, duty-bound to guide its activities and to preside—either personally or through a delegate—over its deliberations. This stipulation, implying as it does the idea that in a state subject to the authority of a Divine Law there can be no radical separation of the legislative and the executive phases of government, constitutes a most important, specifically Islamic contribution to political theory.[7]

From Qur'an and *Ḥadīth* he proves that the leader is obliged "to follow the decisions of the majority of his council", yet he is in a presidential system the only holder of authority which enables him to have non-Muslims in his cabinet. There will, thus, be no "unfair discrimination against non-Muslim citizens" (pp. 55–63). In cases of dispute between Executive and Legislature the matter should go to "a kind of supreme tribunal concerned with constitutional issues" (p. 66).

On the problem of *jihād*, the author insists on its purely defensive character, since Islam forbids a war of aggression, supported by Qur'anic verses. Since war is only permissible in self-defence, the non-Muslim citizen shares with the Muslims the duty to take up arms in defence of the Islamic state. Yet, they are entitled to exemption on grounds of conscience, in which case they pay *jizya*. This is a significant reversal of the orthodox position.[8]

He pleads for free and compulsory education for all citizens, regardless of religion; without knowledge the community cannot watch over the actions of the government (p. 87). Here the principle of equality is applied. But does he envisage a uniform national education for all or an education in Islam for Muslims and another education for non-Muslims?

His ideas about adequate material conditions for all citizens, supported by Qur'anic quotations, are not much different from those which form the basis of the modern welfare state. He derives a social insurance scheme from the time of the *khulafā rāshidūn*. It has nothing to do with the twentieth century; the Muslims' example is the caliph 'Umar and it is, therefore, their duty to complete the work then commenced but neglected in subsequent Islamic history.

He maintains that Islam "is a complete, self-contained ideology which regards all aspects of our existence—moral and physical, spiritual and intellectual, personal and communal—as parts of the indivisible whole which we call 'human life'", hence "its adherents cannot live a truly Islamic life merely by holding Islamic beliefs...the socio-economic laws of Islam" must be enforced (pp. 95 ff.). It is, of course, true that no human group can preserve its identity merely by the profession of a universal ideal; it must try to realise it in a disciplined way of life. But where one cannot agree with the author is in his claim that only Islam is so all-comprehensive. Other religions, and even the secularised West which derives much of its ethic from them, teach the same comprehensive social ideal and try to infuse it into their legislation in a lay state. He is right when he views with scepticism the imitativeness of many Muslims where "the West" is concerned, and when he is similarly critical of the opposition of conservative circles to everything Western. For they confuse the real values of Islam with the social conventions of Muslim society and take refuge in historical precedents.

But is he also right when he charges the West with opposition to an Islamic state? That Islam was misrepresented in the West is true and does not only little credit to past Western scholarship and statesmanship, but is a blot on their honour and integrity. Yet Muhammad Asad can hardly be unaware that, certainly in our generation, Western understanding and appreciation of the teachings and institutions of Islam has made great strides, not least in co-operation with Muslim scholars. There is a danger in making Western historical memories, going back to the Crusades, responsible for alleged present-day suspicion of and hostility towards a misunderstood Islam—culturally and politically. Our own more recent historical and present memories may also militate against a just and fair assessment of Western attitudes and practices of today. His statement:

> By insisting that the political forms and procedures of a contemporary Islamic state must strictly follow the pattern evolved in the early period of Islam (an insistence for which there is not the slightest warrant in Qur'an or Sunnah), these self-appointed "guardians" of Muhammad's Message make it impossible for many educated Muslims to accept the *sharī'ah* as a practical proposition for the political exigencies of our time

seems a trifle imaginative. This is not the place to enter into an argument with the author; but it must be said that the Western outsider (who has in any case no business to pronounce on what Muslims ought or ought not to do in their own house) may perhaps be excused if he pays more heed to the statements of traditionalist orthodox religious leaders than to thinkers like Muhammad Asad who set their face against historical precedent, deny the validity of any legal injunction outside the *nuṣūṣ* and want to re-activate and apply in a twentieth-century setting the primary sources of *Fiqh*, that is, Qur'an and Sunna only, in disregard of the decisions of many generations of Muslim jurists.

His sense of moral obligation and responsibility is clearly expressed in his comment on Sura III, 110: "You are the best community that has been sent forth to mankind [in that] you enjoin right and forbid wrong and have faith in God": "Our being a righteous community depends...on our being prepared to struggle, always and under all circumstances, for the upholding of justice and for the abolition of injustice for *all* people: and this should preclude the possibility of a truly Islamic community ever being unjust to the non-Muslims living in its midst" (pp. 98 f.). His answer to the "conservatives" is "that the Law of Islam is not merely a subject for hair-splitting books of *fiqh* and wordy Friday sermons, but is a living, dynamic program of human life: a program sovereign in itself, entirely independent of any particular environment, and therefore practicable at all times and under all conditions: a program, in brief, that would not only not hamper our society's development but would, on the contrary, make it the most progressive, the most self-reliant, and the most vigorous of all existing societies" (pp. 99 f.).

He advocates "a concise, clearly comprehensible code of *shar'ī* laws", without their elaboration by "conventional *fiqh*". Declaring against the various *fiqhī* systems in existence, he wants "a code of the *sharī'ah* which (*a*) would be generally acceptable to all its Muslim citizens without distinction of the *fiqhī* schools to which they may belong, and (*b*) would bring out the eternal, unchangeable quality of the Divine Law in such a way as to demonstrate its applicability to all times and all stages of man's social and intellectual development" (p. 101). He is against harmonisation of existing *fiqh* no less than against a revision in the light of modern conditions which would become obsolete sooner or later, to be revised again until nothing of the Law of Islam would be left. This would negate the very concept of a Divine Law. His remedy is to separate "God's true *sharī'ah* from all man-made, deductive *fiqhī* laws".

The codification of the *nuṣūṣ* is comparatively easy for "a small panel of scholars representing the various schools of *fiqh*, fully conversant with the methodology and history of the Qur'an and the science of *ḥadīth*", elected by the "*majlis ash-shūrā*". He advocates "historical and technical criticism" of traditions in order to establish their authenticity. As is well known, traditional criticism of the traditions only concerns the *isnād*, chain of traditionists, which must be unbroken, reliable and go back to the prophet himself or to one of his companions. What has been selected should be submitted to "competent scholars throughout the Muslim world" for their comments and criticisms to be "considered on their merits and utilised in the final revision of the collection, whereupon this 'minimum' code of *shar'ī* ordinances shall be submitted to the *majlis ash-shura* for adoption as the Basic Law of the land" (pp. 104 f.). This collection only consists of self-evident texts of command or prohibition. He does not mention the *nuṣūṣ* about women, *ribā* and *ḥudūd*.

Muhammad Asad is frank in his admission that dissension and confusion exist among Muslims as to what constitutes the socio-political teaching of Islam on which they ought to model their Islamic state, and he sees in his proposal for a codification of *shar'ī* ordinances the only way out of the impasse at the eleventh hour. Whether his plan is feasible will depend on the support it will find among like-minded fervent believers in the greatness of original Islam, and on the chances of its realisation in an age of doubt, unconcern and unbelief. To assess with even some accuracy how widespread this unpropitious state of affairs is, a Western student of Islam and the present scene in Muslim countries must live among Muslims for a considerable time. From my visits, especially to Pakistan, I hesitate to judge; it is well-nigh impossible to put oneself into another person's mind, especially where such personal questions as faith and spirituality are concerned. In circles of devout believers, one often encounters a withdrawal from public witness to the social relevance of Islam in the existing political, economic and social situation. To work out statistically the chances of the advocates of an Islamic state of the types we have described so far, or of Islam as a personal faith and example, as advocated by 'Ali 'Abd al-Raziq, Khālid Muḥammad Khālid and others is as futile as it would be misleading: spiritual concerns cannot be evaluated by numbers. For it is the strength and tenacity of convictions held which, in the end, count for more, provided the atmosphere exists for their realisation.

MAUDŪDĪ'S SOLUTION

Next to the radical and deceptively simple plan proposed by Muhammad Asad, the conservative solution of Sayyid Abul A'lā Maudūdī, sustained by great traditional learning, personal courage and militancy, must now be considered. It is another manifestation of the ferment and disquiet that characterise the battle for the minds and souls of the Muslims of Pakistan; a chapter of a significant story which has begun before Pakistan came into being and one which is not yet completed.[9]

Maulana Maudūdī has been a force in Pakistani politics from the establishment of the state. He has from that time on fought vigorously and tenaciously for Pakistan to become an Islamic state, with not only the help of profound learning, but also of a political movement whose unchallenged leader and propagandist he was from the beginning. The views here discussed are to be found in his *The Islamic Law and Constitution*,[10] a collection of his writings and speeches spread over many years, not, like Muhammad Asad's, a single consecutive treatise. Yet, the book is a coherent, cogent exposition of the need for an Islamic state with the *Sharī'a* as its law. Since it owes its origin to the cut and thrust of political debate, it is more forceful in language and more polemical in tone than Muhammad Asad's, and its several parts reflect the constitutional debate in full swing.[11] He stands right in the centre of that debate, and his views are stated with remarkable incisiveness and precision; they represent not only an important contribution to a crucial political debate, but perhaps even more to the literature on an Islamic state in the twentieth century. There is nothing vague or ambiguous in his exposition. His concept of the dynamic nature of Islamic law owes not a little to Iqbal.

The general outline of an Islamic state has been drawn by Rashīd Riḍā and the *Ikhwān al-Muslimūn* with whose strategy and propaganda Maulana Maudūdī has much in common. He works closely together with the *'ulamā* of Pakistan though he has his own political party, the *Jamā'at-i-Islāmī*, with a closely knit organisation on authoritarian lines; he believes in political action beyond the mere statement of the orthodox position on state and government, law and administration. His appeal is to the Muslim masses and he wages a relentless, continuous battle for their political support. But among his followers are also many intellectuals in the universities and the administration. This needs to be remembered when examining his ideas: here is no utopian idealist, but a realistic, clear-headed and determined leader of a political movement who aspires to political power in order to establish, by gradual measures, an Islamic state based on Qur'an and Sunna.[12]

First, we shall consider his views on sovereignty. He starts from the fact "that Pakistan was demanded and established in the name of Islam" and significantly adds "and for the sake of the revival of its glory. It is thus potentially an Islamic ideological state". The man who had stood outside, if not against, the movement for Pakistan, after partition demands an "Islamic ideological state" whose task it is to promote "the Islamic system of life". In order to convert to Islam the newly established state, "still based on and working according to the same secular bases on which it did during the British period", he demands of the Constituent Assembly the acceptance of four demands. The first of these demands unequivocally acknowledges: "That the sovereignty in Pakistan belongs to God Almighty alone and that the Government of Pakistan shall administer the country as His agent."[13] For him, Islam is

> the very antithesis of secular Western democracy. The philosophical foundation of Western democracy is the sovereignty of the people. Lawmaking is their prerogative and legislation must correspond to the mood and temper of their opinion.... Islam...altogether repudiates the philosophy of popular sovereignty and rears its polity on the foundations of the sovereignty of God and the vicegerency (*Khilafat*) of man.[14]

Since the sovereign alone has authority to issue laws, the law of Islam is given by God, the sole lawgiver, as is clear from the Qur'an (Sura XII, 40). His own definition of the Islamic state is "theo-democracy" by which he means the "Kingdom of God", not administered by a priestly hierarchy—as he defines the English term "theocracy"—but by "the whole community of Muslims... in accordance with the Book of God and the practice of His prophet".[15]

Hence, the Islamic state is the *Sharī'a*-state. Legislation is the real problem in a modern Islamic state and, while basically Abul A'lā Maudūdī agrees with Muhammad Asad about the Divine Law as the only possible and valid law in an Islamic state (with

Qur'an and Sunna as its source), he is much more traditional in his approach and use of *Fiqh*. What is the *Sharī'a*? This question might seem strange were it not for the fact that Abul A'lā Maudūdī does not seem to distinguish between the *Sharī'a* as a complete scheme of life (and thus identical with Islam) and as law which—so he says himself—is only a part of such a scheme, which he calls "Islamic Law", "which can neither be understood nor enforced separately" from this "complete scheme of life and all-embracing social order". Of its many parts only that part is called "Law" by him which needs for its implementation the coercive power and authority of the state.[16] Of constitutional and administrative law only the principles are laid down in the *Sharī'a*, its details are left to the Muslims to work out "in accordance with the demands of the age or the country in which they live subject, of course, to the limits prescribed by the *Sharī'ah*" (p. 59). Yet, its detailed injunctions—obviously much more than what Muhammad Asad called the *nuṣūṣ*—

> are such that they can always fulfil the needs of human society in every age and in every country—provided, of course, that the entire Islamic scheme of life is in operation. They are so comprehensive that we can frame detailed laws for every emergency and every fresh problem on their basis, for which the legislature has been given the right of legislation. All the laws thus framed are to be considered an integral part of the Islamic Law. That is why the laws framed by our jurists in the early days of Islam for the sake of "Public Good" [*maṣlaḥa*] form a part and parcel of the Islamic Law [p. 59].

The same applies to the field of international law. It is clear that the area of human legislation is severely limited by including a considerable part of *Fiqh* (if not all of it) in "Islamic Law" in the sense he gives it. This is bound to limit the range and freedom of *ijtihād* in practice—in theory he pleads for its exercise—since the decisions of previous *mujtahids* and, in fact, all previous legislation on the case in point must be taken into account. Thus, Abul A'lā Maudūdī is in complete agreement with the orthodox point of view.

All the same, he explicitly distinguishes between "that part of the *Sharī'ah* which has a permanent and unalterable character, and is, as such, extremely beneficial for mankind, and that part which is flexible and has thus the potentialities of meeting the ever-increasing requirements of every time and age". His classification of the first part comprises the laws derived from the *nuṣūṣ* of Qur'an and Sunna: the prohibition of alcoholic drinks, interest and gambling, the punishments prescribed for adultery and theft and the rules for inheritance; the directive principles, such as the prohibition of intoxicants in general, of all exchange transactions not voluntarily entered into by both parties, and the principle that men are protectors and in charge of women; the limitation in the number of wives, of divorces and in the amount of legacies permitted to a man. All three groups combined give "a permanent complexion to the Islamic Social Order and the characteristic features to its Culture" (pp. 60 f.).

His justification of the *ḥudūd* for theft and adultery, for example, is interesting in that Islamic society is arranged in such a way that because of opportunities of earning one's living, and because of the obligation of the state to look after the poor and needy (*zakāt*), theft is not a necessity. In view of the segregation of the sexes and the facilities for marriage "where virtue, piety and charity are current coins and the remembrance of God and the hereafter is kept ever fresh in men's minds and hearts" punishment must be meted out if the crime of adultery is committed. (He could have added that Islamic law demands four witnesses to prove adultery.) He adds:

> These punishments are not meant for the filthy society wherein sexual excitement is rampant, wherein nude pictures, obscene books and vulgar songs have become common recreations; wherein sexual perversions have taken hold of the cinema and all other places of amusement, wherein mixed, semi-nude parties are considered the acme of social progress and wherein economic conditions and social customs have made marriage extremely difficult [pp. 56 f.].

The flexible part of Islamic law is, according to him, the result of the application of four methods: *ta'wīl*, "probing into the meanings of the injunctions found in the Qur'an and the Sunnah"; *qiyās*; *ijtihād*; and "*istiḥsān* (Juristic Preference): it means framing rules, if necessary, in non-prohibited matters in conformity with the spirit of the Islamic legal system" (p. 62). He rightly maintains that only a pious, deeply learned jurist can accomplish the task of legislation.

In his answer to objections that Islamic laws were antiquated or barbarous, he claims that Islamic law throughout the ages to the nineteenth century is characterised by a progressive evolution. What he does not say is that throughout Islamic history the *Sharī'a* was largely honoured by non-observance, except in the sphere of personal status law. But it was at least recognised in theory as binding on the *umma*. Abul A'lā Maudūdī, then, counter-attacks and points to concentration camps and the atom bomb tolerated and applied by modern man. For him the punishments of Islamic law are divinely ordained and unalterable. But man has the duty to create conditions of life and standards of morality which make the imposition of these *ḥudūd* unnecessary. He equates "modernism" with adherence to a different morality, that of modern civilisation and puts a straight question to these votaries of "modernity": "What are the values that you believe in? Do you believe in the Islamic values of life and standards of morality or those of the modern civilization?" If they choose a different set of values

> it means that you differ with and disbelieve in the Islamic ideology itself. In this case you should have the courage to declare that you reject Islam outright. Is it not foolish to allege faith in a God whose laws you consider as barbarous? Anyhow nobody can remain inside the pale of Islam after holding such an opinion about the law of God [p. 67].

We note how he contrasts "Islamic ideology" with modern civilisation. Extreme as his attitude is, it does also not reveal much understanding for the real dilemma which besets devout Muslims who believe in God, but not in the immutability of Islamic law. Further, it must be pointed out that Maulana Maudūdī ignores as much as do other advocates of an Islamic state that there are Muslims who do not believe in God and can, therefore, not be expected and certainly, if we concede freedom of conscience, cannot be forced to submit to Islamic law. He speaks of Muslims who do not agree with the majority—the majority must agree on the law, this is the meaning of *ijmā'*—and grants them "their own Code in their personal matters"; but they are bound to submit to the "Law of the Land". The same applies to non-Muslims living in Pakistan.

It may be argued that this is entirely fair and reasonable in a lay state with a law in force which every citizen, be he religious or irreligious, can and must accept. Religious law of whatever religion can only be binding on those who *profess* that religion. If, therefore, in an ideological state the "Law of the Land" is Divine Law as this is understood in classical Islam, a serious problem arises, as may be seen from this statement of Maulana Maudūdī:

...it is not fair for the minorities to ask us to throw our ideology overboard and introduce laws which are against our convictions merely for the sake of appeasing them. When we were helpless because of foreign domination, we tolerated the supremacy of un-Islamic Laws. But now when we are masters of our destiny, we cannot replace Islamic Laws by those of any other type without conscious apostasy and betrayal of Islam. Are the minorities really entitled to ask the majority to give up its religion and its way of life?...Is it reasonable that in a multi-religious country all the communities should become irreligious? If the answers to all these questions are in the negative, I find no reason why "Islamic Law" should not become the "Law of the Land" in a country where Muslims are in a predominant majority [p. 71].

It would not be difficult to find flaws in this peculiar reasoning, but logic is not the only guide in human life. Obviously, this deeply religious fighter for an Islamic state cannot even consider a lay state which, in contrast to a secular state, is certainly not anti- or irreligious, but, as a state, is areligious and grants freedom of religion to all its citizens equally. But he would not acknowledge as religion what is the private concern of the citizen; for him religion is Islam as a faith and a way of life for the individual believer and the community, organised in a state under religious law.

He admits human legislation, as we have already seen. But it "is and should be subject to the Supremacy of Divine Law and within the limits prescribed by it". These limits, he explains on the basis of Shāṭibī's *Al-i'tisām*, consist of interpretation, analogy, inference and independent legislation. Interpretation is not permitted where Qur'an and Sunna have laid down clear injunctions. Analogy and inference appear to mean *qiyās*, and independent legislation is *ijtihād* of which Maulana Maudūdī has this to say:

The real law of Islam is the Qur'an and the *Sunnah*. The legislation that human beings may undertake must essentially be derived from this

Fundamental Law or it should be within the limits prescribed by it for the use of one's opinion. For *Ijtihād* that purports to be independent of the *Sharī'ah* can neither be an Islamic *Ijtihād* nor is there any room for such an incursion in the legal system of Islam.

Its function is, he avers, "to impart dynamism to the legal system of Islam by keeping it in conformity with the fundamental guidance of the *Sharī'ah* and abreast of the changing conditions of the world". Among the six qualifications demanded of the person who wants to exercise *ijtihād* the most important is undoubtedly the fourth:

Acquaintance with the contributions of the earlier jurists and thinkers (*Mujtahidīn*) [*sic*!] of Islam. This is necessary not merely for training in the technique of *Ijtihād*, but also for the sake of ensuring continuity in the evolution of law. Of course it is not, and should not be, the purpose of *Ijtihād* that every generation may necessarily destroy or discard what previous generations have built and thus try to build the whole structure afresh.[17]

He makes stringent demands on the character, intelligence, learning and piety of the *mujtahid*. He is at one with the *'ulamā* that only *'ulamā* are qualified to initiate new legislation. But they must have received a legal education such as he outlined.

He has no illusions about the difficulties of introducing Islamic law in Pakistan. In his opinion, British rule resulted in divesting the life of the Muslims of its Islamic character; therefore, Islam must be brought back into it. This can only be done gradually, as he illustrates from the Qur'an. It took the British, he says, a hundred years to replace the *Sharī'a* in force in India before they occupied it by their own code of law.

Change of law is contingent on change of attitudes and economic and social life. Thus, the whole structure of life in Pakistan will have to be changed. This takes time, especially as education must first produce the men capable of running a progressive modern state on Islamic principles. The legal structure cannot be changed until the moral outlook and social habits have undergone a thorough reform in the direction of Islamic ideals.

At the same time, he is opposed to the temporary establishment of a secular state incapable of building up an Islamic atmosphere. He asks: "Can an irreligious state, with Westernized people at its helm, do this job? Will the persons well versed only in running bars and night clubs and movie houses spend their energies in constructing and maintaining mosques?" The answer is firm resolve and a workable plan. The first step, he considers, is for the Constituent Assembly to declare, consequent upon the affirmation of the sovereignty of God—mentioned earlier on—

that the basic law of the land is the Islamic *Sharīʿah* which has come to us through our Prophet Muhammad (peace be on him). That all those existing laws which may be in conflict with the *Sharīʿah* shall in due course be repealed or brought into conformity with the basic law and no law which may be in any way repugnant to the *Sharīʿah* shall be enacted in future. That the State, in exercising its powers, shall not be competent to transgress the limits laid down by Islam [p. 107].

These principles were later incorporated in the Objectives Resolution and the constitution adopted by the Constituent Assembly. It is noteworthy that British rule and legislation cannot have been quite so alien and injurious to Islam if only those laws must be repealed or amended which offend against Islamic concepts. Of more weight is his insistence that these measures are considered interim palliatives until such time as Islamic law can be promulgated in an Islamic state. He thought that ten years would be needed to change the collective life of Pakistan, provided a "comprehensive plan for a thorough reform of all the departments of our national life for which all the resources of the state will have to be utilized" can be devised and implemented.

Thus, the educational system will be re-orientated; all the means of propaganda—the press, the platform, the cinema and the radio—will be used for the purpose of creating a new Islamic consciousness, a new healthy outlook; and an incessant and systematic effort will have to be made to mould the society and its culture into Islamic patterns [p. 109].

In this appraisal of the situation and the measures needed, especially in a new, comprehensive education, he is naturally not alone, and much constructive work has been done by the government in the last few years. Education is in all Muslim countries the key to progress and self-fulfilment of individual and nation.

His main concern is naturally with law, and he advocates an academy of law in order to enable law colleges to teach Islamic law systematically on modern lines. He stresses the need for proficiency in Arabic in the study of *Fiqh*; otherwise Qur'an and *Ḥadīth* cannot serve as the basis of an all-Islamic law which is the final aim of law reform. The next step is the appointment of Islamic scholars and experts of modern legal thought in order to codify Islamic law "section and clause-wise according to the modern patterns". The law-code arrived at is in substance Islamic law, only in form and arrangement is it to follow modern codes. Since not everything included in a book of *Fiqh* is Islamic law, Maulana Maudūdī repeats what constitutes Islamic law and stresses that it consists—apart from clear commandments and prohibitions in Qur'an and Sunna—of what has been accepted by the *umma* through *ijmā'* or by "an overwhelming majority of our own people" from a majority decision of the *'ulamā*. These parts should be compiled by a body of experts into a code to which additions will constantly be made through fresh laws "framed by general consent or majority decision". This code "will be the basic book of Law and all the current books of *Fiqh* will serve as commentaries for this book" (pp. 115 f.). He is certainly determined to preserve the historical continuity of traditional Islamic law: the history of *Fiqh* through "an unprejudiced study of all the major schools of *Fiqh*" will not only show the evolution of Islamic law, but also "point out the lines along which this law can develop in future". The guidance of the jurists of the past should be sought "before making an independent effort and pronouncing a final judgement" (pp. 118 f.).

If we were to ask how can such a law regulate all manifestations of human life and all human activities in the private and collective sectors of state and society in the twentieth century, Maulana Maudūdī would unhesitatingly answer that this was an irrelevant, even entirely wrong question, typical of a human product of modern civilisation. No believer would pose such a question. Modern civilisation, he claims,[18] is based on three fundamental principles which are diametrically opposed to Islam as an ideological state. They are "secularism, that is irreligiousness or worldliness; nationalism; and democracy". For him, they are not only wrong, but "the root cause of all those calamities and troubles in which humanity is involved to-day" (p. 22).

His ideological Islamic state is based on belief in God as sovereign ruler of the whole world; every believer is as the servant of God, His caliph.[19] All caliphs are equal, "this is the real foundation of democracy in Islam". Authority under the divine sovereign is held by the whole community of believers who delegate their "vicegerency" to the *amīr* who, as we know, is the *khalīfa* and *imām*. Maulana Maudūdī never mentions the *imām* nor his function and likewise avoids the title of *khalīfa* for the head of the Islamic state to be established. Muhammad Asad also uses *amīr* as title of the head of state. "The state, according to Islam, is nothing more than a combination of men working together as servants of God to carry out His will and purposes"[20] is Maulana Maudūdī's definition. Its

social conduct and political action...is entirely different from that of the secular state in all its details and ramifications....A state-system based on belief in the sovereignty of God and in a sense of responsibility to Him requires for its successful working a special type of individual mass-character and a peculiar mental attitude.[21]

Therefore, an "Islamic revolution" is needed through propaganda, chiefly by education, preparatory to the setting up of an Islamic state. Every revolution, he tells his hearers, demands a movement, leaders and workers, a definite social consciousness and cultural and moral atmosphere. Thus the French Revolution needed leaders like Rousseau, Voltaire and Montesquieu; the Russian Revolution Karl Marx, Lenin and Trotsky

and thousands of other Communist workers whose lives were cast in the Communist mould. The National-Socialism of Germany could only take root in the moral, psychological and cultural conditions...created by the theories of leaders of thought like Hegel, Fichte, Goethe, Nietzsche and many others including Hitler. Exactly in the same way the Islamic revolution can be brought about only when a mass movement is initiated based on the theories and conceptions of the Qur'an and the example and practice of Muhammad (Peace) which would, by a powerful struggle, effect a wholesale change in the intellectual, moral, psychological, and cultural foundations of social life.[22]

To create such a movement he has worked indefatigably.

What, then, is to be the constitution of the Islamic state as envisaged by Maulana Maudūdī? "There are four sources of the unwritten Islamic Constitution: The Qur'an...; The Sunnah...; The Conventions of the *Khilafat-e-Rashidah* [the reign of the *khulafā rāshidūn*]...; The Rulings of great Jurists...."[23] Abul A'lā Maudūdī deems

> the decisions of the Caliphs [i.e. the *khulafā rāshidūn*] relating to constitutional and judicial problems accepted by the Companions, (as) binding on all and for all times...such interpretations and such decisions must be accepted *in toto*, because the consensus of opinion of the Companions on any matter is tantamount to an authoritative exposition of the law.[23]

The sources for the "golden era" are "the books of *Ḥadīth*, History and Biography", which he seems to accept without applying modern literary and historical criticism to them.

There are technical difficulties in the use of these four sources, he admits: lack of knowledge of Arabic, of familiarity with the arrangement of *Fiqh* books and especially the prevailing system of education with its strict division into entirely traditional or modern-secular, combined with the ignorance of those in power and authority who contest the sole right of the *mullahs* (religious leaders) to interpret Islam. Correctly interpreted by experts these sources give mandatory guidance to Muslims which they cannot overlook if they are and wish to remain Muslims.[23] He contests the claim of modern political science to locate true sovereignty and denies that any human being is worthy and capable of exercising absolute sovereignty. "The prophets alone are the true agencies through whom the directives and the commands of the Almighty are communicated to mankind."[24] The believer is the vice-gerent of the divine sovereign, not—as stated earlier[25]—in his individual capacity, but collectively with all the other members of the community of believers. Islamic vice-gerency has, thus, nothing whatsoever in common with the divine right of kings or with papal authority. "It is the collective right of all those who accept and admit God's absolute sovereignty over themselves and adopt the Divine Code, conveyed through the Prophet, as the *law* above all laws and regulations."[26] The state is bound by this code and has no claim to the obedience of the citizens if it goes beyond the limitations ordained by God (Sura II, 229). Any dispute "should be referred to that fundamental Law which God and His Prophet have given to us...there should be an institution in the state which should undertake to adjudicate in strict accordance with the Book of God and the *Sunnah* of the Prophet".[27]

It is characteristic of his traditionalism that Abul A'lā Maudūdī should conceive of the Legislature in a contemporary Islamic state in terms of the *ahl al-'aqd wa-l-ḥāll*, rendered by him as "Body which resolves and prescribes". He calls "those who do not decide in accordance with the Divine Code, Unbelievers" (Sura v, 44), and "all such pieces of legislation...would *ipso facto* be considered *ultra vires* of the Constitution". What, then, is the purpose of the Legislature? It is "alone competent to enact them [the explicit directives of God and His Prophet] in the shape of sections, devise relevant definitions and details and make rules and regulations for the purpose of enforcing them". Where more than one interpretation is possible the legislators may choose one and place it on the Statute Book. That they must be traditionally learned stands to reason: his idea of the legislature is far removed from the concept of a modern parliament. If no provisions exist, they can enact laws in conformity with "the general spirit of Islam"; but previously enacted laws covering such a contingency must be adopted from the *Fiqh* books. The freedom of independent legislation is, thus, in practice much more restricted than his words would lead us to assume.

Wherever and in whatever matters even basic guidance is not available from the Qur'an or the *Sunnah*, or the conventions of the Righteous Caliphs, it would be taken to mean that God has left us free to legislate on those points according to our best lights. In such cases, therefore, the legislature can formulate laws without restriction, provided that such legislation is not in contravention of the letter and the spirit of the *Sharī'ah*—the principle herein being that whatever has not been disallowed is allowed.

Muhammad Asad expressed the same idea. This does not seem to accord easily with the assertion of an all-embracing Divine Law guiding the believer in all situations at all times.

Abul A'lā Maudūdī defines the purpose of the Executive in an Islamic state as "to enforce the directives of God...and to bring about a society ready to accept and adopt these directives for practical application in its life".[28] The judiciary has the function to adjudicate "in strict accordance with the Law of God".[29]

He further claims the precedent of the *khulafā rāshidūn* who imitated the prophet, for his contention that in Islam Executive,

Legislature and judiciary are under the authority of the head of state, yet they function "separately and independently of one another". While the *ahl al-'aqd wa-l-ḥāll* were previously the legislators they are now only a body advising the head of state "in matters of law, administration and state-policy", that is they have merely consultative status. In present circumstances (which are far from ideal) "we can amend or alter the details of this set-up according to our existing requirements. But the fundamental principles we will have to keep intact".[30]

Maulana Maudūdī puts and answers the question what the position of the Legislature in Islam is by stating that while consultation is laid down in the Qur'an—*shūrā*—it is not clear from Qur'an and Sunna whether the head of state is bound to accept its recommendations or not, but, he says,

> the conventions of the Caliphs and the judgments of the eminent Jurists of Islam...finally guide us to the conclusion that the *de facto* responsibility for all administration rests with the Head of the State. And the Head of the State, although obliged to consult his advisers [the legislature], yet is under no obligation to sanction, follow or adopt their unanimous or even majority verdict or opinion. In other words, he can always exercise his "veto".[31]

Applied to Pakistan, he demands that in the absence of a consultative assembly with the qualifications necessary in an Islamic state, the Executive must be subordinated to the majority decisions of the Legislature. In appearance, this is similar to the practice in a modern parliamentary democracy where the Executive is responsible to the Legislature. But here it is only a temporary measure until the Islamic state comes into operation. Until then he seems to assign the Legislature both consultant and law-making functions with power to overrule the veto of the head of state.

What is important in Abul A'lā Maudūdī's detailed discussion of all questions of constitutional theory and law is his intention—on the basis of the fundamental injunctions of Qur'an and Sunna (which he treats as equally authoritative and binding)—to establish an ideological state. He explicitly differentiates the Islamic ideological state from secular ideological states of the Communist and Fascist types by his emphasis on the idea of justice based on the Divine Law as the guide and final arbiter. The Islamic state has a mission not only among the Muslim believers, but also to the whole human race: the mission of leading mankind to God.

The specific nature of this religious state necessitates the distinction between two kinds of citizens: the believers and the *ḏimmīs*. The latter are adequately protected, by the divine demand of justice, in life, property and freedom of religion. But since they are not Muslims, they cannot subscribe to the Islamic ideology of the state and must, therefore, be excluded from the supreme direction of affairs of state and from the decision of its policy which is prescribed and clearly limited by the Divine Law. They are free—and must be invited by dint of the ideology of the state which aims at the reform of mankind—to join the community of believers. The *ḏimmīs* are a minority, no doubt, but not a racial or national minority. Theirs is a credal minority which, inevitably, restricts their political rights, since in a religious ideological state the source and purpose of politics is to realise the religious demands arising from the religious nature of the state.

Thus, he points out that the treatment meted out to the Negroes in America and the non-Communists in Russia would be unthinkable in Islam. But since the non-Muslims do not fulfil the basic requirements of the Islamic state, namely, faith in Islam, they cannot be appointed to key-posts. Yet he states that "they have an equal share with Muslims in the matter of all civil liberties, and even in economic matters no discrimination is made between a Muslim and a *Zimmi*....Furthermore, the *Zimmis* are exempt from the responsibility of the defence of the state, which devolves exclusively and entirely on the Muslim citizens."[32] "There is no other state which accords such full cultural and human rights to its minorities as the Islamic state", he concludes.

On the question of women's rights Maulana Maudūdī likewise takes his stand on Qur'an and Sunna and (with the help of a literal interpretation of Sura IV, 38, and a *ḥadīth*) denies them the posts of responsibility in an Islamic state, including membership of the Legislature, since there is "a functional distribution between men and women and according to that the fields of politics and administration belong to the men's sphere of responsibilities".[33] But he suggests a separate Assembly for women—elected by suitably qualified women of Pakistan—for welfare, education and medical care.[34]

These statements must be seen against the background of the constitutional struggle in Pakistan on which they have a close and important bearing, since half the population are women, and a sizeable minority consists of Hindus and a much smaller group of Christians. He took a vocal part in the debate between what he terms an Islamic and a national state and challenged his countrymen to come into the open for or against the Islamic state: "to choose a middle course between '*Imān*' (faith) and '*Kufr*' (unbelief) is neither honest nor honourable nor fruitful in the long run".[35]

On yet another hotly debated question, Maulana Maudūdī has taken an identically uncompromising stand, that of joint or separate Muslim and Hindu electorates. The advocates of joint electorates deliberately ignore, he maintains, that "the fundamental factor that has divided and separated various sections of people in our country is the difference of religion". This entails "different principles of conduct, different objectives of life, different values of morality and different modes of living". He equally opposes the two courses open to remove the division: absorption of non-Muslims in the Muslim community, or unification and integration of these diverse communities. The first option is repugnant to Maulana Maudūdī: Islam is a brotherhood open to all who want to join it "and become a part and parcel of our nation". There is no other honest, Islamic absorption of non-Muslims possible, to his mind. The second option would "destroy religion as the main factor shaping culture and civilization and foster a *common secular culture* as the basis of Pakistani Nationalism". This would be followed by framing

> a secular constitution...to let religion live by sufferance and remain strictly confined to the narrow domain of beliefs and devotional practices and even to encourage intermarriages between different communities in order that Pakistanis may not remain divided into separate societies which eventually divides them into separate nationalities.[36]

He insists that it was religion which prompted partition of the Indian subcontinent and that it is religion alone which unites the two wings of Pakistan. Once religion recedes into the background or even fades out, the nation will fall apart. He rejects territorial nationalism and significantly speaks of "our nation" by which he means Islam, thus implying that an Islamic state of Pakistan would be a part of the universal *umma* of Islam. Since an Islamic state is his avowed aim, he had already discussed in 1948 the question of participation of non-Muslims in the Legislative Assembly. He made a distinction between the Council (*shūrā*) advising the head of state on matters of law and administration in conformity with the *Sharī'a*, and "a Legislature of the modern conception". He would (naturally from his ideological standpoint) exclude *ḏimmīs* from membership of the council, but admit them to the Legislative Assembly. Yet he made it a condition that such an Assembly "could not enact any law which is repugnant to the Qur'an and the *Sunnah*" which would also be "the chief source of the public law of the land". This would at the same time ensure that "their participation would not damage the fundamental requirements of Islam".[37]

He also considers the alternative of giving all non-Muslim groups a separate representative Assembly as "a Central Agency through which all the demands for their collective needs may be submitted to the Parliament [otherwise called Legislative Assembly]". They can suggest laws concerning their personal law which, with the assent of the head of state, can be placed on the Statute Book. They may also "submit representations, objections, suggestions, etc. with the fullest freedom in regard to the general administration of the Government and the decisions of the Parliament". The last-named right he would also concede to the separate Assembly of women.

It goes without saying that among his constitutional proposals were specific ones dealing with educational reform and moral training for all services in accordance with Islamic principles and standards of conduct. For the government of an ideological Islamic state is obliged to "establish and promote all that is good according to Islam and suppress and eradicate all that is evil...".[38]

Objections could be raised against Maulana Maudūdī's aims and intentions both from a more liberal, "modernist" religious point of view and from a laicist and secularist position. His ideas may be medieval, but it is undeniable that there is faith and religious conviction behind his detailed exposition and practical proposals. They are presented by a determined political leader who is imbued with religious zeal and fights in the lecture hall, on the platform, on the radio and in numerous pamphlets and articles in his own monthly *Tarjuman al-Qur'an* for an Islamic state as the goal of an Islamic renaissance. That he was imprisoned several times, once condemned to dcath even, is eloquent testimony to the notice the Government of Pakistan takes of this clear-headed religious scholar and forceful leader of a political movement in opposition to it and its policy.

CHAPTER 7

'ALLĀL AL-FĀSĪ: A BLEND OF ISLAM AND ARAB NATIONALISM

By contrast, 'Allāl al-Fāsī is really at home in both Islam and Europe. A Qur'an scholar of distinction, a mature thinker, a rebel and fighter for Moroccan freedom and independence, a representative leader of his people who led his party, the *Istiqlāl* (Independence), to victory and power, he has displayed since the kingdom became independent and sovereign in 1956 high qualities of statesmanship. Equally at home in Muslim tradition and Western civilisation as represented by France, he has achieved in his own thought a harmonious co-existence between the eternal Islamic verities and the *rūḥ al-'aṣr*, the *Zeitgeist*. He has learnt much from Muḥammad 'Abduh and Jamāl al-Dīn al-Afghānī no less than from Voltaire, Montesquieu, Dostoevski and Tolstoi. Flexible and moderate, strong-principled and tolerant, he combines the wisdom of the thinker with the purposefulness of the political leader: an impressive personality who evokes respect and admiration. At the time of my visit he was Minister of Islamic Affairs.

His general position is that of the *Salafīya*—or should we say *Neo-salafīya*?—yet more open to the West, free from polemical and apologetic preoccupations and prejudices. His *Al-naqd al-ḏātī* (Self-criticism)[1] is the confession of faith, informed criticism and plan of political and social action of a rounded, integrated personality. It towers, as far as I can judge, over every other treatise written in recent years by a Muslim author. It reveals unusual depth of insight and penetration, width of vision and classical beauty of style. Love of Islam and of country are superbly blended with understanding of the West and of the *Zeitgeist*, its psychology and human needs in the political, economic, social and cultural spheres. Deep, genuine faith in God goes hand in hand with the firm conviction of a modern Muslim of the dynamism of a flexible Islam, the eternal truth of which represents the highest ideals of rational man. Here is religious humanism at its best. Besides, this remarkable literary document reflects in every line the urbane humanity of a contemporary Muslim patriot who lives in the world of today, yet in his faith and social idealism sees beyond the weakness and uncertainty of a transient world whose enlightened citizens have largely lost their inner peace and security.

He advocates a genuine democracy built on the full co-operation of thinking citizens and based on majority rule in liberty and freedom, economic equity and social justice, all bound together in obedient service to God. The book contains a well thought out and skilfully arranged programme which gradually unfolds through a profound discussion of the various elements which constitute contemporary thought on rational man's destiny as a citizen of a country he loves, a member of the Arab nation and of the community of Islam which he professes and which directs his thought and action.

A liberal democrat in politics, a socialist in economics and a progressive conservative in religion, 'Allāl al-Fāsī combines nineteenth-century liberalism and rationalism with twentieth-century religious socialism of an egalitarian type. This characterisation is naturally only approximate: his is a whole, forceful personality which cannot be divided up into clearly defined and divided components, the more so since the religious and political unity of Islam is the foundation and centre of his philosophy and outlook. But with his stress on reason and reasonableness, on social and cultural progress and on economic equality with a strict limit on individual wealth this leader of an Islamic political party and champion of Islam in a continuous forward movement for right and justice belongs more to the first quarter of this century. Reading what the younger generation of Moroccan Muslim activists write and listening to them, one has the impression that 'Allāl al-Fāsī almost belongs to a passing generation of practical idealists.[2]

'Allāl al-Fāsī's approach is rational and empirical; he is against blind imitation of Western political and social ideas and definitely against modern capitalism as incompatible with Islamic ideas about social justice. But he condemns equally the uncritical rejection of everything modern and European simply because it is modern and European. In the wake of Muḥammad 'Abduh, he insists on Islam's encouragement of the use of reason since it is both *dīn al-'aql* (a religion of reason) and *dīn al-qalb* (a religion of the heart).[3] Though Islam has no priesthood, its religious scholars in the past tended to close their minds to rational inquiry and progress—'Allāl al-Fāsī again and again speaks of Islam as *ḥaraka*, a movement—which is why he opposes "priestly" predominance and authority (*saytara kahnūtīya*).

To do justice to the methodical development of his thesis a full synopsis would be required which follows the architectonic structure of the treatise and reproduces much of its contents, presented in magnificent, measured Arabic prose. This is not possible in the context of this study; it must, therefore, suffice to point out a few salient ideas and suggestions. 'Allāl al-Fasi stresses the power and force of ideas, their thorough testing in the light of reason and experience, of the classical concepts of Islam and of the history of the Moroccan people in the Maghrib. In succession he discusses the various types of *fikr* which means both idea, opinion, thought and thinking. Traditional learning is happily blended with French clarity.

In order to show the supreme importance and topical relevance of religion he distinguishes *fikr dīnī* from *fikr islāmī*: he thus brings out the distinctive features of Islam as being concerned with this life and the next, and concentrates on its moral and social relevance. But he begins with *al-fikr al-'āmm*, public opinion, which he values as highly as Voltaire whom he quotes as saying: "Opinion rules the world, but the intellectuals must guide this opinion from afar" (p. 65). Because he is much concerned with guiding and directing public opinion towards majority rule in a democracy of the patriotic Moroccan people, religion in general, Islam in particular and patriotism, both Moroccan and Arab, in unison must provide this indispensable direction of thought and action. He does not favour totalitarian indoctrination: *taujīya* (direction) is like *tarbīya* (education); and he stresses the need for freedom of thought (*ikhtiyār al-afkār*). But, while there must be free choice, the first duty of thought is to serve the nation, aid its maintenance, promote its march forward and everything that is conducive to progress. This is *fikr ṣaḥīḥ* (sound, right thinking) fed from the springs of Arab civilisation (*ḥaḍārat al-'arab*) and Islamic culture (*ṯaqāfat al-islām*) which are combined in the Moroccan fatherland (*waṭan*) (pp. 87 f.).

Islam is right and useful in and for every age and place, including our own, and is capable of being right for other times and places as well. Sound ideas and right thinking, for which we are working, guarantee, he is convinced, the independence of individual and nation and are responsible for fulfilment, progress and unity (p. 91). He holds that belief in God and in a divine pattern is a basic premise for our intellectual and spiritual striving and well-being; with it freedom seeks happiness. Thus, the religious foundation of all thinking in the service of nation and mankind is essential, which is why religion is today the question of all questions in the world (pp. 98 ff.). While this is true of mankind in general, it is particularly crucial for Morocco (and the whole Arab nation). For he thinks that

> it would be foolish if we risked European political and social doctrines without profound study of the fundamental factors in their formation and the impact of all this on our national experience and our mentality on which Islam has had a great influence.... Religious thought in Islam means complete freedom; it is our most important criterion when we make our choice of ideas and theories [pp. 104 f.].

Here lies the reason, to my mind, for 'Allāl al-Fāsī's objective, positive-critical attitude to the West; he is secure in his faith in God and in his conviction of the excellence of Islam. Hence we find calm and dignity flowing from a position of natural strength in face of the challenge of our time. There is no need here to compensate, or rather overcompensate, for a feeling of uncertainty and unconscious inferiority. It is quite probable that Moroccan experience of French colonisation, but also of French culture, despite his banishment and exile, have contributed to this healthy attitude of a free and independent mind. Hence he speaks so often of freedom (*ḥurriya*), independence (*istiqlāl*), forward march (*sayr ilā-l-amāmi*), revolution (*ṯaura*). His vocabulary is indicative of his mind and attitude to Islam and its absolute values, and to contemporary ideas, theories and movements which must be measured by this immutable standard. For he stresses the origin of Islam in freedom and its intellectual, spiritual and social revolution against Arab paganism and the mercantile aristocratic order of the Quraish (p. 106).

The motive force in all this was religion and divine revelation. He wants to restore that freedom and revolutionary fervour in order to solve the problems of the present age, especially to put an end to its social evils. Here we see his agreement with the modern *Salafīya*, a conservative movement of restoration of that *élan vital*—to borrow a concept of Henri Bergson's—which animated and led to victory the religious and spiritual revolution that was Islam as preached by the prophet Muḥammad (p. 115). He blames the later generations of Muslims for their lethargy and narrow-mindedness which led to stagnation and petrification, the very negation of the principles on which Islam was founded, for, he repeats, "Islam is movement".

This applies in the first place to the affairs of state in which the guiding principle must be public welfare (*maṣāliḥ*) in conformity with the principles of Islam and the requirements of the changing times. The community, he insists, chooses in freedom under God its institutions and form of government. Mutual consultation (*shūrā*)—the full name of 'Allāl al-Fāsī's political movement is *ḥizb al-shūrā wa-l-istiqlāl* (Party of Consultation and Independence)—is the only method to achieve the destiny of the Islamic nation in so far as the Muslims follow what is right, just and good in the light of human experience (pp. 110 ff.). He appeals for courage to follow the dictates of Islam, without fear that progress, as understood today, will harm religion. He equally deprecates the rigidity of those who have stood still, and the neglect of the commandments of Islam by those who want to progress in blind imitation of the West (p. 114).

On the basis of Islam as a religion and as a polity, he next discusses the national idea (or thinking) which is moulded by the attachment to a country (*waṭan* = fatherland) and by the mind and soul of the individual and the community. Ethnic and geographical diversity of Muslim nations is bound in the unity of Islam which is one and the same for all Muslims everywhere (pp. 117 f.).

After *waṭan*, 'Allāl al-Fāsī considers the idea of Morocco or the Maghrib as a whole (North-West Africa) and its importance for the fatherland of Morocco in the fields of history and culture under the influence of successive rulers of distinctive religious views and practices and of different cultures. He discusses similarities and dissimilarities between them and the indigenous genius of the Maghrib, its spiritual pattern and geographical nature. In this way, he establishes the confluence—in North-West Africa—of various patterns and models of thought and civilisation which gives the Muslim Arab Maghribī fatherland and nation its specific character—a character moulded by Islam as well as by this confluence (pp. 121 ff.).

Against this background, he next studies problems of administration in an attempt to define a sound national administration (*idāra ahlīya*) against the background of the French parliamentary system based on the will and desire of a clear parliamentary majority (pp. 126–31). He notes the absence of a democratic organisation in North Africa prior to the establishment of French domination and influence because he realises that the democratic parliamentary system is peculiar to the Latin nations. His statesmanlike quality clearly emerges in his positive, yet critical, evaluation of Western ideas and institutions in relation to the Islamic Arab Maghrib as it developed. This results in his advocacy of a sound governmental machinery which combines indigenous with Western democratic elements. His ideas thus represent a balance which only a mind could achieve which coolly surveyed ideas and institutions imported by a foreign power hostile to national freedom and independence but not blindly rejected for this reason. Such a position would be impossible without the inner security and strength that flow from a deeply religious nature which has its roots in traditional Islam—interpreted as a continuous movement of the mind—and in the history and culture of the Maghrib. To this we must add the deep political understanding and insight, of the spiritual guide and leader of a political liberation movement in Morocco, into the political basis of a free national and individual life.

Naturally, administrative decisions are based on a policy laid down by the government and directed by its functionaries (p. 129). A truly national administration must, therefore, be founded on the free decisions of an independent national government. Hence it is necessary to examine with critical eyes the administration of the European protective power (France) as well as the previous administration. Self-criticism demands recognition of a steady decline due to the absence of the Islamic virtues of social justice and consideration of the public good (*maṣlaḥa 'āmma*). These must be revived and applied in the administration of the future through education by and in the political movement for independence and freedom (pp. 132 ff.).

As a consequence he demands in the next chapter (*al-fikr al-siyāsī*, the political idea: p. 137) political action (control over the ruling power and its actions) by every individual member of the nation. This agrees with the stress he laid earlier on the responsibility which rests on the individual citizen in a parliamentary democracy. In case we think 'Allāl al-Fāsī simply imitated the French system as practised in France, he made it perfectly clear that the Moroccans must be masters of their destiny and country to exercise such political control in conformity with the ideals of Islam and the experience of the Maghrib. He possessed the wisdom and the patience to work with the late King Mohammed V for the gradual transition from absolute to constitutional monarchy, a process continued by the present King Hassan II, as will become clear when we consider the Moroccan Constitution which this ruler promulgated. 'Allāl al-Fāsī states that "the basic idea in politics—concern for the public good—" could only be fulfilled in practice if interest in the conduct of public affairs were awakened in all citizens by creating an informed opinion through explanation of the issues involved among the majority of all classes of the nation. "This is the meaning of popular sovereignty which the various contemporary constitutions have not ceased to proclaim, and this is the meaning of what we have laid down as a basis in the draft 'The Arab Contract' (*al-mīṯāq al-'arabī*); the nation (*al-umma*) is the master of authority (*sulṭa*, power) and its guardian" (p. 137).

Have we here an echo of Rousseau's *Contrat Social*? In Morocco "The Arab Contract" has given authority into the hands of His Majesty the King. Government is based on the partnership between the nation and its leaders. 'Allāl al-Fāsī envisages a Moroccan democracy which is based on the parliamentary order equally dissimilar to the order in England—in his mind an aristocracy—as well as in Russia, and even in France with its model of the great French Revolution or the system of Napoleon. Nor should Morocco follow the method followed today in the majority of democratic countries with their two chambers, an "assembly of deputies" and an "assembly of senators" (pp. 142 f.). While all have something to commend themselves, Morocco must choose what conforms best to its interests. This is not served by capitalism, which is why he rejects the English and the French political systems. The same applies to Fascism. He opts for "true democracy" and wants to accord woman complete equality in the service of the nation; she must have the right to vote and to be elected: "We are not convinced that there is in the religion of Islam anything which permits the denial to her of this right." In support he cites the time of the prophet and of the first caliphs (pp. 142 f.). At the end of Czarist times the question of woman's equality with man was thought about "in the democratic Islamic republics [*sic*] which came into being in the Russian Empire, and the Russians and the West have taken over from there the granting of this right to women" (pp. 142 f.).

He then goes on to discuss the division of powers in a democracy among those who govern, from the eighteenth century onwards. In France, Montesquieu devised the threefold division of authority into legislative, executive and judicial power, which ‘Allāl al-Fāsī considers inadequate for the contemporary situation. Admittedly, Montesquieu's division checked absolute power, but another attitude to division is needed in our time. He favours a distribution according to the influence of the parties of the country, "for the majority party becomes the strongest link between the executive power and parliament and, in general, political organisations have a strong influence on the choice of the *ahl al-ḥāll wa-l-‘aqd* [understood in a modern sense] as is apparent in a democratic system..." (p. 144). ‘Allāl al-Fāsī compares this importance of party organisation to the role of the *‘aṣabīya* in a tribe or community as understood by Ibn Khaldūn. Similarly, in the twentieth century, he holds, one-party dictatorship arose. Democracy has long rested on the two-party system, one forming the government, the other the opposition as England has so successfully demonstrated

> where we find a maturity in constitutional thinking such as we do not find in any other country in Europe and America. But if a multiplicity of parties has the merit of freedom of thought and competition in action it generally leads to a weakening of representative government and loss of the majority which is favourable to stability in government and absence of confusion in the nation. For the election in England or America continually leads to a governing majority (p. 145).

On the other hand, in France and Belgium this often leads to the representation in parliament of a number of parties of equal strength making stable government only possible by some sort of agreement and compromise.

All this shows how 'Allāl al-Fāsī studied Western democratic institutions and procedure to see how their lesson could be applied to Moroccan democracy which he hopes to establish after liberation under the king. The question of party organisation and party discipline interested him particularly; he saw in a strong democratic party the best means to achieve independence and a democratic political order for his nation. Political and social freedom are essential for the working of parties and, more important still, for the education and guidance of the nation and its good order (pp. 147 ff.). England and its parties serve him as model, not France, Central Europe, the Balkans or Soviet Russia. The Turkish Republic withholds, he says, the political, social and religious freedoms from its people; there is no free Islamic society in Turkey, and political associations which oppose the government do not exist. He finds nothing in the Turkish Revolution which his own country could usefully take over; it is not like the great French Revolution. What is best as well as worst in it all stems from European countries. His political insight and historical consciousness would not allow him straight, outright borrowing in blind imitation (pp. 148 f.).

The political parties in the Arab East are to his mind deficient in that they only serve the interests of those in power and do not promote the national liberation which should be their primary objective. Liberation was to lead to a constitutional political order with parliamentary institutions. By contrast, the political parties in the Arab West in Tunisia, Algeria and Morocco are much better (p. 149). They are broadly based, represent the people longing for freedom and independence, and work to achieve both. Speaking about the Moroccan *Istiqlāl*-party in relation to the French and British parties, he thinks that it is midway between the rather weak parties of France and the strong ones of England, in keeping with the needs of its inner organisation and its work for the reform (*tanẓīm*) of the nation (*umma*). Its aim is to gain national and individual freedom for the Moroccan people which is a spiritual nation (pp. 151 f.).

Next he considers the judiciary and emphasises the independence of the Moroccan judiciary in dispensing justice in accordance with the *Sharī'a* as interpreted by the Māliki rite. He passes in review the history of Moroccan legal practice before and since the advent of Islam and speaks out strongly against retaining reactionary, artificial customs and traditions in violation of Islamic ideas of justice and equity. This applies particularly to the treatment of women as a means of enjoyment to be bought and sold at will, without the right to inheritance although one can inherit from them. He is surprised that this is possible while the modern woman in Morocco is doing away with many traditions and customs which are less shameful.

He combats not only customary law and the courts which apply it, but also the consular courts with their capitulations of foreign European, largely French, origin. They present a challenge to the Moroccan national consciousness and impede its march towards freedom and independence. Hence the paramount need is for a unitary system of justice, based on the *Sharī'a*. The state, represented by the king, and the community never considered other, customary or consular, courts as legitimate. In support of the Moroccan nation's deep love of justice—an Islamic virtue—he quotes a statement by L. Massignon made at a function in honour of 'Allāl al-Fāsī in Paris. Moroccan hearts must be filled with a burning love of justice and of freedom, "for law and freedom are both an aid to justice and grounds for equality between men. Let us be worthy of the legacy of our forebears (*al-aslāf*) who lived and died for justice and freedom" (pp. 155 ff.). Therefore, Islam demands obedience to the *Sharī'a*.

It is noteworthy how objectively 'Allāl al-Fāsī discusses what is the most sensitive and delicate problem in contemporary Islam: the law applied in the state. It must be *Sharī'a*-law, but it is also necessary to borrow certain legal concepts and institutions from French and other laws. In his statesman-like attitude he is convinced—despite the supreme excellence of the *Sharī'a* as the result of divine revelation—that a modern state in the twentieth century must supplement it with laws and regulations taken from modern law-codes (presumably because of the mixed law in force under the French protectorate). Yet in view of the foreign capitulations (*imtiyāzāt ajnabīya*), the restoration of the *Sharī'a* is essential. The most serious problem exists in the sphere of criminal and civil law, since the institution of French- and Spanish-Moroccan law courts led to difficulties in relation to *Fiqh* and the *Sharī'a*-courts. The principal obstacle was the rigidity of the *fuqahā* of Islam as well as of the foreign jurists who were opposed to the *Sharī'a* for reasons of politics and diplomacy. Yet Allāl al-Fāsī does not exonerate the Muslim jurists from the charge that they did not face up to contemporary realities with flexibility. He asserts that the welfare of the fatherland requires the institution of a general Moroccan law-code commonly to be applied in the Moroccan courts to all inhabitants of the country. "Its basic sources are the Islamic *Sharī'a* and Moroccan cases with the help of French and (other) foreign law." It must be ratified by His Sherifiyan Majesty after the '*Ulamā* have pronounced by *fatwā* that all its stipulations conform to the general principles of the Islamic *Fiqh*; its name should be "The Islamic Moroccan Law" (pp. 159 ff.). Such a law would be in the best interests of the Moroccan nation at the present time "and be neither incompatible with our religion nor with the requirements of the utmost progress of the most advanced contemporary nations" (pp. 159 ff.).

He defends the *Sharī'a* of Islam against ignorance and fanaticism among many prominent practitioners of foreign laws who do not want to admit the worth of the Islamic *Sharī'a* and its influence even on the laws of Christian and lay countries including French law, dating back to the advance of Islam into southern France in the eighth century. The rule of Islam in Europe lasted until the fifteenth century, he continues. Its influence was specially strong in Spain, France, Italy and Sicily in legislative matters. The Ottomans followed and exerted their influence in Eastern Europe. This claim can hardly be substantiated in the matter of actual laws in force, but nobody would deny the considerable cultural influence on medieval Europe of the advanced Islamic states with their highly developed, superior civilisation.

Of greater significance is 'Allāl al-Fāsī's criticism of those who reject the *Sharī'a* as the proper and suitable basis of contemporary Moroccan law out of religious fanaticism or blind imitativeness, or because they are motivated by the desire to appear very advanced and civilised before the foreigners by separating themselves from everything the *aslāf* left behind.

He appeals to his countrymen to have self-confidence in the sure knowledge of the excellence of their own civilisation, not only in matters of legislation, but also in the field of national reconstruction as a whole (pp. 162 f.).

Next to the legal system it is the economic sphere which presents the most serious challenge to classical Islamic thought and practice. Here too 'Allāl al-Fāsī shows the same open-mindedness and willingness to reform we saw him adopt before. While he shares his view of the dynamism and flexibility of Islam with Iqbal, he appears to be much more prepared in practice to modify time-hallowed teaching and its application to a new situation. It is true, he is determined to stay within the confines of the *Sharī'a*, but tries to find a more liberal interpretation on which he can base his progressive views and is prepared to depart from Mālikī decisions, although he stresses the importance of this regnant school in Morocco as one of the basic components of Moroccan Islamic society. Writing in 1952, before Morocco gained freedom and independence, his stand was still largely theoretical, though none the less influential. Subsequent events have proved how difficult in practice a restoration of flexibility and a liberal interpretation of the *Sharī'a* in conformity with the needs of a twentieth-century state are.

The principal obstacle to a financial structure required by a modern economy is the prohibition of *ribā*, interest or usury, in the Qur'an as in Judaism and Christianity. 'Allāl al-Fāsī, strongly opposed to modern capitalism with its accumulation of capital in monopolist hands, and the consequent control over the national economy, adopts the decision of Muḥammad 'Abduh which allows moderate interest to be taken on non-loan capital on deposit, but forbids interest on credit (*ribā jalī*) in conformity with a *naṣṣ* of the Qur'an. But concealed interest (*ribā khalī*) is allowed or, better, tolerated in certain circumstances, though forbidden by the Sunna, in time of need. But care must be taken so that capital cannot be concentrated in the hands of the rich members of the community to the detriment of the people as a whole (p. 199).

This detailed discussion of economics in Islam is preceded by a general disquisition on the economic problem from 1850 on with special reference to the Christian churches and to Marxism and Russian communism (pp. 187 ff.). His own views are strongly coloured by those of Ibn Khaldūn whom he quotes. His claim concerning Christian Socialism, that no programme ever emerged which agreed with the principles of Christianity and with the needs of the time, is interesting. Only after that he deals with economic thinking in Islamic history (pp. 190 ff.). With the help of the Qur'an and *Ḥadīth* he presents the economic teaching of Islam on wealth, property and expenditure which are all governed by social considerations and concerns. This is clear from his references to Mālikī decisions. One is reminded of Sayyid Quṭb's *Social Justice in Islam*, except that 'Allāl al-Fāsī shows much more practical concern and a more realistic grasp of the complexities of a modern economy. He claims that Islam safeguards the economic equilibrium between the individual members of the *umma*, e.g. in matters of inheritance, in contrast to French law. He further illustrates this by explaining the Islamic law on property, be it held by an individual, a group or company or the Treasury (*bayt al-māl*) for the benefit of the whole community in the state. He singles out landed property, mainly in the hands of the state, with the special case of pious foundations (*waqf*, *awqāf*). Looking at Islamic history, he concludes that the caliphs tried to avoid the creation of big estates in private hands, but blames the authorities of later periods for permitting the emergence of several types of landed property and thus adding confusion in the economic life to that in government and administration. He pleads for the equitable distribution of property and wealth in the interests of the people by a return to the high principles of Islam and claims that in their social spirit they surpass other religions (pp. 212–15).

He hopes to achieve this by the strict enforcement of *zakāt*—a religious duty to relieve poverty—and the imposition of other taxes to obviate the imbalance caused by inequality in incomes. This is a good example of his willingness to make full use of Islamic provisions and supplement them by non-religious, financial measures as they are adopted in our time by the state. He advocates planning, but demands that due consideration be given to the moral and social injunctions of Islam. A fair and workable balance between private and public property is essential for individual as well as national wellbeing, prosperity and happiness. He also stresses the value and dignity of labour above money. Monopoly of any kind is to be avoided, private banking is to be eliminated, and in all private property and enterprise the public good must be the guiding principle. Production, distribution and consumption must be unified nationally, and national wealth must be increased in order to guarantee economic equity and social justice. The public and private sectors of the national economy must be harmonised in the best interests of all concerned. A national banking system must provide loans for private enterprise as well. All sources of wealth must be tapped and developed by the state for the benefit of the whole nation. In all this work of reform the primary aim must always remain the liberation of man (*taḥrīr al-insān*), especially from economic bondage (pp. 223–7). He speaks of "our great intellectual and spiritual wealth. We must examine our conscience and return to ourselves. Even some foreign principles may be followed if they are compatible with what is most holy and strong in our souls: freedom (*ḥurriya*)" (p. 228).

In the chapter on *Social Thinking*, 'Allāl al-Fāsī again shows that this must be determined by the teachings of Islam which are to be applied in a progressive, liberal and liberating spirit. Starting from the composition of the Moroccan nation—Arabs, Berbers, Jews and Africans—he emphasises their basic unity: the first three are all Mediterranean, and the black Africans are so integrated that no differentiation exists and no bar to national unity hampers their common progress towards independent, free nationhood. Religiously, there is also unity, since the Jews number only 2 per cent of the population. Despite religious differences there is no reason why all sections should not co-operate politically and socially in the Moroccan cause to achieve freedom and independence as one nation.[4] A further unifying factor is the Muslims' adherence to the Mālikī rite in law and to the doctrine of Al-Ash'arī in theology. Moreover, Arabic is the common language throughout Morocco, despite local dialects among some tribes.[5]

Concerned with the reform of Moroccan society, he first discusses the importance of the family in state, society and religion and then the social evil of prostitution in its moral, economic and legal aspects (including the outlawing of prostitution in public in various countries) in the form of a historical review beginning with eighteenth-century French literature (Molière, Montesquieu, Voltaire and Diderot).

Now the scene is set for a searching, critical inquiry into the position of woman in Moroccan society. After briefly touching upon her position in pre-Islamic Arabia and the time from the advent of Islam over later developments, he comes to the present time and deplores the rigidity of outdated views which are reflected in malpractices, especially where child marriages are concerned. Reforms are needed to restore woman's full rights in the community. He opposes the opinion of Mālik who gives the guardian or trustee the right to marry off the girl without her prior consent arguing "that this Māliki law is incompatible with the *Zeitgeist*. For the Moroccan woman can no longer accept such an arbitrary interference with her future at a time when she is making progress towards better conditions...we must adopt the view of the majority of the schools of Islamic law which stresses [the need of prior] consultation of virgin, widow or divorcee...". He justifies his departure from Mālik by Qur'anic verses, and thus returns to the original source, the tradition of the prophet.[6] It must be observed that he is careful to remain within traditional law in his attempt at raising the status of woman in contemporary Moroccan society.

Likewise, on the question of polygamy (*ta'addud al-zaujāt*) he draws a distinction between early Islam when one could rely on the conscience of the believer, and the misuse and neglect of the strictly limited Qur'anic permission of a maximum of four wives at one time in the later periods. He points to broken marriages and, as a consequence, uncared-for children in our time in Morocco to justify his plea for the prohibition of polygamy by the state, both on Islamic and social grounds. Interestingly, he bases this plea on the perfect *Sharī'a* itself and explicitly not on the *Zeitgeist*: the Qur'anic condition of equal justice accorded to each wife is in present circumstances not generally possible. For he holds that the verses of the Qur'an are intended for guidance of the *umma* in accordance with time and place (pp. 274 ff.). He gives his opinion "with complete inner confidence, in the belief that the *Sharī'a* of Islam is suitable for every time and place", and hopes that such a reform "will establish justice, enhance the appreciation of woman and her worth, and protect Islam". As usual, he furnishes further arguments both from history and present-day conditions in Morocco. In the first place, justice is not only absolute, but has also a meaning relative to time and place. Just as in education and medical care justice today demands of the state to provide both for everybody (although this was not considered necessary and, therefore, unjust, in earlier times), so is it with polygamy. Secondly, Mālikī jurists endorse and legalise the prohibition of polygamy in certain Moroccan tribes laid down by the woman at marriage in the marriage contract. Lastly, polygamy must be prohibited in Morocco generally so as to make it impossible for certain Berber tribes to marry more than four wives, as is their custom (pp. 277 f.). This, incidentally, agrees with the present trend to gradually eliminate customary law (*'urf* or *'ādāt*) and establish *Sharī'a*-law in matters of personal status. "One law for everybody" is a principle closely linked with the desire and the need to create one nation.

'Allāl al-Fāsī's attitude to divorce (*ṭalāq*)[7] is again in keeping with that of the *Salafīya*: he calls for a return to the prophetic tradition and for the application of Islamic laws governing marriage and divorce with such justice that the rights of the wife in marriage and after divorce are fully safeguarded. He compares these laws with those in force in the West and comes to the conclusion that, although Islam considers marriage a contractual agreement on the part of the husband, and the wife has normally no legal right to demand a divorce as in the West, Islamic law, derived from the Qur'an, is the best and is preferable to Western law. He thinks that to give the wife the legal right to divorce is responsible for the large number of divorces in the West. He quotes Al-Ghazālī in support who permits divorce provided no harm is done to the wife through the husband's unjust use of his right. But 'Allāl al-Fāsī is sensitive to the moral claim of a divorced wife to compensation and adequate protection on account of the equality he concedes woman in an Islamic Moroccan state. He insists that a wife whom her husband has divorced is entitled to compensation in accordance with her status and her husband's financial position, and he bases his view on the Qur'anic injunction: "provide for them, the rich according to his means, and the poor according to his means", although the schools of law differ as to the precise meaning of this injunction. He follows those who consider it an obligation against his own—Mālikī—rite which considers it only desirable. For obligatory compensation protects the wife against the whims of her husband; this agrees "with the public weal which demands the protection and support of woman and restraint of the wilfulness of men in rashly pronouncing a divorce" (p. 281).

This illustrates his attitude to Islamic law throughout: he is at the same time progressive in keeping with the *Zeitgeist* and yet upholds the immutable validity of the *Sharī'a* as far as its primary sources are concerned. Hence he advocates a liberal interpretation and aims at reviving and courageously applying its spirit which from a religious, ethical and social point of view is so perfect, due to its divine origin, that—rightly understood and practised—it fully answers to every need all the time. In the case under discussion, he relies on the Muslim husband's sense of fairness and justice not to misuse his legal right in marriage; if he does, by suppressing and harming his wife, or denying her rights, 'Allāl al-Fāsī grants the wife the right to demand a divorce. This means that he sets clear limits on the free exercise of man's legal rights on moral grounds and recognises woman's equality as a moral, but not as a legal person. This does not quite give woman equality in law; for, while the husband can himself pronounce the *ṭalāq* in his own right, the injured wife must apply to the court for a divorce, and the *qāḍī* alone can institute legal proceedings against the husband. It must be recognised that as long as the *Sharī'a* as prophetic tradition is maintained as obligatory, a radical departure from it cannot be expected. In this respect 'Allāl al-Fāsī's position can perhaps be compared to that adopted by Muhammad Asad, although he pays much more attention to *Fiqh* than the latter and follows its more liberal schools; in this he goes further than Abul A'lā Maudūdī.

Moreover, he regrets the existence of other marriage regulations in force among some tribes in Morocco which are incompatible with Islamic teaching on marriage and divorce; and he demands their abolition as part of that reform which he deems essential to achieve the national liberation of Morocco and its independent statehood as an Islamic nation.

Woman's civil rights should be determined on the basis of complete equality, he continues, as was the case in early Islam. He frankly criticises later developments, particularly because, he claims, neither Greek, Roman, Christian nor Jewish law have accorded woman such a position. In Islam she enjoys a full share in most offices of state with the exception of the Grand Imamate according to the Mālikī school. But she has the right to exercise *ijtihād* and *taqnīn* (legislation) and has a voice in all social and political questions. He wants to see her rights restored in Morocco (and in all Muslim countries) to the extent of the theory of the "Islamic *Sharī'a*".[8] It is to be noted that the *Sharī'a* is his norm and that reform for him means the full restoration and implementation of that norm in private and social life, not simply paying lip-service to the *Sharī'a* as the ideal theory, and certainly not its abolition. He wants to make the equality of the sexes a feature of national Moroccan life by admitting women to offices of state and to positions in all spheres of political, social, economic, cultural and religious life in accordance with "the nature of things". He therefore stresses the need for equal educational opportunities and sharply criticises past neglect in women's education. No integration of woman in the national life in all its spheres and aspects is, however, possible unless the men unlearn their wrong ideas and attitudes to woman as "solely a property which was acquired for pleasure and enjoyment, nothing else" (p. 287).

Within the framework of the *Sharī'a* of Islam, 'Allāl al-Fāsī tries to give directives for the reform and improvement of the components of Moroccan state and society, such as the protection of the family, the home as "the little fatherland", housing, care of parents for their children, care of the state for waifs and orphans in accordance with the Islamic injunctions about guardians and with reference to measures taken by the French. He also deals with grave social evils which must be eradicated, such as addiction to alcohol and drugs.

He then surveys the whole field of education against the background of the aims of national education towards patriotic citizenship. To inculcate love of fatherland (*waṭan*), of religion (*dīn*) and community (*umma*) in the home and in school is a primary requirement of all education and instruction. "To work for human welfare, the establishment and practice of justice and the enjoyment by all men of freedom", these are the true aims of a patriotic education (pp. 329 f.).

Written at a time when most of Morocco was under French and a small part under Spanish protection and government and when Arabic had to compete with French and Spanish as languages of instruction, it is natural that 'Allāl al-Fāsī should stress the imperative need for Arabic as the sole language of instruction. This is the more important since the sciences and other "secular" subjects were taught in a foreign language, French or Spanish. His plea paved the way for the national education in Arabic which is the aim of the government through the Ministry of Education in independent, free Morocco.[9]

This discussion leads to the fundamental problem of religious or secular education which 'Allāl al-Fāsī introduces by a historical survey beginning with the French Revolution. Rightly—though natural in a thinker and scholar of his distinction—he stresses that the battle was not joined against religion, but against the clergy and that "the French republican school was formed in the atmosphere of a political and religious war" (p. 337).

Few religious leaders in Islam make that distinction and admit that a lay state is not necessarily anti-religious, though organised religion is not allowed to interfere in politics. At the same time, it must be remembered that the application of this principle raises more difficulties in Islam if understood in the traditional sense as a religious and political unity, than it does in the West.

He contrasts the French system with the British system and comments on the Butler Act of 1944 and its debates with the result that the state observes neutrality towards religious instruction (but permits voluntary religious schools which it subsidises on certain conditions). He claims that after the Great War French opinion veered towards the British attitude, with growing opposition from the Communists (pp. 338 f.). Needless to say that 'Allāl al-Fāsī is opposed to a purely secular education, both from the point of view of Islam and of the best interests of the child. He holds that religion is and must remain basic to Morocco as "one of the most precious national possessions; it is, therefore, impossible for us to imagine Moroccan schooling that does not care for religious instruction for it is as necessary as language, history, mathematics and other elementary subjects without which no plan of instruction can do" (p. 340).

He opposes dual education in Morocco no less in the sense that one part of the people receives religious instruction in school and the other "a lay education (*tanshi'a lā'ikīya*) far removed from every contact with the spiritual heritage of the nation". Religion must therefore be taught in the Moroccan schools proper as well as in those instituted for foreigners which comprise Moroccan children among the pupils. Both should have one curriculum:

Arabic language, Moroccan history and religion. This is the accepted practice in all nations which have an official religion, he claims; it does not mean that non-Muslim children must study Islam. But it is right that Muslim children should be obliged to attend religious instruction whereas the other children need not. As an alternative he suggests that there should be a fixed time for religious instruction in all schools for the different religions (*milla*) under government supervision and paid for out of its budget. He adduces the Italian example in Libya in support. He considers religious instruction as essential for the spiritual development of all Moroccan children. He dismisses neutrality in education as belonging to the realm of fairy tales. Its practice in France and Turkey only led to the loss of all that was holy to them, and nothing but a return to an order built on positive principles in faith and society will restore their equilibrium. Turkey only imitated France in order to be counted among the Western nations at a time when Europe combined against the East and the Eastern peoples. Since Islam is a liberating force towards a just society it would be wrong to deprive Muslim children in Morocco of the significant spiritual values of Islamic culture. Hence it is imperative to give them a religious education (pp. 340 f.).

He pleads for compulsory education of all Moroccan boys and girls so that they will find fulfilment and satisfaction in the patriotic service of their country and nation (pp. 346 f.).

He frankly faces the many difficulties which beset such a national education: not enough qualified teachers, no suitable text-books, especially of geography, not to mention political difficulties created by the French protectorate and the imperialist ideas and intentions hostile to a general national education. He asks: "Is it not necessary to arouse in the pupils faith in the fatherland and self-confidence?" A clear programme is essential with a curriculum designed to serve the aim of a unitary, but not a uniform, national education. To achieve this aim he is willing to learn from the parliamentary as well as from the popular democracies. He used his exile in Egypt to study compulsory education there, in the shadow of British occupation. He works out detailed plans for primary and secondary education, linked by an intermediary stage, beginning at the age of seven and continuing to the age of sixteen.

While not opposing specialist training he stresses the need—in the context of the struggle for independence and freedom—for a broad general education for all classes of Moroccans, boys and girls, designed to produce not just artisans as the imperialists would like. Foremost attention must be focused in spreading the general culture characteristic of Maghribī Islam by instruction in the Arabic language and literature, Moroccan history, arithmetic and the other basic subjects, including geography, and in religion, as mentioned earlier. Education is the key to a flourishing national life to which all Moroccan citizens of both sexes must make their fullest individual contribution (pp. 352–6). He stresses moral and intellectual instruction while not neglecting physical fitness, yet does not overlook vocational training, the utilitarian aspect of which naturally comes to the fore only after independence in all countries which endured foreign rule. He looks forward to a future of intellectual, moral and social independence, individually and collectively, as the result of an enlightened modern schooling with emphasis on social responsibility in a democracy (pp. 361 f.). With this aim in mind, he devotes a special chapter to adult education which he divides into two branches, the first for illiterates and the second for those who did not complete their primary, secondary or higher education. He sees in the Adult Education Movement of Britain a model to follow as Egypt did in 1945, though for practical ends, whereas Britain concentrates on the Arts and Sciences, especially in the "Workers Educational Association". Here, extension of the frontiers of knowledge and the appreciation of literature and music are aimed at rather than acquiring skills. Nor does he forget Denmark's splendid achievement in this field. He thinks that from a cultural and social point of view the history of Morocco shows that the mosques and colleges provided—with the help of pious foundations (*awqāf*)—free education for all who wanted it and that they could be used, suitably adapted to the present time, to provide that further education he considers essential, "if adopted jointly by the Ministries of Education and of Social Affairs on the English pattern". He cannot see why from now on the administration of *awqāf*, the Ministry of Justice, the Supreme Council of the Qarawīyīn and other religious institutions should not co-operate in this venture (pp. 369 ff.).

In conclusion, we have to ask—on the basis of the foregoing

summary of the views expressed in 'Allāl al-Fāsī's *Al-naqd al-ḏātī* —what part Islam plays not only in his thought, but also in his programme for an independent Moroccan state and society. For the "acid test" of the lofty and sound principles and teachings of Islam is in their application to the public life of a people that has just emerged from foreign rule and tutelage, in the shape of laws and regulations according to the orthodox leaders. This book is not simply a "confession of faith" and of shortcomings; it is more than an "examination of the heart (or conscience)", *imtiḥān al-ḍamīr*, as he explains in the epilogue of his book. If it were nothing else it would be remarkable and singular enough, though not quite as unique as in fact it is. By making this frank and informed scrutiny of a leading thinker's mind and of the Moroccan nation's character and qualities the basis of future action, the author is able to suggest a comprehensive and consistent plan of reforms. He is convinced that nothing less than these essential reforms will suffice to launch his fatherland and nation on the way to independence and keep a steady keel on the exciting, arduous voyage of self-discovery and self-fulfilment after liberation. To this end, he has studied Western contemporary ideas and institutions. For he desires a modern society for Morocco, in tune with the *Zeitgeist*. This does not mean, however, throwing overboard inherited values and blindly imitating what appears as representative of this *Zeitgeist*. A study of the origin and development of Western ideas from the French encyclopedists to Marx, Lenin, Stalin, Hitler and Mussolini, has enabled 'Allāl al-Fāsī to see the underlying political, social and economic ideas and actual conditions as so many factors producing modern Western thought and thinking. It has confirmed him in his conviction that a modern Moroccan society can only be viable materially and significant spiritually if its *ethos* is the expression of its inherited values in their original purity and fully takes into account the heritage and the lessons of a long and chequered history and of a composite culture in which, naturally, Islam dominates. But he realises that North African (*Maghribī*) Islam owes something to the cultures and civilisations of many conquerors before the coming of Islam and since then to French imperialism.

This is clear from the last chapters of the book, particularly the chapters on "The Islamic Community" (*al-tā'ifa al-islāmīya*),

"The Social System" (*al-jihāz al-ijtimā'ī*), "The Trade Unions' Organisation" (*al-niẓām al-niqābī*), "The Need for a National Trade Union" (*ḍarūrat al-niqābat al-qawmīya*), advocating the confluence of the trade unionists with the patriotic (national) movement. Islam is so deeply rooted in 'Allāl al-Fāsī that it enables him to survey the modern Western scene with such inner security and strength that he can concentrate on social reform as the positive result of his *Self-Criticism*. Politics and economics only serve society; political and economic activities aim at social action. The reform of society, Muslim Moroccan society, is the foremost task facing the leadership responsible to "throne and nation".

In his *Summing Up* (*khalāṣa*) the social side of imperative reforms has first place, and it is here that the *Sharī'a* of Islam plays an essential, even vital role not only in matters of personal status, especially that of woman, but also in economics (*ribā* and *zakāt*) and in national education (mosque, college and other religious institutions). Those suggestions of his that have been transformed into action after independence we will see in the next part of this study. Suffice it to say here that without the great courage, wisdom, moderation and faith of 'Allāl al-Fāsī it is doubtful whether Morocco would today be what she is and tomorrow what king, government and leaders of thought aim at. The question what part Islam actually plays in his thought and in his master plan for a far-reaching reform of society is difficult to answer, largely because his approach is that of the modern sociologist and not that of the Muslim theologian. This distinguishes him from all the writers we discussed earlier on. Islam is so much a part of his nature and mind that it cannot be expressed quantitatively in relation to other parts of his strong personality. Undoubtedly, all the emphasis is on society, a modern Muslim society. This emphasis corresponds not only to practical needs which a political leader of his stature would naturally have in mind before all. It is at the same time an answer to the neglect of the sociological approach among the Arabs which he deplores by contrasting it with the fact that Ibn Khaldūn was the first thinker to create a social science. He claims that social thinking was only introduced into Europe by George Adam Smith and Montesquieu and other social scientists (pp. 429 f.). It is interesting in this connection to see 'Allāl al-Fāsī criticise Ibn Khaldūn or rather perhaps defend him by subscribing to the view expressed by a Western writer that, because Ibn Khaldūn lived at a time when autocracy arose in Islam, he was not interested in the social side of Islam. He belonged to a class of functionaries engaged in setting a disturbed order right while neglecting the principles of the *Sharī'a* and its laws. The ruler whom he served was concerned about his own prerogatives and requirements, but not about those of the community—Ibn Khaldūn's characterisation of the power-state.

That this does not apply to Ibn Khaldūn the thinker and author of the *Muqaddima* does—in our context—not matter any more than that 'Allāl al-Fāsī's evaluation and judgement of English democracy or his insistence on the superiority of Islamic over Jewish or Christian law are open to criticism. What matters is his understanding and use of Western ideas and institutions—after considerable and profound study—in his own attempt at setting out the means to reform, recovery and a flourishing political and social community after independence has been won. To be a *salafī* bent on the restoration of the purity of Islam and on the fullest application of its social and moral teachings and at the same time a man imbued with modern ideas and fashioned by a free and open encounter with contemporary French culture must lead to a different emphasis in situations where different problems have to be faced and solved. That he faces these situations and tries to meet them with open- and fair-mindedness distinguishes him from most other nationalist leaders. His religious fervour is evident, so is the fact that it blends with a strong social consciousness and the revolutionary outlook of a modern national guide and leader. Therefore, he is—as far as I know—the first practical thinker who considers Moroccan history from the point of view of social organisation (in the chapter on "The Social System"). In him, a new orientation manifests itself when he eloquently pleads for a revolution in thinking along lines of party and trade unionism (pp. 385 f.).

The reader of his *Epilogue* cannot fail to be impressed by the dignity and humility of the man in face of attack and abuse which he had to endure when "imperialists" or "colonialists" denied Morocco's right to freedom and rejected the first chapters of his book when published. Nor is it surprising to find a quotation from André Gide's *Symphonie Pastorale* (*al-simfūnīya al-rīfīya*) supporting his argument, or a reference to Georges Bernanos. This is all of a piece with the concluding paragraph of the book, a quotation from Ibn Khaldūn with which he ends his *Muqaddima*.[10] Written in exile, *Self Criticism* is not only a vivid testimony to a gallant fighter for human and national freedom and for the things of the spirit. It is also a challenge to all those who want to build Islam into a modern national state as a central force and factor.

PART II

ISLAM IN THE MODERN NATIONAL STATE

12-2

SECTION 1

CONSTITUTIONAL ISSUES

CHAPTER 8

THE ISLAMIC REPUBLIC OF PAKISTAN

In isolating the Islamic question from the other problems facing a newly independent Muslim state we must be clear from the outset that political consolidation, economic viability and social advance—to be brought about by radical reforms in all aspects of society—take precedence over the problem of the place of Islam in public life. And yet, Islamic teachings and institutions, from the formative period to the threshold of the present time, have a bearing on the more practical tasks of securing physical survival and development, social organisation and cultural activity. The importance of Islam as a state- and nation-building factor naturally varies from country to country and depends on their history and on the circumstances of their emergence as sovereign national states.

It was, therefore, necessary to describe the national movements and the views of leading exponents of the several trends discernible in contemporary Islam in order to understand the forces at work today in various Muslim countries.

Disagreement on the nature of the state—Islamic or Muslim, i.e. modern national—apart, all writers, statesmen and politicians with their followers are agreed on the imperative need to implement social justice as taught by Islam in the new society they intend to build up.

Social justice is today a universal demand whatever the inspiration for its realisation is. We are, therefore, justified in asking whether the practice of social justice in modern Muslim states makes them Islamic irrespective of the form in which it is practised, as *zakāt*, enjoined in the Qur'an and defined in the *Sharī'a*, or through the legislation of a modern welfare state. This is significant as an indication of the division of Muslims today into traditionalists who want to build an Islamic state on the basis and with the help of a fully operative *Sharī'a,* and liberals who adhere to the principles of Islam, but want to apply them in a new, modern form. As is clear from the first part of this study, this division runs right through the Muslim world today. It can be seen nowhere more clearly than in Pakistan where, moreover, this and similar questions are constitutional issues. For although the president promulgated a new constitution in 1962, a final settlement concerning the actual character of the Republic of Pakistan has not yet been achieved. The battle for or against an Islamic state is still being fought, as the reintroduction of the term "Islamic" into the title of the state as the result of an amendment clearly shows.

HISTORICAL BACKGROUND

To understand the seriousness and persistence of this struggle, we must go back at least a century to the time of the mutiny in 1857 and its adverse effects on the Muslims in India. In fact, the whole period of Muslim rule in India must be taken into account to appreciate that and why Islam in the subcontinent differs from Islam in the Middle East and North Africa. For, despite the common ground that unites all Muslims rooted in the basic teachings and practices of Islam, there is much in India and Pakistan that is peculiar to their Muslims. The visitor to the subcontinent is immediately struck by this and recognises it as the result of a separate development which is at least partly due to the presence of Hinduism and the inevitably resultant communalism. It is highly significant that communalism seriously hampered the close co-operation of Muslims and Hindus in achieving independence and freedom from British rule. Sayyid Ahmad Khan's conviction that the separation of the two nations was inescapable is based on fact, not on fiction. For it is a fact that only the Western-educated Muslims and Hindus could unite in the common struggle for a free India and could overlook the incompatibility of traditional Islam and traditional Hinduism as two distinct ways of life. But the masses on both sides were separated by religion, culture and language. The gulf that separates the masses from the Westernised intellectuals is certainly one of the main reasons for the fear of the Muslims of being reduced to a permanent minority in a free and independent united India. This more than any other reason is responsible for partition and the tragic circumstances in which two separate national states were born in the subcontinent.

Both Sayyid Ahmad Khan and Mohammad Ali Jinnah began as champions of Muslim–Hindu unity. Yet their deep concern for their own Muslim community and their realisation of the dangers inherent in the numerical weakness of the Muslims and their unfavourable economic situation (partly due to Muslim backwardness in modern education) impelled the former to advise his co-religionists against joining the Indian National Congress and forced the latter to press for a separate state for them.[1] Nor must we forget that the fear of the Muslims was and is paralleled by the fear of the Hindus, due to the long rule of a Muslim minority, especially under the Mughuls, over a Hindu majority. Although freedom from fear is one of the basic freedoms that was to have been secured through the defeat of German National Socialism in the Second World War, pronouncements and noble intentions alone are not enough to rid mankind of deep-seated distrust, especially if it is based on historical as well as contemporary experience on both sides. The several phases of the Muslim–Hindu conflict leading to the partition of the subcontinent and the creation of Pakistan in two parts separated by a thousand miles of Indian territory have often been described and must remain outside the scope of this study.[2] A visit to the subcontinent will soon convince the observer of the unhappy legacy fear on both sides has bequeathed to the two independent nations. Fearful problems were created (some needlessly no doubt) and these bedevil mutual relations and cast their shadows on political and economic affairs to the greater detriment of Pakistan than of the much larger, richer and better equipped India.

As long as these practical difficulties militate against a steady growth of security and prosperity, a peaceful solution which would lead to a flowering of Islam in Pakistan, with which we are primarily concerned here, cannot be expected. It would be wrong to judge the present situation exclusively from the standpoint of practical politics and physical priorities and to dismiss the Islamic issue as a luxury which Pakistan cannot afford. Islam—in whatever form we understand Islam—is, after all, the *raison d'être* of Pakistan. Hence this Islamic issue overshadows the constitutional development and has acted as an irritant from the moment Pakistan was born out of confusion and human suffering in 1947.

One must not only take into consideration the events leading to a separate Muslim state which meant death and tragedy for millions on both sides. We must also remember that Islam has divided as well as united Indian Muslims. The answer to the question "What is Islam?" is determined not only by theological considerations but also by political realities, and at least partly depends on which side of the border a Muslim finds himself. This holds good for the person who has made a free choice no less than for the person who was caught by events and circumstances. Even so, the answer is by no means simple. For not all Muslims in India look upon themselves as "Indian citizens of the Muslim persuasion", that is patriotic Indians who profess the religion of Islam and make their contribution to the Indian state and nation as Muslims. We know that Abul A'lā Maudūdī was at first against Pakistan because, he maintains, the Muslims are not a nation in the Western sense, but "an ideological party very much like the socialists or communists. They should struggle for the propagation and adoption of an Islamic ideological concept in the whole of India, and if they did this it was very likely that within a few years the whole of India would become *Dar-ul-Islam*."[3] To this end, Maudūdī organised his party in 1941.

Likewise, many Muslims in Pakistan look upon themselves as "Pakistani citizens of the Muslim faith", serving their Pakistani state and nation as Muslims without wishing to live by the *Sharī'a* of Islam, adapted to present needs. And yet the two groups do not share the identical motives for their attitude to Islam, for Pakistani Muslims are the majority and Indian Muslims a minority. We are back at the important distinction between Islam as a complete way of life in society and Islam as the personal faith of the individual citizen. But both groups—and their subdivisions—have this in common that they wish to restore the Qur'an to its pre-eminent position as the primary source of Islam and the principal guide in a Muslim's life, in so far as they are believers.

Here it is important to note that the Muslims in the Indo-

Pakistan subcontinent have only comparatively recently been influenced by the "Back to the Qur'an" movement in the wake of the Egyptian "modernists" and the Muslim Brotherhood, a movement which was to bring about a renaissance of Islam in response to the challenge of the Christian West. As stated in the Introduction[4] Muslim India produced a spiritual leader long before the West in the wake of the French Revolution and its seminal ideas roused the Muslim East, in the person of Shāh Walī Ullāh (1703–62) who set afoot a movement which threw up a succession of religious leaders. To him present-day Pakistanis trace their own attempt to get back to the source of inspiration and guidance. Two events made a deep impression on Shāh Walī Ullāh: the parlous state of Mughul power and administration which caused widespread suffering to the peasants, and his two pilgrimages which brought him into close contact with the scholars of Hijāz. Taught by his father, a prominent Sufi, jurist and founder of a *madrasa* in Delhi, he was particularly well qualified to benefit from the scholars in Mecca. He returned from there determined to rekindle religious fervour and bring about a moral regeneration among his Muslim countrymen—descendants from the Arabs whom he revered—by his translation of the Qur'an. The Qur'an was first translated into Persian and later, by two of his sons, into Urdu, so that the ordinary believer could learn to understand its message and live by it. He is a reformer in the tradition of Ibn Taymīya, that is, a restorer of the purity of the Islam of the prophet and his companions and of Qur'an and Sunna: a true *mujaddid* (renewer). His interest in the Traditions earned him the other title of *muḥaddith*. He taught first in his father's *madrasa* and later in his own school *Ḥadīth* and wrote many books and treatises on the whole field of theology and jurisprudence. The outstanding work in theology and *Fiqh* is the *Ḥujjat Allah al-bālighah*, called by A. Bausani a treatise of "religious sociology". It is a rather long-winded treatise, but Bausani skilfully extracted Shāh Walī Ullāh's doctrines from it.

The important feature of this remarkable presentation of the tenets of Islam is that it originated in an Islamic environment free from any European influence decades before the French Revolution. It is this book in particular which is today claimed to have an important bearing on the attitude to Islam in Pakistan, especially among the "modernists" who claim support for their views and intentions from Shāh Walī Ullāh's significant distinction between two kinds of successors of the prophet: one, the inheritor of his political functions and the other who exercises religious authority. Those who inherited his political functions are concerned with legislation, *jihād*, defence, taxation, administration of *waqf*, care for mosques, and so on. The successors to his religious authority have the duty to teach and preach, to study Qur'an, *Ḥadīth* and *Fiqh* and to instruct in them the community, whom they are to guide in their religious activities and to inspire towards spirituality and ethical behaviour. Even if those intellectuals with whom I discussed Shāh Walī Ullāh and his views are right in holding that he was by implication far in advance of his time (evident by his hints and allusions since he could not openly propound revolutionary ideas, which would have aroused orthodox opposition, as have his and his sons' Qur'an translations) it may be doubted whether he advocated a separation of religion and politics. For the political and religious unity of Islam was an axiom with him as with all orthodox Muslims. It seems that the separation of functions was demanded by him within the overall unity of the religious and the political. The prophet has given the world a *sharī'a*, "a total religio-political law",[5] but, although based on revelation, the laws vary with time and people within the one immutable *dīn*. This view allows Shāh Walī Ullāh to take account of political, economic and social reality and, by the *cautious* exercise of *ijtihād*, to arrive at an interpretation of the *Sharī'a* in accordance with *maṣlaḥa*, the public good. It is clear that in his reasoning he is no innovator; he remains within classical Muslim jurisprudence which, in order to arrive at a solution commensurate with the needs of the time, carefully and diligently weighs the opinions of the outstanding jurists and, by a judicious exercise of *ra'y* (personal rational judgement), chooses and develops the opinion which best suits the case. How narrowly circumscribed *ijtihād* is in the view of Shāh Walī Ullāh can be seen in M. D. Rahbar's English translation of the relevant passages of his treatise dealing with *ijtihād* and *taqlīd*, and it must remain an open question whether Pakistani scholars are justified in assuming that "the emphasis on *ijtihād* is Shāh Walī Ullāh's main contribution to modernist speculative thinking in Muslim India".[6] But that he appeals to the prophetic tradition (*ḥadīth*) in preference to *taqlīd* of the jurists of the past is certainly a sign that he wanted to restore the flexibility of Islamic jurisprudence in its formative period before the fourth century of the *Hijra* and thus re-establish that dynamism of Islam which plays such a great role in Iqbal. His stress on *ra'y*, understood by Aziz Ahmad as "reason and argument", is claimed to have influenced the rationalism of Sayyid Ahmad Khan.[7]

We have seen earlier that Maulana Abul A'lā Maudūdī shared with Shāh Walī Ullāh his conservative understanding and use of *ijtihād* which is far removed from the free, unfettered exercise of one's own judgement of the modernists properly so called. Hence it appears that Shāh Walī Ullāh's concept of the *khilāfa*, the succession of the prophet, as two-pronged, *k. ẓāhirī* and *k. bāṭinī* (external and internal, or temporal and spiritual) is perhaps his greater contribution to political thinking and its reflection in constitutional theory and law today. His political awareness prompted him to active intervention in the affairs of the Mughul state by calling on the ruler of Afghanistan to defend the Muslim empire against its enemies, principally the Jats, and to restore effective Muslim rule. This has become known through the discovery by K. A. Nizami of a considerable number of Shāh Walī Ullāh's letters.[8] This is another reason for the renewed interest in him. Nor should we overlook the immediate influence on his and subsequent generations of his Qur'an translation, for it played an important part in the religious revival among Indian Muslims. Together with his interest in *Ḥadīth*—his own school was called *Dār al-Ḥadīth*—it has created a movement carried forward by his four sons right down to 1857 and has stimulated not only Sayyid Ahmad Khan and Iqbal, but also the '*Ulamā* of Deoband, the foremost seat of traditional learning in India, both through his sober mysticism and through his moderate, sane, yet progressive attitude to *Fiqh*. Since Shāh Walī Ullāh was himself influenced by Shaykh Aḥmad of Sirhind, the *mujaddid alf-al-thānī*, many Pakistani intellectuals let the prehistory of Pakistan begin with both.

The significance of this interpretation is clear: it represents an inner, spiritual justification for Pakistan as the independent, sovereign state of the Muslim nation in the subcontinent. Furthermore, this justification is traced back more than two centuries to authoritative thinkers and responsible spiritual leaders working for a renewal of Islam, the Islam of the prophet and his companions. This is superimposed upon the political movement based on the two-nation theory. This movement with its strong economic, social and cultural considerations is fostered and led by emancipated Western-educated intellectuals who, while guided by Islamic principles, acknowledged religion as important only in the final stages leading to partition.[9]

A further, equally important reason for the renewed interest in Shāh Walī Ullāh is that he is as much respected by the orthodox religious leaders and scholars as by the academics. Consequently, those who want to reform and adapt the *Sharī'a* of Islam or to justify new legislation in conformity with Qur'an and Sunna and within the limits of permissible *ijtihād* can refer to Shāh Walī Ullāh for authority. They can do this because they know that those who consider themselves the only experts, on account of their traditional learning, capable of judging whether any proposed measure is admissible or not, will accept his authority. Although Shāh Walī Ullāh cannot be considered on the same level with the oldest authorities in *Fiqh* his standing is assured through his being an indigenous scholar of unquestioned eminence who has been associated with Arabia through his studies. Besides, he has established a school and a tradition which has influenced some of the eminent *'ulamā* who have taken an active part in Pakistan's prolonged efforts at constitution making. It is, indeed, difficult to see how Islam can be kept out of politics in Pakistan however much the quietists among the religious and the advocates of a lay state may wish it.

MUSLIM DIVISIONS IN RELIGION AND POLITICS

It was not many years after the disaster of 1857 that both traditionalists and "modernists" systematically set about to remove, if possible, the weaknesses which the Muslim community in India revealed. The traditionalists were anti-British and determined to counter the English educational system, considered dangerous to Islam and Muslim life, by a great effort to implement higher traditional education in a *madrasa*; they founded Deoband in 1867 to this end.

Moreover, they favoured close Muslim–Hindu co-operation in opposition to the British in government, administration and education. The "modernists" found a champion in the person of Sayyid Ahmad Khan who only partially realised his dream of establishing a Cambridge in India with the foundation of the "Mohammedan Anglo-Oriental College" at Aligarh, the outcome of his "Society for the Educational Progress of Indian Muslims" which he founded in 1870.[10] He recognised the need to offset British neglect of Muslim education after the 1857 revolt and to combat missionary influence and, rightly, saw in a general education comprising general subjects on the Western model and a rational training in Islamic subjects the highroad to political, economic, social and cultural achievement and success. Until 1867 he favoured a common effort of Muslims and Hindus, but the Urdu–Hindi language controversy at Benares in that year convinced him that unity of the two communities was unattainable, and that it was impossible to weld Muslims and Hindus into one Indian nation. Thus, he threw his considerable talents and indefatigable energy into the unstinted support of the Muslim community, principally in the field of education and scholarship. Aligarh fell short of his desire to integrate a three-tier education in English with modern subjects, in Urdu, and in Arabic and Persian. The British administration opposed his plans and he had to be content with the "Mohammedan Anglo-Oriental College" (which later developed into a full university). His rationalist approach to revelation, discernible in his commentary on the Qur'an, aroused the implacable hostility of the orthodox, and, although his views were kept out of the Faculty of Theology, Deoband looked with suspicion at Aligarh, both on religious and political grounds. The latter was due to his endeavour to persuade his Muslim community to seek protection with the British by co-operation with the occupying power, since he was convinced that otherwise the Muslims would be subjected to a Hindu majority of 4:1. In 1886 Sayyid Ahmad Khan set up yet another body, the "Mohammedan Educational Conference" of which A. H. Albiruni says: "It was a powerful instrument of intellectual awakening and general spread of knowledge amongst the Muslims."[11] This Conference also served political ends until the Muslim League was founded. Only two years later, he advised his Muslim countrymen not to join the Indian Congress.

Sir William Hunter, a member of the Indian Civil Service and sometime president of the Education Commission had (in 1871) this to say about the causes of Muslim discontent with their exclusion from the I.C.S.:

How comes it that the Muhammadan population is thus shut out alike from official employ and from the recognised Professions?...The truth is, that our system of public instruction, which has awakened the Hindus from the sleep of centuries and quickened their inert masses with some of the noble impulses of a nation, is opposed to the traditions, unsuited to the requirements, and hateful to the religion of the Musalmans....The truth is, that our system...ignores the three most powerful instincts of the Musalman heart. 1. The vernacular of Bengal used by Hindu teachers, whom the whole Muhammadan community hates....2. The rural schools seldom teach the tongues necessary for his holding a respectable position in life, and for the performance of his religious duties....3. No provision for religious education of the Muhammadan youth....A system of purely secular education...is certainly altogether unsuited to the illiterate and fanatical peasantry of Muhammadan Bengal.[12]

Sayyid Ahmad Khan demanded, before a select committee in 1872, two branches of education for Muslims: one general for all classes, the other to help them to benefit from such "rules and benefits of education adopted by the Government until it is ready to adopt the plan proposed in the first branch". He did not conceal that their own system was out of date: "old books do not teach independence of thought, perspicuity, and simplicity...".[13] It was found that the Muslims fully benefited from government primary and secondary education where it was provided in the vernacular. But in higher schools, colleges and universities the Muslims were either absent or backward. Consequently, measures were taken to remedy this unsatisfactory situation. When Lord Lytton laid the foundation stone of Aligarh, the British effort was recognised in the address presented to him: "The government could neither introduce a system of religious education, nor could it direct its efforts towards contending with the prejudices of a race by whom religion is regarded not merely as a matter of abstract belief, but also as the ultimate guide in the most ordinary secular concerns of life." Neither such an admission nor praise for Britain was welcomed by the traditionalists, nor would they approve of one of Aligarh's aims: "To reconcile oriental learning with Western literature and science."[14] Sayyid Ahmad Khan was consistent in his stress on better Muslim education to secure adequate shares for Muslims in government posts, while at the same time deploring appointment by educational qualifications, as long as the Muslims lagged behind. Likewise, he was against Muslim participation in local government, since the Muslims would be outvoted as a minority of 1:4. The same applied to the national level. Hence he saw the only salvation in British rule which alone could prevent the Muslim minority nation from being dominated by the Hindu majority. In 1888 he declared: "If my nation follow my advice they will draw benefit from trade and education."[15]

Apart from his educational and political work, Sayyid Ahmad Khan expounded his modern outlook as far as Islam is concerned, stressing the need for moral regeneration among his co-religionists, in numerous articles, and especially in his commentary on the Qur'an in Urdu. His motto was: "The word of God (Qur'an) must be in harmony with the work of God (Nature)."[16] Consequently, he emphasised the compatibility of the Qur'an with modern science so that A. H. Albiruni speaks of him as the leader of the modern *Mu'tazilites* and maintains that his Qur'an commentary is equal to the later Arabic commentary by Muḥammad 'Abduh and Rashīd Riḍā, first published in *Al-Manār*. And yet it must be conceded that the orthodox revival connected with Deoband and Lucknow was too strong for Sayyid Ahmad Khan's liberal views to prevail, the more so since the Western-educated Muslims showed little or no interest in his religious endeavours or in Islam as such.

In 1894 an organisation was founded in Lucknow by orthodox scholars under the name of *Nadwat-al-'Ulamā* in opposition to Aligarh's liberalism in theology. This organisation was joined after Sayyid Ahmad Khan's death by one of his most distinguished colleagues, Maulana Shiblī. He changed its curriculum by making English a compulsory subject and was ably assisted and afterwards succeeded by Sayyid Sulaiman Nadwi and Maulana Abul Kalām Āzād. Shiblī was critical of Sayyid Ahmad Khan's modernism in theology no less than of his pro-British policy; nor would he keep religion and politics apart. A. H. Albiruni quotes from an article of Abul Kalām Āzād's, published in 1910, a significant passage which clearly indicates Lucknow's hostility to Aligarh and its determination to wrest the spiritual leadership of Indian Muslims from it: "All the examinations of the causes of our decline and decay lead to the conclusion that there is nobody to shepherd our confused and dispersed flock. But the group of people which the school at Nadvatul-Ulcma is producing through its education and training will bring together and lead this flock which has lost its way." He also quotes Shiblī as saying of Aligarh that it was "an institution for Training in Slavery" and "For the last thirty years efforts have been made to uplift the Muslims in the name of nationhood, but the failure of these efforts is only too obvious. The followers of the Prophet do not respond to the call of nationhood. Appeal to them in the name of religion, and you will see what a splendid response you get."[17]

Whatever one may think of dragging religion into politics, events in Pakistan have proved right Shiblī, the man who is credited with coining the phrase "Islam in Danger"—a phrase which, used by religious leaders, has never since lost its force. Shiblī wanted the *Nadwat al-'Ulamā* to rally and lead the Muslims of India in the vigorous performance of their religious duties. Says A. H. Albiruni: "Shibli did not see the realisation of his dream, but the vision has found other votaries. Shibli—Abul Kalām Āzād —and now, in the more congenial atmosphere of Pakistan, Maudoodi—form an unbroken chain."[18]

Abul Kalām Āzād embarked on a crusade of revivalism with a rare gift of knowledge and emotional appeal, first as editor of *Al-Nadwa*, which propagated the views of the movement led by Shiblī, and from 1912 in his own paper *Al-Hilāl.* He wrote to a friend:

> The Aligarh movement has paralysed the Muslims. The real aim is the promotion of Pan-Islam, which is the true foundation and link for progress and reform of Islam, and, for this there will never be a better opportunity than we have now. Today no local or national movement can benefit the Muslims, even if it be the tall-talk of the (Aligarh) University. So long as the whole world of Islam does not come together in an international and universal alliance, how can small tracts help the forty crores of Muslims?[19]

He castigated in a speech "those heretics and hypocrites who, during the last forty years, had cooperated with the Satans of

Europe to weaken the influence of Islamic Caliphate and Pan-Islam".[20]

Politics apart, Abul Kalām Āzād devoted many pages of *Al-Hilāl* to his advocacy of "Back to the Qur'an" on which he wrote a commentary and claimed that he took only the Qur'an as his guide, not any brand of Indian politics. But his critics were not slow in pointing out that oversimplification and appeal to Muslim emotions while able to kindle enthusiasm could hardly promote real reform and purification. Yet his tremendous influence over many years is a fact, though we might today find (with hindsight) that Abul Kalām Āzād might have roused the pride of the Muslims in the glorious past of Islam, but gave them little guidance, if any, in the tragic conflict of communalism in the face of Hindu revivalism and superior strength. His was a complex personality who could combine pan-Islamism with Indian nationalism in which he played a significant role.[21] Iqbal shared his orthodoxy against Sayyid Ahmad Khan, but became the protagonist for separate Muslim nation- and finally statehood. Abul Kalām Āzād shared with some of the finest Muslim minds the deep conviction that the Muslims had an important part to play in a united, free India and had a large following among his people, especially within the *Jām 'iat al-'ulamā-i-Hind* and the *Khilāfat* movement which were both founded in 1919 and worked closely together. The organisation of the *'ulamā* aimed at securing general Muslim adherence to the *Sharī'a* (in matters of personal status), gained Gandhi's support for the *Khilāfat* movement in protest at British "betrayal" of Turkey and took part in Gandhi's non-violent non-co-operation movement. Abul Kalām Āzād worked wholeheartedly in the All-India National Congress whose presidency he assumed in 1938. He was convinced that the safeguards promised to the Muslim minority were adequate to warrant unreserved Muslim participation in the Congress's fight for the freedom of India. This is the tenor of his Presidential Address in 1940. A. H. Albiruni holds that he changed his views from revivalism and pan-Islamism to cosmopolitanism in his internment during the war, and the Muslim leaders hoped in 1946 that he would make common cause with them. But he opposed, with other *'ulamā*, among them Maudūdī, the formation of Pakistan and preferred to live and work in and for India. Albiruni's comment is interesting and revealing: "The forces which he set in motion in 1913 are being consolidated and led today by Maulana Maudoodi, the leader of 'Islami Jamiat'. All those who want Pakistan to be a theocracy may or may not realise it, but they are following the path originally shown by the gifted Editor of *Al-Hilal*."[22]

COMMUNALISM

The foregoing clearly shows how closely religion and politics are linked, and, before touching briefly on Iqbal, we must pay some attention to the political aspect of the communal problem in India. For political and economic considerations predominated, at least among the political leaders on both sides, and the religious issue was subordinated. There were divisions among Hindus as well as among Muslims, and the All-India National Congress had to steer a careful course between Hindu extremists and Westernised nationalists, just as the Muslim League, founded at Dacca in 1906, was composed of a few orthodox religious leaders and a majority of Westernised landlords and politicians who could at first not command a large following representative of Indian Muslims. The Muslims in India were not only divided in their political loyalties —to Britain, to nationalist India or to neither, they were also disunited in their concept of and attitude to Islam. The vicissitudes of the Muslim–Hindu concord and—mostly—conflict cannot be discussed here. Communalism looms large in the numerous books and studies about Pakistan and India before and after partition. A judicious description and assessment is to be found in Khalid bin Sayeed's *Pakistan. The formative phase.*[23]

What stands out is that mutual fear and distrust, but particularly the Muslim minority's apprehensions leading to demands for safeguards against the Hindu majority, made frank and successful co-operation very difficult. To this must be added that fear and weakness drove many Muslims to seek the protection of the imperialist power, Britain, and thus precluded them from making common cause with the Hindus in the national liberation struggle, which was naturally resented by the latter. This is clearly shown in the shortlived marriage of convenience between these two sections of India which began during the Great War when Britain was at war with Turkey, reached its height with the Congress-supported

Khilāfat movement in 1919—preceded by the Lucknow Pact in 1916 between the League and Congress—and came to an end when the *Khilāfat* movement collapsed with Kemal Atatürk's abolition of the Ottoman caliphate. Hindu support considerably lessened when in 1921 and 1922 Muslim fervour led to communal disorder and death. Nor can revivalism and conversionary zeal on both sides have made for trust, amity and concerted action. On the constitutional plane, neither Muslim agitation for separate electorates—temporarily successful in the partition of Bengal 1909–11—nor M. A. Jinnah's advocacy in 1938 of joint electorates with adequate safeguards for the Muslims, achieved any purpose: the two "nations" did not see their way to a free unitary India in partnership. Muslim disunity, causing weakness so fatal in politics, affected the prospects of a united India much more adversely than Hindu factionalism. Religious fanaticism, fear, dislike and contempt (which periodically erupted into communal disturbances) constituted perhaps after all more powerful an obstacle to unity than distribution of seats in the provincial and central administrations and legislatures, and participation in the civil service on an adequate proportional basis.

Mohammad Ali Jinnah's rise to undisputed leadership of a strong and powerful Muslim League representing the majority of Indian Muslims is not only due to his great political ability and astuteness, but largely to his recognition that mass support could be won only by appealing to his co-religionists' loyalty to Islam. Shiblī was right when he put his discovery to the test: appeal to religion, not to nationhood. The most emancipated political leaders have to pay heed to the sentiments of their followers, the majority of whom are simple orthodox believers. This is true of both sides, Muslims and Hindus. In India, the language question is not to be divorced from religion either.

Urdu and Hindi had come to be for many of their speakers identical with Islam and Hinduism, rightly or wrongly. In a country where the gulf between a small wealthy upper class and the poor, largely illiterate masses is so wide, sophisticated intellectuals can understand each other and can even come to agree in a language equally foreign to the mass of their followers. But when they have to translate the terms of their bargain—politically speaking—into the everyday joys and sorrows, fears and hopes of the masses in their native tongues linked to the beliefs and practices of their respective religions, they realise how much they are still a part of their community and have to take account of this fact. This holds good for pre-partition India no less than for post-partition Pakistan and India. This will remain so until the opportunity of educational and economic equality has been offered and seized and the intellectuals and the simple, naïve minds, the rich and the poor, have grown into one nation. Pakistan has a smaller and less serious minority problem than India. Until fear has been banished from the minds of Muslims and Hindus, together with an assured economic and social security, religion will in all likelihood play an unfortunate part in politics and in individual human lives. The verdict on the creation of Pakistan—inevitable as it seems in the circumstances then prevailing—will depend on the amity between the two nations of the subcontinent which a unitary India could not provide. Yet this amity largely depends on the integration, not migration and expulsion, of the minorities on either side of the border between India and Pakistan. Self-determination has been applied, but every majority area contains at present a minority divided from the majority by religion, culture and language. Can the tolerance of Islam solve the problem? Before trying to answer this question, at least from the constitutional provisions, a few quotations from documents may illustrate the communal problem in India before partition as seen by Muslim leaders.

THE CASE FOR MUSLIM SEPARATISM

Iqbal, poet and philosopher, passionately concerned about the renaissance of Islam as a just social system based on a dynamic religion, said in his Presidential Address to the Allahabad meeting of the All-India Muslim League in 1930: "Communalism in its higher aspect, then, is indispensable to the formation of a harmonious whole in a country like India. . . . The Muslim demand for the creation of a Muslim India is, therefore, perfectly justified." He gave this as his idea of a Muslim state:

I would like to see the Punjab, North-West Frontier Province, Sind and Baluchistan amalgamated into a single state. Self-government within the British Empire or without the British Empire, the formation of a consolidated North-West Indian Muslim state appears to me to be the final destiny of the Muslims at least of North-West India....India is the greatest Muslim country in the world. The life of Islam as a cultural force in this living country very largely depends on its centralisation in a specified territory.

He defended his opinion against the Congress:

...the Muslim demand...is actuated by a genuine desire for free development which is practically impossible under the type of unitary government contemplated by the nationalist Hindu politicians with a view to secure permanent communal dominance in the whole of India....

"Let me tell you frankly", he continues with a reference to a statement by Lord Irwin that the Muslim community had failed to produce leaders,

that at the present moment, the Muslims of India are suffering from two evils. The first is the want of personalities....By leaders I mean men who, by Divine gift or experience, possess a keen perception of the spirit and destiny of Islam, along with an equally keen perception of the trend of modern history. Such men are really the driving force of a people but they are God's gift and cannot be made to order....[24]

Dealing with communalism, he said in the same address:

A community which is inspired by feelings of ill-will towards other communities is low and ignoble. I entertain the highest respect for the customs, laws, religious and social institutions of other communities.... Yet I love the communal group which is the source of my life and my behaviour; and which has formed me what I am by giving me its religion, its literature, its thought, its culture, and thereby recreating its whole past, as a living operative factor, in my present consciousness. ...Nor should the Hindus fear that the creation of autonomous Muslim states will mean the introduction of a kind of religious rule in such states....I therefore demand the formation of a consolidated Muslim state in the best interests of India and Islam. For India it means security and peace resulting from an internal balance of power, for Islam an opportunity to rid itself of the stamp that Arabian Imperialism was forced to give it, to mobilise its law, its education, its culture, and to bring them into closer contact with its own original spirit and with the spirit of modern times.[25]

These are noble sentiments, indeed, but in the prevailing situation perhaps more than a little utopian. But they spring from a deep spirituality and represent the conviction of a Muslim believer, the product of Indian Islam in which Iqbal was so much interested that he kept aloof of the *Khilāfat* movement. With Nietzsche, whom he greatly admired and whose *Übermensch* is claimed to have inspired his concept of the Self, he abhorred nationalism and pleaded for *The Reconstruction of Religious Thought in Islam.*[26] Iqbal significantly differs from the advocates of an Islamic state on the model of the *khulafā rāshidūn* in his rejection of "a kind of religious rule" and in his plea to his fellow-Muslims to adopt his plan for a separate Muslim state at peace with the Hindus, as outlined above, and to remove from Islam "the stamp of Arabian Imperialism".

Various other plans for a separation of the two nations—a notion not accepted by Gandhi—through the formation of contiguous Muslim majority areas into independent states were proposed in the following years until the Lahore Resolution of the Muslim League was moved in 1940 by M. A. Jinnah, rejecting the Federal Constitution proposed by the British Government and demanding

> independent states consisting of Muslim majority regions geographically contiguous (NW and E)...(and) that adequate, effective and mandatory safeguards should be specifically provided in the constitutions for minorities in the units and in the regions for the protection of their religious, cultural, economic, political, administrative and other rights and interests in consultation with them and in other parts of India where the Muslims are in a minority.[27]

For M. A. Jinnah was convinced that the Hindu–Muslim problem could only be solved by allowing

> the major nations separate homelands, by dividing India into "autonomous national" states....(This) will far more adequately and effectively safeguard the rights and interests of Muslims and various other minorities....It is extremely difficult to appreciate why our Hindu friends fail to understand the real nature of Islam and Hinduism. They are not religions in the strict sense of the word, but are in fact different and distinct social orders...never can a common nationality [*sic!*] evolve...there is not one Indian nation...the Hindus and Muslims belong to two different religious philosophies, social customs, literatures. They neither intermarry nor interdine together and, indeed, they belong to two different civilisations which are based mainly on conflicting ideas and conceptions. Their outlooks on life and of life are different. It is

quite clear that Hindus and Musalmans derive their inspiration from different sources of history. They have different epics, different heroes, and different episodes....To yoke together two such nations under a single state, one as a numerical minority and the other as a majority, must lead to growing discontent and final destruction of any fabric that may be so built up for the government of such a state.

To his mind, the present unity is artificial, due to British conquest and bound to collapse with the departure of the British.

Muslim India cannot accept any constitution which must ncessarily result in a Hindu majority government. Hindus and Muslims brought together under a democratic system forced upon the minorities can only mean Hindu raj. Democracy of the kind with which the Congress High Command is enamoured would mean the complete destruction of what is most precious in Islam....[28]

The events leading to the partition of the subcontinent must be seen against this background. Pakistanis derive from it the justification of their action and policy. In the face of inhuman difficulties and almost insurmountable obstacles and with much bloodshed and misery the majority of Indian Muslims have set up their own state, and it is now necessary to review their attempt to frame a constitution expressing their national identity as Muslims.

It is only natural that a student of Islam who comes from Pakistan to India and meets Muslims who have remained in what they regard as their homeland from conviction and design or from sheer physical necessity will encounter diametrically opposed views and opinions on the tragedy of partition. He will do well to take their views seriously and accept their *bona fides* with the same respect as that of their brothers in Pakistan. Men and women of honour and integrity look upon the Indo-Pakistan subcontinent as their home and that of countless generations of their ancestors throughout the ages. Islam has been a great power and spiritual force—alongside Hinduism and to a much smaller extent Christianity—in the common homeland for so long that even the substitution of "medieval" for "Muslim" India, quite apart from forty million Muslims living today in the Indian Union, cannot blot out history. Leading thinkers and statesmen, scholars and scientists together with millions of ordinary, humble folk have made their decision and choice. Are we outsiders to say—even if we knew all the reasons and could objectively weigh the pros and cons—the Pakistanis or the Indians or both are right or wrong? Those Muslims who have opted for India are in a sense hostages to fortune as recurring communal clashes show even if such clashes are isolated and deplored by the leadership. The human situation is often tragic, never easy, and we should respect how human beings like ourselves cope with their problems and try to carve out for themselves and their families meaningful lives in changed circumstances, at least as far as Islam is concerned. Their concept of and attitude to Islam is bound to have changed or is in process of undergoing transformation. This may be of more than local significance in the end. A little will be said on this from observation, later.

THE BATTLE FOR A CONSTITUTION IN PAKISTAN

But first we shall turn to Pakistan and examine how the Muslim nation has been engaged in giving itself a constitution which expresses its ideals and intentions, on the basis of previous experience as a minority in danger—so they are convinced—of being swamped by an alien majority with whom they shared for centuries a common homeland and a good many things as well. By their formation of a separate homeland for Muslims in Pakistan they achieved freedom from minority status with all that means or might have in store for them. While this must not be belittled, it must be supplemented by something more positive than such mere freedom. This complement is provided by Islam: Pakistanis want to live their lives as Muslims; they do not only want to be sole masters of their destiny and have unhindered opportunities in careers of their own choice. On their own in their own state they must assert their identity or, rather, after long stagnation for reasons of inner decay and foreign domination they have to rediscover their individual and social identity as a separate Muslim nation.

Here is the key to the importance—out of all proportion compared with the tremendous problems of sheer physical survival and development—of the constitutional issue. Religion has become an ideology and this at a time when religion is at bay (as many of us think) and has to contend with new, dynamic political ideologies which have little use for traditions such as Islam has created and in its formative phase developed. Many of these traditions were turned into customs out of keeping with social and cultural change, quite apart from the stark fact that the solid basis of faith is today largely weak or lacking without which Islam as a way of life is unthinkable and unworkable. There can be little doubt that Islamic "ideology" is only intelligible against the background of pre-independence Muslim–Hindu relations and the medieval caliphate which gave rise to political theology. Two hostile camps organised themselves with divergent, even incompatible political ideologies, for, as stated in Part I, ideology belongs to the realm of contemporary politics and can only partially be applied to Islam as a political and religious unity expressed in a state-law. The Muslim political leaders, with the exception of Maulana Muhammad Ali and Maulana Shabbir Ahmad Usmani (Maulana Abul A'lā Maudūdī was, as already stated, against a separate Muslim nation and state before partition) had no intention of setting up an Islamic state properly so-called. Yet they could not prevent religion from assuming growing importance among their followers as among the Hindus, which is why it inevitably coloured their political ideology. To that extent, religion also played a part in official thinking. The issue is rather confused because the intelligentsia in politics and the professions use the term "ideology" in the contemporary political sense, wanting a modern national state based on Islamic ideology, while the orthodox and liberal or "modernist" advocates of an Islamic state are determined to make Pakistan Islamic in character and in law, either the *Sharī'a* or a modern law in conformity with Qur'an (and Sunna).

Political nationalism is, as we saw, only the prelude to independence and statehood, it cannot provide the "ideology" on which a nation-state can be patterned and built. If nationalism had been sufficient not only the educated leaders but also the Muslim and Hindu masses could have found in the nationalist struggle that unity which would have carried them forward into a United India. This was, after all, the dream of Sayyid Ahmad Khan, Mohammad Ali Jinnah, Maulana Muhammad Ali in the Muslim camp and of Zakir Husain and Maulana Abul Kalām Āzād in the Indian nationalist camp, and of many others. Muslim–Hindu harmony and common endeavour for a free, united India as the result of the

Lucknow Pact in 1916 did not last long. Jinnah's words at the League session at Lucknow were true, yet utopian: "Towards the Hindus our attitude should be of good-will and brotherly feelings. Co-operation in the cause of our motherland should be our guiding principle. India's real progress can only be achieved by a true understanding and harmonious relations between the two great sister communities...."[29] By skilful diplomacy and compromise the leaders can agree on action, but it is the willingness of their followers which alone can realise it. As the subsequent history leading to separation shows, reasonableness was defeated by emotionalism, suspicion and other imponderables. By 1939 Jinnah blamed the high command of the National Congress, in his appeal to observe 22 December as the "Day of Deliverance" (from the Congress Ministry) as "primarily responsible for the wrongs that have been done to the Musalmans and other minorities". A resolution deplored that they

> have done their best to flout Muslim opinion, to destroy Muslim culture, and have interfered with their religious and social life, and trampled upon their economic and political rights; (and) that in matters of differences and disputes the Congress Ministry invariably have sided with, supported and advanced the cause of the Hindus in total disregard and to the total prejudice of Muslim interests....[30]

Jinnah had started as a nationalist in pursuit of an Indian Dominion united by Hindu–Muslim friendship and co-operation. Force of circumstance made him demand a separate Muslim homeland in 1940. To win mass support and recognition he had to bring Islam into his programme: the League fought for Muslim religion and culture. A separate state was proclaimed to be the only way out to safeguard Muslim interests and to preserve their distinct way of life. This state was to be Pakistan.

It is likely that little, if any, attention was paid to the nature and meaning of such a state for the Muslims of India before Pakistan came into existence, if we are permitted to judge from the debates of the Constituent Assembly of Pakistan. We must even go further and say that, with the exception of Maulana Maudūdī and his supporters, no politically organised body of opinion existed in 1960–1 in that country. Discussions with many members of the professions, including those who had served in the Indian Civil Service before partition, in the universities and with men and women in other spheres made me aware of widespread confusion and vagueness. These are largely due to disagreement on fundamentals.

It must, naturally, be stressed again and again that to keep Pakistan alive and its two disparate parts of West and East Pakistan together, to establish an ordered life and administration out of the chaos in the wake of partition, and to create an economy strong enough to secure political stability was—and still largely is—the paramount need of the hour. In this respect the Pakistanis have done a great deal and have achieved much of permanence and basic soundness. This is no mean feat, and testifies to the energy and enthusiasm with which they threw themselves into a task the magnitude of which they could hardly have envisaged and for which they could not prepare systematically, either physically or mentally. They had little guidance apart from the Government of India Act, 1935, and a very limited experience most of which was not gained in the highest grades of the Indian Civil Service. Moreover, meagre resources hampered their often heroic efforts. It is, therefore, not surprising that the initial enthusiasm gradually petered out and gave way to at least political, if not more general, lethargy. It would not be fair to expect the crystallisation of a clear "ideology" or perhaps rather the transformation of a predominantly pre-partition political ideology which had arisen from a practical situation—communalism—into a positive, nation-building ideal based on the one common factor: Islam.

ISLAMIC OR MODERN NATIONAL STATE?

It is difficult to decide whether the vagaries of the process of framing a workable constitution are due to the so-called Islamic ideology being open to as many different interpretations as movements, parties and people use the term, almost like a magic wand, or to a more deep-rooted disagreement about the aims and objects of an independent Muslim state and nation in the subcontinent which has produced this ambiguous ideology. As the Report on the Punjab Disturbances of 1953[31] shows, there was—and undoubtedly still is—by no means even broad unanimity on what constitutes a Muslim and what is Islam. To my mind, it is not so much the failure of the parliamentary system as such—whether it is suited to Pakistan or not—nor the failure of the politicians to make it work, which disillusioned the intelligentsia and discouraged the drive and energy of the new nation, as this lack of spiritual guidance. For Islam must play a part in the life of Pakistan, and, because of its origin and the reasons for it in pre-partition India, it must give purpose and significance to the Muslims. Overshadowing the fight for physical survival and political progress is the question we have treated in the first part of this book: an Islamic or a Muslim state, a state based upon the law of Islam or a modern national state based on contemporary law, be it a law entirely adapted from Western codes, or a law, partly Western, partly Islamic (traditional or modernised).

What we find reflected of this conflict in the parliamentary debates we encounter no less outside Parliament. Nor were the question solved and the issue closed with the constitution of 1956, nor even with that of 1962. There are forces pitted against each other quite irrespective of the tribunal before which they engage in combat: a National Assembly or a Commission to ascertain views which are then reported, submitted to the president and taken into consideration in the constitution he promulgated.[32] In short, Islam is a live issue pervading the short history of this state and acting as a constant irritant. Islam not only concerns the Muslim majority, it is also of vital importance to the minorities, chiefly the Hindus numbering over twelve millions. The issue of an Islamic state has naturally agitated their minds as is already clear from the debates about a constitution in the National Assembly. In those days there were chiefly two parties, the Muslim League representing the Muslim majority, and the Congress party. The minority problem at once highlighted the fundamental question: What is Islam? If Islam were but a religion, the Hindus and Christians of Pakistan would simply be religious minorities. But if Islam is not only a religious and political unity, but an ideology, a religious or a political ideology or both in one, the position of a religious minority must be different because an ideological state demands that all its citizens accept and work for its ideology. How can a Hindu accept an Islamic ideology? If he cannot subscribe to it what will be his position as a citizen? Yet the decision not only depends on him; it lies rather with the Muslim majority. Will they accept a non-Muslim without reservation? If they do not, how does the equality granted to every Pakistani citizen in theory work out in practice? Is second-class citizenship permissible under the terms of the United Nations Charter of Human Rights, and if not how can a state discriminating between one class of citizens and another be and remain a member of the United Nations? To put these questions already shows the issues involved in all their complexity.

In the case of Pakistan the situation is even more complicated by the fact that Hindus are not, strictly speaking, *d̲immīs*; only the *ahl al-kitāb*, that is, Jews, Christians and Zoroastrians, are accorded protection. But Pakistan as a modern state accords full equality to its Hindu millions in its constitution; are they, then, a political or a religious minority? We see that by looking at the minorities in Pakistan we can obtain some indication as to the character of the state, in addition to other, more specific features.

We have considered earlier the case for an Islamic state made out by Abul A'lā Maudūdī and Muhammad Asad. In a different, less strict, sense Muhammad Iqbal and Ghulam A. Parwez, each in their own way, advocate an Islamic state. Iqbal stands in the catholic tradition of Islamic jurisprudence and stresses the importance and power of *ijmā'* (consensus) and, closely linked with it, *ijtihād*, while Parwez is much more radical in his recognition of the Qur'an alone, and only that part of the Sunna which is in complete agreement with the Qur'an, as legitimate sources of law. Both Iqbal's and Parwez's views are represented in the debates, and we must briefly discuss them here.[33] Iqbal wants to see the idea of *ijmā'* applied in a Legislature and thinks this feasible in view of the impact "of new world forces and the political experience of European nations". He holds that "the transfer of the power of Ijtihad from individual representatives of schools to a Muslim legislative assembly...is the only possible form Ijma can take in modern times...in this way alone can we stir into activity the dormant spirit of life in our legal system, and give it an evolutionary outlook". His modernist recognition of evolution is, however, tempered with his orthodox view that "the Ulema should form a vital part of a Muslim legislative assembly helping and guiding free discussion on questions relating to law. The only effective remedy for the possibilities of erroneous interpretations is to reform the present system of legal education in Mohammedan countries, to extend its sphere, and to combine it with an intelligent study of modern jurisprudence."

His views about legal education have been taken up by Abul A'lā Maudūdī in his projected law college.[34] According to Iqbal, the "closing of the door of Ijtihad is pure fiction...if some of the later doctors (of law) have upheld this fiction, modern Islam is not bound by this voluntary surrender of intellectual independence... equipped with penetrative thought and fresh experience the world of Islam should courageously proceed to the work of reconstruction before them". For him, reconstruction is more than "mere adjustment to modern conditions of life". If it were nothing else, the imitation of Europe would be the answer to the Muslims' problems. For Iqbal holds that Europe is in decline because its idealism, grounded in pure reason, cannot kindle that enthusiasm and conviction which only revelation can give to man's striving. We may not agree with him, but this is his innermost conviction when he writes:

> ...Europe today is the greatest hindrance in the way of man's ethical advancement. The Muslim, on the other hand, is in possession of these ultimate ideas on the basis of a revelation...and in view of the basic idea of Islam that there can be no further revelation binding on man, we ought to be spiritually one of the most emancipated peoples on earth.... Let the Muslim of today...reconstruct his social life in the light of ultimate principles, and evolve, out of the hitherto partially revealed purpose of Islam, that spiritual democracy which is the ultimate aim of Islam.[35]

It would be easy to point out that these opinions are based on misunderstanding and hostility to everything European. Instead, we ought to realise that Western domination as experienced by Muslims in India (and elsewhere) has not only given them a distorted notion of European thought, but has also rekindled their interest in and enthusiasm for the fundamental values of Islam. We may detect in these and similar utterances by leading Muslims a certain naïve romanticism and a utopian element. What matters spiritually is that out of the understandable reaction to Western domination there can come a revival which would benefit not only the Muslims, provided only the Muslims could agree on the right way to revitalise Islam and apply its principles not only in paper constitutions, but in social and individual life in their independent modern states. Nor must we overlook that in Iqbal's case his judgements on Europe are less important than his positive philosophy: the attainment of man's true self through religion, that is, naturally for him, Islam. Classical Islam, centred in the Qur'an, is a dynamic faith and social system. Iqbal justifies "the immutability of socially harmless rules relating to eating, drinking, purity or impurity" as making for inwardness and social cohesion—in other words, Iqbal was not prepared in this matter any more than in any other basic legal injunction to depart from the obligatory legal norm. Yet he does not endorse the view of the *'ulamā* that the orthodox schools of Islamic law have reached finality in their interpretations. No, he admits that

> since things have changed and the world of Islam is to-day confronted and affected by new forces set free by the extraordinary development of human thought in all its directions, I see no reason why this attitude should be maintained any longer.... The claim of the present generation of Muslim liberals to re-interpret the foundational legal principles, in the light of their own experience and the altered conditions of social life, is, in my opinion, perfectly justified. The teaching of the Quran that life is a process of progressive creation necessitates that each generation, guided but unhampered by the work of its predecessors, should be permitted to solve its own problems.[36]

Yet a few lines further, Iqbal defends the laws governing personal status (marriage, divorce, inheritance), quoting from the Qur'an: "And for women are rights over men similar to those for men over women."

The foregoing quotations show clearly the difficulties of a believer at a time of crisis and transition when attitudes must undergo change and the scale of values must be reassessed and rearranged. To say that here are contradictions and ambiguities would be too easy a way out of a real predicament which is by no means confined to Islam. These difficulties help us to understand why drafting a constitution—and not only in Pakistan—as an ideal to achieve and a guide for the direction of state and nation can be such a complicated business. The advocates of a strictly orthodox Islamic state and those of a modern lay state find it easy to state their views with precision and to press their demands. The majority occupies many in-between positions which are much more difficult to define and to defend.

G. A. Parwez, who by the usual nomenclature would have to be described as a "modernist", speaks for many who want a positive application of Islamic principles in an Islamic form blended with contemporary forms of expression. In principle, he adopts a position similar to that of Muhammad Asad in that he would go back to the Qur'an as the only source of true, authentic Islam. A follower of Iqbal in his stress on the dynamism of Islam and of Sayyid Ahmad Khan in his rational interpretation of the Qur'an, Parwez rejects everything except the Qur'an. He calls the laws based on the immutable principles of the Qur'an "bye-laws". The Legislature must decide them by a majority of its members among whom should be some *'ulamā* as well as non-Muslims. The Legislature represents, for him, the *umma* of the present age which differs from its predecessors in the same way as our age differs from bygone ages. Hence the majority of the Legislature are laymen, not learned like the *'ulamā* who as members must have an opportunity to argue their case on the basis of the *Sharī'a*. G. A. Parwez only recognises that part of the Sunna which is in agreement with the Qur'an. Most of the Sunna goes back not to the prophet, but to others who invented *Ḥadīth* in order to bolster up laws made by their generation. He founded a paper *True Islam* to propagate his views against the *'ulamā* who oppose a national state. He did not found a party, but has many followers among the intelligentsia and hopes to win over the masses by education, the key to an Islamic state of Pakistan. He envisages full democracy for Pakistan with a bi-cameral system: a lower house based on universal suffrage and an upper house of the intelligentsia. But as far as I can gather from information received, G. A. Parwez envisages—in the sense of *shūrā*—Parliament largely as a place of discussion and consultation, though this must include the power to pass legislation, his "bye-laws" (as already mentioned). He wants the Supreme Court to act as an appeal court against the violation of Qur'anic principles in legislation. Muhammad Asad holds the same view.

While maintaining the biological, natural difference between the sexes, he would accord woman full equality of opportunity in all professions and callings, including politics. For the Qur'an, he avers, draws no distinction between male and female believers.

He would impose *jizya* on non-Muslims as a kind of tax

analogous to, but in contrast with, *zakāt* (an obligation on all Muslims) which should amount to their entire surplus.

His idealism stands out clearly, so does a certain lack of historical sense in his acceptance—natural in a believer—of the Qur'an and the Sunna clearly attributable to the prophet as actual history, the history of true Islam. But this criticism is naturally Western and applicable to the Qur'an as much as to any other document. A believer does not as a rule acknowledge that the Qur'an may contain injunctions which are time-bound. Yet there are other equally pious and devout Muslims who consider the Qur'anic punishment for theft (the loss of a limb, in the first instance the hand) as inapplicable in our time.

CONSTITUTIONAL DEBATES

But before we consider views and opinions of individuals we must follow the discussion of the constitution in the Constituent Assembly in connection with the "Objectives Resolution" of 1949 which was later embodied in the First Constitution of 1956. In the words of the prime minister Liaqat Ali Khan it contained the basic principles of the constitution to be framed. The relevant passages are:

Whereas sovereignty over the entire universe belongs to God Almighty alone, and the authority which He has delegated to the State of Pakistan through its people for being exercised within the limits prescribed by Him is a sacred trust; This Constituent Assembly representing the people of Pakistan resolves to frame a constitution for the sovereign independent State of Pakistan; Wherein the State shall exercise its power and authority through the chosen representatives of the people; Wherein the principles of democracy, freedom, equality, tolerance and social justice, as enunciated by Islam shall be fully observed; Wherein the Muslims shall be enabled to order their lives in the individual and collective spheres in accord with the teaching and requirements of Islam as set out in the Holy Quran and the Sunna; Wherein adequate provision shall be made for the minorities freely to profess and practise their religions and develop their cultures;...Wherein shall be guaranteed fundamental rights including equality of status, of opportunity and before law, social, economic and political justice, and freedom of thought, expression, belief, faith, worship and association, subject to law and public morality; Wherein adequate provision shall be made to safeguard the legitimate interests of minorities and backward and depressed classes; Wherein the independence of the judiciary shall be fully secured....[37]

This declaration of constitutional principles was passed against the votes of the Hindu minority. It satisfied the orthodox as well as the modernist Muslims, the traditionalists and the Westernisers. What is its real meaning in terms of Islamic political thought? It clearly distinguishes between sovereignty and authority, a sound distinction from the point of view of political science. God's sovereignty is supreme and undivided; He only delegates authority to the state through its people; an authority, moreover, which is limited. There is here no popular sovereignty, and taking the resolution at its face value the student of Islam will read hidden behind "the limits prescribed by Him" the prescriptions of Islamic law, the *Sharī'a*, that is, God's law, and everything man has authority to do must be in accord with it. Maulana Shabbir Ahmad Usmani, one of the *'ulamā* of Deoband, clearly implied this when he saw in the phrase "within the limits prescribed by Him" "the fundamental difference between an Islamic State and a secular materialistic State".[38]

It is difficult to see how the assertion of the sovereignty of God can be reconciled with the next paragraph of the resolution (which speaks of the "sovereign independent State of Pakistan") except by the assumption that the latter expression is a technical term taken over from Western constitutions by those who drafted the resolution in an attempt to please both sides.

The third paragraph no less than the first aroused suspicion and opposition in Hindu quarters. B. K. Datta of the Congress party objected to the intermingling of religion and politics which, he claimed, "belong to two different regions of the mind". He further objected to the qualification of "democracy...and social justice" by the phrase "as enunciated by Islam" since it created "...a ruling race, the patricians of Pakistan, and condemned the minorities to an inferior status. The nation would remain communally divided into two houses, the minorities tasting neither democracy, nor freedom, nor equality, nor social justice, but being merely tolerated...."

Evidently, the non-Muslims were not satisfied with the assurances of the prime minister and of the foreign minister (Mohammed

Zafrullah Khan) that they would be admitted to service in the government and administration of Pakistan as equals. In our context, the statement of M. Zafrullah Khan is worthy of note since it comes from a devout and learned Aḥmadī:

The conception that religion and politics occupy distinct spheres which should not be permitted to overlap is born of failure to grasp the full significance of religion.... Its function is to establish and maintain the most harmonious relationship between man and his Maker on the one hand and between man and man in all aspects of their relationship on the other. Politics is only one aspect of the relationship between man and man. Those who seek to draw a distinction between the sphere of religion and the sphere of politics as mutually exclusive, put too narrow a construction upon the functions of religion....

Yet one can sympathise with the representatives of the minorities in their apprehension lest an "ideological" state might relegate them to the status of second-class citizens who would be discriminated against. Maulana Shabbir Ahmad Usmani spoke in favour of an Islamic state—the Objectives Resolution envisaged such a state in the opinion of the *'ulamā*—and defined it thus:

The Islamic State means a State which is run on the exalted and excellent principles of Islam...it can only be run by those who believe in those principles. People who do not subscribe to those ideas may have a place in the administrative machinery of the State but they cannot be entrusted with the responsibility of framing the general policy of the State or dealing with matters vital to its safety and integrity.

If these principles were confined to Islam and not the common possession of the civilised world today, one might perhaps share the non-Muslims' apprehensions. On the other hand, it is difficult to see how the learned Maulana Usmani can hold them exclusive to Islam and exclude non-Muslims from participation in the running of the state on an equal footing, as long as Islamic principles only and not their expression in the *Sharī'a* as the only valid form are concerned. If we consider a famous speech of Mohammad Ali Jinnah's, it will become clear that much of the confusion between an Islamic and a modern national state is due to loose thinking and imprecise wording. For it seems difficult to claim the architect of Pakistan as an advocate of an Islamic state as we have defined it—

with ample quotations—in the first part. These are the Qaid-i-Azam's words, spoken in the Constituent Assembly in 1947:

If you work in co-operation, forgetting the past, burying the hatchet, you are bound to succeed, if you change your past and work together in a spirit that everyone of you, no matter to what community he belongs, is first,...second and last a citizen of this State with equal rights, privileges and obligations, there will be no end to the progress you will make...we are starting with this fundamental principle that we are all citizens and equal citizens of one State. You may belong to any religion or creed or caste—that has nothing to do with the business of the State. ...I think we should keep that in front as our ideal and you will find that in course of time Hindus would cease to be Hindus and Muslims would cease to be Muslims, not in the religious sense because that is the personal faith of each individual, but in the political sense as citizens of the State.[39]

Surely, this sane but idealistic tone and opinion belong to a statesman who has no intention of establishing an Islamic state, but a modern national state on the principles of equality and—as is clear from other of his speeches—social justice as taught by Islam. Principles are one thing, applied traditional law based on these principles something different. However, the confusion has arisen because different people mean different things by the same words they use. G. W. Choudhury discusses this question in his *Constitutional Development in Pakistan* and significantly states that "while, at least until 1954, it was generally agreed that Pakistan should aim at becoming an Islamic State, there was no agreement as to the meaning of the term 'Islamic State'".[40] He contrasts the views of the *'ulamā* with those of the Qaid-i-Azam whom he quotes as saying: "In any case Pakistan is not going to be a Theocratic State to be ruled by priests with a divine mission. We have many non-Muslims, Hindus, Christians and Parsis, but they are all Pakistanis. They will enjoy the same rights and privileges as any other citizens and will play their rightful part in the affairs of Pakistan." The first governor-general of Pakistan was echoed by its first prime minister, who stated, when presenting the Objectives Resolution, that

the ideals that prompted the demand for Pakistan should form the cornerstone of the State. The investment of power in the people eliminated any danger of the establishment of a theocracy....If there are any who still use the word "theocracy" in the same breath as the polity of Pakistan, they are either labouring under a grave misapprehension or indulging in mischievous propaganda. When we use the word "democracy" in the Islamic sense, it pervades all aspects of our life. It relates to our system of government and to our society with equal validity because one of the greatest contributions of Islam has been the equality of all men.[41]

Yet it is not cynicism, but the recognition of *Realpolitik*, which prompts us to add that all too often some men are more equal than others. To arrive at a balanced view, we must weigh the opinions expressed in public carefully and, moreover, remember that no matter how enlightened and tolerant the leading circles (ministers, administrators, members of the Constituent Assembly, university teachers and judges) are, it is the ordinary citizens whose experience in daily contact shows how far equality is possible and in existence in the prevailing atmosphere.

The debate about the Islamic character of the constitution went on unabated over the next years as is reflected in several reports. First, the Interim Report on Fundamental Rights, accepted in 1950, lists among these the prohibition of discrimination on grounds of religion, race and caste, and lays down that every duly qualified citizen of Pakistan is eligible for state service, women as well as men. (Exception was only made for the head of state who must be a male Muslim; this was objected to by some Hindu representatives.) Another fundamental principle was freedom of conscience and the free exercise of religion, which includes the right to propaganda. Every denomination is permitted to manage its own affairs, and religious instruction in educational establishments is obligatory on members of that community only. No citizen can be forced to pay taxes for any religion other than his own.

This is clearly in accord with modern concepts, but not strictly with classical Islamic doctrine which allows freedom of religion to *ahl al-kitāb*, but not the propagation of any faith other than Islam and, at least in theory, places certain restrictions on the size, height and number of churches and synagogues and forbids the erection of new places of worship. Agitation and violence against the Aḥmadīya sect and the attempt to exclude it from the *umma* of Islam show that orthodox intolerance against any deviation is difficult to eradicate. But the same does not necessarily apply to other faiths.

The next document of considerable bearing on our problem is the Report of the Basic Principles Committee which was set up by the Constituent Assembly. It appointed several subcommittees, among them the "Board of *Ta'līmat-i-Islamīa*" "to advise on matters arising out of the Objectives Resolution and on such matters as may be referred to them by the various Sub-Committees".[42] As was to be expected of *'ulamā* the board's advice on the person and qualifications of the head of state represents the classical theory of the *Khilāfa* with the *ahl al-'aqd wa-l-ḥāll* electing the head of state and the *'ahd* (contract) between him and the people. The board were willing to transfer the functions of the *ahl al-'aqd wa-l-ḥāll* to the Legislative Assembly, provided its members were the most learned and pious the people could elect as their representatives. The board insisted on a Committee of Experts to examine all laws in relation to the *Sharī'a*. Legislation was limited to matters not provided for in the *Sharī'a*, and the head of state should have a Legislative Council to advise him. Such advice would naturally be the duty of the *'ulamā*. But since *shūrā* is only consultation, the Legislative Council can only advise, and the head of state may or may not accept advice tendered. Thus, even their accommodation to modern notions of the separation of the Executive from the Legislature does not grant the substance of this separation, since the decision rests with the chief executive. The Legislature has no power.

Despite their desire to meet the wishes of the religious leaders the government and their supporters in the Constituent Assembly were not favourably inclined to the Board's recommendations, though the wording of the "Basic Principles" has a distinct Islamic connotation and emphasis. The preamble should contain the Objectives Resolution, and the "Directive Principles of State Policy" were to implement that resolution. These laid down that "Facilities should be provided for them [the Muslims] to understand what life in accordance with the Holy Quran and the Sunnah means and the teachings of the Holy Quran to the Muslims should be made compulsory". Drinking, gambling and prostitution were prohibited. *Ribā* was to be eliminated "as and when it may be possible to do so". Islamic moral standards were to be promoted and maintained; *zakāt*, *waqfs* and mosques should be properly organised. "Suitable steps should be taken for bringing the existing laws into conformity with the Islamic principles, and for the codification of such injunctions of the Holy Quran and the Sunnah as can be given legislative effect duly safeguarding, as has been enjoined by the Holy Quran and the Sunnah, the personal laws of the non-Muslims." The state "should endeavour to discourage among Muslims parochial, tribal, racial, sectarian and provincial prejudices as well as other similar un-Islamic feelings and inculcate in them the spirit to keep foremost in their minds the fundamental unity and solidarity of the Millat and the requirements of the ideology and the mission for the implementation of which Pakistan came into being".

It is, then, explicitly stated that the foregoing are guiding principles which should be applied in legislation and in the administration of the state, "but they shall not be enforceable in any court of law". Of great significance is the so-called Repugnancy Clause, long a bone of contention and fraught with grave difficulties: "No Legislature [federal or provincial] should enact any law which is repugnant to the Holy Quran and the Sunnah." It is made clear that "wherever these expressions—Holy Quran and Sunnah—occur shall mean, when applied to any sect, such interpretation thereof, as is recognised and accepted by that sect". The Supreme Court (not a board of experts, as recommended by the board of *Ta'līmat-i-Islamīa*) was given exclusive jurisdiction to determine whether or not a particular law is repugnant to the Holy Qur'an and the Sunna.

So far, both guiding principles and provisions are in accord with the principal reason advanced why the Muslims in India should have a homeland of their own where they could live as Muslims for whom Qur'an and Sunna should be the norm of their individual and collective lives. But we note that the word "ideology" is used to express in a political term the ideal: a religious ordering of the entire life of the Muslims of Pakistan. Political theology influences thinking and formulation.

The bold statement that no law must run counter to Qur'an and Sunna is, however, supplemented by an escape clause (ch. III 10(1)) which lays down that its provisions should not apply to fiscal and monetary measures, laws relating to banking, insurance, provident funds, loans and other matters affecting the existing economic, financial and credit system, except after the time and in the manner prescribed in subparagraph (2) which stipulates the appointment of a commission, after twenty-five years, which should report on the steps and stages needed to bring the exceptions named into line with the principal provision. The next paragraph suggests that an organisation should be set up "for making the teachings of Islam known to the people, and for '*Amr-bil-maruf*' and '*Nahi-anil-munkar*'".[43]

The name of the state should be "the Islamic Republic of Pakistan". This designation has given rise to conflicting interpretations: was Pakistan to be an Islamic state based on the *Sharīʿa* or a modern national state based on Islamic principles?

That the head of state should swear "in the name of Allah That I will faithfully discharge...and that in my public and personal life, I will endeavour to fulfil the obligations and duties enjoined by Islam" is to be expected after the foregoing. This is also demanded of Muslim ministers and members of the Federal and Provincial Legislatures. Non-Muslims are required to take an oath wherever required "either in the name of Allah or should make an affirmation".

Among the "Fundamental Rights of Citizens of Pakistan" we note that:

> Every duly qualified citizen shall be eligible to appointment in the service of the State irrespective of religion, race, caste, sex, descent or place of birth...provided further that it shall be lawful to prescribe that only a person belonging to a particular religion or denomination shall be eligible to hold office in connection with any religious or denominational institution or governing body thereof.

Freedom of conscience and the right to profess and propagate religion are guaranteed, subject to public order and morality. Notably, Pakistan has outlawed untouchability as "inconsistent with human dignity". Its practice is unlawful and an offence.

The committee had a difficult task which it tried to discharge so that conflicting views and interests could be given due consideration and be reconciled in an agreed version to be placed before the Constituent Assembly. The "Islamic Republic of Pakistan" was to be an "ideological" state. This ideology was defined as "principles of democracy, freedom, equality, tolerance and social justice as enunciated by Islam shall be fully observed". It is to be noted that there is no mention of an Islamic state nor of religious principles and law. On the face of it, everybody should be able to subscribe to this programme, since these principles are, to repeat, the common possession or at least aspiration of the whole civilised world. Yet one can argue that the phrase "as enunciated by Islam" only makes sense if the law of the state embodies and realises these lofty principles. Here the real problem starts: is this law to be in strict accord with Qur'an and Sunna as interpreted in the *Sharī'a* or are Qur'an and Sunna only to serve as the guide to a new interpretation in the form of a new, modern law? A subsidiary question is no less important: Who is to decide—the *'ulamā* or a modern legislature consisting largely of laymen? We shall come back to this problem.

The Report of the Basic Principles Committee was issued in 1952 and debated at length in the Constituent Assembly before being passed in 1954. This debate more than echoes the earlier one on the Objectives Resolution, not least because the actual constitution was to be agreed upon. Hindu speakers attacked the Islamic character of the constitution, and B. K. Datta reminded members that Mohammad Ali Jinnah had seen no need for an Objectives Resolution. He claimed that the new provisions "go very far beyond it and totally negative its spirit". Again, he insisted that a constitution had to be either Islamic or parliamentary, not both at the same time. In his support he cited Muslim political thinkers of the ninth to twelfth centuries who, he mistakenly claimed, tended towards the idea of the sovereignty of the people in opposition to the ideal of the Islamic state. Moreover, he is wrong in attributing to Al-Ghazālī the definition of political science as dealing "with the proper order for the State affairs of the mundane category" as applying to Islam. It is simply an echo of Plato and Aristotle, and the Islamic polity does not fall into this category. In his view, the sovereignty of God and the sovereignty of the people are—rightly—irreconcilable, and there is force in his taunt that the Committee "undertook the task, abandoned a thousand years ago as absurd, of reconciling two irreconcilable principles". Not distinguishing between sovereignty and authority—in the Objectives Resolution delegated by God to the people—B. K. Datta understands that resolution to give sovereignty over the state of Pakistan to its people. He says:

Is the God of our conception incapable of working through the will of the chosen representatives of the people of Pakistan? If not, then why make God or His words, or His special agents intervene at every stage of our state affairs? Why then empower the Third House...the Mullah House, which is, to boot, a nominated House, to interfere in matters of legislation and curtail popular sovereignty...? The Committee is apparently unable to place reliance on the good sense of the collective body to exercise check and supervision over the sovereign Parliament and even goes to the absurdity of allowing a single Muslim member, if he so chooses, to obstruct and hold up every legislation for some time at least.

The contrast between the medievalism (or, from the orthodox point of view, timelessness) of the *'ulamā* under the leadership of Maulana Sayyid Sulaiman Nadwi (the head of the *Nadwat-al-'ulamā* at Lucknow) and Mufti Muhammad Shafi, and the contemporary advocate of parliamentary democracy, could not be expressed more clearly; nor could one have put the finger more pointedly on the inconsistencies of a compromise solution.

B. K. Datta also doubted how the proposal "for bringing the existing laws into conformity with the Islamic principles" could be implemented in view of different interpretations of the Qur'an by different Muslim sects.

How [he says] will the body that will be entrusted to redraft the laws of the country—or for that matter the body that will be attached to the Head of State—be distributed among the sects? If four or five *'ulamā* reshape the existing laws so as to make them conform to the *Sharī'a* according to their light, where is the guarantee that four hundred or five hundred other Maulanas, Maulvis and Mullahs will not declare the favoured four or five infidels?...Democracy and religiosity cannot go hand in hand. Democracy, as we all know, grows by criticism. But bring in religion and you make people intolerant of diversity of views.

He opposed the provision that the head of state must be a Muslim, since he would be that in any case, seeing that the Muslims are in a majority of more than six to one over the minorities. Looking at other Muslim countries, he quotes—in support of his plea to separate politics from religion—General Neguib's reply to the demand that the new constitution of Egypt should be based on Islamic principles: "Religion is for the individual, but country for all. Cross and Crescent will shine together in the Egyptian sky."

Another opponent of the Islamic character of the proposed constitution, R. K. Chakravarty, complained that it was "Islamic so far as convenient to the makers and, thus, neither thoroughly Islamic nor thoroughly modern". He charged the committee with creating "six classes of citizens instead of one" and by introducing separate electorates making one of them a perpetual majority. Other Hindu speakers approved of the Islamic constitution. Several Muslims were sharply critical of the report, calling it "hypocrisy" and a "denial of Islam" since it broke "a treaty with the minorities" by proposing separate electorates. Mian Iftikharuddin, dissenting Muslim member of the Basic Principles Committee, thought that the report betrayed both Muslim and minorities' interests "by the parochialism of the proposed constitution" and opposed the tribunal of *'ulamā* saying: "the only tribunal before which we can go—however fallacious, however backward—is the tribunal of the people". In 1949, during the debate on the Objectives Resolution, he was against the Islamic character of it since he opposed communalism and held that "the fight in this country is not going to be between Hindus and Muslims. The battle in time to come will be between Hindu-have-nots and Muslim-have-nots on the one hand and Muslim and Hindu upper and middle classes on the other."

On the paragraph guaranteeing freedom of conscience and religion, Mahmud Husain made an interesting comment on the Muslim majority and the non-Muslim minorities: "We possess common nationality, which is a legal concept, but we are not the same nation, which is a sociological concept. We are *not* one nation, and yet we are citizens of the same State."[44]

Another noteworthy feature of the debate is the part played by the two women members. Both Begum Shah Nawaz and Begum Ikramullah pleaded for the application of the principle of *ijtihād*, and the latter wanted to see a reform of the law on marriage and divorce: polygamy should be restricted and divorce made more difficult (there had been a large increase in divorce since partition) and women should be allowed to inherit their father's entire property in the absence of sons. She pleaded that there was nothing irreligious or un-Islamic in such a reform. In fact,

President Ayub Khan issued in 1961 an ordinance restricting polygamy and regulating divorce as the result of pressure by APWA (All Pakistan Women's Association) which led to the appointment of a commission in 1955 to make recommendations to the president.[45]

On behalf of the government, the law minister, A. K. Brohi, answered some of the criticisms levelled against the report. He asserted that the "Directive Principles" were more than "pious wishes"; they represented the programme of the government but were not legally binding. He extolled Islam as "not a religion among religions, but the one final, universal religion...all that is good and great in the twentieth century derives its power and inspiration from what is contained in the message of God delivered to His Prophet thirteen centuries ago". He held that non-Muslims need not believe that God exercised the sovereignty of the state; the law for them was but the product of the Constituent Assembly. A minority had no choice anyhow, and it may be doubted whether his argument was very convincing and helpful. He accepted an amendment to refer adjudication to the Supreme Court instead of a Mullah Board in relation to the Repugnancy Clause. He deplored the absence of any attempt by reputable experts in Muslim law to present to the world a treatise "showing how we are going to deal with the specific concrete problems of law: I mean both domestic and international law. Such a study would be relevant to the current inquiries about the punishment of crime, the position of women, the doctrine of *riba* and similar matters...it is our fault that we have not been able to give a clear enunciation of the Islamic Law." It is true that the *'ulamā* were preoccupied with the principles and submitted in 1951 a twenty-two point demand to the Basic Principles Committee about an Islamic state in conformity with the *Sharī'a*.

He made the further point that the preamble was not substantive law: constitutional law only supplied "the *mode* and the *manner* in which the sovereign power within the State could be distributed". The use of the term "sovereign power" is significant, so is that of the terms "Muslim Law" and "Muslim state" in his answer to a question about the place of Hindu personal law under an Islamic constitution: "The Muslim law of a Muslim State is not antipathetic to, is not incompatible with the due expression of the personal law of the non-Muslims in a Muslim State." This is good orthodox doctrine, and the *'ulamā* make this point with utmost clarity in their twenty-two basic principles of an Islamic state. A. K. Brohi also made the interesting point that the constitutional framework expressed in the Basic Principles, including the preamble, had nothing to do with the Qur'an: "We do not say that everything you find here is Quranic....The ideology is Quranic, the programme is Quranic, but when we get down to the business of distributing sovereign power...we have adopted a federal form of government."[46] The *'ulamā* favoured a presidential system in which all executive power is vested in the head of state who can, naturally, delegate authority, if he likes. This comes from the classical doctrine of the *Khilāfa*. At their convention in 1953 the same group of *'ulamā* discussed and agreed on amendments to the report. Presided over by Maulana Sayyid Sulaiman Nadwi, the mind and drafting hand of Maulana Abul A'lā Maudūdī can be seen as clearly as in their 1951 suggestions. This time, they dealt with practically all aspects of the Basic Principles as adopted in 1954 by the Constituent Assembly. Those amendments affecting the Islamic character of the state must be briefly touched upon.[47]

Opposed to what they call "the system of education as obtaining during the British regime", they would substitute the clause in the Directive Principles of State Policy about teaching of the Qur'an by: "The teaching of the Holy Quran and Islamiyat be made compulsory for every Muslim and the system of education be so reformed that it may enable the Muslims to mould their lives in accord with the Holy Quran and *Sunnah*." The addition of "and Islamiyat" in the first sentence is to be found in the 1962, but not in the 1956, Constitution.[48]

They found the clause dealing with drinking, gambling and prostitution too imprecise and wanted to substitute for it the following: "Intoxicants, gambling and prostitution in all their various forms be completely prohibited through proper legislation within a maximum period of three years from the date of enforcement of the constitution." In the 1956 Constitution the formulation is: "The State shall endeavour to prevent prostitution, gambling and the taking of injurious drugs; and prevent the consumption of alcoholic liquor otherwise than for medicinal and, in the case of non-Muslims, religious purposes."[49] This has become even weaker in the 1962 Constitution: "Prostitution, Gambling and the taking of injurious drugs should be discouraged. The consumption of alcoholic liquor...should be discouraged."[50]

In their attempt to put teeth into the Islamic clauses, the *'ulamā* suggested this wording for the clause about bringing existing laws into line with Islamic principles: "Suitable steps should be taken to bring existing laws into conformity with the Holy Quran and the *Sunnah* within five years." They also clarified and amplified the proposed codification, notably by specifying that "laws regarding the personal matters of Muslims should be made in the light of the Holy Quran and the *Sunnah* as are held valid by the respective schools of thought among Muslims and the followers of one school of thought should not be bound to follow the interpretation of another, and that no such law should be made as may create obstruction in the performance of its religious rituals and duties". In trying to maintain the *Sharī'a* according to the four orthodox rites, the *'ulamā* ignore the widespread desire among orthodox Muslims today to arrive at a uniform Islamic law consisting of laws chosen from any of the four orthodox rites for their compatibility with the modern age. The *'ulamā* of Pakistan are evidently opposed to any liberalisation and modification within existing Islamic law. This clause has not been included in either of the two constitutions.

Next, they would have "the economic policy of the State based on the Islamic principles of social justice". They also suggested additions to the Directive Principles, such as: "Proper and effective arrangements should be made for the promotion of Islamic learning and culture." This has been adopted in the 1956 Constitution: "the President shall set up an organization for Islamic research and instruction in advanced studies to assist in the reconstruction of Muslim society on a truly Islamic basis."[51] The 1962 Constitution contains a similar provision, calling the organisation "Islamic Research Institute" and defining its purpose as "to undertake Islamic research and instruction in Islam". They further demanded that

> the State should ensure that in the selection, appointment and promotion of Muslim candidates and employees, Islamic character and observance of the tenets of Islam are given due consideration....In the training of the Muslim employees of the State...special arrangements for their moral and religious training and education should be made, so

that the moral standard of the state employees of Pakistan...be high enough. All facilities should be provided to the Muslim employees of the State for carrying out their religious duties and observing the tenets of Islam.

Neither constitution incorporated these nor the following demand: "The propagation of atheism and infidelity and the insulting or ridiculing of the Holy Qur'an or the *Sunnah* should be prohibited through legislation."

The group of *'ulamā* found the Repugnancy Clause too negative and proposed to add to it "and the Qur'an and *Sunnah* be the chief source of the law of the land". Nor were they satisfied with the procedure laid down in the Directive Principles for preventing legislation repugnant to Qur'an and Sunna. Such laws should be submitted to "a Board consisting of not more than five persons well versed in Islamic Laws" by the head of state. It should be noted that this board has no power of veto; it simply expresses an opinion which is neither binding on the head of state nor on the Legislature. The bill when resubmitted can—but must not—be amended. In either form it has to be passed again by a majority of members "present and voting which should include the majority of the Muslim members present and voting". The *'ulamā* wanted the Supreme Court to adjudicate in this as in other constitutional matters which were to be submitted to the Supreme Court if contravening any provision. Moreover they suggested replacing certain clauses by others of which the first would run:

To deal with constitutional objections raised under section 3 [Repugnancy Clause] against laws enacted by a legislature or other issues concerning interpretation of constitution in this behalf, there should be appointed five Ulama in the Supreme Court who, along with some judge to be nominated for the purpose by the Head of the State in consideration of his "*tadayyun and taqwa*" (religious zeal and piety) and his knowledge of Islamic law and learning, should decide whether or not the law in dispute is in conformity with the Qur'an and *Sunnah*.

Three of the *'ulamā* dissented from this proposal and favoured instead "a Board of experts of Islamic law ('*Ulama-i-Pakistan*)" to whom the matter objected to should be referred "and the Legislature should be bound by the verdict of this Board". They considered an association of five *'ulamā* with the Supreme Court merely in order to interpret the Qur'an and Sunna useless. The Constituent Assembly wrote the Repugnancy Clause into the 1956 Constitution in this form:

(1) No law shall be enacted which is repugnant to the Injunctions of Islam as laid down in the Holy Quran and Sunnah, hereinafter referred to as Injunctions of Islam, and existing law shall be brought into conformity with such Injunctions.

(2) Effect shall be given to the provisions of clause (1) only in the manner provided in clause (3).

(3) Within one year of the Constitution Day, the President shall appoint a Commission—

(*a*) to make recommendations—

(i) as to the measures for bringing existing law into conformity with the Injunctions of Islam, and

(ii) as to the stages by which such measures should be brought into effect; and

(*b*) to compile in a suitable form, for the guidance of the National and Provincial Assemblies, such Injunctions of Islam as can be given legislative effect.

The Commission shall submit its final report within five years of its appointment, and may submit any interim report earlier. The report, whether interim or final, shall be laid before the National Assembly within six months of its receipt, and the Assembly after considering the report shall enact laws in respect thereof.

(4) Nothing in this Article shall affect the personal laws of non-Muslim citizens, or their status as citizens, or any provision of the Constitution.[52]

Clause (3) makes no reference to the first part of clause (1), that is, no machinery has been devised to receive objections to any new law on grounds of repugnancy. In the Report on Basic Principles the Supreme Court was given power of adjudication, as was stated earlier. Moreover, the exemption of fiscal and monetary matters, etc., is not mentioned. The '*ulamā* took exception to this exemption and wanted the following wording substituted for that in the report: "The provisions of this chapter should apply to money bills after the expiry of a period of 5 years from the date of enforcement of the Constitution." Their reasoning was:

If the State accepts the supremacy of the dictates and commandments of Allah and His prophet, as is evident from the wording of Section 3, there is no reason why the financial matters of the State should be placed beyond the jurisdiction of Allah and His Prophet. Islam is the best guide for us in all matters. It is so in the case of financial problems too. We are not at all prepared to accept a clear vote of no-confidence against Islam in one of the Sections of our Constitution.[53]

The 1956 Constitution in fact incorporated the Objectives Resolution in its preamble and in its "Directive Principles of State Policy". It mentions among other Basic Principles of the report not enforceable in any court that: "Steps shall be taken to enable the Muslims of Pakistan individually and collectively to order their lives in accordance with the Holy Quran and Sunnah." Further recommendations concerned the teaching of the Qur'an, "to promote unity and the observance of Islamic moral standards; and to secure the proper organization of zakat, wakfs and mosques.... The State shall endeavour to eliminate *riba* as early as possible."[54] Minority rights are to be safeguarded and special care is to be shown to the backward classes and scheduled castes.

In the second schedule, under the heading "Oaths and Affirmations", the framers of the constitution adopted a secular form of words, contrary to the wishes of the *'ulamā* and to the wording in the Report of the Basic Principles Committee. The president, ministers and members of the Legislatures simply swear or affirm that they "will bear true faith and allegiance to Pakistan".[55]

The name of the state is "the Islamic Republic of Pakistan". This corresponded to the wishes of the *'ulamā* who stated in their *Amendments*: "The appelation of Islamic Republic is just to indicate that it is a Republic which is based on the principles of Islam—something which has already been specified in the Objectives Resolution, and Section 3 of thc Report too leads to the same conclusion."[56] This raises the question of the meaning and significance of the Islamic provisions of this consititution in the light of the larger question we have discussed throughout this book: what is an Islamic state?

N. Zakaria[57] says: "We in Pakistan wanted not only a democratic constitution but also an Islamic constitution....The Sovereignty of God is an unquestioned basis of our Constitution and as such the Federal and Provincial Legislatures are debarred from enacting such laws which would be contrary to the Principles of the Quran and *Sunnah*." When discussing the Islamic provisions of the constitution, he says: "Although Islam is recognised as the

State religion [*sic*!] and the Islamic provisions have a strong symbolic force for the Muslims, the Constitution is modern in character and does not make an attempt to establish a theocratic state." It would seem that the Islamic provisions are, indeed, more symbolic than real; they appeal to the strong emotional attachment of Pakistanis to Islam, but not being enforceable in law their practical influence on law and life is not easily discernible. The just discussed Repugnancy Clause seems to bear out this impression.

Maulana Sayyid Abul A'lā Maudūdī forcefully expressed after the presentation of the draft constitution how meaningless this provision was and suggested a different formulation. He claims that this article "forms the only basis on which will rest the possibility or otherwise of establishment of an Islamic Order in the country", and rightly states: "When we ponder over the procedure enumerated in Clause (3) of this Article we feel that this Clause takes away almost all that was provided for in Clause (1)." He says that in its present form it does not meet "the demand of the people for an Islamic Constitution". But while he and his followers as well as the *'ulamā* have a clear idea of what an Islamic constitution and an Islamic state should be—namely a constitution and state based not only on Islamic principles, but also on Islamic law with Qur'an and Sunna as its sole source!—the "modernists" would be content with a constitution and a state law based on Islamic principles and an Islamic ideology as defined in the Objectives Resolution. "The people" at large have an even vaguer notion, and their demand for an Islamic constitution, assumed by Maulana Maudūdī and N. Zakaria, was undoubtedly satisfied by the preamble and the Directive Principles of State Policy, of which N. Zakaria rightly says that they "are a sort of manifesto of the inspiration of the State of Pakistan and the main object of their incorporation was to set a goal for all governmental activities".[58]

Maulana Maudūdī's formulation did not find an entry into the constitution as adopted. His relevant clause (1) reads:

> No law shall be enacted which is repugnant to the injunctions, directives and the basic teachings of the Holy Qur'an and the *Sunnah* (hereinafter referred to as the Injunctions of Islam) and if any objection is raised in any legislature that a Bill or any part of it is repugnant to the Islamic Injunctions, it shall be decided upon by the majority of the Muslim members of the Assembly.

We have seen in our detailed discussion of Maulana Maudūdī's views in part I of this book that he considered the interpretation of Qur'an and Sunna by the companions and the decisions of the caliphs as authoritative and, therefore, binding on all Muslims everywhere and at all times, including our own. At the other end of the scale is G. A. Parwez who only accepts the Qur'an and that part of the Sunna which agrees with it and, presumably, rejects previous interpretations. So does Muhammad Asad. Is it surprising that successive governments of Pakistan were not in a hurry to implement the Islamic clauses of the Directive Principles as far as law and legislation are concerned?

The Liberals are certainly in a majority, but they are, naturally, divided in their attitude to and acceptance of traditional law. Says I. H. Qureshi: "It has been recognized in all Muslim countries that in many respects the mutable part of the *Shar* requires considerable overhauling, and the immutable bases need a new interpretation."[59] He insists that Islam is

> not a code of certain rigid laws or even legal concepts...but a dynamic force, a concept of life, not of law, a guidance for the springs of thought and action and not a static code of action. In other words, Islam is a live and dynamic ideology and not a dead, unprogressive and static collection of injunctions and prohibitions. It requires a new interpretation at every stage of our development and cannot be content merely with precedents and past usage. Islam does not discard precedents and traditions, but it lays emphasis upon the progressive unfolding of the creative instincts of mankind in accordance with the eternal principles defined by revelation.[60]

In the same context, he calls Islam the motive force of the polity of Pakistan and says that the prophet has given an ideology to his people.

This is typical of the modernist attitude of many Western-educated Pakistanis in the liberal professions and is so far the only attempt to bring about a synthesis between Islam freshly interpreted, and Western civilisation. It is in its attitude to Qur'an (and Sunna) near to that of G. A. Parwez and shared by many intellectuals in the civil service and the academic and legal professions. To the Western student of Islam it seems, however, that both in theory and in practice, there are fundamental obstacles to a real synthesis—in so far as it is possible—which are not sufficiently taken into account, perhaps even not recognised as existing. On the theoretical side, there is, as pointed out already, if not outright opposition then certainly considerable reluctance to apply the same historical and literary criticism to the Qur'an as are applied to the Bible in the West. The nearest one gets to this kind of criticism is in respect of the Sunna. But even G. A. Parwez appears, as far as I can judge, to take a somewhat subjective view in his acceptance of the Sunna in so far as it agrees with the Qur'an and the rejection of the bulk of *Ḥadīth.* Despite all "modernism" the basic attitude seems to be still medieval; in other words, political theology still dictates views and attitudes. It is difficult—particularly for an outsider—to be explicit in this matter, but what I have in mind is the view of a distinguished Pakistani judge with whom I had occasion to discuss this problem, that, as quoted earlier, the penalty for theft though laid down explicitly in the Qur'an was inapplicable today. This example is perhaps not entirely apt, since there is, though in very different circumstances, the precedent of the caliph Omar setting aside this penalty in time of famine, often adduced by the defenders of the *Sharī'a* as obligatory and, therefore, applicable today. This is probably one of the precedents and traditions which I. H. Qureshi would not disregard. The argument from precedent—strictly speaking—stems from an orthodox attitude which accepts tradition as the inevitable corollary of belief. What, then, about the argument from silence, the theoretical admission that what is not forbidden is permitted? This is sound as far as it goes. But to my mind the Qur'anic injunctions about the inheritance of wife and daughters—apart from a husband's gift to his wife during their married life—are not covered by either principle. While it is true that Muḥammad brought about a great improvement in the status and rights of woman compared with pre-Islamic Arabia, and that a just settlement was achieved in the conditions of the times, our own age demands complete equality for woman. How, then, can a corresponding reform of Personal Status Law in regard to woman be justified on the basis of the Qur'an?

These are some of the difficulties in the practical field on which no agreement is in sight. Yet both kinds of obstacles are only relevant against the background of religious faith; and a modern state pledged to grant fundamental rights must include among these freedom of thought and opinion which includes freedom not to believe just as much as freedom to hold beliefs different from the majority population.

The acid test—we find again—is law, and the dilemma of Muslims is a real one. That the framers of the constitution while accepting the name "Islamic Republic of Pakistan" at the behest of the *'ulamā* did not mean this to be an Islamic state whose law was Islamic law is clear from statements made by A. K. Brohi in 1952: "The problem of constitution-making in Pakistan has become complicated due to the false emotional associations that have been formed, due to what I call a wrong insistence on the slogan, viz. that the constitution of Pakistan would be based on the Islamic law." Yet replies to critics of his views led him to state: "I have never said that I do not want Islamic constitution in this country: all I have said is that having regard to the accepted notion of what constitutional law is, it is not possible to derive from the text of the Quran any clear statement as to the actual content of the constitution of any State." This is correct. Yet a further reply, "if there be any clear and direct statement in the Quran as to what our constitution should be like, then of course it has got to be followed",[61] highlights the dilemma in that the Qur'an, though acknowledged as the general guide and exemplar, does not always answer the needs of contemporary constitution-making. We must add that what A. K. Brohi said of constitutional law applies to every other sphere of Islamic law likewise, since divinely revealed law is one, indivisible and comprehensive.

It would, then, appear that those who want to apply the principle of separation of politics and religion, whether they are believers or not, at least face up to the realities of the present situation even if they are at variance with Muslim tradition. The Objectives Resolution and the Directive Principles of State Policy as passed by the Constituent Assembly in 1954 may be considered as a part of an Islamic constitution in the sense that the name of the state contains the word "Islamic" as a qualifying adjective of the Republic of Pakistan; the sovereignty of Allah and Islamic principles are stressed; it is specified that the Muslims should be enabled to live by the "teachings and requirements of Islam, as set out in the Holy Quran and the Sunnah", and it is laid down that no law, new or existing, should be repugnant to Qur'an and Sunna;

ribā should be eliminated, and drinking, gambling and prostitution prevented.

Yet what has been incorporated of these Islamic intentions and provisions in the Constitution of 1956 not only falls short of precision, but has been weakened in the non-enforceable and, what is more important, in the enforceable part in respect of the Repugnancy Clause.[62] In terms of Islamic political thought, as represented by Ibn Khaldūn, the Islamic Republic of Pakistan would in the light of this constitution resemble an Islamic *mulk* rather than the *khilāfa*. For its personal status law is *Sharī'a*-law, it professes allegiance to the principles of Qur'an and Sunna and to Islamic injunctions, but its civil and criminal law is that which existed prior to partition in India and may be likened to Ibn Khaldūn's *qawānīn siyāsīya*. Ibn Khaldūn's ideas, after all, reflect his observations and experiences of Muslim states of his own and earlier times. The constitution represents a reasonable compromise in existing circumstances. Yet it cannot be denied that it means different things to different people; traditionalists and modernists interpret it in accordance with their own views.

Why are the Islamic provisions in the 1956 Constitution weaker than in the Directive Principles of State Policy as passed by the Constituent Assembly in 1954? It is unlikely that the second Constituent Assembly, though of a different composition from the first, was less favourably disposed to the demands of the religious groups. It is, therefore, more plausible to look for the stiffening of the opposition to the *'ulamā* (or at least a stronger disinclination to listen to their demands for an Islamic state) to the situation brought about by the anti-Aḥmadīya agitation and the Lahore disturbances in 1953. These deplorable events clearly show how the deliberate, provocative injection of a religious issue into an already difficult political and economic situation can lead to an explosive situation which only prompt and determined government action can control. The affair must also be seen in conjunction with the campaign of the *'ulamā* for an Islamic state and constitution in which Sayyid Abul A'lā Maudūdī played a leading role. A court of inquiry, consisting of Mr Justice M. Munir, president (later chief justice of Pakistan and recently law minister), and Mr Justice M. R. Kayani, a Shī'ī, was appointed in 1954 to inquire into the Punjab disturbances and published a report, known as the *Munir Report*.[63] This report not only surveys the actual events and the history of the anti-Aḥmadīya agitation which began long before partition when the movement had its headquarters in Qadian, but also deals in part IV with the concept of an Islamic state and with the question "What is Islam?". It is not surprising that the learned judges pulled no punches and couched their findings in non-legal terms often using strong language since politics were as much involved as religious issues. The report not only shows the complexities of defining Islam and an Islamic state in our time revealed by the testimony of leading Pakistani *'ulamā*, but also the close connection between religion and politics due to the religious and political unity of Islam in the classical theory. It must have had considerable influence on the constitutional debate.

The agitation against the Aḥmadīya sect was led by the Ahrar, a religious group, opposed to Pakistan before partition on political as well as religious grounds and at that time in league with the Congress Party. They found willing allies in some of the most distinguished *'ulamā* of Pakistan in 1952–3, since the Aḥmadīya was not recognised by these groups as a Muslim sect so much as considered heretics outside the pale. The doctrinal bone of contention was the alleged claim of the sect's founder Mirza Ghulam Ahmad to be not only the promised Messiah and *Mahdī*—replacing Jesus who will not return, and the Messiah of Islam—but also a prophet (*nabī*). It is the accepted Islamic doctrine without exception that Muḥammad was the seal, the last of the prophets. Hence the doctrine of *khatam al-nubbuwat* (literally: the seal of prophethood) is at stake. The founder of the Aḥmadīya sect explicitly stated on various occasions that he unreservedly recognised this doctrine and that he who denied it was not a Muslim.

The Aḥmadīya is today split into the Qadianis and the Lahoris; the former have their headquarters at Rabwah on the Pakistani side of divided Punjab, and their present Khalīfa, Mirza Bashir-ud-Din Mahmud Ahmad, flatly denied in a statement to the press in 1953[64] the allegation that the Aḥmadīya did not believe in the doctrine. All the same, his group seems to accept him as a prophet *in a certain sense*, as is clear from the Khalīfa's book *Ahmadiyyat or True Islam*.[65] He argues that, since all religions expect a "Promised Prophet" and Mirza Ghulam Ahmad combined all the characteristics necessary for the various Messiahs in his own person and answered to all the prophecies of previous prophets, he was also a prophet though to the Muslims from whom he hails he was their "Promised One", the *Mahdī*. The founder himself made no such claim to prophethood; he acknowledged Muḥammad as the *khatam*, the seal of all prophets, and only claimed that he was a *muḥaddath* to whom God had spoken, and the *mujaddid* of the century, just as in Islam every century had its *mujaddid* (renovator).[66]

Maulana Muhammad Ali, to whom we owe an English translation and commentary on the Qur'an and many other writings, also wrote a refutation of Iqbal's condemnation of the Qadianis as non-Muslims in which he quoted other statements by Mirza Ghulam Ahmad which show that the latter insisted on being a *muḥaddath* who, however, could be called a prophet *metaphorically*: "The promised Messiah, on account of his being a *muḥaddath* can be called a prophet metaphorically", or, "If *muḥaddathiyyat* is called prophethood metaphorically, it does not mean a claim to prophethood".[67] These are the founder's own words. Maulana Muhammad Ali mentions, however, that, while the Lahore section of the Aḥmadīya movement "sticks to that position", the Qadianis—this was in 1934—hold that the founder of their sect was a prophet and he who does not believe in him is a *kāfir*, unbeliever.[68] In the statement by the present Khalīfa, already referred to, this is denied in these words: "...any person who believes in him [Muḥammad] as the last prophet (Akhir-ul-Anbia) and accepts the Holy Quran as the last Book of God for the guidance of mankind has a right to be called a Muslim...." Both sections of the Aḥmadīya are, as far as one can judge, actively engaged in proselytising with fervour and energy; both produce a considerable literature explaining the tenets and practices of Islam as a universal faith of peace and brotherhood. Rabwah counts young men from many lands among those studying in its college as I found during a lively lecture-discussion.

The foreign minister of Pakistan at the time of the anti-Aḥmadīya agitation and riots was Zafrullah Khan, a Qadiani, and one of the three demands of those who led the agitation was his dismissal because, they claimed, the Aḥmadīs denied the doctrine of *khatam al-nubbuwat* and were therefore outside the pale of Islam.

The second demand concerned the dismissal of all Aḥmadīs from key posts in the administration; and the third demand wanted the sect to be declared a non-Muslim minority which was to be given a seat in the Legislature on a separate list.

From personal knowledge I can testify to the deep religious faith of the Aḥmadīs; their sincerity and earnestness are beyond doubt, as is their strict observance of the traditional *Sharī'a*. They claim that their *khalīfa* is invested with a purely spiritual authority and, with 'Ali 'Abd al-Rāziq, they deny any interest in politics. They live as a closed, well-knit and devout community in Rabwah, practise strict segregation of the sexes, but believe in and realise a sound education of girls in order to enable them to be good mothers. Women should nurse women, and they may teach. I would not have been welcome in the Girls' College at Rabwah, where male teachers are hidden from view. My wife visited the college instead. They share with most strict Muslims antagonism to the West, largely on moral grounds, and blame the Western mixing of the sexes for widespread moral laxity. They are convinced that they can win the world for Islam, but do not express views on how a world-wide religious community can establish a world government. Here, too, they seem to be in agreement with 'Ali 'Abd al-Rāziq who, it will be remembered, desires world-wide religion, but is opposed to world government. The Rabwah community is a closely knit, dedicated community, full of religious zeal and with a strong sense of purpose. No doubt, some of this special atmosphere and cohesion, also noticeable wherever one meets Aḥmadīs, is due to their status as a minority since they keep very much to themselves.

The inquiry conducted by the two judges brought to light, in the words of the *Report*, such disagreement about fundamentals among the *'ulamā* interviewed that they felt constrained to state: "We put this question (What is Islam and who is a *momin* or a Muslim?) to the *ulama* and we shall presently refer to their answers to this question. But we cannot refrain from saying here that it was a matter of infinite regret to us that the *ulama* whose first duty should be to have settled views on this subject, were hopelessly disagreed among themselves."[69] They subjected the *'ulamā* appearing before them to a searching questioning on all aspects of an Islamic state, its foundation, scope and functions; on the position of non-Muslims in an Islamic state; on the nature and obligation of *jihād*; on the possibility of legislation; and on the permissibility of painting, sculpture, mixed acting, and so on. The result of this was that—divergences of the views apart—the judges presented a coherent picture of what an Islamic state is and what it entails for its Muslim and non-Muslim citizens in rights and duties with due regard to Pakistan's obligations as a member of the United Nations and in international law, e.g. in the treatment of prisoners of war in a *jihād*. This interesting part of the *Report* which arose out of the anti-Aḥmadīya riots and the above-mentioned three demands cannot be reproduced here.[70]

This inquiry was necessary because it became apparent that the demands were based on the conceptions which the opponents and attackers of the Aḥmadīs held of Islam:

> ...throughout the inquiry every one has taken it for granted that the demands were the result of the ideology on the strength of which the establishment of an Islamic State in Pakistan was claimed and had been promised from certain quarters. The point which must be clearly comprehended to appreciate the plausibility or otherwise of the demands is that in an Islamic State, or, what is the same thing, in Islam, there is a fundamental distinction between the rights of the Muslim and non-Muslim subjects, and one distinction which may at once be mentioned is that the non-Muslims cannot be associated with the business of administration in the higher sphere.[71]

The learned judges end this section of their *Report* with conclusions showing their deep concern about the dangers of what they consider to be unrealistic dreams and lack of clarity of thought and appreciation of the realities of the present situation. A few quotations may follow because they confirm the impressions of Western students of Islam and the Pakistani scene, sympathetic students who lack the inside knowledge born of prolonged residence in Pakistan and—so I am convinced—the right to pass judgement on fellow human beings struggling hard to build a state and nation amid appalling difficulties.

The authors of the *Munir Report* justify their preoccupation with the issue of an Islamic state by the need to present "a clear picture of the numerous possibilities that may in future arise if true causes of the ideological confusion which contributed to the spread and intensity of the disturbances are not precisely located".

They deplore the lack of loyalty of officials, of respect for property and of a sense of public duty, and state: "If there is one thing which has been conclusively demonstrated in this inquiry, it is that provided you can persuade the masses to believe that something they are asked to do is religiously right or enjoined by religion, you can set them to any course of action, regardless of all considerations of discipline, loyalty, decency, morality or civic sense."

They then make this important observation: "Pakistan is being taken by the common man, though it is not, as an Islamic State. This belief has been encouraged by the ceaseless clamour for Islam and [the] Islamic State that is being heard from all quarters since the establishment of Pakistan." Recounting the glorious achievements of early Islam in its victorious sweep over large parts of the world they say:

> It is this brilliant achievement of the Arabian nomads...that makes the Musalman of today live in the past and yearn for the return of the glory that was Islam....Little does he understand that the forces, which are pitted against him, are entirely different from those against which early Islam had to fight, and that on the clues given by his own ancestors (the) human mind has achieved results which he cannot understand. He therefore finds himself in a state of helplessness, waiting for some one to come and help him out of this morass of uncertainty and confusion. ...Nothing but a bold reorientation of Islam to separate the vital from the lifeless can preserve it as a World Idea and convert the Musalman into a citizen of the present and the future world from the archaic incongruity that he is today. It is this lack of bold and clear thinking, the inability to understand and take decisions which has brought about in Pakistan a confusion which will persist and repeatedly create situations of the kind we have been inquiring into until our leaders have a clear conception of the goal and of the means to reach it.[72]

THE DECEASE OF THE ISLAMIC REPUBLIC

The 1956 Constitution brought no appreciable change. The administration battled on while the politicians, with few exceptions, sought position and influence and were divided and often forgetful of the need of the hour. Who cared for the welfare of the state and gave a sense of purpose to the people? Parliamentary democracy —allegedly inspired by "Islamic principles of social justice"— ground on fitfully until General Mohammad Ayub Khan, with the help of the army, seized power in 1958 and set up a benevolent military dictatorship under martial law.[73] He set himself the task of creating order and efficiency and of doing away with widespread corruption. No doubt, it needed a strong arm to right things and, if possible, rekindle the enthusiasm, dedication and wholehearted effort which marked the birth and early life of the new state. When I visited the country in the autumn of 1960 I was impressed by the physical picture Pakistan presented, and by the determination and energy of the administration, headed by Field-Marshal Ayub as president. The re-establishment of democracy was the president's declared aim and firm promise. A beginning was made with the basic democracies in an attempt at establishing democracy "from the grass roots", not by allowing the several parties to re-form. That the president of Pakistan has acted from patriotic reasons throughout is beyond doubt; that he conceived of guiding and administering a state and ruling the people as a military operation is equally certain. He said, as reported in *Dawn*, that: "It was his desire to see the country as organized as her army."[74]

The basic democracies are a kind of local government: in the towns all their members are elected, in the rural areas two-thirds are elected and one-third is nominated. In the opinion of Khalid bin Sayeed, the officials dominate them; he quotes G. A. Parwez's view that the basic democracies were akin to the Islamic council of advisers (*shūrā*) and that Western-type democracy was unsuitable for Pakistan.[75] It is precisely for this reason that the application of the term *shūrā* to the Legislative Assembly is ambiguous unless the latter is merely an advisory body. The politically conscious, and especially the Western-orientated, Pakistanis want, in fact, a Western-type parliamentary system and want to give the Legislature power of decision and control of the Executive. This extends to the adjudication of repugnancy. While I. H. Qureshi, for example, declares Muslim law to be sovereign, he assigns all legislative activity to the Assembly. This was already the view of Iqbal: *ijmā'* and *ijtihād* in a modern state belong to the representatives of the nation (*umma* or *milla*). As far as the five-tier system of basic democracies is concerned, there is little doubt that the power and influence of the elected members are steadily growing as they are gaining experience, and the president's purpose to rouse the ordinary men and women of Pakistan to their responsibilities and to a share, however modest, in the running of their country has already borne fruit.[76] Whether they will lend themselves to the emergence of real democracy on the national level—they form the electorate for the National Assembly and for the president—under the presidential system, adopted in the 1962 Constitution, remains to be seen.

VIEWS AND ATTITUDES

But before dealing with this constitution, I must give a brief summary of the views and aspirations which I learned from many Pakistani men and women in personal conversation, discussion and in lectures. The first point to make is that, quite naturally, the attitude to Islam and its role in a modern national state varies greatly between the generations. The older generation shows, almost without exception, a much stronger, even if more emotional than intellectual, attachment to Islam. The degree of Westernisation in outlook and political consciousness naturally also varies. There is, however, hardly anyone who does not want to see Pakistan built on Islamic principles of brotherhood, equality and justice, whether they call this—mistakenly—an Islamic state or not. There is considerable difference of opinion as to the part traditional Islamic law is to play. This applies even to judges and lawyers generally. With few exceptions—those who are inclined to the views of Sayyid Abul A'lā Maudūdī—they consider existing laws on the whole in agreement with Qur'anic principles. Again, most are agreed that Personal Status Law which is *Sharī'a*-law must be adjusted to meet changed attitudes to woman's rights and to her place in society. To this end, the All-Pakistan Women's Association has been working over the years.[77] The members of this organisation predominantly belong to the upper middle classes and the higher income groups and are devoted to the welfare of all Pakistani women, to raise the standard of living and working and to safeguard and, where necessary—as in matters of polygamy, divorce and inheritance—to improve the lot of women generally. They have well-run and successfully working schemes of vocational training, including arts and crafts, and do admirable work in the educational sphere. The reason given for remaining a rather exclusive band of workers and for not opening its ranks to women of all classes is that they want to stay clear of politics. It is to be expected, though, that with the extension of educational facilities this maternalistically directed group of ladies will gradually widen its membership and thus grow into a really national organisation. This need not necessarily be on Western lines, but could conform more to the *genius loci.* APWA is represented in international women's organisations and plays an increasingly important role in Pakistan.[78]

To return to the general problem of law, there is in addition to the people who advocate the adaptation of existing laws, another school of thought which wants the law of the state, i.e. its civil and criminal codes, eventually to be *Sharī'a*-law. Those who hold this view do not underrate the difficulties, but are convinced that it has to be done since Pakistan ought to be an Islamic state just in the legal sphere. They advocate the bold but responsible exercise of *ijtihād* by a body composed of *'ulamā* and lay judges imbued with the spirit of Islam. They consider this necessary in order to preserve their religious and cultural heritage in the modern world. They have no illusions about the immensity of the task which will take a long time and needs careful planning and preparation. Nobody wants to entrust it to the *'ulamā* exclusively, and it is certainly a departure from orthodox Islam to associate lay judges with the business of law-making, as well as to place the actual legislation in the hands of the elected Legislature.

All jurists were agreed that the findings of the *Munir Report* deserved special attention, and some felt that the comments made on it by the *'ulamā* and by Maulana Maudūdī ought to be taken into account. There is no doubt that Western notions have been generally accepted by men who in many cases were already members of the judiciary before partition. This applies, among others, to such matters as preventive detention, arbitrary imprisonment on which Maulana Maudūdī, himself a victim to such measures on several occasions, has repeatedly raised his voice. There is also widespread agreement among eminent judges on the inescapable need to make the entire corpus of law compatible with the Qur'an, fully conscious of the fact that only five legal injunctions in the strict sense are to be found therein. They differ over the degree to which they can accept the Sunna. The majority are critical of *Ḥadīth* and share G. A. Parwez's view, though some admit that it is difficult to ascertain precisely what is and what is not prophetic

Sunna. Those traditionally learned among them who possess a working knowledge of *Fiqh* are naturally more conservative and would give more scope to the *uṣūl al-fiqh* (the principles of Islamic jurisprudence) in arriving at a *Sharī'a* brought up to date and applicable to present-day needs. A critical attitude is most marked where Islamic history is concerned: here it is understood that the validity of the *Sharī'a* has largely remained an ideal except in Personal Status law.

Interesting variations could be observed in conversation with academic law-teachers. While there existed a consensus of opinion that an Islamic state was essential, their approach to Islamic law was critical and historical and they stressed that *ijtihād* should be exercised by the Legislature and not by the *'ulamā* as a distinct group. They stressed the adaptability of the *Sharī'a* with examples from its early history, which furnished many precedents, and averred the possibility of achieving, without much difficulty, a modern law in keeping both with Islamic moral and legal principles and contemporary concepts. In their view, the existing Anglo-Muhammadan law is on the whole consonant with Qur'an and Sunna. Among the exceptions is the case of legitimacy. In Muslim law only a child conceived and born in wedlock is legitimate, hence the existing British (Anglo-Muhammadan) law needs revision since it recognises legitimacy as long as the child is born in wedlock. Ibn Qayyim al-Jawzīya is frequently quoted, especially his definition of the *Sharī'a.*[79] Some favour full implementation of traditional Islamic law which is flexible enough to be applicable to modern conditions and, therefore, does not need any modification or adaptation. Some defend the penalty for theft, since in a modern welfare state everybody is adequately provided for. Interpreting the penalty as only applicable to a habitual thief—quite correctly—I have even heard a view that Islamic law was more humane and reasonable than British law which inflicts heavy terms of imprisonment and banishment on an ascending scale. Inevitably, a certain apologetic and anti-Western attitude was discernible here and there.

On the other hand, it is significant that acknowledged authorities in their respective academic or judicial fields who are devout, practising Muslims are strongly in favour of strict separation of religion from politics. "Maulvis" are—in the view of one eminent judge who certainly does not stand alone in this matter—ignorant of contemporary problems and needs and, therefore, incapable of satisfying economic needs and social aspirations by and within the old *Sharī'a* system. He is convinced that the *Sharī'a* cannot be the basis of the law of the land. It would limit the authority of the people and discriminate against non-Muslims: both are incompatible with a contemporary state. While the moral code of religion is beneficial to citizenship, a modern moral code should be in conformity with the attitudes, concepts and needs of the times. Religion is and should be the private affair of the individual; Turkey is a valuable example. We find here the valid distinction between absolute and conventional justice, already drawn by Aristotle in relation to law.[80]

A number of intellectuals are convinced that religion in its orthodox form is on its way out and does not attract Western-educated youth nor can it satisfy their aspirations. This is largely, but not entirely, the case. However, even among the older generation there is not always that clear distinction between an Islamic- and a Western-type, modern national state, nor are the *'ulamā* mentioned in the *Munir Report*, the only group lacking unanimity in answering the fateful question "What is Islam?".

One jurist even sees in Islam not a religion but a social system. Yet state and society should be regulated by the chosen representatives of the sovereign people whose sovereignty is, however, limited by the sovereignty of God and His *Sharī'a*! *Ijmā'* and *ijtihād*—within the limits of Qur'an and authentic Sunna—should be exercised by the representatives of the people who decide and make laws. Islam—in his view—fulfils the same function as the constitution in the United States, in fact it *is* the constitution: surely a thoroughly orthodox position! The *Sharī'a* consists of two parts, it is held: the inviolable, unalterable, fundamental laws based on the Qur'an and authentic *Ḥadīth*; and the laws promulgated by *mujtahids* of every generation. The latter are not unchangeable and, therefore, not binding. The same view was expressed by I. H. Qureshi, quoted above. *Fiqh* is perhaps worth considering, but it is by no means binding on the present generation. But who decides the meaning of the Qur'an and the authenticity of the Sunna? The answer is presumably the Legislative Assembly or the lawyers who, in this jurist's view, must be free to legislate within the limits imposed by Qur'an and Sunna, in conformity with the popular will, the aspirations and the spirit of the age, and the requirements of modern life. This liberal view is widespread, but—we are bound to admit—imprecise as long as the meaning of the Qur'an and authentic Sunna is not clearly established and not free from inconsistency because no real integration between tradition and modern thought has been achieved.

The Islamic provisions of the constitution may after all be more than a concession to the religious leaders' desire for an Islamic state and to the sentiments of the people, whoever is meant by this term. For it is conceivable that a sound knowledge of what life in accordance with the requirements of Qur'an and Sunna means, will in due course enable the legislators to decide and make the requisite laws which are both in spirit and in fact Qur'anic *and* contemporary. The Central Institute of Islamic Research is expected to play an important part in the dissemination of such basic knowledge,[81] in conjunction with other Islamic Research Institutes in Pakistan.

Making allowance for the situation prevailing at the time when Pakistan came into existence, it is understandable that responsible leadership in government, administration, the universities and the liberal professions stakes all on education; this is neither escapism nor a facile postponement of decision and action. The two reasons for this view are large-scale illiteracy which is being vigorously attacked and, as a result, receding, and—among the Western-educated middle age group and the youth—ignorance of Islam and what it means and stands for. It is for this reason that a number of the younger university and college teachers though they wish to see Pakistan as an Islamic state—whether based on the principles as well as the injunctions of Islam, or only on the principles—are convinced that the time is not yet ripe for it and, therefore, advocate a lay state. Their hope is education. This view is widely shared by members of the legal profession as well. The example of Turkey convinces Maulana Maudūdī and the *'ulamā* that setting up what they consider to be a secular, Western-type state will thwart all chances of an Islamic state at a later date.

The politically active and the civil servants among the intelligentsia are principally concerned with the economic stability and social advancement of Pakistan; they see the economic and social factors as the original driving forces in the idea of Pakistan and they see religion as either an important afterthought (albeit of decisive importance in rallying support for the Muslim League and its stand and fight for a separate homeland for the Muslims) or as one of several factors alongside economic and social needs and aspirations, but one which must—now Pakistan is in existence—not interfere with the physically and mentally healthy building up of a viable state and society. It is this latter group which appears to have stood out against the all-out demands of Maulana Maudūdī and the activists among the *'ulamā* and are most likely responsible for the watering down of the Islamic provisions. This is made clear by a comparison between the two constitutions of 1956 and 1962. Yet at the same time the religious forces are battling on and try to make what is encouraged into a positive commandment and what is discouraged into a definite prohibition.

The observations here offered are typical, but it would be wrong to generalise: there are not only many middle-of-the-roaders, there are among the categories mentioned many individuals who hold opposite views. The result is that the picture lacks sharp outline in view of the fluidity of the situation.

The youth of Pakistan is equally divided, but naturally the positions taken up tend to be more extreme. There are the staunch upholders of tradition and of traditional Islamic law at the one end, and a majority of secularists at the other. What is more general is ignorance of the Islamic heritage with a consequent lack of interest in Islam combined with an outward-looking attitude of mind which lives in the present and looks to a future in which Pakistan should take her place as a modern nation working for the unity of the world. It is in the youth that the influence—negative from an orthodox Muslim standpoint—of British institutions and rule is most marked. Theirs is often a secular attitude and they look to the West for inspiration and guidance. This also applies to many younger people in the civil service and in the professions who are often Oxford- or Cambridge-educated. During my visit the Constitution Commission was seeking, receiving and sifting evidence by interview and questionnaire to ascertain what kind of constitution the intellectuals and the literate people generally wanted. The Islamic provisions apart, interest chiefly centred in the system of government, presidential or parliamentary; one or two Houses of

Parliament; unitary or federal form of government; universal suffrage or limited suffrage dependent on qualifications; the position of women; and the position of minorities.

The majority of students, especially in Lahore, seemed much more interested in national and international politics than in Islam. There was a distinct feeling abroad of "first things first", namely the physical development of Pakistan within the United Nations. Many thought that nationalism should not be stressed so much in our age of internationalism and interdependence; they want to be a part of the wider world, why talk about Islam? Religion is the private affair of the individual, and some thought religion—as they imperfectly understand it—had little to contribute to good citizenship. Enthusiasm was found to transcend religious and national barriers; material questions in relation to one's career were uppermost in many people's minds as they are everywhere else in the world. A consciousness of Islam and its principles and values, a knowledge of Islamic history and a sense of belonging to a distinctive culture that is Islam were rarely in evidence.

An interesting feature of this view-finding journey was local and regional differences met within the same country. Thus, Karachi, where we began our inquiry, seemed to be possessed of a strong Islamic awareness among the staff and students of the university, though it would be dangerous to draw conclusions from a certain segment without covering the whole academic population. The group known as *Jamiyatul Falah* (which publishes the *Voice of Islam*) is conservative-progressive and in favour of a limited modification of the *Sharī'a* through *ijtihād* where necessary, based on the classical concept of the religious and political unity of Islam. On the solid basis of the revelational character of Islam as an all-embracing way of life its members showed in varying degree a preparedness to modify and adapt. All stressed the need for a return to Islam through education, hence their publication *Voice of Islam*, and deplored the neglect of intelligent religious instruction and the damage British secular education had done to their admittedly inadequate religious education. This group is fully aware, together with all responsible intellectuals—traditionalist as much as modernist, *'ulamā* and professional men and women—of the wide gap between a thin top layer of educated and the broad ignorant masses under the influence of the mullahs.

Discussions and friendly talks with leading jurists were most stimulating and helpful in Karachi during a second visit (which fell in the month of Ramadhan with all that that means for a practising Muslim) on our way back from Malaya to Iran. Opinions among devout Muslims varied from the impossibility of a fully fledged Islamic state to its possibility in the future after thorough education leading to a revival of religious consciousness and fervour based on a fresh interpretation of the Qur'an. There is full awareness of the need to preserve the principles, but applied in accordance with present-day thinking and needs. Within strictly defined limits, political and economic exigencies of our time (e.g. credit on interest) must be accepted in the national as well as the international field in accordance with Pakistan's membership of the United Nations. Full equality of citizenship without discrimination is considered essential. The search for a solution arrived at by a harmonious combination of faith and intellectual affirmation is honestly and relentlessly being conducted, and if my impressions are correct, such a solution is being sought more on the lines of G. A. Parwez than of Sayyid Abul A'lā Maudūdī and the *'ulamā*. Faith goes with unquestioning observance of ritual as a matter of course. The intellectual search is conducted with the scientific tools of historical and literary criticism, except where the Qur'an is concerned. It is realised that the key to any solution is education: to this all search inevitably leads back. Yet this very method is suspect to the traditionalist as Western and, therefore, un- if not anti-Islamic! The Central Institute of Islamic Research has been the butt of orthodox attack on many occasions. The old and the new, rigid traditionalism and progressive, deeply religious "modernism" are still poles apart, and so are both from the advocates of a lay or even a secular state. Within the modern universities I visited—Karachi, Lahore and Peshawar—the atmosphere is that of a generation in transition. Women students attend the same lectures, but sit together in a cluster, sometimes separated from the men students, some in *burka* (veiled), either inside and outside the university, or only outside. Socially they do not mix, though I attended a meeting of the Political Science Group at Lahore (University of the Punjab) where girls took part, but sitting in one group together. In Peshawar, the separation was more pronounced still. Here the general impression was—a reluctance to discuss the

Islamic issue apart—that an Islamic state with as full an implementation of the *Sharīʿa* as is feasible in our time was a necessity to justify Pakistan. In Lahore, it was the opposite, although all thinking people know that Islam, however understood, was, is and must remain the *raison d'être* of Pakistan. Opinion among men students was divided on the question of equality of women, polygamy and divorce. I heard a plea for polygamy as an economic need in agriculture. My reply that modern methods would achieve better results than two more hands did not satisfy my questioner. It is true that the individual smallholder cannot discard time-honoured, but outmoded methods without financial support and training.

On balance, I should say that among the academic youth there is a minority in favour of an Islamic state in substance, not just in name. The majority are divided in their allegiance to Islam from personal faith to indifference and outright rejection as being out of date and dividing men instead of unifying and leading them to a world state. The universalism of Islam does not appeal to them. Many take the separation of religion and politics for granted: they want a modern constitution and law, with Islam as the private affair of the individual. In fact, their knowledge of Islam is thin, if not non-existent. Islamic feeling is vague and emotional; Islam as a force in public life is not even considered; partly, no doubt, out of ignorance of what it stands for.

An interesting example of a Muslim state as understood by Ibn Khaldūn is Swat State under its ruler Major-General Miangul Jahan Zeb. We visited him in his capital Saidu Sharif where he rules with an Advisory Council of Elders consisting of fifteen elected and ten nominated members. Justice is dispensed partly in accordance with Islamic (*Sharīʿa*) law and partly tribal customary law. Criminal law is largely tribal, e.g. a thief will not have his hand cut off. Islamic law is modified in that the ruler introduced land reform in respect of succession, determining the minimum size of land held as a smallholding of 2½ acres. This holding cannot be split up into smaller fragments; this would be uneconomic. Such a holding is either held collectively by the heirs or one heir buys the others out. The Advisory Council meets every three months and makes recommendations. (The Islamic *shūrā* (council) goes back to Arabian tribal custom.) The ruler himself meets every day between 100 and 200 of his subjects, singly or in groups, to hear their grievances and listen to their views. He also dispenses justice in a modern, progressive spirit. He believes in gradualism and wants a Muslim, but not an Islamic state.

He would like to see the Government of Pakistan give the religious leaders and dignitaries a scientific *and* religious education. For he is convinced that the practice of the Islamic virtues in the spirit of the modern age can greatly contribute to the solution of its manifold new problems. His enlightened paternalism suits his people living in one of the most beautiful corners of Pakistan, a kind of Switzerland which one reaches travelling over the Malakand Pass, one of the routes which Alexander the Great's army took. An Italian archaeological expedition under Professor Tucci brought magnificent pieces of Gandara art there to light. Besides, Swat is one of the most fertile parts of West Pakistan and produces an annual revenue from lands, forests and customs dues of approximately two million dollars which the ruler uses for constant improvements, especially for medical and educational services. Purdah is a purely economic matter in that only the rich keep their women folk in purdah. Once the girls have completed their education, which is modern, they discard the veil. The Wali, as his title as ruler of Swat State is, built a hospital with free service which employs male nurses only, so that women are reluctant to be in-patients there. The girls train mainly to become teachers, and schools are free. He also established a college which bears his name. At the time of my visit there were 400 students enrolled preparing for the B.A. Degree in affiliation with Peshawar University. He pointed out that without credit—naturally against interest—he could not have built schools, a hospital, a college and other civilised amenities.

Perhaps my impressions gained in many conversations and lecture-discussions are better summed up at this stage by saying first and foremost that meeting fellow human-beings struggling with difficult problems in both the material and the spiritual spheres imposes care and discretion on the student of Islam. We are not dealing with texts of bygone ages—perhaps unfortunately?—but with living men and women and living issues in a situation which changes all the time while the problems become greater, not smaller. The first adjustment one has to make is that Islam in the Indo-Pakistan subcontinent is *sui generis* on account of centuries of proximity with Hinduism and of long Muslim minority rule over a Hindu majority. The decline of Mughul power, the advent of Britain and the 1857 mutiny all contributed to a decline which a certain revival, largely in conjunction with the *Khilāfat* movement in which religion played no less a part than politics, could not halt and turn to more than a predominantly economically and socially based movement towards Muslim home rule. Religion only played an active part in the final stages of the fight for Pakistan. Mixed up in a political movement, Islam had to become involved in day-to-day politics which, in turn, inevitably led to its use as a pawn in the political game. This was and is unfortunate because this fact often colours the attitude of the leadership towards Islam as they encounter it in its representative dignitaries and scholars. The latter, especially, often possess more traditional learning than worldly wisdom and experience. But being drawn into the political battle they are bound to take up a position more rigid than is good for sound political, economic and social development and for the inner renewal and fresh flowering of Islam as a religious way of life.

I am almost inclined to think that only Sayyid Abul A'lā Maudūdī and his *Jamā'at-i-Islāmī* have a well-defined objective and work for it with single-mindedness of purpose and determination, making use of means copied from totalitarian political philosophies and movements. Before all, they have a clear concept of the state they want Pakistan to become: an Islamic order. This viewpoint is wholly unacceptable to the political leadership of Pakistan, to the president and his government no less than to the majority of the Western-educated and orientated intelligentsia in the civil service and the professions. It is difficult to gauge the extent of religious belief and practice among this influential group on whose shoulders the survival and development of Pakistan rests. No man can look into another man's mind and soul; we can only judge by their words and deeds. Everybody must, whether he likes it or not, profess his or her allegiance to Islam, and the difficulty is that—as said so often before—Islam must play a part—how big or how small is another matter—in the building up of an independent state for the Muslims in Pakistan.

Accustomed to think in terms of classical Islam with law in the centre, one must stress less the theory of the jurists whose idealisation of the *Sharī'a* preserved Islam, and take more note of the actual state of affairs in the Umayyad and Abbasid caliphates and, last but not least, in the Muslim states in India from the Middle Ages to the end of the Mughul period. While in theory the religious and political unity of Islam has always been maintained, political reality clearly demonstrates the cleavage between the ideal and the actual: we find Muslim states, but no Islamic state, not even under Aurangzeb. We need only read Ziauddin Barani[82] of the fourteenth century to realise the dual system of Muslim rule in medieval India and remember Shāh Walī Ullāh's twofold succession of the prophet: temporal and spiritual. It is significant that the liberal-minded among the intelligentsia should seek support for their views in the ideas of Shāh Walī Ullāh, and that the orthodox should look to the formative first phase of Islam in Arabia to justify their concept of an Islamic state. Whether they use—ambiguously—Qur'an and Sunna and avoid mentioning the *Sharī'a* or not: they mean a state based on and centred in a divinely revealed law, with due regard for *Fiqh*.

Muhammad Asad, G. A. Parwez and many who think like him occupy a sort of middle position which is difficult to define precisely. Their numerical strength I was unable to estimate, but I am inclined to think that those I have met form the most hopeful element—from the point of view of a living Islam—in the confused, frustrating situation I found in 1960–1. Here is honest and serious analysis and criticism which springs from deep faith and patriotic responsibility. Patriotism, a sense of civic duty and responsibility has always been the keynote of President Ayub's speeches and appeals to the people of Pakistan in the name of Islam and by frequent use of the term "Islamic ideology". The test of the profession—on the lips of many people—of the Islamic ideals of brotherhood, equality and social justice is in the conscious effort to translate them into reality in the daily needs of Pakistani state and society. Of this, not much can be detected outside the devoted band of civil servants in the administration, the Planning Commission, Research Institutes, APWA and similar organisations. In the educational field much planning and research is being carried out.[83] The crux of the problem is and remains the place, if any, of the *Sharī'a* in the life of the state, not in the demands of the orthodox or in the rejection of the modernists and adherents of a lay state. In spite of the Islamic provisions, Islam is not the state religion. But it has been used and sometimes misused for political ends.

Islam must unite West and East Pakistan since nothing else can promote national unity. East Pakistan has been restive since the inception of the state, for political and economic reasons. The Bengali Muslims felt aggrieved and claimed to be discriminated against in funds which were not commensurate with the revenue their jute production brought in, and in their representation in the services, civil and military, of the Republic. This was my distinct impression after a memorable stay at Dacca. Equal representation of West and East Pakistan in the National Assembly and since the 1962 Constitution also alternate sittings in both wings should help, together with other measures, to promote unity. Muslims in East Pakistan are, generally speaking, more strongly attached to Islam than the Muslims in West Pakistan. Hence Islam is essential to give spiritual content to Pakistani nationalism, or (as the leading religious and political leaders say) Islam forms the ideology of the nation. Bearing in mind the meaning of ideology as a political "creed", we realise that the wheel has come full circle, and we have reached the point from which we started: the problematic nature of Islam which cannot be resolved unless and until the role of Islam as a set of guiding principles and/or a complete religious and political system and way of life, expressed in law, has been defined.

Convinced of the necessity of an Islamic state for Pakistan before visiting the country, I soon realised that this may after all not be a solution, at least not immediately, and, if at a later date, only if a real synthesis between the tenets of Islam and the physical and spiritual needs of modern life can be worked out by the Pakistani nation in such a way that there is room for agnostics, atheists and adherents of other faiths on a basis of complete equality and in a spirit of wholehearted service to the one nation composed of different people. Whether Islam can be adapted to that extent is a big question which raises doubts, especially if Islam is understood as an ideology to which only Muslim believers can subscribe.

Speculation is not very helpful, especially if there is so little concrete evidence on which to build it. If an opinion must be ventured it is this: a lay state guaranteeing freedom of religion, particularly in an age of doubt and unbelief such as ours, offers a better chance to a people divided in religious belief, culture and customs. Perhaps the signs are that the Qaid-i-Azam's vision of a future Pakistan in which Muslims and Hindus are only divided by religion, but united in the service of their common country, has a better chance of realisation in a state whose principles are spelt out in the preamble of the constitution as the successor of the Objectives Resolution.

THE CONSTITUTION COMMISSION AT WORK

The next stage in our report is a brief discussion of the Islamic issue as it presented itself to the constitution commission set up by the president. Its terms of reference contained this charge: "And, having further taken account of the genius of the people... to submit constitutional proposals...advising how best the following ends may be secured: a democracy adapted to changing circumstances and based on the Islamic principles of justice, equality and tolerance...."[84] Consequently, the members under the presidency of Mr Justice Muhammad Shahabuddin dealt in a special chapter with the "Preamble and Islamic Provisions" and stated[85] in para. 183: "The preponderance of opinion (96·64 %) is in favour of adopting this preamble...." They take note of the discussion in the first Constituent Assembly during which Hindu members opposed the references to Islam and make some pertinent observations in para. 184:

> It is stated by some that it is not correct to say that the objective, from the outset, was that Pakistan should be an Islamic State, but that the main cause for the Pakistan movement was the desire to avoid domination by the Hindu majority, and in this respect reliance is placed on the absence of any reference to an Islamic State in the Lahore Resolution. The majority opinion, however, is otherwise and in its support various pronouncements of the Quaid-i-Azam as well as of the Quaid-i-Millat [Liaqat Ali Khan] are pressed into authority. As to what exactly the view, in this regard, was at the inception is an academic question, because, even if it is taken that in the beginning the objective was not an Islamic State, it cannot be doubted that the majority in this country now desire an Islamic way of life....[86]

It may be seriously doubted whether "an Islamic way of life" is identical in meaning with an "Islamic State" and also whether the majority spoken of in fact represents the majority of the people or only those who sent in answers to the commission. For we must remember that the advocates of an Islamic constitution, both orthodox and liberal, made full use of the facilities available to make their views known to the constitution commission. They collected signatures for the answers they prepared to the commission's questionnaire and sent them in. Thus, nineteen *'ulamā* published *Answers to Constitution Commission's Questionnaire* in the form of a pamphlet which also contained their *Basic Principles of an Islamic State* of 1951, discussed above, and a form at the end to be detached, signed and forwarded to the president of the commission by all readers who agreed with their demands. In their answer to question 34 they state:

Firstly, that Pakistan has come into being by virtue of the sacrifices of the common Muslims. Furthermore, next to the Grace of God, it is only the determination of the common Muslims that can guarantee its existence and strength. No non-Muslim has brought this country into being.... Secondly, barring a few high-grade State servants and a paltry number of people of prosperous families, the general Muslim populace desire to make and see this country flourish as an Islamic State whose laws should be Islamic, whose system of government should be Islamic, whose educational system should be Islamic. It is for this object that the Muslims sacrificed their lives, property and honour to establish Pakistan. Their sole interest in the establishment of Pakistan was this objective alone and for this purpose only they are interested in the continued existence of Pakistan. There can be no greater enmity towards this State than to destroy this interest of its people. After creating frustration and disillusionment among the common Muslims, what support can a handful of such people lend to this State as are embarrassed by the very name of Islam—their religion...?

This comes from learned orthodox scholars who were certainly not in the forefront of the battle for Pakistan. They claim to speak in the name of "85% of the Muslim population of this country", and admonish "the learned members of the Commission" to

realize that the Muslims do not merely expect this State to assist them in the "study of the basic values of Islam" [the subject of question 34]; they have been studying these values even before the establishment of

Pakistan and shall, God willing, continue to do so in future. They had created a new and independent State after so many sacrifices and sufferings not merely for the sake of this thing. What they desire is to make Pakistan a full-fledged Islamic State and for this purpose the minimum that can satisfy them is that clauses 24 to 26, 28, 30, 32(*a*), 197 and 198 should be kept intact as they were incorporated in the late Constitution. It need not be mentioned that from the Islamic standpoint even these clauses are defective and inadequate and a good deal more is necessary.

In answer to question 39—the establishment of "a democracy adaptable to changing circumstances and based on the Islamic principles of justice, equality and tolerance"—they draw the commission's attention to the "22 Basic Principles of an Islamic State...from this the Commission will know what exactly are the Islamic principles of justice, equality and tolerance and how [such] 'a democracy...' can be established". The *Munir Report* is certainly not of this opinion.

Finally, in answer to question 40—inviting suggestions—they state:

> An overwhelming majority of the people of this country are desirous of introducing the Islamic laws. Hence it is not enough merely to provide in the Constitution that no law shall be enacted which is repugnant to the injunctions of Islam as laid down in the Holy Quran and Sunnah. It should be positively provided that the primary and chief source of the laws of the country would be the Holy Quran and the Sunnah.[87]

Maulana Sayyid Abul A'lā Maudūdī was one of the nineteen *'ulamā*, and he aims to win the masses through his powerful propaganda. These *'ulamā* neither have, nor could they prove to have, the support of the vast majority of Muslims for an Islamic state as they understand it, since the masses are largely illiterate and inactive; they desire before all better material conditions.

G. A. Parwez's followers also issued material setting forth their views on an Islamic constitution. They distributed a short pamphlet, entitled *Basic Provisions of an Islamic Constitution for Pakistan*, based on the Qur'an alone, for signature and dispatch to the constitution commission. In their reply to the commission's questionnaire, also published in pamphlet form, they set out their demands for an Islamic state, with an Islamic constitution, based on the Qur'an alone. The *Basic Provisions* reflect the ideal Islamic state of G. A. Parwez's concept in fourteen Articles of which the salient features are these: (1) "Sovereignty shall belong to God to the complete exclusion of any one else." (2) "Supreme authority shall vest in the Holy Quran, which will form the basis of the State and nothing repugnant thereto shall be acceptable." (3) "Formulation of government shall be the corporate duty of the Ummat to be discharged by mutual counsel." (4) "The Ummat, as one compact whole, will form the government and Sects and parties will be banned completely." (5) lays down that everybody fit to perform state duties shall be equally eligible, provided he is capable and his life "conform(s) to the Quranic teachings". (7) states as the primary qualification of "The Head of State, Members of the Advisory Council, Ministers, members of the Legislature, Executive Officers and other functionaries and every one else howsoever connected with State business: (i) knowledge of the Quranic Fundamentals and injunctions". (8) "The Legislature shall have the power to formulate by mutual consultation, laws for the State, as required, subject to the proviso that it will keep always within the four corners of the Quranic Fundamentals which shall never be violated or transgressed, and that no law will be framed which is repugnant to them." (11) "For the fulfilment of God's responsibilities towards man, sources of sustenance, means of production and surplus wealth with individuals shall be placed, as deemed necessary, under State control as a trust, so that they may be available for use towards the development of citizenry, that is for introducing Nizam-e-Rabubiyyat or Quranic Economics." (13) "Every citizen shall enjoy the fundamental rights assured by the Holy Quran...." The last Article deals with non-Muslim citizens.

This Qur'anic Constitution assigns executive powers to a president who is advised by a council—in conformity with the principle of *shūrā*—and presumably promulgates the laws formulated by the Legislature if he approves of them. This can only be implied in the absence of any explicit statement. A noteworthy feature of this scheme is the equation of "Quranic Economics" with "Nizam-e-Rabubiyyat" (*niẓām al-rubūbīya*), the divine order or law which seems to mean an economy based on the Qur'anic principles of justice, equality and brotherhood, under state control.

The *Answers to the Questionnaire* are naturally more concrete inasmuch as they have to translate the *Basic Provisions* into specific answers to specific questions. Since we are concerned with principles in the first place, a detailed discussion of measures suggested by these liberal exponents of an Islamic state cannot be entered into here. What is important, to the exclusion of everything else, is their insistence on the supremacy of the Qur'an whose precise meaning in terms of law is to be decided by reference to the Supreme Court as the highest legal authority under the Qur'an. Its decision is binding and overrides the differences of interpretation by the four orthodox rites. This presupposes an expert knowledge of the Qur'an on the part of the judges. They are obviously competent to decide what "the Law of God" is; this is referred to in the answer to the first question which also demands: "4. (i) The State shall be guided in its legislative or executive policies by the principles of the Quran. (ii) The State shall, as soon as may be practicable, bring all laws in consonance with the principles of the Quran." In answer to the second question, the adherents of G. A. Parwez reply:

> The only way to prevent recurrence of the costly mistakes of the past would be by adopting an Islamic Constitution. It is [the] Quran alone which has the loyalty of all Muslims irrespective of their other differences. The moment [the] Quran becomes the foundation of our new Constitution the stability that we seek shall be achieved. It is also necessary that the power of the State be so distributed amongst its various organs, that each section of society is secured effective participation and control in the matter of policy making.

This is presumably to be achieved by universal suffrage which they advocate for all adults irrespective of sex for the "House of Representatives" by direct vote, and for the "Senate" by "limited franchise through Vocational Institutions..." (p. 9 of their *Answers*). Their ideological position is clearly expressed in their answer to the thirteenth question (joint or separate electorates for Muslims and non-Muslims): "Pakistan came into being on the basis of two-nation theory. The *sine qua non* of this ideological principle is separate electorate. Muslims should alone vote for those who would represent their distinct ideology and non-Muslims who do not accept this ideology, should elect their own representatives when needed." They refer to their answer to the fortieth question on the position of non-Muslims in an Islamic state; and it is particularly important and of the greatest interest that they there justify differentiation between Muslim and non-Muslim citizens by an appeal to the authority of the Quaid-e-Azam. This shows quite clearly how important Islam in the struggle for a separate homeland for the Muslims of the sub-continent during its decisive phase was; and also that Mohammad Ali Jinnah changed his views after partition. As the acknowledged leader of the majority of Indian Muslims who desired to live their lives as Muslims in an independent state, he stressed the differences between Muslims and Hindus and used them as a justification for the demand for home rule. At the same time he gave an assurance "that the minorities must be protected and safeguarded to the fullest extent...". This quotation from his published speeches is cited by them and they claim Qur'anic authority for it while at the same time stressing that he excluded them from the Muslim nation since he said:

Hindus and Muslims, though living in the same towns and villages, had never been blended into one nation: they were always two separate entities....Pakistan started the moment the first non-Muslim was converted to Islam in India. As soon as a Hindu embraced Islam he was outcast not only religiously but also socially, culturally and economically....Throughout the ages Hindus had remained Hindus and Muslims had remained Muslims and they had not merged their entities. That was the basis for Pakistan....They [Islam and Hinduism] are not religions in the strict sense of the word, but are in fact different and distinct social orders, and it is a dream that Hindus and Muslims can ever evolve a common nationality....

To their mind, these and similar utterances they quote "reflected the true Quranic spirit", and they aver: "In working for Pakistan, Quaid-e-Azam used no political stunts but built on firm Quranic principles." Finally, they claim that he favoured an Islamic state when he said:

There is a special feature of the Islamic State which must not be overlooked. There, obedience is due to God, which takes practical shape in the observance of the Quranic principles and commands. In Islam obedience is due neither to a king, nor to a parliament nor to any individual organisation. It is the Quranic provisions which determine the principles of our freedom and discipline in political and social spheres. In other words, Islamic State is an agency for enforcing Quranic principles and injunctions.[88]

We saw earlier on when discussing the debates of the Constituent Assembly that the founder of Pakistan spoke differently as governor-general of sovereign, independent Pakistan. The statesman minimised the differences between the Muslim majority and the Hindu minority in his appeal for national unity of equal citizens professing different religions which he apparently understood in the contemporary sense as the personal affair of the individual citizen.

The commissioners themselves defend a constitution based on religion with the argument, among others, that minorities would be safer under a religious than a secular constitution—especially an Islamic one since "Islam gives them [the minorities] a guarantee of equality, freedom and justice, which is far more effective being a matter of ideology than a mere declaration of secularity". We note the expression "a matter of ideology" by which they probably mean what they state in order to justify an Islamic constitution: "Islam permeates the life of a Muslim and does not allow politics to be kept apart from ethics as is the case in countries with secular constitutions."[89] Two observations are called for here: their claim that secular states do not base their politics on ethics is unproven; and while the claim that Islam permeates a Muslim's entire life is good classical doctrine and has, therefore, attributed to it what is called an "Islamic ideology", this certainly does not apply to non-Muslim minorities living under an Islamic constitution as understood by the advocates of an Islamic state. This is clear from the *Answers to the Questionnaire* of G. A. Parwez's movement which means to make second-class citizens out of the minorities at least in one important respect, namely by debarring them from holding high public office if the interpretation of the following passage of their views on non-Muslims in Pakistan is correct:

> ...whether a Constitution is framed on the basis of the political objective that the creation of Pakistan implied or that of the ideology of the Muslim people, there is no escape from a Quranic Constitution. The position of non-Muslims in Pakistan would be that they would have justice and equality guaranteed by the Fundamental Rights, but they shall not have a say in running the Government or in formulating ultimate policies of an ideological State. They would always be welcome to remove the disability by accepting the ideology....[90]

In their *Basic Provisions*, Article (14) guarantees the non-Muslims fundamental human rights, but states explicitly: "By the reason that non-Muslims refuse to subscribe to the Islamic Ideology they shall have no claim to participate in the working of the State, whose only function is to give shape to that Ideology",[91] which seems to go even further and to exclude them from all public offices, not only from such key posts as, for example, the position of chief justice of Pakistan, which has been held for many years by a Roman Catholic.

Fundamental as the differences between the *'ulamā* and Maulana Maudūdī's *Jamā'at-i-Islāmī* party on the one hand, and G. A. Parwez's liberal movement on the other are, they have in common the desire to make Pakistan an Islamic state under Islamic laws. In principle at least, it is irrelevant whether Islamic law is to be based on Qur'an and Sunna in the words of the *'ulamā*, or in the much more traditional form of Maulana Maudūdī, with full utilisation of *Fiqh*—though it may be inferred from the reactions of the *'ulamā* to the "Muslim Family Laws Ordinance" (quoted later in this chapter) that they adhere to the *Sharī'a* just as much as he—or whether Islamic law is to be newly framed, based on the Qur'an alone, as is the opinion of G. A. Parwez—his by-laws framed by the Legislative Council.

This is what is meant by political theology; that is, theological concepts of the sovereignty of God, the revelation of His will, and man's obedience to Him and His law flowing from His revelation, determine political thinking and action. Nor does the nomenclature matter, be it theocracy, theodemocracy (Maudūdī) or nomocracy (the rule of divine law). What alone matters is that the religious groups in Pakistan, both orthodox and liberal, want Pakistan to be a state founded on and centred in religion. That Muhammad Asad and G. A. Parwez's movement are more open and attuned to the inexorable demands of a contemporary state and more prepared to meet them than the rigidly orthodox *'ulamā* or Maulana Maudūdī, like the *Ikhwān al-Muslimūn*, does not alter this basic fact. I merely state this as my opinion, irrespective of what my own attitude to an Islamic state in our time is and of my respect for friends in Pakistan who desire an Islamic state.

The commissioners include in their *Report* a long dissertation on tolerance in Islam to justify the retention of the preamble of the old constitution in the new constitution to be promulgated by the president. They do not recommend differential treatment of non-

Muslims in respect of government service nor the demand found in the *Basic Principles* and the *Answers* of G. A. Parwez's followers that state officers and employees should without exception possess among other qualifications "knowledge of the Quranic Fundamentals and injunctions".[92] In 1952, Maulana Maudūdī made a similar demand for moral training in Islamic principles, and the *'ulamā* in 1951 and 1953.

The important point about the commission's recommendations concerning Islamic provisions is their emphatic conviction that the Qur'an should be the basis of belief and practice of the Muslims of Pakistan: "Islam is not merely incessant prayers and meditations but actual social life lived in accordance with the ideal";[93] and they recommend a discipline based on the moral teachings of the Qur'an. They do not mention Islamic law in this context. They remark on the conflict between belief and action so much in evidence, and blame it for the desire of "some of our young generation [who] regard religion of no practical value, with the result that they express themselves in favour of a secular state".[93]

The "mullahs" come in for censure as being responsible for the dichotomy between faith and action through their inadequate preaching and teaching. The commissioners aver: "We have no doubt whatsoever that Islam meets our requirements to the full."[93] They see the remedy in the work of the Central Institute of Islamic Research as the necessary first step by linking it with the problem of moral regeneration by means of religion in opposition to secularism. They state:

> We have thus an ideology [from the Qur'an] which enables us to establish a model welfare-state, and history shows that such a state had been established [as] a model in the early days of Islam. If the modern generation doubts the efficacy of Islam, that is due to their lack of appreciation of the universal applicability of the Quranic teachings and a lack of knowledge of the Islamic history. The remedy lies in acquainting oneself with the principles of Islam and with the Islamic history and not in discarding religion. Those, who talk glibly of secularism in Pakistan, overlook the fact that, by a mere change of expression, one's conduct does not change. If there is any chance of reforming ourselves it lies only in drawing inspiration from Islam. Liberal secularism of the West, which seems to attract the modern generation, is itself based on the traditional discipline which was developed when religion was a force

in those countries. The standards of social welfare, presented by Islam, are by no means lower than those adopted in the West. If we do not follow the principles of Islam, a mere change in nomenclature is not going to be of help. We therefore consider that it is imperative that we should understand those principles and acquaint ourselves with the history of their application to the affairs of the world. For this purpose, literature on a large scale, explaining the basic values of Islam in the light of modern knowledge, should be produced and made available to every person who can read and understand. It was obviously for this purpose that the late Constitution provided in its Article 197 for the setting up of an organisation for Islamic research, and instruction in advanced studies, to assist in the reconstruction of Muslim society on a truly Islamic basis.[94]

This is practical idealism and makes sense as long as one can believe in the healing power and efficacy of education, and provided the expression "in the light of modern knowledge" means a strictly scientific non-polemical and non-apologetic approach to, and study of, the classics of Islam in Arabic and Persian, and particularly of Islamic history, with the tools of historical criticism. It can, if so carried out, not fail to produce a new generation of conscious, knowledgeable Muslims. But how can it affect now the present generation of university students, graduates and younger civil servants, among whom—admittedly—the trend towards secularism or at least laicism is strongly noticeable?

It is highly significant that in answer to the question whether the Repugnancy Clause should be included in the new constitution "an overwhelming majority, 97·23 %, favour the adoption of this provision...".[95] The commissioners' comment is no less revealing:

We do not think that this majority has fully considered the difficulties involved in this question. A minority of 1·63% took the attitude that no Islamic provision is required..., 1·14% consider that the laws should be brought in conformity only with the Quranic principles and that the expression "Sunnah" should be deleted from the Article. As against this there is the view, expressed by some, that the Quran without Sunnah would give rise to controversy with regard to the interpretation of the Quran, as Sunnah is really an interpretation and a commentary of the Holy Book.[95]

They go on to mention the difficulties involved in deciding the authenticity of traditions and register the view of the official delegation that if a more specific provision was considered advisable it may be laid down that no law should be enacted which is repugnant to the principles of Islam as enunciated by the Holy Quran and Sunnah with the right of Ijtihad to meet the requirements of the times and the needs of present day society....As regards Ijtihad, there are, again, different views. There is also the question as to whether it is necessary at all to disturb the general law, that is law other than personal law, that has held the field for such a long time in this sub-continent, and, in this connection, the fact that, in most of the Muslim countries, the general law has not been brought into strict conformity with the Quran and Sunnah becomes relevant.[95]

In other words, they take a practical, realistic view—we saw earlier that Anglo-Muhammadan law is by and large considered compatible with Islamic principles—and their reference to other Muslim states points in the same direction. They turn to Iqbal in support of their opinion that basing legislation on *Ḥadīth* is difficult, by citing his quotation from Shāh Walī Ullāh to the effect that

the law revealed by a prophet takes especial notice of the habits, ways, and peculiarities of the people to whom he is specifically sent....His method is to train one particular people, and to use them as a nucleus for the building up of a universal Shari'at. In doing so he accentuates the principles underlying the social life of all mankind, and applies them to concrete cases in the light of the specific habits of the people immediately before him. The Shari'at values (Ahkam) resulting from this application (*e.g.*, rules relating to penalties for crimes) are in a sense specific to that people; and since their observance is not [an] end in itself, they cannot be strictly enforced in the case of future generations....[96]

It is to be remembered that Iqbal was interested in the Muslims of the subcontinent, not in Arabia, and the conclusion to be drawn from this quotation—which seems to be the opinion of the commission too—is that at least some laws based on *Ḥadīth* are time-bound and not necessarily valid at other times in other lands. However, the commissioners say that not everybody shares this view. They also reject the view that non-observance of "the essentials of faith" should be punishable because the Qur'an does not prescribe "punishment which the state can inflict, and if we prescribe such punishments in this respect we shall not be acting in conformity with the Holy Book".

In Malaya, Muslims found eating in a restaurant during Ramadhan should be and often are apprehended by the police and fined.

The commission understandably concludes that no definite steps can be taken to change the laws in force at once, and envisages two stages which should be taken to make the necessary changes: first, "to create a climate wherein different schools of thought could evolve unanimity with regard to the fundamentals of Islam as far as traditions are concerned," and secondly "the drawing up of the principles, which should be regarded as the standard to which the laws of the country should conform". To this end, they suggest the formation of a commission which should co-operate with similar commissions in other Muslim countries, since this was a matter which concerned the whole Muslim world. In their opinion, "that Commission will have to advise as to whether instructions given by the Prophet with reference to local conditions should necessarily be followed literally in the various countries regardless of the local customs to which people of those countries have all along been accustomed, or, only the principles have to be adopted".[95] In other words, the crucial question whether the *Sharī'a* has to be adopted as the law of the land, or whether only Qur'anic principles have to be observed in framing new laws or rather adapting existing laws, has been left open. It is noteworthy that the views of this commission come very close to a historical–critical approach to the Qur'an. The setting up of a commission appears to be the only measure possible at this juncture, since it means that the overriding importance of the Qur'an is accepted and the insistent demands of the advocates of an Islamic state, both orthodox and liberal, are, if not met, at least recognised. This realistic suggestion led to the establishment of an "Advisory Council of Islamic Ideology". How far this council corresponds to the commission's suggestions we shall discuss in connection with the new constitution. We shall find that what the commission envisaged is partly the business of the Advisory Council and partly that of the Central Institute of Islamic Research, both institutions to work closely together. It can be stated here already that, probably on account of the persistent agitation in orthodox circles and of the much gentler advocacy of the liberal group, the full implementation of the commission's more cautious procedure contained in their careful suggestions would not have satisfied these movements. Yet the more definite and immediate measures proposed in the new constitution are severely limited in their impact on the Legislature, which in the adopted presidential system has in any case a narrowly circumscribed authority.

An outstanding feature of this *Report* is the preoccupation of the commission with the "Basic Values of Islam". It is their deep conviction that whichever system of government is to be adopted, and whatever law is to be enforced in the Republic of Pakistan—these are the principal questions, together with the inquiry into the failure of the parliamentary system, they have to investigate and to answer—it is Islam, its principles, teachings and its history to which Pakistan will have to turn in order to live meaningfully. Political theology has crept into their minds. It is therefore not surprising that they attach such paramount importance to the right kind of education on all levels. If education is under constant review in such highly developed countries as Britain, and if it is realised here that the welfare state cannot be maintained and improved without a well-educated citizenry, we are not surprised to see education treated as a political problem of first priority in newly established, underdeveloped countries. The question of the role of Islam in the public life of a modern national Muslim state is therefore closely linked with the other question: the role of Islam in national education. Hence the seemingly exaggerated space Islam as the nation's guide in politics and in education occupies in framing a constitution. This is clearly the reason why jurists and political leaders are so much concerned with theology and so hampered by the prevailing uncertainty and division of opinion in their deliberations on what is in the West a political problem pure and simple which can safely be left to constitutional lawyers.

This should go a long way towards understanding why Islam is such a problem in Pakistan, quite apart from what the reasons were for its coming into being (economic, social, or religious or all of them together). We can also understand why a decision on whether Islamic provisions should be written into the constitution, and if so what they should contain, presented such difficulties for the constitution commission. As if it were not enough that they have to devise a system, a form and a machinery of government, a legislature and a judiciary which guarantee the life of state and society, and human rights to every individual citizen, they have in addition to assume the role of theologians as well, as the *Munir Report* and the *Report of the Constitution Commission, Pakistan*, clearly show. No wonder, then, that the writers of the latter report found it necessary to censure the religious functionaries in mosque and school for failing to provide the necessary basic knowledge of the fundamentals of Islam.

The members of the commission fully realise that their suggestions of a research institute to produce the requisite literature, and of a commission to bring existing laws into conformity with Qur'an and Sunna, are both long-term measures. Moreover, they know that such literature "would not reach the bulk of our population which is uneducated", and "the work of the Commission...does not by itself make one a good Muslim", and therefore they ask what can be done for the uneducated:

> at present their knowledge about Islam is what the Imam of their mosque spreads among them and, unfortunately, an average Imam, even if he has a full knowledge of the ritual, is not capable of explaining the principles of Islam in the context of modern conditions. He has to depend on the bounty of one or a few rich members of the limited society he serves and cannot therefore afford to criticise any action which does not infringe the ritual however anti-social and un-Islamic in effect it may be. Due to lack of proper training and education and want of security of employment the average preacher carries on following the line of least resistance by keeping on the good side of the powerful section.[97]

The *Munir Report* castigated the *'ulamā*, the *Constitution Commission Report* the mullahs. The answer to the latter problem is, again, education, and the commission recommend that the universities should arrange courses in religious studies (Qur'an, *Ḥadīth* and *Fiqh*) for the proper training of Imams. Without such training, nobody should be appointed Imam; and once appointed he ought to be adequately paid.

ISLAMIC PROVISIONS IN THE 1962 CONSTITUTION

When we now consider the Islamic provisions of the constitution imposed by President Ayub in 1962 we will do well to remember the long tug-of-war that has been going on about an Islamic constitution and an Islamic state. Even if these provisions were not rather isolated and overshadowed by the substantive clauses of both the 1956 and the 1962 Constitutions and would not, by their isolation alone, raise doubts in our minds as to their efficacy, the long-drawn-out battle would lead us to the same doubts.

This paradox of satisfying the aspirations of the advocates of a religious state by writing Islamic provisions into an otherwise legitimately and overwhelmingly modern political document on the one hand, and on the other hedging these provisions round with assertions of the overriding power and authority of the Legislature or the government, tantamount to making them innocuous, is not at all puzzling. We need only recall the preceding discussion of what Islam is and what an Islamic state is to which no clear, unequivocal answer could be elicited. The clearest of all the answers is that of Maulana Maudūdī, and that is—in spite of modern-sounding formulations—representative of that static Islam which, from our modern vantage-point, we are pleased to call medieval, whereas everybody talks about and demands a dynamic Islam.

The preamble to the President's Constitution asserts the sovereignty of Allah as did the previous constitution of 1956, with this difference: the people of Pakistan exercise authority as a sacred trust—under God's sovereignty—in both, but in the first constitution this authority was limited, "within the limits prescribed by Him"; this has been left out in 1962. The new constitution simply states that "the Muslims of Pakistan should be enabled, individually and collectively, to order their lives in accordance with the teachings and requirements of Islam". These were defined in 1956 by the addition of "as set out in the Holy Quran and Sunnah".

The rights of the minorities are safeguarded in both. In 1962 "the backward and depressed classes" of 1956 are omitted, but their special needs are stressed later on. Fundamental rights are guaranteed in both Constitutions, but clause (*e*) in 1962 adds "consistently with the security of the State" to the universally accepted limits of "public interest and morality". Whereas the president "in exercise of the Mandate given to me. . . by the people of Pakistan" promulgated the new constitution, "we the people of Pakistan in our Constituent Assembly. . ." performed this act in 1956.

In 1956 the name of the state was "the Islamic Republic of Pakistan"; in 1962 simply "the Republic of Pakistan". It was to be expected that the advocates of an Islamic state would wish to restore the epithet "Islamic", and this was actually achieved, together with the restoration of the above-mentioned limitation imposed on the authority of the people, namely "within the limits prescribed by Him".[98] What was termed "Directive Principles of State Policy" in the first constitution now bears the name "Principles of Law-making and of Policy".

The Islamic provisions are basically the same in both documents, only in the new constitution they are separated and dealt with under the two chapters headed, "Principles of Law-making" and "Principles of Policy". In the former, it is stipulated that

> the responsibility of deciding whether a proposed law does or does not disregard or violate, or is or is not otherwise in accordance with, the Principles of Law-making is that of the legislature concerned, but the National Assembly, a Provincial Assembly, the President or the Governor of a Province may refer to the Advisory Council of Islamic Ideology for advice any question that arises as to whether a proposed law disregards or violates, or is otherwise not in accordance with the Principles of Law-making.[99]

The first of these Principles reads: "1. Islam—No law should be repugnant to Islam."[99] It is indicative of the importance attached to Islamic ideology and content that the law minister in presenting the first Amendment Bill declared that with these two changes (nomenclature and divine limits to human authority) "all major ideological requirements in the Constitution would be met".[98] He is also reported as having stated that: "All existing and future laws have been brought within the purview of [a] clause barring legislation dealing with [matters] repugnant to the Holy Quran and Sunnah."[98] This statement curiously enough does not agree with the first principle of law-making, just quoted. Mian Abdul Bari for the opposition regretted that the Repugnancy Clause in the present constitution was not couched in the same terms as in the 1956 Constitution, which had provided that "no law shall be enacted which is repugnant to the injunctions of Islam as laid down in the Holy Quran and Sunnah". The Law Minister in his reply agreed to substitute the word "shall" for "should", but insisted that the matter would not be justiciable.[98]

Presumably, the two reports in *Dawn* taken together can be interpreted as indicating a reversion to the 1956 Constitution in the wording of the Repugnancy Clause. Yet, now as then, it is not enforceable in a court of law. Moreover, the Legislature is not bound by the advice of the Advisory Council of Islamic Ideology and therefore need not withhold or repeal a law repugnant to Qur'an and Sunna. This makes this Islamic provision quite ineffective, though laying government and Legislature open to attack and causing agitation and unrest, thus throwing an additional burden on the administration. For it is at least doubtful whether those intellectuals are right who see in the reintroduction of the word "Islamic" nothing but a meaningless change in nomenclature. Even if the figures quoted from the Report of the Constitution Commission do not reflect the actual state of affairs (that the overwhelming majority wants an Islamic constitution) this reintroduction and "shall" in place of "should" in the Repugnancy Clause must mean a good deal to a good many people in Pakistan. That it does not matter in so far as the conduct of affairs of state is concerned is beside the point, since the friction caused between the religious groups and the government must, as already stressed, increase existing difficulties.

In another respect, the new constitution—like the old—cannot be entirely satisfactory to orthodox Muslims: Article 7 of the Principles of Law-making guarantees not only freedom of religion, but the propagation of all religions. Islam, as cannot be stressed too much, is the most tolerant religion, but, while it tolerates the faiths of the *ahl al-kitāb*, it does not permit propaganda, and apostasy is a heinous crime. The provisions of Article 7 are comprehensive and fully protect other religions. Article 12 is equally liberal: "No law should, on the ground of race, religion, caste or place of birth, deprive any citizen of the right to attend any educational institution that is receiving aid from public revenues."[100] Taken together with Article 7, which exempts adherents of any religion from paying taxes to be used for any other religion or denomination, tolerance could not go further.

The first Principle of Policy largely corresponds to Article 25 of the 1956 Constitution, which is usually referred to as the Enabling Clause. It reads: "1. The Muslims of Pakistan should be enabled, individually and collectively, to order their lives in accordance with the fundamental principles and basic concepts of Islam, and should be provided with facilities whereby they may be enabled to understand the meaning of life according to those principles and concepts." "Fundamental principles and basic concepts" take the place of "the Holy Quran and Sunnah" of 1956. On the other hand, as already stated, "Islamiat" is added to the "Holy Quran" in subclause 2. Both constitutions explicitly say that—to quote Article 3 (Fair Treatment of Minorities) of 1962—"the members of minorities should be given due opportunity to enter the service of Pakistan".[101] Article 18 (Elimination of Riba) simply states: "Riba (Usury) should be eliminated."[102] The earlier version read: "The State shall endeavour to eliminate *riba* as early as possible."[102] The president thus decided a point of dispute of long standing, whether *ribā* means interest or usury, in favour of the latter. No time limit is mentioned either. The clauses about prostitution, gambling and drinking were briefly discussed earlier.[103]

"Part X. Islamic Institutions" is intended to give effect—within the limits already stated—to the Islamic provisions of the Principles of Policy. They are the president's responsibility and entirely in his discretion:

There shall be an Advisory Council of Islamic Ideology. The Council shall consist of such number of members, being not less than five and not more than twelve, as the President may determine. Members of the Council shall be appointed by the President on such terms and conditions as the President may determine. The President shall, in selecting a person for appointment to the Council, have regard to the person's understanding and appreciation of Islam and of the economic, political, legal and administrative problems of Pakistan.... The functions of the Council shall be—(*a*) to make recommendations to the Central Government and the Provincial Governments as to means of enabling and encouraging the Muslims of Pakistan to order their lives in all respects in accordance with the principles and concepts of Islam; and (*b*) to advise the National Assembly, a Provincial Assembly, the President or a Governor on any question referred to the Council under Article 6, that is to say, a question as to whether a proposed law disregards or violates, or is otherwise not in accordance with, the Principles of Law-making. (2) When, under Article 6, a question is referred by an Assembly, the President or a Governor to the Council for advice, the Council shall, within seven days thereafter, inform the Assembly, the

President or Governor, as the case requires, of the period within which the Council expects to be able to furnish that advice. (3) Where the Assembly...considers that, in the public interest, the making of the proposed law in relation to which the question arose should not be postponed until the advice is furnished, the law may be made before the advice furnished.[104]

Not only is the function of the Council—the commission recommended by the constitution commission in a rather emaciated form—purely advisory, but also the government need not even wait for such advice to be tendered, if the public interest demands the promulgation of a law.

It is further laid down—in chapter 2 of this part x—that:

(1) There shall be an organization to be known as Islamic Research Institute, which shall be established by the President. (2) The function of the Institute shall be to undertake Islamic research and instruction in Islam for the purpose of assisting in the reconstruction of Muslim society on a truly Islamic basis.[105]

As in the first constitution, oaths of office demand simply "true faith and allegiance to Pakistan".[106]

Political theology has scored a Pyrrhic victory in the battle for an Islamic constitution, and an Islamic state properly so called is as long a way off as in 1949. The effective governmental leadership, as distinct from the leadership of the political parties, upholds the ideal of a "Muslim society on a truly Islamic basis"—whatever this may mean in terms of legislation—but continues, on the practical plane, to conduct the business of state and to build up a sound economy in the "public interest" (the Islamic *maṣlaḥa*!) as it understands it. We must realise that it is extremely difficult for the government—infinitely more difficult than for any Muslim government in the other countries I have visited—to govern effectively on an even keel, beset as it is by the political theology of the religious movements and Islamic parties on the one hand, and by Western-educated politicians and members of the liberal professions, who genuinely want a parliamentary system with parliament in effective control of the Executive, on the other hand.

The Islamic provisions apart, the President's Constitution certainly has a contemporary character giving him wide powers, much wider in fact than the American Constitution confers on the American president, since executive authority is exclusively vested in him. The checks and balances written into the Constitution of the Islamic Republic of Pakistan are weak, and doubly so under a strong, energetic president. These aspects of the constitution must remain outside our purview. Suffice it to mention in passing one feature in conclusion which usually is the essential prerequisite of a democratic system: universal suffrage. There are perhaps good reasons why Pakistan could not now adopt universal suffrage, chief among them still widespread though diminishing illiteracy—yet this was no obstacle in India. The electorate is composed of the members of the Basic Democracies, but the demand for universal suffrage continues to be made, not least by the *Jamā'at-i-Islāmī* of Maulana Maudūdī. From the point of view of modern constitutional law one can hardly call the Constitution of Pakistan Islamic, mainly because Article 6(2) explicitly secures any law against an effective challenge in the name of Qur'an and Sunna. The function of the *Sharī'a*, even if we were to accept its modern equation with Qur'an and Sunna only, to the exclusion of the other principles of *Fiqh* and of *Fiqh* itself as in any way binding, is, to repeat, purely advisory. The fact that the preamble and the Principles of Law-making express universally accepted ideals and ideas does not make the justiciable part of the constitution—and this is what really matters—Islamic, notwithstanding the identity of these ideals and ideas with those enunciated by Islam in Qur'an and Sunna.

That the observer of the Pakistani scene is forced to these conclusions may be seen from the weighty pronouncement of the minister for law and parliamentary affairs, Mr Justice Muhammad Munir of *Munir Report* fame, and a former chief justice of Pakistan.[107] He informed his audience that the president had appointed eight members of the Advisory Council of Islamic Ideology in conformity with the constitution and referred to the difficulties involved in the appointments, since the qualifications demanded of such members were "cumulative and not alternative". He said: "...persons having an understanding and appreciation of Islam and also of the economic, political, legal and administrative problems of Pakistan could not be easily chosen. Anyhow, an effort has been made to comply with this constitutional requirement." In view of the advisory function of the council under Article 6, he made this point:

...it was necessary to have on the Council persons who not only have requisite understanding and appreciation of Islam, but have also a thorough grasp of Constitutional Law, because under the principles of law-making, though the first principle is that no law should be repugnant to Islam, there are 15 other principles which have no direct relationship with Islam and [are] in the nature of an enunciation of human rights recognised by the United Nations of which Pakistan is a member. These principles can be given effect to only if a constitutional and juristic approach is made to a question as it arises. The President has, therefore, included in the Council two eminent persons both of whom have been judges of the Supreme Court and who can also appreciate the religious side of the problems that are likely to present themselves. One of these gentlemen had once before been deputed by the Government to bring the existing law into conformity with Islam while the other had been selected as Chairman of the Islamic Laws Commission whose function was to prepare a code of the injunctions of Islam. Another member of the Commission has been engaged for several years on research in Islamic Law as Director of the Central Institute of Islamic Research and has high academic qualifications in Western education. The remaining members are learned divines who are experts in the Shariat and Fiqh and who understand the problems with which Muslim philosophy is confronted today.

Two observations are called for here. One is that the president has acted upon the stipulation in the constitution and has tried to find the best persons available for a task which is not the easier for its merely advisory nature. The other observation is meant to underline the complexity of the matter because it is taken out of its legitimate medieval context and is placed within our time, which demands, as Mr Justice Munir rightly stresses, "a constitutional and juristic approach". The religious concern of political theology arising out of the first principle of law-making has to be weighed against and brought into relation with fifteen other non-religious principles of law-making to which Pakistan is committed as a member of the United Nations, irrespective of its ideology—itself the outcome of political theology.

The law minister also dealt with the rules of procedure of the council, which

should provide that when a matter is referred to the Council, it should require the Islamic Research Institute to collect the material and undertake other preliminary work. The Institute should then formulate its own opinion and, together with the material on which it is based, send it to the Council. Thereafter, the Council should not only consider the opinion of the Institute but also undertake, where necessary, an independent study with the assistance of other learned divines who may be specialists in the branch of law to which the problem relates.

The religious and political nature of Islamic law is clearly recognised since the council is advised to consult political, economic or administrative experts.

The Council may well have a standing body of such advisers [the Governor of the State Bank of Pakistan and the Chairman or Deputy Chairman of the Planning Commission are mentioned]. Having thoroughly sifted the material and discovered the essential principle, it will be for the Council to apply it to the concrete situation and to return an opinion. In returning the opinion, the Council should forward to the referring authority the proceedings of the Islamic Research Institute, the opinion offered by the advisers and its own opinion. If the Council is not unanimous, it should forward all the opinions by its members.

The law minister then reminded his audience that the council was only an advisory body and that the final authority rested with the Legislature which decided.

The council has yet another function: to recommend measures designed to enable and encourage the Muslims of Pakistan "to order their lives in all respects in accordance with the principles and concepts of Islam". Mr Justice Munir went on:

The Council shall thus be a standing body engaged in discovering the principles and concepts of Islam, and the deviations or departures from such principles and concepts current among the Muslims of Pakistan. Here it may have to draw a distinction between the discretionary and the mandatory [hence the importance of having learned judges among its members] and to determine the area of human action in which complete freedom is given by Islam to the individual or society.[108] If Muslim society is to be reconstructed on a truly Islamic basis, such basis will have to be determined and declared with precision which is an essential attribute of law enabling it to claim obedience. In this connection, the shift from the old to the new modes of life and activity will have to be located and appraised in the light of the relevant forces and responsibilities of reversion or variation to be judged. There are two ways of making men order their lives in accordance with certain concepts, namely, (i) voluntary effort to induce people to mould their lives in the desired manner, and (ii) legal compulsion to make them to do so. Both these methods are open to the Council to be recommended to the Government in the form of concrete proposals, but it will be for the Government to decide whether in the circumstances the proposals are feasible. One more point regarding the Advisory Council of Islamic Ideology is that it is a creation of the Constitution and has therefore to function within the limits, and it is not entitled to ignore or disregard any provisions of the Constitution.

Yet, while as a modern jurist and a minister of the government Mr Justice Munir stresses the political and juristic limits within which the council is confined and can function, as a modern Muslim he passes comment on the novelty of such a constitutional arrangement, which is highly significant and deserves mention and careful notice. He says:

It is to my mind the first instance where, in modern history, an effort is being made to bring Islam in impact with modern political, legal, ethical, social and economic conditions and to present new and unanticipated problems for solution to a jurisprudence which for almost one thousand years has been in a static condition in the belief that the rules embodied therein are eternal, which are capable of application to all given situations, irrespective of variations of time, place and conditions. In other words, the experiment being tried here is intended to generate a process to apply Islam to present conditions which, as respects the production, distribution and consumption of wealth, and the conception of the State and of its relationship with the individual and with other states in times of peace and war, are entirely different from the conditions in which the jurisprudence took its birth and developed.

This is clearly an attempt at applying the classical doctrine of divinely revealed law being the law of the state to fundamentally different conditions in the modern world without recognising the eternal validity of that law as it developed historically until it became static. It does not matter whether this happened a thousand years ago, as Mr JusticeMunir thinks, or only with the advent of British rule over India, as Maulana Maudūdī holds: the principle is the same. But, while Maulana Maudūdī is a classical representative of political theology, Mr Justice Munir seems to be prepared, at least in principle, to allow theological considerations to influence political decisions and action, as is clear from the continuation of his press statement: "We shut our eyes to realities if we suppose that the present age does not hold a challenge to Islam and we misunderstand Islam if we think that it does not hold a challenge to present values." The same duality—for in modern man the two sides are not component parts of a unity under divine sovereignty any longer—meets us in his further statement:

> The process to be adopted by the Council will, in essence, be judicial interpretation and will have to be performed in definite legal terms as one law, when in conflict with another, has to yield to or override the latter. But no judicial interpretation, however rational, can ignore or mutilate the text unless the text itself be held to have been meant for a different situation or a temporary purpose.

Is this an attempt to exclude theological premises and arguments and keep proceedings on a strictly legal plane? This would be my interpretation. And yet, if "the text" refers to the *naṣṣ* of the Qur'an—as seems likely—does his statement suggest that this text should be set aside if inapplicable on any other count than belief in revelation and its eternal validity? We might think of the penalty for theft, and it is possible that this was in Mr Justice Munir's mind.

It is clear from this remarkable utterance of the law minister soon after the promulgation of the new constitution that, no matter how restricted the power of the Advisory Council of Islamic Ideology and its influence on actual legislation are, its creation and advisory function are an earnest of the intention of those who hold the real power in Pakistan to recognise, if not legally to implement, that the state is based on Islamic ideology. Institutions like the Council and the Islamic Research Institute may be considered but a token—not to say a concession—by the Western-educated and -oriented political leadership and intelligentsia. But they cannot prevent the religious leadership from taking in any case the Advisory Council seriously and as a symbol, if not more, of an Islamic state to come. Moreover, these religious parties and groups persist in interpreting especially the Repugnancy Clause as mandatory in spite of Law Minister Khurshed's explicit reiteration that it is not justiciable, even with the substitution of "shall" for "should" in its wording.

Events since the time the constitution came into force, especially since the formation of parties was again permitted, would indicate that the will and determination to make Pakistan an Islamic state governed by Islamic law have lost nothing of their impetus. It would be wrong to see in this nothing but manœuvring for position and gaining political advantages, as the nation-wide celebrations of the birthday of the prophet Muhammad on 14 August 1962, which coincided with the fifteenth birthday of Pakistan, show. Ministers and former ministers, like A. K. Brohi, university professors and respected religious leaders appealed to the masses to emulate the prophet and realise the ideals of Islam. On the other hand, a comparison between the speeches made by prominent *'ulamā*, including members of the *Jamā'at-i-Islāmī*, and those by lay speakers reveals the cleavage between traditional orthodoxy, which is unremittingly anti-West, and the more liberal, moderate approach from the president downwards. *Dawn*'s leading article expresses the situation neatly:

The danger we must guard against is the attempt of this orthodoxy—in the name of religion—to impose a tyranny which is really calculated to create a climate for the emergence of their own dictatorship. At the other extreme lies an equally dangerous menace—that of aggressive and ruthless materialism which regards the very mention of the word Islam as a relic of superstition. Our Revolution strove for a balance between the two opposing extremes; and in the affairs of the State and in other fields of national life it has throughout been its architect's well-meaning endeavour to support a movement away from the excessive concentration on the dogmatic aspects of Islam but not in any way disregarding the true tenets of the religion. But this is a task in which the enlightened ulema, the country's Central and provincial legislatures and the intelligentsia in general will have to take a more substantial share than has so far been noticed.[109]

The president himself had made a strong appeal, which was reported in *Dawn*, a few days earlier,[110]

President Ayub said that Pakistan was a Muslim country and had been established with the object that its people should march with the times and the people of other countries, and at the same time lead their lives in the Islamic way. These things, he warned, could not be done by mere talking. Work and constructive work was needed for that....He said that there was a vast difference in the thinking of literate and illiterate people in the country. The educated people were getting away from religion because the way in which religion was presented to them made them run away from it....In order that the people might lead their lives on the Islamic pattern, and at the same time keep pace with the modern world, the Islamic Ideology Board had been set up.... Then there was the Islamic Research Institute.

Speaking of the procedure to be adopted by the Advisory Council, the president stated:

This would provide the country with the course on which to move for the betterment of the country and the people. This course had not been adopted in any Muslim country so far, and [he] expressed the hope that in the next five or ten years a clear cut Islamic way of life would be manifest...this was the only course open to save the people from a slavish mentality. These institutions [Council and Research Institute] would help in the creation of a real Islamic atmosphere in Pakistan. He said these institutions had a philosophy behind them and they would serve as centres of such philosophy which would take the Muslim world out of the abyss into which it had fallen. The President observed that if this had not been done the people would have drifted away from religion, with the advance of education...Pakistan had been established on an ideology of religion and that Islam alone was "our cementing force".... He warned the people that if they did not realise their duty in preserving this ideology, the country would be full of Muslims in name but not in fact.

It is significant how the president sees in these two institutions the indispensable means to make the people conscious of their heritage and to model their lives on Islamic ideology. Thus, if their influence on the laws in force and to be made is rather problematical, in the educational field their influence should be felt much more strongly. This makes sense, but the intrinsic difficulty of applying political theology in our time has so far not been solved, if a solution is at all possible. Without considerable reform Islam as a way of life cannot be modernised. Any attempt at even the most moderate reform is, however, being opposed and fought by those who want to apply medieval political theology unadulterated, as the attempt to have the Muslim Family Laws Ordinance repealed by the new parliament clearly shows.[111] It is difficult to understand why restrictions on polygamy and strict safeguards in divorce should arouse the hostility of the '*ulamā* unless it were for the fact that personal status law has always been *Sharī'a* law and its *pièce de résistance*. The measure has been branded as un-Islamic: Maulana G. Ghaus, a member of the Provincial Assembly, is reported in *Dawn* as stating at a public meeting: "that the Family Laws were unacceptable to the people and would never be accepted by the Ulema of the country" and he

> challenged the competency of the Islamic Advisory Council which, he said, was constituted of persons who had no "knowledge of Islam, Shariat or Sunnah"....Maulana Ghaus deplored the "immodesty and shamelessness" of women. The meeting unanimously adopted a resolution calling for immediate repeal of the Muslim Family Laws Ordinance as they were against the dictates of Islam....The resolution also urged the Government to appoint "competent persons" to the Islamic Advisory Council to ensure that all Islamic laws are protected.[111]

Of the eight members of the council four are *'ulamā*!

A day earlier four members of the West Pakistan Provincial Assembly and three editors of Lahore (two of weeklies, one of a monthly), including the ex-general secretary of the *Jamā'at-i-Islāmī*, issued a statement to the press condemning demonstrations by women in favour of the ordinance, containing the following passage:

> Instead of letting the Assembly decide this purely academic and religious issue after a cool consideration of the whole affair in the light of the teachings of the Holy Quran and Sunnah, a section of our women-folk, whose entire life is a standing challenge to even the most fundamental teachings of Islam, have started a campaign to get this issue decided in their favour by force of demonstrations and other such like tactics.... We wish to make it clear to the people responsible for creating this such [*sic*!] situation that, if they want to decide this issue by demonstrations, the general Muslim populace can make much bigger demonstrations and gather momentum in their favour.[112]

Comment would be superfluous.

The six women members of the National Assembly appealed to the government "to see that women have adequate representation on the Advisory Council of Islamic Ideology". These women members also stated:

> We sincerely believe that the question of Family Laws is not that of women's special interest only, but a question in which the entire nation...is vitally interested. The entire nation is bound to be affected as a whole if half the population, constituting a most vital section of the nation, is deprived of the rightful position in the onward march of the nation....[113]

In a thoughtful article, S. M. Abdullah[114] rightly stresses the close connection of this question of woman's rights and freedoms with the tremendous economic and social changes in the wake of Westernisation. Besides, it is also a class question in so far as only women of the upper and well-to-do classes chafe under the old dispensation, whereas the overwhelming majority of women belonging to the masses of ordinary people not only accept their lot, but are said to view the educated woman with suspicion and disapproval. The whole question of the place of woman in contemporary Muslim states will be briefly discussed in a separate chapter.

In the context of the present discussion two facts stand out. In the first place, a modern, Westernised government decides a question of Islamic law and not the traditional custodians of this law, the *'ulamā*. The already quoted Maulana Ghaus, M.P.A. and general secretary of the West Pakistan *Jamiatul Ulema-i-Islam* (which organisation constituted itself into a political party) demanded that the majority of the council should be made up of "ulema whose opinion could be considered as the 'last word' in religious matters", while attacking the government for "working against the Islamic principles in the 'name of family laws and art'", and declared the President "should immediately set up a Board of Ulema to put the President's declared intention of making laws in accordance with Islamic principles into practice".[115]

On the same day four religious leaders in East Pakistan took up a suggestion alleged to have been made by Begum Shah Nawaz that the "Qazi court system, as was practised during the golden era of the Caliphate", should be established in Pakistan, for, they held, "the present judiciary system...had failed to serve woman". They want to see "special courts for trying cases relating to the rights of women, as granted by Islam, to help them secure justice easily, cheaply and quickly". They appealed "to Begum Shah Nawaz and other APWA leaders not to support the Muslim Family Laws Ordinance. The Shariat courts and not this ordinance will safeguard the rights of women."[116]

The second point is that this issue clearly demonstrates how closely linked questions of religious law are with politics, particularly in modern Muslim states. They not only are constitutional matters, or the concern of lawyers, but also deeply affect social and economic life, and it is for this reason that they assume such importance.

Another controversial measure adopted by President Ayub's government is family planning in order to check the enormous population growth of Pakistan. A National Research Institute of Family Planning and central and provincial Family Planning Councils were set up, and practical measures are aided through films, the press and the radio. Foreign aid in the form of capital, consultants and equipment has been given. The charge that family planning was un-Islamic is countered by the government with the opinion that, since the Qur'an does not contain a clear injunction against it, it is justified: this follows the principle of Islamic jurisprudence—"what is not forbidden, is permitted".[117]

It is altogether noteworthy that the president of Pakistan has taken quite a few steps to further religion under martial law which the democratic governments, it seems, were afraid to take for fear of repercussions from the orthodox side. Among these is the "Auqaf Ordinance" of 1959, which placed the administration of these pious bequests—or at least about 700 of them—under a government department, as in other Muslim countries. The department succeeded, by a proper administration and through pooling of resources, to make money available for the payment of senior *Khatibs* on the provincial civil service scale. It also established educational institutions which will be discussed in the appropriate chapter on education.[118]

These measures in the interest of live religion must be balanced against the resistance of the government and the intelligentsia to establishing an Islamic state based not only on Islamic principles of brotherhood, equality and social justice, to which democracy is added for good measure—and on which everybody seems to be agreed—but on Islamic law, whatever precise meaning is given to it by orthodox or liberal interpretation.

In conclusion, it must be repeated that Islamic ideology is understood differently by the contending forces in Pakistan just as Islam is differently understood. The government, led decisively by the president and the Western-educated intelligentsia, is opposed by the *'ulamā*, Maulana Maudūdī's party (the *Jamā'at-i-Islāmī*) and other more moderate Islamic parties, and the gulf between the two sides is very wide. Not that there are no areas of agreement between intelligentsia and the other side in such matters as universal suffrage and popular representation—albeit for different reasons. Thus, the *Jamā'at-i-Islāmī* wants it in order to gain power by constitutional means, pack the legislature with its supporters and gradually change existing laws with the aim of achieving one uniformly Islamic law.

The real dividing line is the attitude to Islamic law, and it is difficult to see how an accommodation could be brought about. Unfortunately, the issue is befogged by this "Islamic ideology" which has gained recognition in the new constitution at least in the "Advisory Council of Islamic Ideology", quite apart from frequent mention in speeches by the president and his ministers. This shows how political theology has gained an entry into the leadership of the state, and tends to aggravate the political difficulties and dominate the scene to the exclusion of other problems which some consider of more vital importance for the development of Pakistan. Islamic ideology also helps the traditionalists to play politics and there may well be today the danger again—which President Ayub saw and declared after his *coup d'état* in 1958—that the politicians before the Revolution dragged in the name of Islam only to desecrate it. In his speeches he has repeatedly stressed that Islam must furnish the moral and spiritual values of the nation, but in the service of a progressive and prosperous Pakistan which he tries to rouse the people to build. Unfortunately, the language the people at large, poor and uneducated, understand is that of Imams and *Khatibs*, commonly referred to as "mullahs". The learned *'ulamā*, as is evident from the quotations earlier on, in and out of Parliament, claim to represent the people. They have given little evidence of rousing the masses to exert themselves in the direction the government and the administration are moving to achieve economic and social betterment. As long as the *'ulamā* and those who think like them and follow them attack the Advisory Council of Islamic Ideology and the Central Institute of Islamic Research, and are not prepared to move away from their narrow medievalism by declaring every reform to be *bid'a* (innovation = heresy) and un-Islamic, no co-operation, much less national unity and common endeavour, can be expected.

The 1962 Constitution tries to bridge the gulf between the theological and the rational approach to politics. Though there need be no incompatibility between the two on the basis of faith, no bridge can be built to link religion and politics, as long as one side means principles and the other side means law (not to forget that, while in the Middle Ages faith bound all together, in our time faith has lost its universal appeal and power). Are we therefore driven to the conclusion that only the separation of religion and politics offers a solution? I am unable to answer with a clear "yes" or "no" because Pakistan is a special case without parallel in any other Muslim country, certainly in none of those I visited. The history of the Muslims in the Indo-Pakistan subcontinent and the birth of Pakistan demand (so it seems to me on the strength of my experience) recognition of Islam, not so much in its constitution as in its building up not as an ideological state, but as a modern Muslim state which must rely on the fundamental values of Islam.

These values can only be expressed in law if a liberal interpretation enables all shades of Muslims as well as the non-Muslim minorities to live under it without conflict of conscience and without discrimination. Such a happy state of affairs must remain an ideal to be striven for at least for some time to come, but as an aim it may be the only bond which can unite all Pakistanis in one nation. Nobody would underrate the difficulties in the path to that goal. It would require a reform of Islam which nobody seems to envisage. Short of such a reform, a lay state with Islam as the state religion of the majority with freedom of conscience and freedom to practise any or no religion appears at present the only possible alternative, not only to an outsider, but also to some devout Muslims in Pakistan I was privileged to meet.

It may be doubted whether the generation which founded Pakistan, and is at present still mainly responsible for its upbuilding, will be able to achieve a definite solution either way. But it is certain that not even the younger generation and their children will be able to settle the problem of Islam in Pakistan without an intensive training in *Islāmīyāt* in a presentation commensurate with the twentieth century, which may be many things, but is certainly not a century of faith in God pervading individual and social life. Even in Muslim lay states Islam is recognised as an important factor in education for citizenship, Islam as faith and, particularly, Islam as civilisation and as a civilising force, as an essential part of the mental make-up of the individual citizen and of state and society. Islam gives content and meaning to their nationalism. Islam is in transition today, and it is quite possible that in order to find its proper place in a Muslim national state it will have to be transformed before it can once more become a spiritual force of consequence to Muslims and the world at large.

APPENDIX TO CHAPTER 8

SOME RELECTIONS ON ISLAM IN INDIA TODAY

It would be more than presumptuous were I to pontificate on the position of Islam and of the Muslims in India, a secular state with a well-functioning parliamentary democracy. The Muslims are a minority who were once rulers of a Hindu majority; today they are Indian citizens of the Muslim persuasion. They owe and give loyalty to India, their nation and state. Islam is their private concern, whether as a religion or as a cultural heritage. The right to write about the Indian Muslims is based on long, friendly conversations with representative Muslim scholars and statesmen whose attitude to Islam is conditioned by their passionate concern and love for India. Quite a few of them were in the forefront of India's struggle for freedom and independence and they were united with Hindu Indians as nationalists. Their common purpose shaped their outlook: they fought and worked and are still working for India as Indians; that they are Muslims is of as little importance as being Hindus is for their Hindu fellow-citizens, at least in theory. But is this really so? Have we not heard that communalism was a potent factor in the conception and realisation of a separate homeland for the Muslims of the subcontinent? Hence a qualification must be made to the effect that the statement applies in the first place, if not exclusively, to the Western-educated élite: Abul Kalām Āzād, Zakir Husain, Humayun Kabir on the Muslim side, Gandhi, Nehru and Radhakrishnan on the Hindu side, all emancipated modern Indians, either agnostics or of varying degrees of religiosity from orthodoxy to liberalism. We must add to these many university professors in the arts and the sciences and high-ranking civil servants and diplomats. To the masses on both sides it is hardly applicable. Speaking to Indians who belong to the Hindu majority, whether they are orthodox or liberal or non-professing Hindus, one learns that among the teaming millions of humble, poor, uneducated folk Hinduism is strong, and this has inevitable repercussions on the wellbeing and practical equality of the millions of observant Muslims in the same station in life.

We visited Delhi, including the *Jamia Millia Islamia*, a mixed Muslim–Hindu model educational establishment of unique character under Muslim direction (see also pp. 356 f.); the Muslim University at Aligarh, which then had 70 per cent Muslim and 30 per cent Hindu students; Patna with its wonderful Khuda Bukhsh Library of unique illuminated Arabic and Persian manuscripts and its remarkable museum; Hyderabad with its Osmania University and its Institute of Indo-Middle East Cultural Studies; Benares with its Muslim weavers; and Calcutta.

It may be objected that, since the views of a large cross-section of the Muslims in India were not obtained, the views here summarised are neither typical nor reliable. To this I can only say—without mentioning any names for the reason given in the Introduction—that the views freely expressed to me are those of thinking Muslims who have not only a clear concept of Islam, but also of Indian Islam, only even more so than the Pakistani Muslims. For Islam in medieval India—we have seen before that in India they do not speak of Muslim, but of medieval India—serves them to a large extent as a justification from history for their present attitude and interpretation.

Orthodox opinion which—in some cases at least—is almost if not entirely identical with that of Maulana Maudūdī's *Jamā'at-i-Islāmī*. It holds to the classical concept of the religious and political unity of Islam, distinguishes between *Dār al-Islām* and *Dār al-ḥarb* and between believers and *d̠immīs*. Willing to discard some of *Fiqh*, it believes in the feasibility of restoring original Islam with the *Sharī'a* based on Qur'an and Sunna, and wants to keep personal status law as it has been. This view seems rather utopian in present-day India.

The majority opinion starts from the claim, based on the history of Islam in medieval and Mughul India, that Islam in India has always been a personal religion, divorced from government and administration. The *Sharī'a*, they aver, was never the constitution, never the law of the land; it could not have been in the presence of other religious and cultural groups, even if ruled by Muslims. They quote in support Barani for pre-Mughul Muslim rule and Shāh Walī Ullāh for the Mughul period. But even if an Islamic state had existed then, it is impossible and undesirable in the twentieth century under entirely different social and economic conditions.

Islamic studies flourish at the universities of Aligarh, with its Institute of Islamic Studies, of Calcutta and Hyderabad, and the Institute of Indo-Middle Eastern Studies produces a series of monographs and texts. Nor must we forget the quarterly *Islamic Culture* with a fine library and a group of able scholars. Agnosticism is widespread, but it goes hand in hand with a live consciousness of a cultural heritage of great significance and personal value. Agnosticism often goes with left-wing politics: the conviction is widely held that only a radical social revolution can prepare the ground for a renewal of Islam. The alliance of the Muslim rulers with the Rajput feudal lords is stressed in defence of the thesis that Islam never was a social force for good in India; the rulers were not interested in the lot of the masses. Nor do those who think like that hold the *'ulamā* and *fuqahā* in honour, because in their opinion they were obscurantists who barred any progress in thought by suppressing philosophy. Yet this view is combined with a genuine appreciation of Muslim ethics and Islam's high standard of personal conduct.

From here a line goes to those who have developed a kind of religious philosophy based on the abiding values of Islam as a personal faith wholly compatible with and complementary to Indian patriotism and wholehearted service to the Indian state and nation as fully equal citizens. The teachings of their Muslim faith enable them to make a significant contribution to the solution of India's many problems, not least the caste problem. That Islam is free from the caste ideology with its teaching of brotherhood, equality and social justice, compassion and charitableness is an asset which, so they believe, can and must be turned to the solution of pressing social, economic and cultural problems. In this teaching, which they are trying to live up to, lies their claim to, and exercise of, equality with the Hindu majority.

There are others who are convinced that Islam has no contribution to make to our largely economic and social problems. Like other religions, Islam is finished in their opinion. They look to socialism to bring about a classless as well as a casteless society.

These views, to repeat, are held by the Western-educated intellectual élite. Inevitably, though perhaps more unconsciously than deliberately, their attitude is influenced by their situation as Muslims in a minority in an officially secular India. Their sheer intellectual power, ability and unquestioned, trusted loyalty secure them full equality, which becomes more qualified the lower one gets in the social scale. These outstanding men do not deny the difficulties and admit discrimination here and there, but they honestly believe that India has greater and more important problems to cope with than that of its Muslim minority, and they are determined to work for their solution. One difficulty is, however, freely admitted (though its seriousness is evaluated differently by different people) that is, the language problem. Urdu is the language of Islam as faith and culture. But the Muslim children must learn Hindi to be able to compete for jobs, to carve out a career for themselves. This is naturally bound to affect their religious instruction, which is extra-curricular.

It is to be expected that Muslims who opted for India and stayed in their posts to help build up a free, independent India view the creation of Pakistan with scepticism, if not disapproval. They stress that Muslim communalism arose late, under British rule only, and that Islam entered into the political movement of Muslims at a late hour. Many think partition was a mistake, the result of politicians' ambitions; they show concern for the success of Pakistan. Among non-Muslim Indians one could hear the view expressed that federation with maximum autonomy for both India and Pakistan was the only solution, though unlikely to be achieved in our generation. It was held that the principal reason for a separate Muslim state—this was said by the same scholar—was Hindu refusal to sit at one table with Muslims and that there exists in fact a personal incompatibility between Muslims and Hindus, except in the higher strata of Westernised, emancipated society.

This was in the winter of 1960–1, and it is a sad reflection on *Homo sapiens* to have to admit that the situation has steadily deteriorated. It seems that personal incompatibility is increasing and fanned into communal antagonism. This is not the work nor the wish of the leadership at the top, but one begins to wonder whether those Muslim intellectuals and Indian patriots were not after all right in their idea that nothing short of a radical social revolution will solve the problem not only of Islamic renewal, but of communal harmony as well. One suspects that the latter was uppermost in their minds and, without going into the politics of this question, it seems reasonable to assume that Islam as the faith of the individual and as the source of his social conduct stands a better chance in a truly secular India than if it is up against orthodox Hindu revivalism, which can only harden Muslim separateness and sharpen communalism.

Another observation may be made in conclusion. The number of Muslims in India is more than three times the number of Hindus in Pakistan. Consequently, the minority problem is different in India from that in Pakistan, and one wonders what effect the stress on Islamic ideology has on the Muslims on the other side of the border. While this thought cannot influence the Pakistani decision between Islam as the private concern of the individual citizen and an Islamic state on the pattern of the *'ulamā* or of G. A. Parwez, it may be worth pondering whether two lay states granting freedom of religion and encouraging the realisation of the ethical teachings of religion in the personal and especially in the social spheres would not more easily be able to compose their differences and live in peace and amity together as sons of the great subcontinent of India and Pakistan? Ideology is a political concept, even if its contents be religious, and it can be dangerous in national no less than in international relations.

CHAPTER 9

ISLAM IN MALAYA

At the time of our visit, the Malays who are Muslims formed a little over half of the population of the Federation of Malaya,[1] and the slightly smaller half consisted largely of Chinese, Buddhist or Christian, and to a much smaller extent of Tamil-speaking Indians. It was, therefore, reasonable to expect that amid the strains and stresses inherent in such a mixed population an Islamic state based on an Islamic ideology would not be the most appropriate institution. The Malays are a gentle, friendly people living mostly in the countryside and making a living by agriculture, largely rice and paddy planting, and by fishing. Commerce is almost entirely in Chinese hands, and industry, largely tin mining, in British hands, although the Chinese have begun to take an interest in industry as well, bringing capital from Hong Kong and the Chinese mainland. There is an upper stratum of Western-educated Malays who man the government and administration; the army and the police are also largely recruited from Malays. Political power is in Malay hands, but economic power in those of the Chinese and the British. We know that politics and economics cannot be kept separate, naturally, and the Malay government was and is making special efforts to secure a share of industry and commerce for the Malays.

In the Federation itself there was no special problem, but Singapore with 70 per cent of its population Chinese presented difficulties since a merger with Malaya was being considered. The government of Singapore tried to do its best for its four hundred thousand Malays by special concessions like providing free education for all Malay children, helping the fishermen, who are mostly Malays, declaring Malay the national language and having a Malay as head of state.[2] Singapore has learnt from the independence of India and Ceylon, which took place earlier, that communalism does not disappear with colonialism. Hence its government has given priority to the cultural problem in order to keep racial and religious peace and to control communalism. Yet there was—in 1961—a pan-Islamist faction composed of rather disparate elements:

Westernised intellectuals, economically advancing and advanced businessmen, teachers, and an active, articulate group of orthodox Malays. The pan-Islamism of the intellectuals is said to be politically progressive, but their political ideology creates a social problem as far as family ties and customs are concerned. Religious pan-Islamism shows itself in a certain rigidity which favours communal solidarity and impedes social and cultural integration. It was very difficult to see clearly because economic advance appeared to militate against the rather static orthodoxy in belief and practice, and to loosen the communal bond provided by Islam.

A greater Malaysia in which Muslim accessions balance Chinese domination in Singapore may solve the dilemma, provided Islam comes to grips with economic and social change. In Malaya proper, communalism was not in evidence. Whether it is a problem beyond the natural stresses mentioned earlier I could not say, since I concentrated on the position of Islam and on the attitudes and views of the Malay Muslims in my travels through several of the states under a Malay sultan and the two former British governorates of Penang and Malacca, which now have a Malay governor.

Contrary to what happened in Pakistan, Malaya was spared a constitutional struggle with Islam as a burning and dividing issue. Like Pakistan, Malaya was under British rule and domination, but the transition from colonial to independent, sovereign self-rule was smooth and orderly. Although Malayanisation was then in full swing and nearing completion, British senior civil servants were still carrying on and trained Malays to take over completely. The British permanent secretary to the Ministry of Education and his Malay colleagues efficiently arranged my programme in advance and gave me every possible help. This enabled me to see how Islam functioned in Malaya on all levels. The separation of state and religion is anchored in the Constitution of the Federation of Malaya. This lays down that Islam is to be the state religion and declares the head of state, the king or Yang di-Pertuan Agong, also head of the Muslim religion in the states of Penang and Malacca as provided for in their constitutions. In the princely states of the Federation the sultan is the head of the Muslim religion, in accordance with their constitutions.

Now, a brief survey of the relevant provisions and articles of the Malayan Constitution, promulgated in December 1957, will illustrate the position of Islam:

Part I, "The States, Religion and Law of the Federation", Article 3 states:

(1) Islam is the religion of the Federation; but other religions may be practised in peace and harmony in any part of the Federation. (2) In every State other than Malacca and Penang the position of the Ruler as the Head of the Muslim religion in his State in the manner and to the extent acknowledged and declared by the Constitution of that State, and, subject to that Constitution, all rights, privileges, prerogatives and powers enjoyed by him as Head of that religion, are unaffected and unimpaired. (3) The Constitutions of the States of Malacca and Penang shall each make provision for conferring on the Yang di-Pertuan Agong the position of Head of the Muslim religion in that State.[3]

Part II, "Fundamental Liberties". Of importance in our context is Article 8:

(1) All persons are equal before the Law and entitled to the equal protection of the Law. (2) No discrimination against citizens on the ground only of religion, race, descent or place of birth in any law or in the appointment to any office or employment under a public authority or in the administration of any law relating to the acquisition, holding or disposition of property or the establishing or carrying on of any trade, business, profession, vocation or employment....(5) This article does not invalidate or prohibit (*a*) any provision regulating personal law; (*b*) any provision or practice restricting office or employment connected with the affairs of any religion, or of an institution managed by a group professing any religion, to persons professing that religion....

Article 11:

(1) Every person has the right to profess and practise his religion and, subject to Clause (4), to propagate it. (2) No person shall be compelled to pay any tax the proceeds of which are specially allocated in whole or in part for the purposes of a religion other than his own. (3) Every religious group has the right—(*a*) to manage its own religious affairs; (*b*) to establish and maintain institutions for religious or charitable purposes; and (*c*) to acquire and own property and hold and administer it in accordance with law. (4) State law may control or restrict the propagation of any religious doctrine or belief among persons professing the Muslim religion. (5) This Article does not authorise any act contrary to any general law relating to public order, public health or morality.

Article 12:

(1) Without prejudice to the generality of Article 8, there shall be no discrimination against any citizens on the grounds only of religion, race, descent or place of birth—(*a*) in the administration of any educational institution maintained by a public authority, and, in particular, the admission of pupils or students....(2) Every religious group has the right to establish and maintain institutions for education of children and provide therein instruction in its own religion, and there shall be no discrimination on the grounds only of religion in any law relating to such institutions or in the administration of any such law; but federal law may provide for special financial aid for the establishment or maintenance of Muslim institutions or the instruction in the Muslim religion of persons professing that religion. (3) No person shall be required to receive instruction or to take part in any ceremony or act of worship of a religion other than his own (pp. 511–14).

These provisions correspond to Article 7 of the Principles of Law-making of the Constitution of the Republic of Pakistan 1962 (p. 7), except that Islam being the state religion of Malaya is accorded preferential treatment in two respects: Article 11 (4) gives the states the right by law to control or restrict proselytising among Muslims, and Article 12(2) enables Muslims to receive financial help under federal law. The latter provision is interesting in that religion is under the jurisdiction of the states which are responsible for adequate provision for Islam, as will be shown presently, even in the two governorates where the king of the Federation is the head of the Muslim religion.

Part IV, "The Federation", specifies in chapter 1, Article 32: "There shall be a Supreme Head of the Federation, to be called the Yang di-Pertuan Agong, who shall have precedence over all persons in the Federation and shall not be liable to any proceedings whatsoever in any court."[4] This is a modern concept and incompatible with Islamic law which places the head of state (*khalīfa*) under the *Sharī'a* like every other Muslim. The Pakistani Constitution provides for the impeachment of the president before the National Assembly, which is, however, not a court of law.[5] The supreme head of the Federation of Malaya is elected from among the rulers of the states for five years during which time he ceases to function as ruler of his state, except that he remains its religious head.[4]

He swears an oath of office in the name of Allah and affirms: "Further we do solemnly and truly declare that We shall at all time protect the Muslim religion and uphold the rules of law and order in the Country."[6]

Chapter 2, "The Conference of Rulers", is convened to elect the supreme head and his deputy and "to agree or disagree to the extension of any religious acts, observancies or ceremonies to the Federation as a whole".

Chapter 3, "The Executive", states that all executive authority is vested in the Yang di-Pertuan Agong who shall act in accordance with the advice of the Cabinet. He is the supreme commander of the armed forces of the Federation, appoints the prime minister and on his advice other ministers. The Cabinet is collectively responsible to Parliament (pp. 516 ff.). The oaths of the prime minister and the other ministers do not make any reference to God (p. 608). Legislative authority is vested in Parliament (p. 529). The rulers of states exercise authority as head of the Muslim religion or in relation to the customs of the Malays (p. 538).

Of the "Financial Provisions" Article 97(3) is relevant: "If in accordance with State law any Zakat, Fitrah, Bait-ul-Mal or similar Muslim revenue is raised, it shall be paid into a separate fund and shall not be paid out except under the authority of State law." The annual financial statement does not show any sums received by way of Zakat, Fitrah and Bait-ul-Mal or similar Muslim revenue (p. 554). There is state supervision of the Islamic provisions, but they are administered by an appointed council, as we shall see presently. The ninth schedule gives the legislative lists and assigns to the federal list the duty of Parliament to make laws concerning: "Pilgrimages to places outside Malaya", which are organised by the Department of Religious Affairs in the several states. Muslim courts are outside the competence of the Federal Parliament and the business of those of the states under the state list, as are provisions concerning "Muslim Wakfs and Hindu endowments" (pp. 618–22). The full text of the provision for Muslim law included in the state list is relevant:

Muslim Law and personal and family law of persons professing the Muslim religion, including the Muslim Law relating to succession, testate and intestate, betrothal, marriage, divorce, dower, maintenance, legitimacy, guardianship, gifts, partitions and non-charitable trusts;

Muslim Wakfs and the definition and regulation of charitable and religious trusts, the appointment of trustees and the incorporation of persons in respect of Muslim religious and charitable institutions operating wholly within the State; Malay custom; Zakat, Fitrah and Bait-ul-Mal or similar Muslim revenue; mosques or any Muslim public place of worship, creation and punishment of offences by persons professing the Muslim religion against precepts of that religion, except in regard to matters included in the Federal List; the constitution, organization and procedure of Muslim courts, which shall have jurisdiction only over persons professing the Muslim religion and in respect only of any of the matters included in this paragraph, but shall not have jurisdiction in respect of offences except in so far as conferred by federal law: the control of propagating doctrines and beliefs among persons professing the Muslim religion; the determination of matters of Muslim Law and doctrine and Malay custom (p. 623).

The constitution also lays down—in part IX—"The Judiciary", Article 153(1): "It shall be the responsibility of the Yang di-Pertuan Agong to safeguard the special position of the Malays and the legitimate interests of other communities in accordance with the provisions of this Article...."

As far as I could observe and ascertain no religious discrimination exists in Malaya. This is certainly due to the happy combination of constitutional clarity and precision and the peaceable, friendly disposition of the population. The Malays, as a whole, willingly accept religious jurisdiction in matters of ritual and family laws, unless they adhere to Malay customary law. The tendency is to replace, wherever possible, Malay customary law by *Sharī'a* law, but the *Qāḍī* recognises Malay custom. Western-educated Malays may chafe under the orthodox interpretation of Islamic law; and we shall see that, especially in the matter of inheritance and succession, rigidity can be and is frequently avoided within limits. But by and large, the Malay, especially in the rural areas—and that is where he mainly lives—accepts the discipline of Islam and makes a happy, easy-going impression.

Yet in Malaya, too, we find the younger generation gradually changing and wanting a more liberal interpretation of Islamic law. In Kuala Lumpur, the capital with the University of Malaya, the atmosphere is certainly free and more critical. But it is remarkable that state and religion work harmoniously together in a determined effort to create a Malay nation. A tremendous effort is being made on a nation-wide scale to spread a working knowledge of Malay in the people through periodic drives. A magnificent language institute trains teachers of Malay; it is provided with the most up-to-date equipment for linguistic study.

Turning to the constitutions of the states of the Federation, we find in *The Laws of the Constitution of Perlis*[7] whose ruler was in 1961 the Yang di-Pertuan Agong of the Federation, that it begins: "In the name of GOD, the Compassionate, the Merciful, PRAISE be to GOD, the Lord of the Universe, and may the benediction and peace of GOD be upon Our Leader Muhammad and upon all his Relations and Friends." Article 10 deals with the composition of the "Council of Succession" and lays down that of the "five male members not members of the Ruling House of Perlis one shall be the Mufti and not less than one other person learned in the Muslim law". Article 12 stipulates that "the person to be chosen and appointed shall be a male of mature age, sound mind, a Perlis Malay, a subject of the State of Perlis, professing the Muslim Religion *Ahli Sunnah Waljama'ah* [that is an orthodox Sunnī], of good but not necessarily of Royal blood...". But Article 17 lays down: "Save as otherwise provided in Article 12 the Sovereign shall be a person who is a Malay, of Royal blood, a descendant of Perlis Sovereigns, a male, and of the Muslim Religion *Ahli Sunnah Waljama'ah*." Hereditary succession is, thus, not automatic, but depends on the "Council of Succession" which is bound to "confirm the Heir-apparent or Heir presumptive... as Sovereign unless after a full and complete inquiry the Council shall consider him to have some great and serious defect derogatory to the quality of a Sovereign, such as infirmity, blindness, dumbness or possessing some base qualities on account of which he would not be permitted by *Hukum Shara'* [the laws of the *Sharī'a*, that is] to become Sovereign Ruler". If neither of these two heirs is eligible, the council "shall confirm the next in order of succession of the other Heirs and so on, always subject to the same power to refuse, until the Council has confirmed one of the other Heirs to be the Sovereign" (Article 11). Failing this, Article 12 is to be applied. Such a person having become "the Sovereign, the Throne and Sovereignty of Perlis shall descend lineally and by primogeniture to his male issue". Constitutional law in Islam does not know the law of primogeniture.[8] Article 34 lays down that:

"The executive authority of the State shall be vested in the Ruler but executive functions may by law be conferred on other persons or authorities." The ruler appoints the Mentri Besar (prime minister) who must be "of the Malay race and profess the Muslim Religion" (Article 35). The same conditions apply to the state secretary who "shall be the principal officer in charge of the administrative affairs of the State" (Article 36). The Mentri Besar must enjoy the confidence of the Legislative Assembly (Article 37). The Legislative Assembly must have a majority of elected members; the ruler may appoint a smaller number of other persons.

It is noteworthy that close attention to the constitutional provisions of the *Sharī'a* in matters of physical fitness and character of the ruler goes together with modern requirements demanded of the prime minister and of the Legislature.

There is, moreover, a "Special Provision Relating to Malays" in Article 70(1):

It shall be the responsibility of the Ruler to safeguard the special position of the Malays and the legitimate interests of other communities in accordance with the provisions of this Article. (2) The Ruler shall, subject to the provisions of Article 39 [by which he is, with certain exceptions, bound by the advice of the Executive Council] exercise his functions under this Part and State law in such manner as may be necessary to safeguard the special position of the Malays and to ensure the reservation for Malays of such proportion as he may deem reasonable of positions in the public service of the State and of scholarships, exhibitions and other similar educational or training privileges or special facilities given or accorded by the State Government and, when any permit or licence for the operation of trade or business is required by State law, then, subject to the provisions of that law and this Article, of such permits and licences.

The Article further stipulates that no person enjoying public office or educational facilities, as mentioned, or possessing a licence for trade or business should be deprived of them, nor should their renewal be refused. It further states: "(9) Nothing in this Article shall empower the Legislature to restrict business or trade solely for the purpose of reservations for Malays." Under the heading "Impartial Treatment" Article 71 says: "All persons of whatever race in the same grade in the service of the State shall, subject to the terms and conditions of their employment, be treated impartially."

While Malaya is definitely a Muslim state—but not an Islamic state—it should be noted that these two Articles of the constitution try to safeguard the Malays, but not at the expense and to the detriment of non-Malays. That the Malays are Muslims is irrelevant since public service and the carrying on of trade and business are in no way connected with a person's religion, with the two exceptions mentioned. The same applies to educational facilities, especially facilities of higher education which qualifies for the higher echelons of public service. But the fact that special provision is made for the Malays clearly shows their vulnerable position in these spheres and the concern of the government to secure for the Malays adequate representation and participation in the running of their state and economy.

A Department of Religious Affairs is a constitutional requirement in every state, and in Penang and Malacca. It is the result of a law passed by the Legislative Assembly of the state. Thus, according to an "Enactment to make provisions for regulating Muslim religious affairs and to constitute a Council to advise the Yang di-Pertuan Agong in matters relating to the Muslim religion in the State of Malacca", to be known for short as "Administration of Muslim Law Enactment, 1959", a *Majlis* or "Council of Religion, Malacca" was set up by "the Governor with the advice and consent of the Council of State" consisting of a president —*ex-officio* also the president of the Religious Affairs Department—as principal executive officer, the Mufti and not less than five or more than nine Muslims. All members of the Majlis must be males over twenty-one years of age and professing the Muslim religion. The secretary of the Religious Affairs Department shall be *ex-officio* secretary of the Majlis. Its members are "public servants for the purposes of the Penal Code". The Mufti is to be appointed by the Yang di-Pertuan Agong; among his duties is the chairmanship of a legal committee of the "Council of Religion, Malacca", which shall have "two other members of the Majlis, and not less than two or more than six other fit and proper Muslims who are not members of the Majlis".[9]

The Legal Committee is to consider requests any person may make for the issue of a *fetua* (*fatwā*) or ruling on any point of Muslim law, and the chairman shall issue a ruling agreed upon by the committee unanimously. In the absence of unanimity the matter is to be placed before the full Majlis "which shall...issue its ruling in accordance with the opinion of the majority of its members".[10]

A civil court can submit any question of Muslim law before it to the Majlis which refers it to its legal committee for an opinion to be certified to the requesting court on its behalf.[10] "Ordinarily the orthodox tenets of the Shafeite [*Shāfi'ī*] sect" must govern the rulings, unless they would be against the public interest. In that case, "unless the Yang di-Pertuan Agong shall otherwise direct", the less orthodox *Shāfi'ī* tenets are to be followed. If neither tenets accord with the public interest "the tenets of any of the three remaining sects namely Hanafi, Maliki or Hanbali as may be considered appropriate" shall be followed, provided the head of the Muslim religion has sanctioned such procedure. "Any ruling... shall, if the Yang di-Pertuan Agong so directs, be published by notification in the *Gazette* and shall thereupon be binding on all Muslims resident in the State."[11]

These regulations show that a modern procedure is adopted in the application of the *Sharī'a*: a ruling cannot be given by the traditionally qualified Mufti alone, but by a majority of the council, unless the legal committee is unanimous. The Mufti is normally the only expert in Islamic law in the Majlis. Departure from the *Shāfi'ī* rite to which the Malays subscribe is still valid in Muslim law as long as a more liberal interpretation agrees with one or other of the three other orthodox rites.

The setting up of *Sharī'a* courts logically follows from the applicability of Muslim law in all matters pertaining to Islam in force in Malaya. The head of the Muslim religion appoints a chief *qāḍī* and as many *qāḍīs* as are required in the state. The ordinance calls them "Kathi Besar" and "Kathis" and lays down precise rules governing the functioning of these religious courts. Such courts may try both criminal and civil offences committed by a Muslim and may inflict the appropriate punishments, provided these are limited to two months' imprisonment or a fine of two hundred dollars (Malay) in criminal cases, and in civil cases to one thousand dollars, unless "the amount in dispute or value of the subject matter is not capable of estimation in terms of money".[12] Civil cases concern personal status law (betrothal, marriage, divorce, claim to property arising out of any such matter, legitimacy, guardianship, maintenance, *waqf*, *nazr* (vow)).

Provision is further made for an appeal committee against judgement by a religious court under certain conditions.[13] The language of the proceedings of the *Sharī'a* courts must be Malay. Prosecution, defence and evidence are in accordance with Muslim law, but in form correspond to criminal and civil court proceedings of the state. While the religious courts can impose prison sentences, they must naturally hand the sentenced person over to the state authorities for imprisonment in a state prison. This can be done through a police officer or an officer of the *qāḍī* court.[14] In case of non-compliance with a judgement or order of a religious court, the latter may—on its own accord or at the request of any person who was to benefit under the judgement—"send a certified copy of such judgement or order to any Magistrate's Court..." in the place of the religious court "together with a request to the Magistrate that such judgement or order may be executed". If more than one thousand dollars are involved the judgement is sent to a sessions court and its president is asked to execute it.[15] The court of the Kathi Besar has a standing equal to that of a magistrate's court.

Religious dues, such as *zakāt* and *fiṭra*, are payable into the General Endowment Fund (*Bayt-al-māl*) of the Majlis, but "shall be accounted in a separate account of the Fund".[16] The Majlis is empowered to collect "monies or other contributions for any charitable purpose for the support and promotion of the Muslim Religion or for the benefit of Muslims in accordance with Muslim law...".[17]

Further provisions relate to mosques, marriage and divorce, registration of divorces, serving of notice to a husband that his wife desires a divorce upon application by the wife to the *qāḍī*, and to maintenance of dependants.[18]

In short, in matters of personal status orthodox Sunnī Muslim law is in force throughout the Federation by state law. For what has just been described for Malacca is (with certain variations but generally following this pattern) the law in all parts of the Federation. The variations concern the composition and number of members of the "Council of Muslim Law"; e.g. "the Administration of Muslim Law Enactment, 1960" of the state of Negri

Sembilan is promulgated by H.H. the Yang di-Pertuan Besar (sultan) with the assent of the ruling chiefs and the advice and consent of the Legislative Assembly; in the state of Trengganu by H.H. the Sultan and with the advice and consent of the Council of State, here the ordinance is called "The Administration of Islamic Law Enactment, 1955 (1375 [A.H.])".

In Negri Sembilan the chairman is a member of the State Executive Council; among the members are: the Mufti, the chief Kathi, the inspector of religious schools, four members of the State Legislative Assembly, and "five other members of whom at least one shall be a Non-Malay Muslim".[19] H.H. is to appoint the Mufti for his state "on the recommendation of the Public Service Commission...provided that before acting on the recommendation...H.H. shall consider the advice of the Mentri Besar and may once refer the recommendation back to the Commission in order that it may be reconsidered".[20]

This ordinance, moreover, specifies the offences under Muslim law as follows: non-attendance of male Muslims of fifteen years of age and over "at midday prayers on Friday at a mosque of a kariah [the area within which the mosque is situated] in which he ordinarily resides shall...be guilty of an offence punishable with a fine not exceeding twenty-five dollars [it is generally five dollars]", unless there are good reasons, such as rain, long distance, sickness, etc. Next, "the purchase, sale or consumption of any intoxicating liquor; the partaking of food, drink or tobacco in daylight during Ramadan...".[21] Desertion of wife or her ill-treatment are punishable by imprisonment and/or fine, just as is a wife's disobedience. Sexual irregularities and offences (fornication, incest, etc.) are punishable by law.[22] Fornication includes adultery and "on conviction before a competent court" the man is sentenced to imprisonment or a fine; the woman incurs half the penalty. These penalties do not correspond to those imposed by the *Sharī'a*, nor is the procedure the same since Islamic law demands four witnesses to adultery. Thus, penalties are more in line with contemporary conditions.

Teaching any doctrine of the Muslim religion without written permission of the Majlis is liable to imprisonment or fine. If anybody "propagates any religious doctrine or belief other than [that] of the Muslim religion among persons professing the Muslim religion [he] shall be guilty of an offence cognizable by a Civil Court and punishable with imprisonment for a term not exceeding one year or a fine not exceeding three thousand dollars".[23] This rule reflects the status of Islam as protected state religion, hence the culprit is tried before a civil court.

Islam is further protected against the spreading of false doctrines, issuing of *fatwās* by persons other than the Mufti, possession, printing, publishing and selling of religious books contrary to the teachings of the four orthodox rites, misuse of the Qur'an, insults against the Muslim religion, contempt of the lawful authority of the head of the Muslim religion and/or of religious functionaries, or of the Majlis. All these acts are punishable offences, as is non-payment of *zakāt* or *fitra* and incitement to neglect religious duties.[24]

One further point is important: Muslims are forbidden to contract a civil marriage. This was already so under British rule, as is clear from the "Civil Marriage Ordinance, 1952" enacted by the British High Commissioner and their Highnesses the Rulers of the Malay States with the advice and consent of the Legislative Council. Article 3(2) declares: "No marriage one of the parties to which professes the religion of Islam shall be solemnized or registered under this Ordinance."[25] Civil marriages must be monogamous.[26]

Naturally, the "Married Women and Children (Maintenance) Ordinance, 1950" does not apply to Muslims either. But in Negri Sembilan its provision for the maintenance of illegitimate children is in force, obviously an extension of Muslim law which only demands maintenance of legitimate children.[27] Non-payment by the father is punishable by a term of imprisonment.

So far we have only dealt with Muslim law, but in some states of the Federation customary law is strongly entrenched. Thus, the state of Pahang established, by a constitutional enactment, a "Council of Religion and Malay Custom" under the "law relating to the administration of the Law of the Religion of Islam and Malay customary law". The same applies to Trengganu. In Pahang, for example, constitutional provision is made for rulings in both Islamic and Malay customary law.[28] In Trengganu the council has a president, and the Department of Religious Affairs a commissioner, as head, whereas in Negri Sembilan there is personal union between the two heads. While the laws and regulations are the same throughout the Federation, procedure and nomenclature differ from state to state.

Thus, we find in Trengganu the Appeal Court called "The Shariah Appeal Court", and H.H. the Sultan shall appoint four members to a Committee—in other states called the Legal Committee—in addition to "not less than three *Ulamas* of the Majlis", with one of its members as chairman to be elected for each meeting. "The Majlis shall take notice of and act upon all written laws in force in the State, the provisions of the *Hukom Shara*ʿ and the ancient custom of the State or Malay customary law." The Mufti is to advise on any point of Islamic law and

> in making and issuing any ruling upon any point of Islamic law or doctrine...the Mufti shall ordinarily follow the orthodox tenets of the *Shafeite* sect: provided that if the Mufti considers it to be in the interests and welfare of the Muslim community he may issue the *fetua* within the tenets of any of the four sects. In making and issuing any ruling upon a point of Malay customary law...the Majlis shall have due regard to...Malay customary law applicable in the state and in the event of the point in any manner concerning Islamic law shall refer the matter to the Mufti for his advice.[29]

We note that in this state—and also, for example, in Pahang—the Mufti need not, as in Negri Sembilan, distinguish between the orthodox and less orthodox rulings of the *Shāfiʿī* rite. Rulings according to Malay customary law are only binding on Malay Muslims, but not on foreign Muslims residing in those states where customary law is applied.

As a rule, decisions by the Majlis or the Department of Religious Affairs are forwarded to the head of the Muslim religion through the Mentri Besar or the state secretary who is always the head of the administration. Trengganu stipulates that the chairman of the "Shariah Appeal Court" must "hold or have held the office of Magistrate", and that "nothing in this Enactment contained shall affect the jurisdiction of any Civil Court and, in the event of any difference or conflict arising between the decision of a Court of the Chief *Kadzi* (*qāḍī*) or a *Kadzi* and the decision of a Civil Court acting within its jurisdiction, the decision of the Civil Court shall prevail".[30] The first condition means that form and method of state courts should be applied to religious courts, and the second establishes the authority of the state as overriding that of a religious court, that is, as paramount.

On the whole, the Malays are satisfied with the separation of religion from politics and with the application of the *Sharī'a* only to personal status law. But a group of orthodox Muslims want to go further and establish an Islamic state governed by the *Sharī'a* throughout. They are mainly organised in the Pan-Malayan Islamic party which, at the time of our visit, formed the Government of Trengganu and Kelantan which have practically an all-Malay population. Here an attempt is made to bring the existing state legislation into line with Islamic law. The taking of interest (*ribā*) is forbidden. The financial provisions for the "Corporation"—the name in Trengganu for the Department of Religious Affairs in the other states—exclude from the "General Endowments Fund" (*Bayt-al-māl*) *inter alia* "the interest on all deposits left by the Corporation in the State Treasury so long as they remain in the custody of the State Treasury". This interest cannot be used for "charitable purposes for the support and promotion of the Religion of Islam or for the benefit of Muslims in the State in accordance with Islamic law". It "shall be paid by the Corporation to the State Treasurer for the benefit of the State".[31] The financial assets of the state of Kelantan are entrusted to the state bank which transacts business on a co-operative basis, with profit and loss sharing, but without charging interest. It is maintained by the government that economic progress is possible within the Islamic system, without having recourse to the capitalist system with investment, credit, and so on. Islamic teachings are not opposed to the public interest nor to the welfare of the people which it is the task of the Islamic state to promote. How to implement democracy is a matter for interpreting the principle of *shūrā*. As members of the Pan-Islamic party they took over the government after their electoral victory and they must apply Islamic principles and injunctions to the full. The revenue of the state consists of *zakāt* and *fiṭra*, but the government will not accept *zakāt* from the proceeds of gambling or betting or other unlawful gain.

There is neither any need nor any intention to reform Islamic law. They favour the exercise of *ijtihād* to legislate for new cases, but not to modify existing medieval law. The *'ulamā* declare themselves not to be of *mujtahid* standard, although they admit that new legal decisions on the basis of the Sunna are required in cases for which no precedent in *Fiqh* exists. They are not committed to al-Shāfi'ī, but, as laid down in the Muslim law enactments, consider themselves free to apply Ḥanafī, Mālikī or Ḥanbalī law as the case may be. They want to purify Islam from non-Islamic accretions, but they will not go any further.

The *muftis* and *qāḍīs* throughout Malaya are usually foreign trained, some are actually non-Malays. They train either at Al-Azhar in Cairo or in Mecca. In Selangor, for example, the Mufti comes from Mecca. Many teachers are Al-Azhar trained, those teaching Arabic usually come from Egypt. There are few indigenous scholars. Great hopes are placed in Al-Azhar trained teachers, but it appears that they comply after their return with the wishes of the ultra-conservative *muftis* and *qāḍīs*. Any loosening up, any more progressive interpretation of tradition must wait—this is the general opinion—for the younger generation until they take over from their elders. Malaya also possesses a Muslim College in Klang in the state of Selangor which trains religious teachers and functionaries. In 1961 its principal was also head of the Department of Islamic Studies in the University of Malaya at Kuala Lumpur. I understand that this is no longer the case. It would be easier to integrate Islamic studies in the humanities generally if there were a head of the department who has no connection with a theological college. At the time of my visit—during a reception in honour of the rector of Al-Azhar—there was a suggestion made by him to establish closer links between Klang and Cairo by naming the college "The al-Azharite Muslim College of Malaya". Individual *muftis* issue *fatwās* not necessarily based on the ruling *Shāfi'ī* rite, but practise limited *ijtihād* by applying their *ra'y* to Qur'an and Sunna. This varies from state to state. Among the younger orthodox generation there is unanimity that Islamic law should be uniform, not split up into *maḏāhib* (the four orthodox rites).

While it is the general intention that the state should not use its coercive power to force a Muslim to go to litigation in a Muslim religious court, the Department of Religious Affairs in Selangor, for example, claims full and exclusive jurisdiction over Muslims of the state. If a widow does not accept her share in the estate of her deceased husband under Muslim law, because she is otherwise fully equal to her husband in matters of franchise, social status and economic opportunities, and appeals to the state High Court, the judge invites the Mufti to assist him and passes judgement according to Muslim law.

In Selangor there is no customary Malay law in force, and no conflict is felt to exist between religious and secular law. This is borne out by the case just reported and by the fact that the Mufti of the state, while applying *Shāfiʿī* law, is prepared to issue *fatwās* in order to meet present-day needs to some extent—not in the case reported, though—by going back to the Qur'an and Sunna.

In Negri Sembilan customary law is applied in some parts of the state. Here matriarchal succession is in force. Landed property is reserved for matriarchal succession only, and the government, through the Department of Religious Affairs, recognises the *lambaga*, an official skilled in the interpretation of the customary (*ʿādat*) law. What a wife inherits from her mother belongs to her; if she dies without female heir the property falls to a niece. But landed property acquired during married life is halved between husband and wife. On the husband's death one-half goes to the widow, whereas his half goes to sons or daughters, less one-eighth for his widow, according to Muslim law. Yet there is quite generally in Malaya an escape clause in operation. For the partners may agree on the succession, irrespective of Muslim law, and such a settlement—provided it was made during the lifetime of both—is recognised by the *qāḍī* on the death of the husband. In frequent discussions with *qāḍīs* I asked whether there was not a real danger that Muslim law would one day cease to be applied in this instance, because succession had been settled outside it by a private agreement between husband and wife. The invariable answer was that such a contingency would not arise since the Muslim wives were quite satisfied with one-eighth of the husband's estate. As long as the wife's inheritance does not exceed one-third of her deceased husband's estate, Muslim law is vindicated.

In Malacca and Penang, in Kedah, Perak and Perlis and the aforementioned Selangor and Negri Sembilan the religious leaders and scholars were all agreed in their strongly held conviction that Islam is as valid and all-comprehensive today as in its heyday. Nothing has changed. While they say that Islam is flexible enough to take in its stride social and economic changes, they do not seem to realise the economic and social revolution which is taking place before their eyes. The strict enforcement of Islamic law in matters of religious duties, the existence of *qāḍī* courts, the efficient functioning of the Mufti in every state and a well-organised network of religious schools under the authority of the Departments of Religious Affairs must not deceive us into overlooking that, especially in urban surroundings among the ministers and the civil servants, university and state school teachers, stirrings are afoot and liberalisation is desired, especially in such matters as succession and *ribā*. The latter will become more of a problem as and when the Muslim sector becomes more involved with commerce and industry. In other words, the near absence of a Malay Muslim middle class—for which education under British rule is largely blamed—conceals the cracks in the seemingly solid edifice of practical and practised Islam.

In all Muslim countries where the majority live in the rural areas traditional Islam is strong, and it is no other in Malaya where a healthy religious life is very much in evidence. Here and there, among the intellectuals and among the younger members of government and administration, one can detect a certain restiveness over the ultra-conservatism of the older generation of religious functionaries. But these men, usually Western educated, though not always, are not playing any active part in bringing about a change. They hope that a younger generation will liberalise what is to them an inherited faith and practice without much intellectual questioning and inner conflict. They are born Muslims and accept Islam as part of their inheritance and of their personal life. What strikes the Western student of Islam most in Malaya is the almost universal acceptance of Islam and of Muslim law in the sphere where it is in force. The organisation of religious life and the administration of Muslim law, under the authority of efficiently run Departments of Religious Affairs as an integral part of public administration, are certainly impressive. Apart from friendly and on my part searching talks with *muftis*, *qāḍīs*, teachers and administrators, many long, well-organised and conducted meetings, under the chairmanship of the secretary of state, were clearly indicative of the close integration of religious affairs in the fabric of the state. Social occasions in the homes of Mentri Besars, deputy Mentri Besars and state secretaries afforded me excellent opportunities of seeing Islam in action through informal exchanges of views in a most hospitable and relaxed atmosphere. They were a valuable complement to, and sometimes a necessary corrective of, the more official formal meetings and visits to government departments, mosques and religious schools.

As was to be expected, the civil servants would not discuss religious issues, but would normally leave such discussion to the president and secretary of the Departments of Religious Affairs and the religious functionaries. Ministers were among those who stressed the need for liberalisation and progressive education in conformity with the tendencies and needs of the present. In some respects, social gatherings were a good pointer to a new economic and social order in process of emerging. Sometimes, men and women would sit in different parts of a spacious room in an official residence, sometimes one would sit round the table at a common meal in European fashion. A social revolution which will produce a Malay middle class is in progress, but everything is very gradual and gentle: evolution would be a more correct way of describing it. The educated Malays expect the religious leaders and functionaries gradually to accept woman's equality and the free social meeting of the sexes generally, as it is already to be met with in the home. In Malaya, as everywhere else, hope is concentrated on education. Islam is certainly not a problem as in Pakistan.

The separation of state and religion seems to be working well in that each respects the sphere of influence and activity of the other, and both manage to co-exist amicably without friction and rivalry. The only party with a strong interest in religion is the Pan-Malayan Islamic party, but it is unlikely that it will capture power at the centre, even though it is strong in the north-east, as we saw. The composition of Malaya's citizenry is not conducive to an Islamic state.

Generally speaking, Islam is at present strong enough as the state religion to be a barrier to Communism. It is so without being made into a political ideology in competition with Communism. Islam is native and natural to Malaya. But as education is extended it is imperative that religious education must keep pace with "secular" education if Islam is to remain a force in the life of the new generation. This should not be impossible of achievement, and a parallel existence of state- and Muslim law should continue to work smoothly and be beneficial, provided the latter takes account of social and economic change and builds these changes into the law by a fresh interpretation on a larger scale than the traditionalist *muftis* effect at present. Otherwise, Muslim law might lie fallow in certain matters such as private settlement of inheritance, as we discussed a little earlier. Another point at issue is whether to accept *zakāt* from *ribā*; as we saw, most states prohibit it, but Negri Sembilan allows it on the principle of not inquiring into its origin, but of accepting it *bona fide*. Polygamy is another such matter. In the largely rural areas it is quite customary for a man to have two, even three, wives. Provided that the Muslim law of maintenance—the father's responsibility—is enforced, divorce will be controlled. The divorce rate—so I was told—in Negri Sembilan is lower than in Kelantan and Singapore, for instance, because Negri Sembilan enforces the maintenance order.

An interesting detail is the fact that in Penang Muslim law was abrogated by the British for fifty years or more, and has only been gradually restored, after Muslim protest, in the personal sphere. Yet the application of Muslim law alone will not guarantee a live faith as an integral part of a whole personality. This personality is, outside religion, conditioned and formed by the good and bad influences of modern life which is spreading throughout the Federation as the government proceeds with the economic building up of the Malays. The religious leaders are not alone in blaming the British for having neglected the Malays by providing only an English education which was barely enough to fit the Malay youth for the lower cadres of the civil service—exactly the same as in the Indo-Pakistan subcontinent. The educated Malays also blame the British for the "backwardness" of the Malays, for the same reason. Muslim education must, therefore, make great strides in order to keep pace with secular instruction. For unless a sound knowledge of the fundamental tenets of Islam and its interest in this world through its social ethics is handed out to the children and adolescents in a form which is equal to the teaching of secular subjects, the next generation of Malays cannot be expected to remain loyal to the observance of Muslim law in matters of family, succession and taxes. In Malaya, as in other newly independent, sovereign Muslim states, there is no barrier against Communism other than a live, dynamic Islam as far as the Muslim part of the population is concerned.

CHAPTER 10

SOME OBSERVATIONS ON ISLAM IN IRAN AND TURKEY

IRAN

A constitutional régime was set up in Iran in 1906 with the granting of a constitution to which was added in 1907 a number of fundamental laws. Article I declares Islam (that is, Islam according to the tenets of the Shīʿī sect of the Jafarite Ithna ʿAsharī which the Shahinshah (emperor) must profess and propagate) the official religion of Iran. Article II specifies that the Legislative Assembly (*majlis*) can at no time contradict the Holy Islamic prescriptions nor the laws made by the prophet. The Assembly owes its existence to the expected—last or twelfth—Imam, to His Majesty the Shahinshah of Islam under the supervision of the *ʿulamā*, and to the whole Iranian nation.[1] For this purpose a committee of five of the most learned *ʿulamā* must be established to watch that all the laws promulgated by the Assembly are, in fact, in accord with Islamic law. They must also be aware of the exigencies of the time. They are to be chosen from among twenty suggested to the Majlis by the *ʿulamā* themselves, by unanimity or a ballot of the Assembly. They are full and equal members of the Assembly. The decisions of this committee are final and binding. This Article cannot be modified until the reappearance of the *Mahdī*, the twelfth Imam. In 1949 the Constituent Assembly voted a procedure for the revision of Articles of the Constitution, but explicitly exempted this Article II from such a revision.[1]

As far as I could ascertain during my brief stay in Iran, this Article was neither implemented by the late Shah, the founder of the Pahlavi dynasty, Reza Shah, nor has it been by his son, the present Shahinshah. Article XVIII lays down that education is free, but nothing must be taught which is forbidden by religion. All schools, public or private, are under the control of the Ministry of Education (Article XIX). There is to be freedom of press and publication, except for anti-religious books and publications damaging to the Islamic faith (Article XX). Free association is guaranteed so long as such gatherings do not aim at provoking religious or social unrest and disturbances, and are not contrary to public order (Article XXI).[2] The other fundamental rights of the citizens of Iran do not concern us here.

There is the threefold division of powers into Executive, Legislature and Judiciary which are independent of each other. But it is noteworthy that legislative power is shared between the Shahinshah and the two Houses of Parliament, the Majlis and the Senate. In that way the emperor actually wields unlimited executive power and, at the same time, limited legislative power (Article XXVII). The nation is sovereign, all power emanates from it. Sovereignty is entrusted by divine favour through the nation to the emperor through the Constituent Assembly (Articles XXXV and XXXVI).[2] The Shahinshah must, before his accession to the throne, swear an oath on the Qur'an in the name of God, in which he promises, apart from the usual matters, to propagate the *Ithna 'asharī* religion (Article XXXIX). The ministers of the government must be Muslims of Iranian descent and nationality (Article LVIII). The Shahinshah is not responsible to anybody, but his Ministers are responsible to both Chambers (Article XLIV).

The Judiciary is twofold, religious and lay, each with its own courts and tribunals. In other words, *Sharī'a* courts exist and function alongside state courts. Public law is the responsibility of the state, religious law as far as cult and personal status law is concerned is administered by the *qāḍī*. The highest religious authority is that of the chief *Mujtahid* of Qum.

It is claimed—according to my information—that state-law, though arrived at by partial adaptation of foreign law, is in accordance with Islam. The legislative activity of the Assembly is certainly carried on without the committee of *'ulamā* exercising its functions. On the other hand, the *mujtahids*, especially the chief among them, are taken into the confidence of the government or the Shahinshah, if not actually consulted. The religious scholars I met stress the flexibility of the *Sharī'a* and emphasise that the *Shī'a* has throughout practised *ijtihād* and is practising it today. This view was confirmed in other quarters: the gates of *ijtihād* have never been closed, but have been kept wide open. If the government applies the laws in force no friction between it and the religious leaders need arise since the Iranian laws are not—to use a phrase from the constitutional battle in Pakistan—"repugnant to Qur'an and Sunna". The *Mujtahid* of Qum is universally recognised. Yet my impression was that Islam as a force in public life was not much in evidence, and that the separation of state and religion was a fact. The people at large are observant and fervent believers. The intellectuals are, like elsewhere, divided. They distinguish between fundamentals and traditional forms and seem to favour reforms.

A phenomenon peculiar to Iran is the apparent revival of a mystical philosophy; and any dichotomy between the teachings and practice of Islam and present-day attitudes and ideas is resolved by this philosophical Sufism. This is widespread among the educated, especially the academic profession. They stress that there is an unbroken tradition of the philosophy of *ishrāq* (in the sense of mystical illumination) from Ibn Sīnā over Suhrawardy to Shirāzī under the Safavids; it even continued into the period of the Kajars, the predecessors of the present ruling dynasty. This philosophical Sufism, so it is claimed, is capable of giving an intellectually satisfying and logically cogent answer to the problems of being and existence, of the universe and man in it, from the sixteenth century onwards. If I dared venture an opinion—based on many discussions, but not on the analysis of literary texts—it would be that this philosophical bridging of the gap between traditional Islam and twentieth-century problems of faith and modern scientific concepts is feasible within a relatively small, select circle of intellectuals. It is perfectly compatible with the devout practice of traditional Islam in a society which is bound to change under the impact of economic development and its inevitable complement—a social revolution. If it were possible to make a distinction between society on the one hand and politics and economics on the other, as is done by distinguished scholars in the traditional and the modern sense of the term, it might be possible that the skilled exercise of *ijtihād* might provide an entry, indirectly at least, of a modernised Islam into public life. But is it possible to make such a distinction? A modern academic education in theology—Tehran has a distinguished Theological Faculty—may produce "modern" *mujtahids* whose initiative may lead to a fruitful accommodation between traditional *Fiqh* and modern legal thought and practice as well as between the rich and the poor, the Western-educated élite and the unsophisticated believing masses. Since education is government-controlled and universal, this may be achieved. The visitor is certainly impressed by the drive, energy and efficiency of the responsible educationists for a modern, integrated education and by the natural strength of traditional Islam. Unfortunately, I was unable to meet Tehran University students as the university was closed owing to some unrest. But my contacts with students in Shiraz and Isfahan incline me to think that opinion is divided between strict adherence to tradition and a rather detached Western-oriented attitude which must seek an accommodation with Islam.

The question of Islam is closely linked with the economic and social development of modern Iran, but the strength of religious feeling and of traditional observance in a majority of the people suggests that Islam will find its place in a new society in which wealth and skills are more evenly and justly distributed. In any case, Islam as faith and as a moral guide for the individual should and can determine the conscientious performance of his duties as a citizen if it is presented to him as relevant to this age.

TURKEY

The genesis of the Turkish Republic as a modern national state within European civilisation founded by Kemal Atatürk and prepared by successive movements has been treated in ch. 3 of the first part of this book. Here we are concerned with a brief summary of the constitution of this lay state from the point of view of Islam and its classical political thought. The keynote is struck in Article 3: "Sovereignty belongs to the nation without conditions and restrictions."[3] This is not only unequivocal and clear, it is a momentous assertion that the Muslims of Turkey have conferred upon themselves full, undivided and unlimited popular sovereignty. No sovereign above the Turkish nation is recognised as is the case in Pakistan. Even Malaya still maintains—in its constitution—a link with Islam and divine sovereignty; for the king of the Federation as well as the rulers of its member-states owe as heads of the Muslim religion allegiance to Allah, and Islam as the official religion of the Federation involves acknowledgement of the sovereignty of God as is clear from the quoted constitution of the state of Perlis, the preamble of which refers to God as the "Lord of the universe". Even the Iranian nation delegates its sovereignty by divine grace to the Shahinshah. While it is arguable that in constitutional law sovereignty in Iran is legally vested in the nation, morally it belongs to God at least by implication, as in Malaya, and explicitly in Pakistan. Article 2 of the Turkish Constitution states that "the Turkish state is republican, nationalist, popular, etatist, laic and evolutionary".

The Grand National Assembly alone represents the nation in whose name it exercises sovereignty (Article 4). Legislative and executive power are concentrated in it, but it only exercises the legislative power itself, whereas it exercises the executive power through the president of the Republic and his council of ministers (Articles 5–7). The Judiciary is independent, in the name of the nation (Article 8).

All Turkish citizens, men and women, have the right to vote from the age of twenty-two and can be elected deputies from the age of thirty (Articles 10 and 11). The oath is secular: "I swear on my honour..." (Article 16). Islam is not mentioned in the constitution, but Article 75 permits the performance of religious ceremonies as long as this does not violate security and public morals and is not contrary to law. Article 87 states that neither religion nor race exclude from citizenship anybody born in Turkey or abroad of a Turkish father.

This is unadulterated Western doctrine and, together with the presidential system, also Western practice. With the permission to the opposition to organise a party and the handing over of the government to it after its electoral victory, Turkey can justifiably claim to be a Western parliamentary democracy.

It is worth noting that Islam did not disappear at once from the constitution and from civil and penal law. At first Islam, as state religion, was still recognised in the law no. 364 of 29 October 1923,[4] and the *Şeriat* courts were abolished in 1924.[5]

The new constitution (law no. 334 of 9 July 1961) adopted by the Constituent Assembly after the 1960 Revolution confirms the secular character of the democratic, social Republic, and lays down in Article 19 of part 2, section 2, "The rights and duties of the individual", (iv) "The rights and freedoms of thought and belief", (*a*) "Freedom of thought and faith":

Religious education and teaching shall be subject to the individual's own will and volition, and in the case of minors, to their legally appointed guardians. No person shall be allowed to exploit and abuse religion or religious feelings or things considered sacred by religion in any manner whatsoever for the purpose of political or personal benefit, or for gaining power, or for even partially basing the fundamental social, economic, political and legal order of the State on religious dogmas....

While protecting the lawful and legitimate free exercise of religion, the second sentence emphatically excludes religion from any influence on public life. Moreover, Article 153 of part 4, "Miscellaneous Provisions", is specially designed to "safeguard... the Reform Laws: No provision of this Constitution shall be construed or interpreted as rendering unconstitutional the following Reform Laws which aim at raising the Turkish society to the level of contemporary civilisation and at safeguarding the secular character of the Republic which were in effect on the date this Constitution was adopted by popular vote...." After enumerating these laws, Article 154 with equal impartiality safeguards "The Office of Religious Affairs" which was and is still designed to guarantee and provide for the free exercise of religion on a voluntary, personal level. It states: "The Office of Religious Affairs, which is incorporated in the general administration, discharges the function prescribed by a special law."[6]

And yet, what strikes the visitor to Turkey most, if he is a student of Islam, is the fact, already remarked on, that Islam is still a problem in Turkey after forty years. Quite apart from the legal measures taken by the Republic to prevent Islam being exploited for political ends, its disappearance from public life, and its position as a tolerated religion which is entirely the affair of the individual, seem to have left a vacuum. There is general agreement among the intelligentsia—my information comes exclusively from academic circles—that the Republic must remain a secular state, that its structure as built by Kemal Atatürk must be preserved, and that political power as well as the law must be left in secular hands. Religion is and must remain the private concern of the individual. The role of religion is recognised in the personal sphere, it is even conceded that religious education is valuable and should be provided by the state, but it should be in the hands of lay teachers. The training of these teachers who as a rule teach other, general subjects should not be placed under religious authority in a theological college of the traditional type, but should be undertaken by a theological faculty in a university, such as the one founded at Ankara University in 1949, which should be developed and extended. As yet, Ankara teaches the traditional Islamic sciences in a more or less traditional fashion alongside the academic disciplines of Comparative Religion, Philosophy and Psychology of Religion, History of Islamic Art, and modern languages necessary for such a study.[7]

There does not seem to be any attempt as yet at integrating the two streams, the traditional and the contemporary critical. The student is instructed in both and has to use his own judgement in correlating them and, if possible, in arriving at a synthesis. The scholars engaged in teaching in this faculty are fully aware that such an integration must eventually be achieved through their teaching and guidance. The scientific approach to religion is no substitute for faith, but in our age nothing less than such an approach will lead to a rational faith in harmony with the *Zeitgeist*. In any case, as long as Islam is being taught by teachers trained in other subjects as their main teaching tasks, they cannot convey the abiding values and specific doctrines of Islam in any other way. It is to be expected that Turkey which has opted for modern European civilisation—which means post-French Revolution separation of state and religion—sees in Islam a religion in principle like modern Christianity. Yet the opinions are still divided whether this concept can be reconciled with classical Islam and its history. It is true that the Ottoman legal system, with its division into *qānūn* and *Sharī'a* law, to some extent paved the way for the adoption of foreign codes long before the foundation of a secular republic. But the abolition of religious courts dealing with what had always remained untouched (personal status law) inevitably gave rise to the fateful question: "What is Islam?" Even if Islam is now only a personal religion, the traditionalist would expect that the law affecting personal matters would have to be *Sharī'a* law to be administered by religious judges, with or without reform. Turkey is not the only Muslim country which abolished religious courts, but even the Turks who experienced the Kemalist revolution and insist on the separation of Islam from politics are not all agreed on the character of Islam and its role in Turkey. Turkey also has traditionalists and "modernists".

On the whole, it can be said that the approximation to Western ideas in religion has proceeded furthest in Turkey. This is natural within the Turkish philosophy and its aspiration to be an integral part of Western civilisation. But it must be stressed that this does not include the recognition of the Jewish and Christian elements of the foundations of that civilisation. It is, to repeat, post-French Revolution laicised, if not secularised Western civilisation. Once Islam is put on the same level with religion in the West, that historical continuity, without which no faith can develop and in adaptation survive, is lost.

The effect of such a loss cannot yet be seen, but if I am not mistaken there are signs visible among the student generation who grew up without religious teaching and, at least a number of them, without religion in the home, that they are searching for something to believe in. This may be Islam, presented in a way that will appeal to youth today and in their mother tongue, since a knowledge of Arabic is no longer general; for some time it was not even allowed to be taught. In this context, the Faculty of Divinity of Ankara University has a great opportunity and responsibility. But more likely the answer may be sought in materialism or Communism.

Islam has certainly no direct influence on the political, economic and social life of the nation, and an indirect influence on public life through its effect on the individual's social behaviour and on the fulfilment of his duties as a citizen can only happen where Islam is practised as a personal faith. Among the younger generation, one comes not infrequently across the equation of religion with reaction. There is a real apprehension lest any restoration of Islam to its former place might open the door wide to reactionary influences in the guise of religion. What is reported here on the basis of conversations and discussions only refers to intellectuals in the cities, it has no validity with regard to the Anatolian peasants or, to judge by those who fill the mosques at prayer, many city-dwellers of not only middle and old age as well. Tradition and force of habit count for something, but they do not by themselves explain a still strong attachment to Islam in the general population.

The question of reform is, therefore, in Turkey not of the same significance as, say, in Pakistan or Malaya or Morocco. But educated Turks are concerned about its need, though this concern is qualified both by its being considered a long-term business, perhaps a hundred years, and also and mainly because Islamic law is no longer applied and applicable. Therefore, reform in many minds is replaced by reinterpretation: what is needed is a modern presentation of the basic tenets and teachings of Islam as faith in a personal, moral, one and only God. The ethical and social values must be stressed in their relevance to the formation of character and good citizenship. Viewed from this angle, the teaching of Islam in schools gains in importance. But where such a role is envisaged for Islam as part of the national education, there is unanimous agreement that it should be under the control of the state, and instruction in Islam should be entrusted to lay teachers in conformity with the constitutional definition of Turkey as a lay and evolutionary, nationalist, democratic Republic.

POSTSCRIPT

Since this study is an attempt at relating personal observations to the general problem of Islam in crisis and transition, I have felt justified in writing these few remarks, although I am fully aware that they are no more than impressions largely gained from friendly exchanges with colleagues and students in Iran and Turkey during my brief stay.

CHAPTER II

ISLAM IN TUNISIA AND MOROCCO

TUNISIA

Islam in North Africa is *sui generis*; it arrived thirteen centuries ago as a conqueror and added a new layer of civilisation to already existing ones: Phoenician, Roman and Byzantine which had imposed themselves on the indigenous Berbers who are still here today. Besides, it suffered French occupation in recent times, but benefited by French culture and civilisation. As a consequence, Islam is less rigid today in the Mediterranean area than it was under Almoravids and Almohads. There are many monuments to its valour and prowess, but also to its spirituality. But it has also suffered stagnation over the last two centuries through internal decay and, more lately, foreign domination.

Yet there is a special atmosphere about North Africa, Tunisia and Morocco in particular—the war in Algeria prevented me from visiting it. National awakening and liberation leading to sovereign independence are not unconnected with Islam, both positively and negatively. It appears that nationalism, Maghribī Arab nationalism, has discovered a new relationship to Islam which has preserved its purity despite Maraboutism—the religious orders with their cult of saints and their fanaticism and stagnation. It has crushed Maraboutism and tries to build Islam into its new national character as an important constituent. It is naturally not the medieval Islam with its claim to determine policy and to provide the law of the land. It is rather Islam as faith and/or culture and civilisation. Despite significant differences between Islam in Tunisia and Morocco, a synthesis between the spirituality and moral imperative of Islam and French humanism is being aimed at and striven for in both, but more consciously so in Tunisia. There is a Muslim, if not a traditionalist Islamic consciousness abroad, perhaps not very articulate, but clearly to be felt nevertheless.

As far as Tunisia is concerned, undoubtedly the French protectorate promoted the withdrawal of Islam into itself since its concentration on French education and the consequent neglect of Arabic and Islamic instruction was very detrimental to a revival of a largely stagnant Islam, with the exception of such famous seats of Islamic traditional learning as Kairouwan and the Zaituna in Tunis.

The Tunisians are a forward- and outward-looking nation today; they set about building a modern state with energy and determination. Alert and hardworking, they seem to take a road not dissimilar from secular Turkey, but without the radicalism of the Turks where Islam is concerned, even though they have effectively excluded the conservative religious element from the conduct of state. The constitutional position of Islam is clear; the Tunisians are Muslims by religion and patrimony and this is built into their law (and into their national education) without being *Sharī'a* law dispensed in religious courts. This is the work of President Bourguiba, his Cabinet and the National Assembly based on the Neo-Destour party.

The preamble of their republican, democratic constitution begins with the Qur'anic "In the name of Allah the Merciful, the Compassionate" and declares:

We, the Representatives of the Tunisian people proclaim that this people...are determined on...remaining true to the teachings of Islam (*ta'ālīm al-Islām*), to the ideal of a Union of the Great[er] Maghreb, to their membership of the Arab Family...and on the establishment of a democracy, based on the sovereignty of the people (*siyādat al-sha'b*). ...We, the Representatives of the free Tunisian people, draw up with the grace of God this Constitution (*'alā barākati-Llāhi hāḏā-l-dustūr*).[1]

Article 1: "The Tunisian State is free, independent and sovereign, Islam is its religion, Arabic its language and the republican system is its régime." Article 2: "The Tunisian Republic is a part of the Great[er] Maghreb and is working for its unity...." Article 3: "Sovereignty is vested in the Tunisian people...." Article 5: "The Tunisian Republic guarantees freedom of the individual, freedom of religious belief, and safeguards the rights of all religious worship, as long as it does not endanger public safety." Article 6: "All citizens are equal before the law." Article 18: "The people shall exercise legislative power (*sulṭa tashrī'īya*) by means of an Assembly, called 'The National Assembly'." Article 37: "The President of the Republic is Head of State and his religion is

Islam." He begins his oath of office, according to Article 41, with the words: "I swear by Almighty God...." Article 42: "The President of the Republic has executive authority in accordance with the laws of this Constitution. He should safeguard the Constitution." Article 43: "The President of the Republic shall draw up the general policy of the country and control its execution. He shall keep the National Assembly informed of the development of this policy. The President of the Republic shall choose the members of his Government who are responsible to him."

This constitution is that of a Muslim, but not of an Islamic, state. The presidential system adopted is not that of the United States of America (any more than is that of Pakistan), but is suited to the strong personality and leadership of Habib Bourguiba. The disenfranchisement of Islam as far as government and administration are concerned has been accepted by the people who follow enthusiastically their liberator and the founder of their independent state. The older generation must have received many a shock, but the religious leaders can no longer command the allegiance of the people at large, due, it is claimed, to their collaboration with the French under the protectorate. The president is head of state, but although Islam is the official religion and he is a Muslim he is not head of the Muslim religion, as for instance the king of the Federation of Malaya and the sultans as rulers of the constituent states are. The claim which was advanced that President Bourguiba *ex officio* can interpret the law as a *mujtahid*, and that such measures as the abolition of the *Sharīʿa* courts and the administration of Muslim family law by lay judges, are justified through Islamic constitutional law has no basis in that law. It would be different with political laws: Ibn Khaldūn was born in Tunis. For the law of the Tunisian state is not *Sharīʿa* law and the head of state is not a *khalīfa*, notwithstanding the noteworthy assertion in the preamble that Tunisia is determined "on remaining true to the teachings of Islam". This claim is by no means a mere assertion, a figure of speech, safely tucked away in the preamble to the Tunisian Constitution. It is correct to say that not only the Tunisian family law—despite some modifications—is Mālikī law, apart from the obligation of civil marriage as alone legally valid. It is claimed that the civil law also contains many provisions from Mālikī and other orthodox, even some from Shīʿī, sources. This code is based on the "Code Civil et Commercial Tunisien" of 1899 to the compilation of which Santillana greatly contributed. The French burned all the copies they could lay hands on, and I was unable to obtain a copy despite the efforts of the minister of justice. This code is a compound of *Sharī'a* law and Italian, French, German and Swiss, even Roman law.

We have here the novel situation that a lay state, modern in conception and outlook, consciously and deliberately bases its law as far as possible on Islamic law. But law-making is in the hands of modern jurists, not in those of the *'ulamā*, although one or other of them is being consulted. The idea is that everybody in Tunisia has the right to exercise *ijtihād* without claiming all the time that they want to go back to Qur'an and Sunna. The National Assembly is like any other modern legislature, but at the same time considers itself the legitimate heir to the *mujtahids* of traditional Islam. Tunisians claim to be conscious Muslims in spirit, but recognise no obligation to adhere to the letter of *Fiqh* nor to the *uṣūl al-fiqh*. Nor does one encounter the concept of "Islamic ideology". Conscious of the impossibility of fulfilling the stringent conditions of *ijtihād*, they make bold to adapt and change Islamic law, and adopt, where necessary, laws from modern European legal codes and systems. Yet they try to remain loyal to the principles of Islam.

This attitude has its roots in the tradition of the Collège Sadiqi which was founded by Khereddine,[2] prime minister of the Bey of Tunis before the protectorate of France. Here a synthesis is aimed at between traditional Muslim culture and French humanism, not two parallel streams which never meet, but a confluence of two cultures deliberately fostered. Practically the whole ruling class and the administration passed through this school. National feeling saved them from succumbing to the brilliance of French spirituality, even if they continued their higher education in France and graduated in Paris at the Sorbonne. If one were to ask them "what is Islam?", "what sort of a Muslim are you?", they would probably react like an Englishman when he is asked in what his Englishness consists. Islam is a birthright with them, a natural component of their human self. This gives them a freedom and self-assurance one rarely meets in Muslims in other parts of the world.

And yet, interesting and undoubtedly highly significant as this phenomenon is, there are thoughtful Tunisians of the younger intellectual élite who deplore the absence of deep thinking and searching which go to the root of the problem of faith in our time. To them Islam has become problematical as has religion to many people all over the world. They are not sure whether this bold, adventurous spirit animating the builders of the Tunisian nation—necessary and beneficial as it is—does not hide doubt and uncertainty which endanger the future of modern Islam as that of all religion. The pace at which Tunisia transforms its society is terrific: settling Bedouin Berbers in village communities, developing its slender resources, building schools and hospitals, emancipating the women, and many other aspects of the physical and spiritual building up of the people into a nation.

Religion is not the most important of the problems, and Islam is taken for granted since the Tunisians are Muslims. But as in Ibn Khaldūn's Muslim state, religion is an important factor, alongside others. Here and there, doubts arise, though. To hear a new interpretation of Ramadhan makes one wonder how Islamic the Islam of some of the intellectual leaders in Tunisia is: "God does not want us to deprive ourselves of food and be, thus, incapable of work. Work is a social duty which we have to take seriously; it must come first. If we want to show our earnestness and sincerity as Muslims, we should work harder in the month of Ramadhan than at any other time of the year. This would be a token of our faith and of our civic responsibility." This is certainly a novel understanding of Ramadhan. Its observance in Tunisia is, like so many other expressions of religion, a matter of the generations and of the classes. The older people probably all observe Ramadhan strictly; the working classes mostly, including government employees like drivers who would never touch food, drink or tobacco until sunset without any slackening whatever in the performance of their duty. In 1962 during our visit, I had many opportunities of observing this, and in general it may be said that a large part of the population practised both fasting and working.

Those in efficient and effective charge of cultural affairs and of education believe that within a decade or so there will emerge a new Tunisia in which free citizens will take Islam as seriously as their civic responsibilities. Islam will be their personal faith without any gulf existing between faith and reason. Some think on the lines of the *Falāsifa*, like the philosopher and educationalist in charge of Teachers' Training for Higher Education, M. Mahjoub Ben Milad.[3] Others are convinced that a reform of Islam must come if Islam is to be and remain a force in a Muslim's life. But such a reform must come from within, not from the government above. How this can come about is something of a problem since *muftis* and *qāḍīs* and *'ulamā* generally have disappeared from the scene; they are no longer needed. Perhaps reform will come from a new generation of graduates of the Theological Faculty of the University of Tunis. In 1961 the government incorporated the Zaituna, hitherto a Theological Training Seminary or Muslim University under the direction and guidance of M. Ben Achour, in the University of Tunis, founded in 1958. The transformation of an institution of traditional higher education into a University Faculty of Theology as a modern academic discipline is not only an interesting experiment, it also shows the determination of the government and Neo-Destour party to modernise Islam and build religion into a modern national state. The elimination of Maraboutism was a decisive step in that direction. The incorporation of Islamic law in state law—as far as compatible with modern notions of law and jurisprudence—was even more important and far-reaching. The Constitution of 1957 still included the Mufti of Tunisia among the members of a committee to organise and watch over the election of a president of the Republic.[4] The office of Mufti of Tunisia was later abolished. Liberalisation is the watchword, next to modernisation, and there is the determination to keep "clericalism", a concept and a word hardly applicable to Islam, out of public life for good. Talks with ministers were illuminating in this respect, as were those with the deans of faculties and professors of the university whose Faculty of Letters is aptly called after Ibn Khaldūn. As stated before, there is a distinct Muslim consciousness to be felt and the intention is there to see Islamic principles applied in the moral, social and legal spheres, but without considering the letter of Islamic law. That there is a serious problem here is clear, and most likely these scholars are aware of it, although it is not allowed to obtrude and invade and perhaps impede the rapid transformation of Tunisian society in progress. Cultural activities, centred in the "Maison des sociétés culturelles" in Tunis, are lively and attract large audiences.

French-trained, these audiences are not only composed of professional men and women like medical specialists and practitioners, economists, engineers, literary critics and others, but contain a large number of young people, not all students, who are generally interested, knowledgeable, open-minded and enthusiastic about culture and learning. All have a Muslim outlook deeply ingrained in their being, but not related to and often opposed to strict observance of ritual and law. The students at the Faculty of Letters are serious and much concerned about Islam in all its aspects and in the wider context of national and world affairs. They ask, in an acute awareness of the crisis of Islam, internal as well as world-wide, whether traditional Islam is compatible with nationalism and patriotism. The overwhelming majority are convinced Muslims in a liberal sense, with a strong emotional attachment to Islam and stress the cultural heritage of which they are proudly conscious and from which they derive an intellectual indebtedness. Being patriotic Tunisians, they are passionate participants in the "Tunisian experiment": the reforms President Bourguiba effects in Tunisian society by sweeping away time-hallowed traditional laws and customs. They do not put the question "will he succeed in blending modern requirements with the Islamic heritage and a living faith?", but one can sometimes feel its presence in their young, eager minds. Islam is certainly much stronger entrenched in the personality than in the corresponding age group in Pakistan for instance. The outside observer cannot draw any definite conclusions in the midst of a fluid situation—the most characteristic feature of which is movement, a general movement in which Islam is much involved. He is reminded of 'Allāl al-Fāsī's "Islam is movement" in nearby Morocco. It would be premature to weigh the disappearance of *muftis* and *qāḍīs* and of the Sufi orders against a personal status law for all Tunisian citizens, Muslims and Jews, except Christians, which is—with some modifications—pure Mālikī *Fiqh*, administered, as already mentioned, by lay judges under the authority of the Ministry of Justice. Similarly, it would be premature to weigh the absence of mosques in the new Berber villages, complete with stone houses, school, library and dispensary, against the presence of Islamic elements in the civil code, or the interest in the cultural heritage of Islam against the remarkable activity of the Department of Antiquities in digging up the pre-Islamic past of Tunisia: Phoenician, Byzantine and Roman with some of the finest mosaics in the Museum of Sousse and *in situ*. It would be equally rash to see in the new awareness of the ethical and social values of Islam an impending Islamic renaissance. Any assessment can only be provisional and hypothetical. But two more factors will have to be taken into account which we have not considered so far: the strong and active women's movement towards real equality in every aspect of Tunisian life, and the *Neo-Destour* party with the trade union movement.

This nationalist party is, so I was assured, at least in its leadership, fashioned by the Collège Sadiqi and its tradition—the expression "la tradition Sadiqienne" is often used. It is further claimed, rather surprisingly, that this tradition is largely responsible for the success of the nationalist movement in rallying the masses and uniting them behind Habib Bourguiba. In turn, this mass support enabled the movement to achieve independence and the president to introduce his reforms. The party, though not a religious and political party like the *Istiqlal* of 'Allāl al-Fāsī in Morocco, is not anti-Islam, and if not neutral, is definitely reformist where traditional Islam is concerned. It is laic, and it would be correct to say that religion is of secondary importance in its programme and its political work, though the importance of Islam is recognised—for political reasons?—and many leaders and members of the party are practising Muslims. The religious leaders, with few exceptions, are discredited and out of touch with the people and their needs in our time. If they had called upon the masses to defend Islam—we remember the cry "Islam in danger" in Pakistan—there would have been no response. Therefore, the masses have followed the president and accepted his logical arguments in favour of reforms (emancipation of women, family laws, etc.). This is, at least, what I ascertained in conversation with ministers, party and trade union leaders.

The seriousness of purpose, the drive and energy and the enthusiasm of the Tunisian people are certainly striking. Islam is not left out; this is particularly clear from their national education, as we shall see later. What the result will be, a new flowering of Islam as a personal religion influencing individual action in social behaviour, or a deepening and widening secularisation, remains to be seen. The government is determined to free Islam from the shackles of outdated traditions and wants to replace the formal, external interpretation—as they seem to understand tradition—by a new, dynamic and personal spiritual interpretation which would release human energy and enthusiasm for service to the nation. That many of the older generation are shocked, they consider only natural but of no significance. The people at large want a modern faith—or, shall we say, authentic Islam in a modern dress?—in harmony with contemporary ideas about the good society and the individual Muslim's place in it and in the modern world at large. It is—rightly—stressed that the Tunisians are no fanatics; they are gradualists who believe in and apply the evolutionary principle or, as one minister put it to me: "The Tunisians have taken the passion out of religion (ont dépassioné la religion)." What is needed is to adapt, reform, renew religion in the framework of modern ideas, as another intellectual put it. What matters is: will the intellectuals be able to give a lead, as the president has so far given, to the masses on whom the renewal and survival of Islam after all depends? This is the great question. Will education find the right answer?

There is, however, for the whole Muslim world a question far deeper and much more difficult which must be answered before education can even begin. It is the question which lies hidden and buried under bustling activity and slogans, political, social, even cultural, and which is but an extension of the question behind the first part of this study: "what is Islam?", namely, "what does Islam mean today?". Where is the modern Muslim thinker who asks and answers this fundamental question, who lives and thinks in the twentieth century?[5]

MOROCCO

In Morocco the same tendencies are at work as in Tunisia, only less pronounced and more gradual. Here the religious groupings are sharper than in Tunisia; rigid orthodoxy is strongly entrenched, especially in the famous Qarawīyīn in Fes, and the influence of the *'ulamā* is by no means negligible. But here, too, the Sufi orders are discredited and disorganised. There is a strong progressive element among school and college teachers, civil servants and professional men which is strongly influenced by 'Allāl al-Fāsī and his *Neo-salafīya*.

The youth is divided and often confused, largely through lack of knowledge of Islam, its tenets and its history. There is a strong left-wing movement whose adherents have little use for Islam. The intelligentsia is largely reformist, many are strongly under the influence of their French education and tend to favour a separation of religion and politics. Among the top-ranking judges (Cour de Cassation, Appeal and Supreme Courts) the opinion is expressed that personal status law should remain Mālikī law, suitably attuned to modern concepts and needs, but that civil and criminal law should follow modern codes, embodying as much Mālikī law as is compatible with modern concepts and needs. This view, to my mind, is only partly due to religious considerations. Legal continuity and stability count at least as much, for gradual change and modification is strongly favoured, in contrast to some of the Tunisian reforms. The gap between the European, the almost exclusively French-trained intelligentsia, and the *'ulamā*, even the younger ones, some of whom trained at Al-Azhar, is wide. Few have studied both the traditional Muslim sciences and modern methods of research and criticism. Though the people fully participated in the national struggle for freedom and liberty they share on the whole the outlook of the *'ulamā*. For them, the king is the *amīr al-mu'minīn* and even the *khalīfat Allah* elected by the council of *'ulamā* with *bay'a* (oath of loyalty), whereas the educated élite recognises him as the monarch, first the absolute, and now the constitutional king. Yet many of the educated class (unlike the Tunisians), are traditional in observance, with a keen interest in the preservation of Islam as a faith and ritual in a modern, progressive political order. Some favour inner reform, but realise that it needs time until a new generation of scholars takes the place of the older religious leaders and dignitaries whose mind is closed to the aspirations and needs of our time and who find full satisfaction and sufficiency in orthodox Islam. Some hope for a new apostle to renew Islam and restore its universal appeal and application. Highly intelligent and alert, many of the young seem uncertain and confused. Their ignorance of Islam can only partly be blamed on the French who were as little interested in Muslim education in Morocco as they were in Tunisia. Discussions were always lively, but mostly inconclusive.

This was, however, not the case with the girls of the Lycée *Umm al-banīn*. They are very religious and cannot imagine that anything which the prophet said and commanded could ever be set aside. But they want full equality as far as social status and economic opportunity are concerned. They want full emancipation and to be free to continue their work after marriage. This condition is to be written into the marriage contract. They definitely no longer hold with the centuries-old idea that woman belongs in the home. Needless to say that some young men, though they approve of education for girls, do not welcome this spirit of independence and economic competition, even though the girls stress that physical differences between the sexes lead to different occupations, but on a basis of full equality. The attitudes of the young students and their natural curiosity and interest in politics and the building up of free, independent Morocco contrasted, in spite of the inconclusiveness in questions Islamic, with the static certainty, almost complacency, of the learned professors of Fes and Marrakesh, who with great dignity and deep conviction thought preaching and teaching Islam was all that was needed. In fact, sermons are relayed and often broadcast. In this way the religious leaders often take part in politics. Unlike 'Allāl al-Fāsī who favours the equality of woman with the assurance of her full share in society and economic and political life, the traditionally learned professors in Fes—which is still the spiritual centre of Morocco in the traditional (Qarāwīyīn) and modern sense (Collège Moulay Idris, the nursery of the Moroccan modern élite), and in Marrakesh (Collège Ben Youssef)—consider the present phase in the position of women abnormal. In their view woman belongs to home and hearth and her children; but they are in favour of a modern education for girls so that they can in married life help their children's education. Yet despite remarkable modernisation of the Qarāwīyīne, for example, by adding a department for girls and by the affiliation of its Department of Islamic Law to the University of Rabat as part of its Law Faculty, the outlook of its distinguished teachers seems to be predominantly traditionalist. Language and other difficulties would not allow me to ascertain any modernist trend, although there are among its teaching staff a fair number of young scholars, mainly from Egypt, but also from Lebanon, Syria and Iraq. Unfortunately, I did not meet any of the students, many of whom come from all over Africa to this famous seat of Muslim learning.

On the question of woman's inheritance, the *'ulamā* strictly adhere to *Fiqh*: man inherits more, they aver, because he has greater responsibilities than his wife; he is the breadwinner. Men and women are different and have, consequently, different functions and responsibilities. This view is not by any means restricted to the older generation.

There is, however, some appreciation in these circles of a religious crisis due, in their minds, to the absence of religious education during the French protectorate which is also responsible for the difficulties in applying the *Sharī'a* strictly in every field. But they believe that intensive religious education can and must remedy this situation.

An important part in the preservation of Islam as a vital factor in the consolidation and progress of the young independent kingdom of Morocco fell to the *Istiqlal*, the party led so long and decisively by 'Allāl al-Fāsī. The fact that the late King Mohammed V sided with the nationalist movement gave the Istiqlal added power, strength and prestige. From our description of the ideas of 'Allāl al-Fāsī in the first part it is clear that Islam played a decisive role in the fight for liberty, freedom and independence under the king. The *Istiqlal* differs in this from the *Neo-Destour* in Tunisia.

Yet there occurred a split in the party after independence and a number of the younger members left it. They opposed the declaration of the party in 1955 that it favoured the separation of state and religion. Idrīs al-Kattānī opposed this laicism in a sustained attack on this betrayal of Islam which, unlike Christianity, stands for the religious and political unity of the *umma* and thus subjects the state to the law of Islam which through *ijtihād* can meet any and every situation. He quotes Turkey as the classic example of the failure of laicism in a Muslim country. He opposes any change in Personal Status Law and throughout his book propounds the ideas we have met with in Abul A'lā Maudūdī and the Muslim Brotherhood,[6] naturally with special reference to the Greater Maghrib. There are, thus, sharp differences of opinion about the character of the new Morocco which show themselves in different concepts of Islam and its role in the public life of the nation. Islam is not the only problem, but it reflects, alongside political, economic and social questions and differences in dealing with them, the critical state of mind of a people who want to combine loyalty to Islam with active participation in the modern age to which they belong. This can also be seen in the evolution of the Moroccan Constitution.

Nationalist feeling gained force during the French protectorate from 1912. Its last decisive phase dated from the strong policy of Marshal Juin in 1950, and King Mohammed V's banishment to Corsica made him the embodiment of his people's struggle for their liberty. He was an absolute Muslim ruler who wanted to become a constitutional monarch in a modern state. He promised in a *Dahīr* [*ẓahīr*] (a royal proclamation) in 1958, not only economic and social reforms, but also new political institutions to enable the people to participate in the administration of their country. Already in 1951, the king had declared his intention to set up a democratic régime, "the principles of which conform to the liberal spirit of Islam and guarantee a peaceful and calm life to individual and society alike". Based on the national sovereignty expressed in the person of the king who guards it, he now establishes a constitutional monarchy assuming himself the office and duties of President of the Council (of ministers) the ministers of which are responsible to him as sole holder of the executive power. He also retains the legislative power which he will exercise through organs specially to be created by him. He grants the people the fundamental rights of freedom of expression, of the press, and of assembly and association. He considers it in the best interests of the nation and alone compatible with true democracy to grant representation in stages. In place of the tribal system unsuitable to the times, he makes the commune, "the new social and political cell", the base of organisation of the régime of modern Morocco. To this end, municipal and communal elections are to be held, to be prepared by a commission which has to work out an electoral law and a law conferring public liberties. Once these assemblies are functioning, a National Deliberative Assembly is to be created with certain clearly defined responsibilities, including the discussion and voting of the budget. Its membership is to be elected by the communal and municipal councillors from their midst. Such an Assembly is to be followed by a National Assembly elected by universal suffrage. He concludes the proclamation with an appeal to the people to give proof of their political maturity, sense of civic duty and love of country by co-operating with the king in the implementation of these important constitutional measures in stages for the good of the country.[7]

This proclamation was followed by further declarations of King Mohammed V in 1960 to which his son and successor, H.M. King Hassan II referred in his *Dahīr* of 2 June 1961 containing the "Fundamental Law for the Kingdom of Morocco". In it, the king refers to "the spirit of authentic democracy which has its foundation in the teachings of Islam" which inspired him to promulgate the "Fundamental Law", prior to the granting of a constitution. This was done towards the end of 1962,[8] and its preamble and General Principles embody the Articles of the "Fundamental Law". The preamble states *inter alia*: "The Kingdom of Morocco, a sovereign Moslem State [*dawla islāmīya*],[9] whose official language is Arabic, shall be a part of the Great[er] Maghreb." Of the "Basic Principles" the following are relevant in our context: Article 1, "Morocco shall be a constitutional, democratic and social monarchy"; Article 2, "Sovereignty shall pertain to the nation and shall be exercised directly by means of referendum [*istiftā*] and indirectly by the constitutional institutions"; Article 3, "The political parties shall participate in the organisation and representation of the people. There shall be no one-party system";[10] Article 4, "The law [*al-qānūn*] shall be the supreme expression of the nation's will. All must be bound by it..."; Article 5, "All Moroccans shall be equal before the law"; Article 6, "Islam shall be the religion of the State, and the State shall guarantee to all the freedom of worship";[11] Article 7, "The motto of the kingdom shall be: God, Country and King".

We note that Islam is the official religion of the state and that the law of the state is called *qānūn*, not *Sharī'a*. This latter point underlines the sovereignty of the nation, which is both a departure from the proclamation of King Mohammed V and from Islam which by definition must and does accord exclusive sovereignty to Allah.

The "Political Rights of the Citizens" guarantee the human freedoms as in all modern democratic constitutions, including equal rights for women in Article 8: "Men and women shall enjoy equal political rights. The right of suffrage shall be held by all citizens of both sexes, who have attained their majority, except those deprived of civil and political rights"; Article 12 declares: "All citizens may undertake,[12] with equal opportunity, public functions and employment".

The "Economic and Social Rights" include: Article 13, "All citizens shall enjoy equal rights of education and of employment"; Article 16, "All citizens shall contribute to national defence".[13]

The king's rights and duties are set out in a separate chapter. We note Article 19: "The King, Amir Al Mouminine [Commander of the Faithful], the symbol of national unity, guarantor[14] of the perenniality and continuity of the State, shall safeguard the respect of Islam[15] and of the Constitution...." He is in every respect a constitutional monarch; he not only appoints the prime minister, but also the other ministers, and presides over the council of ministers. He promulgates laws which he may submit to a referendum after the bill was discussed in both Houses of Parliament (Articles 26 and 73). Article 47 lays down that "Legislation shall be passed by Parliament". If a bill is not passed and the king submits it to a referendum which approves it, the House of Representatives shall be dissolved (Article 75) by the king. The members of the House of Representatives (*majlis al-nuwwāb*) are elected by universal suffrage. The Upper House, called "the House of Counsellors" (*majlis al-mustashārīn*), is elected in a different way. Two-thirds are elected by an electoral college composed of members of prefectoral and provincial assemblies and communal councils in each prefecture and province. One-third is to consist of members elected by the Chambers of Agriculture, of Commerce and Industry and of Handicrafts, and also of trade union representatives (Article 45). The government is responsible both to the king and to parliament (Article 65). The Judiciary is independent of both the Executive and the Legislature (Article 82). The constitution can be revised by the prime minister and parliament, and such revision becomes final after a referendum approving it (Articles 104 and 107). But Article 108 stipulates: "Neither the monarchical system of the State nor provisions relating to the Moslem religion may be subject to constitutional revision."

As far as the "Islamic" provisions of the constitution are concerned they are no stronger than those contained in the Tunisian Constitution, apart from the duty of the king who is styled *amīr al-mu'minīn* like the caliph, to defend religion (*dīn*). The king is a practising Muslim and attends the Mosque near his palace every Friday for prayer, clad in national robes and riding a white charger. Morocco is a Muslim country, but it is not an Islamic state.

SECTION 2

CHANGES IN LAW AND THE EMANCIPATION OF WOMEN

CHAPTER 12

CHANGES IN LAW

The constitutions which we have considered have afforded us as nearly as circumstances allow to discover what kind of a state Muslims in the countries visited are building after victory over foreign domination or tutelage. While discussing these constitutions, we have drawn certain conclusions largely based on the law in force and on the attitudes and views of different groups of citizens of modern national states which they hold in respect of the *Sharī'a* of Islam. The question of change and adaptation had to be treated in general with as much detail as was necessary in order to illustrate these differences. Now it remains to describe summarily some changes in more detail, changes which concern personal status law which, to repeat, has always been that part of the *Sharī'a* which was observed by all Muslims. One of the main reasons for this hold of tradition throughout the ages is naturally that it was connected with religious customs even though marriage in Islam is primarily a legal contract followed by a religious ceremony. Divorce and inheritance are also legally regulated. Another no less important reason was that personal status law was outside and far removed from politics. It need therefore not be disturbed and, moreover, together with cult and ritual preserved the religious character of the personal and, often also, of the social life of Muslims. It is only since this society has begun to undergo profound changes through contact with the West that moral, social and legal—as well as political and economic issues—have arisen, which singly or combined call for change and adjustment to bring these laws in line with a different social order in our time. Modern Muslim family law has been treated by experts in great detail, especially by

J. N. D. Anderson and J. Schacht.[1] Here only a few examples can be given to illustrate the relevance of personal status law to politics.

We begin with the "Muslim Family Laws Ordinance, 1961"[2] promulgated by President Ayub of Pakistan "to give effect to certain recommendations of the Commission on Marriage and Family Laws". Article 4 deals with succession and assigns to the grandchildren the share of either of the parents deceased before the grandfather. This is also the law in Tunisia and Morocco. Next, the ordinance decrees compulsory registration of marriages before *nikāḥ* (marriage) registrars, appointed by Union Councils under the Basic Democracies. Contravention is punishable with simple imprisonment of up to three months or a fine of up to one thousand rupees or both. Article 6—"Polygamy"—has aroused the determined opposition of the orthodox circles, quite apart from the dissent of Maulana Iḥtishām al-Haqq from the majority report of the commission of which he was a member. This Article stipulates that nobody can take a second wife in addition to his existing wife without the previous permission of the Arbitration Council which consists of the chairman of the Union Council and a representative each of the parties concerned. If a man contracts another marriage without such permission he must immediately pay the entire amount of the dower (*mahr*) due to the existing wife or wives, and on conviction upon complaint he may be sentenced to up to one year imprisonment or have to pay a fine of up to five thousand rupees (£375) or be punished with both. Article 7 specifies that a divorce must be notified to the chairman of the Union Council, otherwise the same penalties as for Article 6 will be imposed. Within ninety days of such notification the chairman must constitute an Arbitration Council to bring about a reconciliation between husband and wife. Further, a wife divorced by *ṭalāq* (the husband pronouncing divorce) can remarry her husband without having contracted another marriage in the meantime, unless *ṭalāq* was pronounced three times. A marriage can also be dissolved by means other than *ṭalāq*, according to Article 8. This gives a wife who wants a divorce, even though the right to divorce has not been explicitly delegated to her, the opportunity to apply for it. One of the worst social evils arising from divorce at the whim of the husband is often destitution of the wife, as the husband is only obliged to maintain the children of the marriage, but not his divorced wife. Therefore, Article 9 is of equal importance:

If any husband fails to maintain his wife adequately, or where there are more wives than one, fails to maintain them equitably, the wife, or all or any of the wives, may in addition to seeking any other legal remedy available apply to the Chairman who shall constitute an Arbitration Council to determine the matter, and the Arbitration Council may issue a certificate specifying the amount which shall be paid as maintenance by the husband.

To safeguard the wife in respect to the dower paid for her on marriage and due to her, Article 10 lays down that, unless details about payment are specified in the marriage certificate of the *nikāḥ* registrar or in the marriage contract, "the entire amount of the dower shall be presumed to be payable on demand". Article 12 amends the Child Marriage Restraint Act, 1929, by raising the marriageable age of girls from fourteen to sixteen years of age and reducing that of men from twenty-one to eighteen.

It is clear that this ordinance greatly improves the position of a divorced wife both legally and financially, and that it restricts, but not prohibits, polygamy. It is therefore surprising that such a storm should have broken over this regulation as if men had suddenly been deprived of a vital right. The real reason for the opposition becomes clear when we look at the "Minute of Dissent" by Maulana Iḥtishām al-Haqq: it is mainly because initiative and jurisdiction have been transferred to state authorities instead of remaining in the keeping of the religious authorities. His objections cannot be understood unless the views expressed by the commission, himself excepted, are studied first. They invoke the principle of *ijtihād* without being *'ulamā* in these words:

As nobody can comprehend the infinite variety of human relations for all occasions and for all epochs, the Prophet of Islam left a very large sphere free for legislative enactments and judicial decisions even for his contemporaries who had the Holy Qur'an and the Sunnah before their eyes. This is the principle of Ijtihad or interpretative intelligence working within the broad framework of the Qur'an and the Sunnah.[3]

The Maulana charged the commission with undermining "the accepted tenets of Islam and the fundamentals of Islamic Shariat" and with doing what was "irregular and unconstitutional".[4] They possess "neither detailed knowledge of the Islamic teachings and injunctions nor are they versed in the interpretation and application of those laws". What they did amounted to "contravening the Holy Qur'an and the Sunnah and in ridiculing the Muslim jurisprudence, and calling their action as *ijmā*' in the Report they have debased the technical term of 'Shariat'". He opposed restrictions on divorce and said: "If we proceed to bar the lawful way of *ṭalāq* or limit it by making the intervention of Court compulsory, men would naturally turn to the other methods...to bring about the dissolution of marriage. God forbid! vice and adultery would become the order of the day and Muslim society would sink to the lowest depths of disgrace...."[5] He vehemently denounced restrictions on polygamy as aping the West. Plurality of wives was lawful in Islam and should be maintained, but at the same time its abuse must be eliminated.

The agitation for the repeal of the ordinance was of no avail, and the ordinance is still in force. That Maulana Iḥtishām al-Haqq was not alone, but represented the '*ulamā* generally, is clear from the protest meetings discussed above.[6] Apart from the issue of Islamic law and the competence or otherwise of those who introduced the changes (which is a serious matter of principle and practice) there are also psychological and social problems involved which have a close bearing on the whole question of the emancipation of Muslim women. This was well stated by S. M. Abdullah[7] who makes the point that on the whole Pakistani society was monogamous and that bigamy existed mainly among the Western-educated, well-to-do upper class. He does not deny that polygamy and divorce present a serious problem, but he fears that legislation alone cannot cure the existing ills and that litigation favours the wealthy class which alone can afford it and will increase under the ordinance. On the other hand, Anis Mirza[8] defends the ordinance as restoring to a Muslim woman the rights and protection bestowed on her by the Qur'an itself. He also maintains the right of *ijtihād* for every Muslim; it was not the prerogative of the '*ulamā*. His question "Do the opponents of the Family Laws know of the hapless destitution of thousands of women and children who are victims of the three fatal pronouncements of '*Talaq*'?", raises doubt in the mind that abuse of polygamy and divorce is mainly practised by the Western-educated wealthier classes; child-marriage is widespread among other classes. The ordinance itself, the fact that six years elapsed from the appointment of a commission to inquire into the existing, unsatisfactory laws until something was done about it, and the taking up of positions for and against clearly show Pakistani society, like Muslim society elsewhere, in transition and crisis like Islam itself.

Tunisia adopted a code of Personal Status Law in 1956 which claims to be Islamic law, brought up to date by certain modifications and changes. It is also published with a Commentary which takes note of Qur'an, *Ḥadīth* and *Fiqh* and has a Preface by the then minister of justice in which he stresses that legislation must reflect the mentality and aspirations of the nation. Hence the new code testifies to the spirit of the educated Tunisian youth.[9]

The regulations governing marriage, for example, are accompanied by copious notes designed to show their provenance from and compatibility with *Sharīʿa* law. Thus Article 3 makes marriage dependent on the mutual consent of both partners, which is claimed to be derived from the Ḥanafī rite. A marriage to be valid must be contracted before a civil registrar. Religious marriage is not accepted in law. Article 18 prohibits polygamy. Article 19 prohibits the remarriage of a wife whom the husband divorced three times. Divorce can only take place before a civil court at the request of either spouse, and after reconciliation attempted by the judge has failed. Damages and maintenance are awarded by the judge. The laws of succession correspond to the *Sharīʿa* on the whole, but are more differentiated and extend the right to succession beyond the limits laid down in Islamic law.

It remains, however, an open question whether the secular legislator deliberately modelled the civil Personal Status Law on the traditional religious law or whether precedents were afterwards sought and discovered in Mālikī and Ḥanafī law. Moreover, the civil authority is the only legitimate and recognised authority in the state, and religious jurisdiction is abolished. A comparison with Pakistan, not to mention Malaya where, as stated earlier, *Sharīʿa* law is still supreme and largely unchanged, is instructive.

It is interesting to note that whereas the *ahl al-kitāb* were always permitted to have their own jurisdiction in matters of family laws, Tunisia has placed Muslims and Jews who are Tunisian citizens under one and the same "Code du Statut Personnel", thus demonstrating the supremacy of the state as legislator uniformly for all its citizens irrespective of religion. Only in matters of cult and ritual is there Jewish autonomy. Foreigners apply their own national law in matters of personal status.

In Morocco personal status law is the traditional *Sharī'a* law which is administered by *Sharī'a* courts. It is Mālikī *fiqh* which was suspended under the French protectorate. Certain modifications have been effected with a view to further changes, but everything is done in stages. Thus, under certain safeguards, a man is permitted to have more than one wife, but, so I am told on good authority,[10] the aim is definitely monogamy. The rigidity of the *'ulamā* and their lack of understanding of modern trends is regretted. The same is said of the rabbis, and the opinion was expressed that there should be one law for Muslims and Jews—as in Tunisia—as a token of a citizenry united in one nation, instead of a majority and a minority living under their own personal status law. There is naturally no objection to, nor interference with, the maintenance of their separate cult and ritual.

Turkey abolished Islamic personal status law with the abolition of the *Şeriat* courts in 1924. The Swiss Civil Code was adopted in 1926, with certain minor concessions to Islamic concepts and customs.[11] Civil marriage is alone legal; yet in the rural areas religious marriage is very widespread, and the civil authorities had again and again to legitimise such marriages in order to safeguard the children of such illegal unions. Polygamy is a punishable offence.[12]

The modernisation of the Muslim family law is not primarily secularisation; this it is, more as a concomitant, and it is inevitable through the social changes in the wake of a modern economy with full participation of women in factory, office, nursing, teaching and the professions. It is a necessary condition, an essential part of woman's emancipation.

CHAPTER 13

THE EMANCIPATION OF WOMEN

Even in highly developed and advanced countries, like those of Europe, it has taken a long time and a determined struggle for woman to come into her inheritance as a free and equal human person. Besides, the example of the oldest Western democracy in the modern sense of the term, Switzerland, shows that woman can be emancipated, modern, free and equal even without having the elementary human right of a say in matters which affect her personally, as well as nationally, through the vote. It is well to remember these truisms when we approach the problem of the emancipation of woman in Islam—in some of the countries of our inquiry.

In the first place, we must make an important distinction between a comparatively small group of Western-educated women, wives and daughters of Western-educated intellectuals, and the vast majority of uneducated, largely illiterate women whose labour is badly needed in the economic development of newly independent countries. What has taken decades or even centuries to mature in the West must be telescoped into a few years or at best a decade or two in order to make a difference to the standard of living, not to speak of higher things. To banish hunger in the worst cases, or to raise a people from bare subsistence level to a position in which the mind can be fed as well as the body in more fortunate cases, the full participation of every able-bodied woman is desperately needed. This is not contradicted by under- if not unemployment of the men for which there are psychological reasons as well as others owing to economic backwardness.

Moreover, emancipation depends on the local conditions and *mores* of a people. Referring back to the agitation in connection with the Muslim Family Laws Ordinance in Pakistan, it is true that the women who demonstrated and fought for years to effect changes are mostly the Western-educated ladies of well-to-do, socially advanced and arrived families. But they did not fight for themselves alone, they are fighting for all women, even the inarticulate, illiterate, frightened wives of the poorest of the poor. But to fight for civil and political rights is only one, though an important, aspect of the women's organisations. Their main activity is in the field of education, in the widest sense of the term, in order to raise the women to a level commensurate with their responsibilities in a modern state. Should we therefore not consider their activities under the head "Education"? It will be better to discuss it in conjunction with the broader question of women's emancipation, because we are not here concerned with formal education of infants and children up to university graduation, but rather with self-help and voluntary organisation of what we are used to call "further education" which covers vocational training as well as intellectual and moral instruction. In Pakistan this work is being done by APWA,[1] and it has a significance which transcends the feminine sphere, important enough as that would be; it has a national significance because it arose out of the chaos and suffering of the early days and months and years of Pakistan's difficult beginnings. We have seen a good deal of APWA's work in Lahore where we took part in a national conference. The women who organise and execute the varied activities of APWA are Muslim women fired by patriotism which many of them proved by giving succour to the homeless and destitute when Pakistan was born. The organisation covers all Pakistan, East as well as West. In fact, Muslim women were active in the movement for a Muslim homeland in the subcontinent long before 1947. It is said that out of an originally political struggle a social welfare movement grew.[2] It established a Cottage Industries section which aims at preserving native skills in arts and crafts and takes a keen practical interest in women's education. The girls are being prepared for a number of professions and APWA helps them to find employment in the above-mentioned occupations and also as secretaries, telephonists, doctors and lawyers. There is a good deal of prejudice against women in such employment, not dissimilar to the attitude current before the First World War in the West. Marriage is usually a bar to continuing in employment, but married women resume work when the children are old enough or do part-time work (as everywhere else). Prejudice is rife among orthodox circles which insist on the segregation of the sexes, even in offices, schools and colleges. It is interesting to find just those who preach "Back to the Qur'an" and the Golden Age of the first four right-guided caliphs denying women that freedom of movement and activity which women in early Islam enjoyed. There is no need all at once to advocate, even less to practise the complete independence, self-reliance and freedom of the Western professional women, often unmarried. Woman achieved her liberty and independence not over night in the West either. But to equate a working woman with social contacts with the other sex with a "bad girl" whom one would not marry is a prejudice to be met with even among Western-educated and -oriented young civil servants and professional men. Women are covered by existing labour laws, and special provision is made for pregnant women and mothers with young children. A field in which Pakistani women pioneered is family planning, at first on a purely voluntary basis, later with government support and in 1962 there were about five hundred centres attached to hospitals and dispensaries.[2]

While social work in all its aspects is their natural and most obvious activity, Pakistani women play a part in politics as well; six seats are allotted to them in the National Assembly. They take their full share in most walks of national life, including teaching posts in the universities. The Department of Social Work of the University of the Punjab is headed by a woman. Peshawar has a woman Reader in Political Science. That they are a force to be reckoned with, they proved in their prolonged fight for a change in the family laws. There is no doubt that, given favourable conditions of steady development in Pakistan, the women will overcome prejudice and opposition and contribute together with the men towards the welfare of their state and nation.

In Turkey today women in the big cities are completely equal; in the countryside the movement towards emancipation has still to gain momentum and succeed.[3]

In Tunisia, the "Union Nationale des Femmes de Tunisie" links its birth and work with the promulgation of the "Code du Status Personnel" in 1956, hailed as the turning-point in the emancipation of Tunisian women. It is a nation-wide movement, inspired by the dynamism of President Bourguiba who shows a special interest in its work. Devoted to the welfare of women as part of the welfare of Tunisia, the Union of Tunisian Women co-operates with similar organisations in Africa and is affiliated to the International Council of Women. The constitution has granted them the vote, and their Mme Présidente was a National Front candidate and was elected to the first Parliament. They are politically very active, together with other national organisations under the general leadership of the *Neo-Destour* party. They are also much concerned with basic education of girls, vocational training and welfare work. Above all, they effectively combat illiteracy among women in a hundred centres, with the support of the Ministry of National Education. They train young girls to take their place in the life of the nation and supply them with the necessities of life during training in four centres in Tunis alone. They train social and health visitors to look after the women in need and provide clothing for women to enable them to shed the veil. They publish a woman's journal (*Faiza*).

There is no sphere of national life to which they do not make a significant, contribution, and they share with the Tunisian men that drive and enthusiasm which is so characteristic of President Bourguiba's new Tunisia. Their organisation is extremely efficient, their leaders work untiringly and ceaselessly to reach every Tunisian woman—educated or not, rich or poor—and inspire them with love of country to be expressed in work, to make them conscious of their dignity and human worth in their own right, and thus enable them to make their distinctive contribution to the welfare of Tunisia. Visiting their headquarters one is reminded of an army headquarters, with charts and tables and statistics and expert answers ready for all possible questions. Does Islam influence their outlook, play any part in their work? This question is difficult to answer absorbed as the National Union of Tunisian Women is in practical economic, social, cultural and political work alongside the *Neo-Destour*. They share the general disapproval of the collaborationist "clergy", but they are conscious of the teachings of Islam about social justice and the dignity of the human person. In Tunisia, Islam has a share in national education, otherwise it is the private affair of the Tunisian citizen whose first duty is to work for his country.

Morocco is in the field of woman's emancipation pursuing the same objectives, but, again, much more gradually and cautiously.

Its women's movement is not so militant and politically conscious and active as the corresponding movement in Tunisia. It is rather like APWA in Pakistan. The Moroccan is more conservative and more deeply attached to religious forms. The greatest obstacles in the path of Moroccan women leading to full emancipation are ignorance and illiteracy. Hence the leaders of the women's movement are trying to combat both. They welcome the reforms in the family laws as a step in the right direction, but stress that the laws of succession and inheritance need changing. This is thought to be a matter of time, and is bound to come. Women generally are said to be completely in the dark about their rights in marriage and divorce; they must be enlightened, with the help of the personal status law (briefly discussed earlier on) which requires the consent of the first wife to her husband marrying a second wife, and the voluntary consent of the girl to enter into matrimony. The importance of the family was stressed, especially in the present time of transition when a feeling of security is essential for the wellbeing of the young. Apart from patient education of the women and appealing for better facilities for girls, the movement also runs women's co-operatives, and provides vocational and domestic science training, on lines similar to APWA's Cottage Industries but catering rather more for feminine needs. The daughters of the educated classes, including the traditionally learned, study at the university and many go into teaching. Once married, few women carry on a profession, but many do voluntary social work. There are, naturally, secretaries, typists and telephonists in Government offices, in commerce, trade and industry.

Only the orthodox Moroccans resist the changes in social customs, such as the mixing of the sexes, due to the employment of women. But gradually a transformation already discernible in its initial stages will make Muslim society as contemporary as the modern institutions which have been adopted. This need not militate against Islam. There is nothing un- or even anti-Islamic in the emancipation of women. On the other hand, one cannot say that any of the measures taken and still to be taken to ameliorate their position and to integrate them in a modern society are directly inspired by Islam. There may be even a danger in the undeniable fact that, particularly in the matter of reforms of the family laws, Islamic law is seen to be outmoded and standing in the way of woman's complete emergence into modern life. To meet this possible danger education must be so devised as to build Islamic teachings into the national education as an integral part. For the real danger to Islam does not come from changes in the law or from the emancipation of women; it comes from agnosticism, atheism, materialism and Communism.

SECTION 3

THE PLACE OF ISLAM IN NATIONAL EDUCATION

CHAPTER 14

ISLAM AND EDUCATION IN PAKISTAN

The role of Islam in education varies from country to country and depends on the place of Islam in the life of state and society in each of them. We are not so much concerned with the private sector of education and religious instruction of Muslim children, but primarily with public or national education. Here, too, we mus distinguish between facilities such as Turkey offers to the children of parents who want religious education for them on the one hand, and compulsory education such as is laid down in Pakistan for all Muslims. The dividing line between instruction in Islam as a religious faith and in Islam as the patrimony of the nation and a decisive or at least important element of its culture and civilisation is often not sharply drawn. This is due to the attitude towards Islam which is itself not always unequivocal, as we have repeatedly seen. We must therefore expect to see a certain ambiguity reflected in the educational field as in other aspects of national thought and life. Besides, we must not forget that every government is forced by circumstances to emphasise the utilitarian aspect of education which inexorably first demands to combat illiteracy, and to provide for vocational and technical training without which the national economy cannot be sound.

We should therefore be prepared for difficulties, some of which at least we encounter ourselves in our highly developed, often affluent societies in the West. I mean the "Two Cultures" controversy which arose over the recession of the humanities in favour of science and technology and the rather lame and largely ineffectual efforts at redressing the balance and achieving a healthy equilibrium. We should, therefore, understand the gravity of the educational problem in newly established independent states which have only recently emerged from foreign rule or tutelage which was characterised by a blatant neglect of "native" education. Imperialism, no matter how progressive and well meaning, made no attempt at integrating the new education, which it offered for reasons of politics as well as of modern civilisation, and the social and cultural traditions of the people it ruled directly or indirectly. As far as Islam is concerned it must however be remembered that Muslim education was backward and static as was Islam itself, notwithstanding the various attempts in the wake of "modernism" and missionary propaganda—which as we have seen are interdependent—at a renaissance of Islam through the "Back to the Qur'an" movement.

The case of Pakistan is in this respect again *sui generis*. We recall the efforts of Sayyid Ahmad Khan in the direction of a new, rational explanation of the Qur'an in order to establish the compatibility of religion and modern science and to bring to a new generation of Indian Muslims both a religious revival and an accommodation, if not an integration, with Western culture and civilisation. We recall too the conservative and orthodox attempts at Deoband and Lucknow, in particular the revivalist efforts of Shiblī and Abul Kalām Āzād.

Against this background, the present efforts in Pakistan must be seen, together with the fact that Pakistan, as she emerged in 1947, must build Islam into the fabric of its state and society in some form or other. Thus education became quite naturally a constitutional issue. The Objectives Resolution and the Principles of State Policy explicitly mention a knowledge of the Qur'an and "Islamiat" as essential for Muslims. Hence education in the religious subjects becomes a requirement without which these principles cannot be implemented. There does not seem to be available any other means for creating an awareness of Islam as something which concerns every Muslim and which lends meaning and purpose to his life. The much stressed "Islamic ideology" cannot become something real, and that driving force it is supposed to be in Pakistani life, without a knowledge of the tenets of the faith and of its literature which a contemporary Muslim can understand, appreciate and recognise as meaningful for his or her personal and social life.

It is a sign of how seriously this issue is taken in Pakistan that less than three months after the military *coup* the Government of Pakistan appointed a "Commission on National Education" which President Ayub inaugurated on 5 January 1959 with an address which "stressed the need for a reorganization and reorientation of the existing educational system so as to evolve a national system which would better reflect our spiritual, moral and cultural values".[1] The commission was not only given terms of reference, but was also set a time limit within which to accomplish its difficult task. That it succeeded is due in no small measure to its members' hard work and their sense of urgency, but also to preparatory studies carried out at educational conferences and special inquiries from 1947 onwards. While the report naturally stresses the utilitarian value and importance of a planned, comprehensive education on a national scale, it also forcefully underlines the paramount importance of character training. Thus, it states:

> The desire for a homeland for Muslims on the subcontinent grew out of their wish to be in a position to govern themselves according to their own special set of values. In other words, our country arose from the striving to preserve the Islamic way of life. When we speak in this context of the Islamic way of life, we have in mind those values which emanate from the concept of a universe governed by the principles of truth, justice, and benevolence, where human relationships are based on the ideal of human brotherhood, and where all these are rooted deeply in religious belief. The moral and spiritual values of Islam combined with the freedom, integrity and strength of Pakistan should be the ideology which inspires our educational system....National unity and religious values have to be translated into deeds in a manner that all our citizens can accept and join in the common effort. Islam teaches honesty and active participation in the removal of distress and poverty. ...From our concept of justice and brotherhood there derives the desire to create a social welfare-state. Our greatest need as a people is to improve constantly our standard of living, which at the moment is among the lowest in the world....[2]

These statements sound the keynote of the objectives of a national policy for education. We note that Islamic principles are to guide national education on all levels.[3]

The commissioners thoroughly discuss higher education.[3] They recommend that Islamic Studies "with their inter-departmental characteristics should be consolidated and developed, bearing in mind their value for our own students and for scholars from foreign countries".[4] Muhammad Afzal Husain has this to say about this important subject: "The comprehensive discipline labelled as Islamic Studies is of the utmost importance to us, who wish to evolve an Islamic State. We have decided to adopt a legal system which corresponds to the Quran and the Sunnah. We wish to produce a social organization which will be truly Islamic." Remarking on the self-confidence man is gaining through increasing control over natural forces, he concludes:

> Man is drifting more and more, and with ever increasing speed, away from the natural conditions. His life and his reactions are becoming artificial. He is becoming conditioned by his self-created surroundings. An educated person seeks rational explanation of ethical principles, and for tenants [tenets?] of his faith. It is for the specialists in Islamic Studies to answer the complicated questions posed and provide solutions of the complex social problems that are developing.... Islam as a comprehensive social and spiritual system has to deal with society as intimately as science.... In the field of Islamic Studies the prerequisites for a postgraduate course should cover a very wide field, extending over ethics and philosophy, science and psychology, economics and sociology, history and geography, and one cannot ignore laws. The Islamic Studies course thus conceived will be the toughest of the disciplines....[5]

To staff such a department and to produce competent graduates who can in turn teach in secondary and, most importantly, also in primary schools as well as tutors in adult education, presents one of the most difficult problems. The universities alone cannot cope with this problem, and this was one of the main reasons which prompted the government to implement the provision of the 1956 Constitution to establish centres of Islamic research and to support already existing institutes devoted to Islamic Higher Studies and Research. Before we review these briefly, we must refer to the "Government Resolution on the Report of the Commission on National Education".

It is a statesman-like document that shows the determination of the government to implement with a sense of urgency and responsibility the recommendations of the commission as far as practicable. They assign to education the primary task of inculcating a sense of patriotism and civic responsibility in every member of

Pakistan's young generation receiving a national education. They say about the great need of Pakistan:

Great stress is to be laid [in national education] on the need for a change in attitude among our people, on a greater demonstration of personal, professional and public integrity, and on readiness to render service to the community. Due emphasis must be given to the role of the educational system in the training of character, the preservation of the ideals which led to the creation of Pakistan, the strengthening of the feeling of a unified nation, and the perpetuation of the principles of truth, justice, benevolence, and brotherhood which are rooted in the spiritual value of the Islamic way of life.[6]

There is no glossing over existing obstacles and faults in character and in higher education, following the critical examination contained in the commission's *Report*; but these cannot here be discussed. Despite the ineluctable concentration on the need to produce the necessary number of scientists, technologists, lawyers and doctors for industry, the civil service and the community at large, there is the frank recognition that the quality of the graduates must be improved and that a level commensurate with that in the long-established universities in Europe, America and Russia must be achieved.

It is natural that civics should form an important subject in secondary education together with other general subjects "to give every pupil the knowledge he needs to live a useful and happy life" (p. 11). Eight years' compulsory schooling in primary education is envisaged in two phases. During the first phase five years are aimed at, and this is to be extended to eight years during the second five-year period. The achievement of this target is linked with the economic improvement of the country and the development of the Basic Democracies (p. 14).

Special attention is to be paid to women's education. While stressing the role of wife and mother by providing training in home crafts, "technical and vocational schools should provide courses of training for women taking up careers". Such careers naturally include those requiring university training (p. 15).

As far as languages in use in Pakistan are concerned, the aim is to make Urdu and Bengali the two national languages for West and East Pakistan respectively; while allowing for Pushto and Sindhi in West Pakistan in the lower forms they are to be replaced as languages of instruction by Urdu from class VI onwards. It is reckoned that fifteen years will elapse before Urdu and Bengali can become "effective media of instruction at the university level" (pp. 18 f.).

The government's decision on religious education deserves full quotation:

Religion is the most vital civilizing force in the history of mankind. It broadens sympathies, inculcates a spirit of tolerance, self-sacrifice and social service, and removes artificial distinctions between man and man. To ensure that the advantages of religious education are properly utilized the teaching of religion should be organized in the following manner:—

(*a*) Religious education should be an integral part of the educational system.

(*b*) Several religious faiths are professed and practised in our country, and their teaching should be confined to those who profess them. Religious education should do nothing which would impair social and political unity in the country. It should foster human brotherhood, justice, equality, and the dignity of man and emphasize the importance of practical goodness, piety and virtue.

This declaration by liberal-minded modern men will have to be taken to heart by those charged with teaching their faith to their pupils if the high aim expressed in the last sentence quoted is to be realised to the good of the country. The comment may be permitted that this declaration breathes the spirit of universalism inherent in the ethical teachings of Islam, but it may be doubted if its implementation would be so easy in an Islamic state, as envisaged by those orthodox ideologists who practise political theology.

(*c*) The teaching of religion should have three clear-cut stages: (i) The compulsory stage; (ii) the optional stage; and (iii) the research stage.

(i) Religious education should be a compulsory subject of study for all Muslim students for the first eight years, that is, in the primary and middle classes. At this stage the emphasis should be on the teaching of the Quran and the life of the Prophet and all controversial matters should be excluded. The Quran should be read with translation, but the boys should be free to buy any translation they like and the teacher should not attempt any interpretation of the text.

(ii) It should be an optional subject in classes IX and X.

(iii) In intermediate classes it should become a component part of Islamic Studies which should be offered as an optional subject. At the university stage Islamic Studies should be an optional subject.

(*d*) Universities should produce scholars of the highest quality in Islamic Studies, capable of interpreting Islam and presenting it as a body of thought that can meet the challenge of modern times and fulfil the requirements of a modern scientific society.

(*e*) An Institute of Islamic Studies should be established (p. 16).

Presumably (*e*) means the Central Institute of Islamic Research in Karachi, which is to assist the universities with the material on which the teachers of Islamic Studies, trained at home or abroad, can base their critical interpretation of Islam which (*d*) rightly considers essential. This is in fact the greatest need in Muslim countries today. They possess scholars of the highest ability and technical knowledge of the Islamic languages and literatures. But in order to achieve the reorientation desired and essential for a living Islam in our time, the modern historical and literary criticism as current in the West must be fearlessly applied to the religious sources and to the historical literature. This requirement cannot be met overnight; it is a long-term process on which will depend whether the intentions of the intellectual élite in Pakistan for whom the Government Resolution speaks in (*d*) can be realised. Even so, it is a truism to state that intellectual awareness, satisfaction and—last but not least—affirmation of faith are of no avail unless faith in God is a precondition. Without it, the best teaching of religion is not sufficient to produce modern believers whose faith is secure against the challenge of the many "isms" which vie with each other for men's minds and souls. We all know that faith cannot be commanded, it can only be encouraged, deepened and led to social action where it exists. The section on religious education presupposes the adherence of every Muslim in Pakistan to the faith of Islam, and it is to be noted that religious instruction during a Muslim child's first eight years of school is compulsory. No allowance is made for humanists, agnostics and atheists. Even if they are in a minority, the compulsory nature of religious instruction, however understandable and positively to be welcomed, subjects the minority to a conflict of conscience. However, we must not view this question from our Western point of view, but rather take into consideration the situation in Pakistan as the result of its coming into being. And yet, absence of faith and challenge to it are not confined within the frontiers of Western countries and Russia.

Bearing in mind the vulnerability of religion in our time, a further difficulty arises: with the same proviso—the special situation of Muslim countries, in particular of Pakistan—it is regrettable, even if it is inevitable, that especially during the difficult years of adolescence when the young, growing mind—growing in dimension and in doubt—is in greatest need of spiritual guidance the teaching of religion is only optional. One can therefore only hope that the elementary teaching of Islam is of such quality and standard that the boys and girls of the upper forms will wish to continue with their religious education; if not formally—because of lack of time necessarily taken up with more pressing, practical subjects fitting them for higher education or a career—then by informal contact with enlightened, understanding teachers who will help them when they want to examine critically the doctrines and ethical and social teachings of their faith.

Where are the ideal teachers of Islam and how can they be supplied? It appears that the main responsibility falls on the Central Institute of Islamic Research. From a statement published on its establishment by the Ministry of Education, we get an idea of its purpose:

With a view to organise research on Islam, to give it a rational and scientific interpretation in the context of the modern age and to bring out the achievements of Muslims in the fields of History, Philosophy, Science and Culture, the President is pleased to establish a Central Institute of Islamic Research. The objectives of the Institute shall be—(i) to define Islam in terms of its fundamentals in a rational and liberal manner and to emphasize, among others, the basic Islamic ideals of universal brotherhood, tolerance and social justice; (ii) to interpret the teachings of Islam in such a way as to bring out its dynamic character in the context of the intellectual and scientific progress of the modern world; (iii) to carry out research in the contribution of Islam to thought, science and culture with a view to enabling the Muslims to recapture an eminent position in these fields; (iv) to take appropriate measures for organising and encouraging research in Islamics, history, philosophy, law and jurisprudence, etc.....

To secure coordination of research in these fields the Central Institute of Research may grant affiliation to the following: (i) Institute of Islamic Culture, Lahore.[7] (ii) Islamic Academy, Dacca. (iii) Iqbal Academy, Karachi.

The Central Institute's first director, Professor I. H. Qureshi, was engaged during my visit in establishing a research library and appointing Research Fellows to the Institute. The journal of the Institute began publication under the title of *Islamic Studies* in 1962. Its first issue contains this interesting comment on the four objectives of the Institute:

In doing so, the Government of Pakistan has acted upon a need felt by all Muslims, namely, the need to understand Islam, the satisfaction of which is requisite for any intelligent self-application to Muslim tasks and duties. The age of Muslim awakening, like the age of Muslim decline, is past. Today, the Muslim World stands on the threshold of a new age, the age of doing. Muslims the world over have had their fill of ideational patterns of awakening: apologetic for the past, explanation of Muslim decline, exhortation to rise up to the standards of the fathers.

Dismissing "the foreign imperialist" as not dangerous, the declaration proceeds:

Indeed, in the age of doing, the Muslim World runs the risk of a far more serious peril, the peril of doing something other than Islam, of achieving objectives other than those of Islam. The strategy of doing presupposes a clear consciousness of the Islamic ought-to-be; and it is the enlightening, deepening and crystallizing of this consciousness that is today's greatest need....The Muslim today is possessed of the strongest will to mould himself and the world into the divine pattern God has provided....The Muslim is by nature committed to God's cause in the world. For him it is platitudinous to assert, and pointless to be asked, whether or not Islam is his ideology, and the Islamic life his highest objective. For him there can be no doubt but that this is so. The question which troubles his inmost conscience and for which he is in search of an answer is rather, "What is the meaning of Islam? What is the nature of the divine pattern? the content of the Islamic life? the momentum and style of Islamic will?" This earnest and disturbing inquisitiveness of the Muslim of today constitutes his modernism, his contemporaneity....To know Islam, therefore, is the first duty of the Muslim, as man. As a Muslim, it is even more than his first duty. It is his *islam*, his Islamic act *par excellence*....To help the Muslim fulfil this primal duty, this Institute was created....As its voice this journal means to uncover the worthy ideas in our Islamic tradition, but with a view to revaluating them, first, in the light of the divine pattern itself, and second in that of the contemporary and future need of the *ummah* for its realization.

The close link between the Institute and the Islamic Advisory Council mentioned earlier[8] secures to Islamic research its *Sitz im Leben*, its topicality. Unfortunately, it also draws it into the political battle about an Islamic state. It is therefore a good thing that the other research institutes mentioned can pursue their task without political distraction. I can say from observation how valuable the work and resultant publications of the Institute of Islamic Culture in Lahore are for the uncovering of the spirit and meaning of Islam today.

To illustrate the place of Islam in secondary education, we quote from the *Report of the Curriculum Committee for Secondary Education*:

> ...special attention has been paid to the formation of character and to the development of a sense of civic duty, patriotism and self-sacrifice. ...The Schemes of Studies...are designed to combine an appreciation of the moral and spiritual values that constitute our national heritage and a progressive outlook on life, leading to the strength and solidarity of Pakistan. And all this has been inspired by the spirit of Islam; the spirit of universal brotherhood of man, of justice, of tolerance, self-sacrifice and practical goodness. This is the spirit of Islam that is not limited to any time or clime; that inculcates those fundamental values towards which human civilization must move to realize its purpose; those fundamental truths that underlie all natural processes and are the goal of intellectual endeavour. It is the spirit of Islam which removes all duality between mind and matter and which reconciles the demands of the body and the soul, making proper use of all aspects of the individual's life—the intellectual, the moral, the aesthetic and the spiritual—the ultimate goal of man.[9]

About the teaching of Islamic history the *Report* has this to say: "The moral and spiritual values of Islam provide the ideology of Pakistan and occupy an important place in all aspects of our life...." It suggests teaching Islamic history up to 1258, the date of the fall of the caliphate, but also

> the history of Islam or Muslims in the Indo-Pakistan sub-continent. An interrelated study of these two histories is expected to give the students a full knowledge of the history of Islam as it shaped their present and to fulfil the purpose of general education to be given at the

Higher Secondary level....This approach in the presentation of Islamic History in the educational system of Pakistan is different from the traditional approach which considered Islamic History to comprise the history of Islamic peoples in countries like Egypt, Arabia, Spain, Turkey and Iran, and ignored the fact that [the] history of Muslims in the Indo-Pakistan sub-continent was as much the history of Islam as that of other countries where Muslims lived. The present approach is expected to imbue the students with the real spirit of Islam, according to which excellence as a Muslim depends upon good conduct and qualities of head and heart rather than on birth. Students of Islamic History, as now presented, will develop confidence in themselves and instead of looking for leadership to other Muslim countries, will try to lead others in the presentation of Islam.[10]

The emphasis on Islam and Muslims in the subcontinent is significant and akin to the views of Iqbal.[11]

No less indicative of the liberal and progressive spirit of the learned educationists who are responsible for this *Report* under the chairmanship of the philosopher Taj Muhammad Khayal is the passage about the syllabus in Islamic Studies, a compulsory subject up to class VIII and optional afterwards:

The syllabus for Islamic Studies...has been drawn up with particular emphasis on Islam as a universal code of morality and a progressive social order, which can meet the demands of all times. Besides inculcating faith in and reverence for God, the Quran and the Prophet, special importance has been attached to Islamic virtues, both individual and social. Stress has been laid on moral and practical goodness and not on superstition and rituals. Sectarian controversies have been avoided. Particular emphasis has been laid on the inculcation of Islamic virtues like truthfulness, justice, toleration, forgiveness, mercy, honesty, readiness to enforce the right and resist the wrong, simplicity, self-sacrifice, social service and the search for knowledge. Islam has been presented as a progressive social system and a universal code of morality.[12]

The committee suggested a well-rounded, comprehensive syllabus—deploring "an unfortunate prejudice in the country against Art and the development of an aesthetic sense"[13]—with emphasis on social studies and integration of Islamic Studies in character training and promotion of civic sense through the development of Islamic virtues.

There are naturally Departments of Islamic Studies at the universities and at colleges which pay special attention to religious instruction. The government's interest in matters Islamic is also shown in making available funds from the *Awqāf*, administered by a government department, to establish a Shāh Walī Ullāh Academy at Hyderabad for the publication of his works and the propagation of his teachings, and also a *Jamia Islamia* at Bahawalpur, a theological college on the postgraduate level to which *Madrasas* affiliate. Here an attempt at a synthesis between traditional and modern teaching is made.[14]

Though not founded on a religious basis and with the object of furthering Islam by sponsoring an Islamic education, women's colleges must at least briefly be mentioned. In deference to orthodox opinion and feeling, there is a separate medical school for women and there is also the "Islamia College for Women" at Lahore in response to a great demand for higher education among Muslim girls, even those in purdah. The principal and the entire staff are women.[15] At the time of our visit only about 15 per cent of the students wished to make use of their education, mainly as teachers, but also in social welfare. They are strictly orthodox, want an Islamic state and are convinced that the Qur'an does not make new developments difficult, if rightly understood in its exact wording. Much scope is left, they feel, for improvement in conditions generally, including women's rights. They accept family planning and favour universal suffrage with more women entering politics. Most of those who intend to take up a career want to work among women.

Next APWA founded a college, in addition to primary and high schools, near Liaqatabad in 1954 which gradually and steadily grew into an institution of higher education with its students obtaining the B.A. Degree of Karachi University.[16] Significantly, most of the girl students come from poor parents who could not normally afford to send their children to college; and the staff has to make great efforts to train them for their degrees. In 1962 it counted 350 students who are looked after by a staff of 22. There are well over a dozen colleges for women in Pakistan, chiefly for home and social sciences, designed to help women's emancipation and full participation in national life.

Lastly, a special educational establishment, set up in 1952, deserves mention: the *Jamia Talim-i-Milli* at Malir City, Karachi, directed at the time of our visit by Professor Mahmud Husain, its founder, who is also joint editor of *The Jamia Educational Quarterly*. It is not only a valuable experiment in progressive education in the context of the spiritual needs of the young state of Pakistan; it has also a notable history in that it owes its inspiration to the *Jamia Millia Islamia* in Delhi which was founded in 1920 at Aligarh and transferred in 1925 to Delhi and was directed for many years from 1928 on by Dr Zakir Husain, a leading Muslim Indian educationist. But the Malir institution is by no means a copy of the Delhi venture. The *Jamia Millia Islamia* was born in the middle of India's struggle for liberty and freedom and—as a result of Gandhi's call for a boycott of state schools and colleges—was founded by teachers and students of the Anglo-Oriental Mohammadan College at Aligarh when it sought to be advanced to university status by the British Government.

> Education in the Jamia Millia was to integrate Indian culture internally and also with the culture of the West. Muslim and non-Muslim students would learn to represent the values of their religion and of their moral and cultural traditions, and would distinguish themselves because of their refinement, modesty, thoughtfulness and competence.[17]

It was from the beginning a co-operative effort of teachers, students, their parents and supporters of a new departure in education which was inspired both by the ideals of Islam and the needs of a national basic education. In 1938, it established a Department of Adult and Social Education in addition to its existing primary and secondary schools which are run on modern lines associating the pupils with the government of the school by letting them run it for one day in the year. In the same year a Teachers' Training Institute was also founded. It added an Institute of Arts Education and since 1951 is recognised as an Institute of Higher Education with the right to confer the B.A. Degree. At the time of our visit, it was a flourishing intercommunal educational institution which still experiments under the guidance of Professor M. Mujeeb. It is an impressive, comprehensive Muslim enterprise which breathes a special, happy atmosphere. During the celebrations of its fortieth birthday, it was stated:

> The tradition of doing pioneer work is strong as ever; we still have adventure in our blood. In one way or another, and especially in the unexplored regions of cultural and emotional integration, you will find

us making continuous and significant advance. This is another way of saying that the Jamia Millia will remain Muslim in name and Muslim in character, for this name and this character is not the assertion of a civic right but the open and unconditional acknowledgement of a civic duty, a duty that devolves upon us because we are Muslims and because we are citizens of India. We must continue to create...an atmosphere in which religions, as the expression of moral and spiritual ideals, provide, because of their differences, an occasion and an inducement to mutual appreciation among their believers....[18]

This was in 1960 and is typical for the attitude of many leading Indian Muslims to Islam as a faith like others, separated from politics.

In a way, the task of the *Jamia Talim-i-Milli* in Muslim Pakistan is easier, but it shares with the Delhi institution the source of its inspiration and the aim of a contribution to national education *sui generis*. It consists of a primary school, a secondary school and a college with intermediate and B.A. classes, and in 1959 added an Institute of Education for the training of teachers. The latter is one of the most urgent needs of Pakistan today, especially in connection with the reorganisation of national education. At the time of our visit, new buildings were going up to house new ventures and ensure the organic growth of a remarkable educational experiment.

The civilising force of religion is today not so strong as it was in a past liberal age. Institutions like the *Jamia Millia Islamia* in Delhi and, in different circumstances in Karachi, the *Jamia Talim-i-Milli* still draw their inspiration and their strength from religious and political liberalism. In religion as in politics, liberalism has to fight an intransigent orthodoxy which is backward looking, and a militant humanism, atheism and materialism which are all attuned to the space age and offer a young generation (in so far as it has this longing) something which appeals more strongly to its desire for roots.

Even if religious education had at its disposal all the most modern and attractive tools in the shape of cogent argument, scientific presentation with obvious relevance to the multitude of physical and spiritual challenges and stresses, its success could not be expected in the immediate future. The fact is that the needs of such an education are so far ahead of modern research by Muslims into Islam in all its facets that neither enough suitable text-books nor the teachers who can use them to the best advantage of their students are available. There are, however, two factors which can obviate this imbalance to some extent and perhaps until such time as the necessary teachers and text-books are available. One is the solid core of orthodox believers whose observance of cult and ritual guarantees, at least temporarily, the survival of religion even if it is not very much alive and not facing outward through giving a lead in good citizenship. The other factor, though not confined to the orthodox majority, is the influence of the home. Family ties are very strong, and example has a great influence on the younger generation, provided the parents show understanding for the problems of the times. In Pakistan APWA can do much to further Islamic consciousness in the women it reaches who can then set an example to their children. The school, as we saw in the *Report of the Curriculum Committee*, can bring Islamic virtues and ideals into play in teaching civics, but only if the conditions mentioned are fulfilled, that is, providing the right type of teacher and the right kind of text-book exist. Education is a long-term business, complex and dependent on many predictable and more unpredictable human factors, unlike a well-planned and smartly executed military operation with a limited objective. And yet, all hopes are focused on the success of a nation-wide system of technical and moral training for which Islam is to supply the spiritual source and values. Islam is consciously called into service to produce good citizens. This offers a great opportunity to release its spiritual power and ethical and social values. But it can also be a means to further the secularisation of Islam by divesting it of its God-centredness and by concentrating on its practical value and usefulness in a world which more and more yields to materialism. Even if this happened, the service of Islam would be very valuable.

If an outsider is allowed to comment on the situation in Pakistan in this respect, he will have to admit that some of the fears of the orthodox groups are justified. But implicating Islam in practical politics and, while paying lip service to its perfect suitability to any age, opposing any change in its traditional structure and form does not seem to be very helpful. All the same, orthodoxy is performing an important holding action, and one can only hope the progressive, liberal elements will evolve a positive, modern Islam before those for whom this is intended as a rallying point and justification for their separate state- and nationhood have drifted away.

APPENDIX TO CHAPTER 14

SOME REMARKS ON RELIGIOUS EDUCATION IN MALAYA

In Malaya, religious instruction for Muslims is under the authority of the Department of Religious Affairs in every state of the Federation. Usually, the teachers in religious schools run by this department were trained in Islamic schools not only in the traditional religious sciences but also in general subjects. This training is preparatory to an intensive Islamic training in the Muslim College of Klang, entry to which is by competitive examination. The college aims at fitting its pupils, both male and female, for the teaching of Qur'an, Islamic history, *Fiqh* and Ethics. As mentioned before all hopes are directed towards this college, but I was unable to attend lectures and classes there and cannot say whether the attitude to religion is modern on the part of the teachers nor whether the teaching methods are modern and designed to enable the pupils to face contemporary problems and situations in a spirit of flexibility and accommodation.

Frequent visits to various religious schools allowed me a good insight into their working. Arabic is everywhere the language of instruction in all religious subjects. In primary schools the teaching of Arabic takes up a large part of the syllabus. Subjects taught comprise the Qur'an, *Ḥadīth*, Ethics (chiefly Al-Ghazālī) and some Sufism, and teaching is on traditional lines. Teachers of Arabic are often Arabs from Egypt, Iraq or Saudi Arabia, but before long the Malays will be able to take over from them. In most schools, Ethics and Sufism are taught on the secondary level only. Incidentally, if a graduate of an Arabic school wants to proceed to the university for higher education, he must first attend a state secondary school for further education to university entrance. In the state of Perak with Kuala Kangsar as its capital, the inspector of religious schools was most helpful. He had arranged an elaborate programme of meetings and visits to religious schools, both for boys and for girls in Ipoh, Padang Rengas, Kuala Kangsar and as the highlight a visit to Ehya Sherif Institution, Gunong Semanggol, in the company of the president and secretary of the Department of Religious Affairs, and the inspector of religious schools who accompanied me throughout. Quite a few of the teachers throughout Malaya are Al-Azhar-trained. Usually there is a seven-year curriculum in two phases, which is both thorough and comprehensive. The teaching of Arabic is excellent, and the ability of the pupils to read religious texts (Qur'an, *Ḥadīth*, *Fiqh*, Ethics) is quite remarkable, especially at Ehya Sherif where secular subjects taught include an introduction to sociology and economics.

Unless the discrepancy between Islamic teaching and economic reality is removed through reforms and a modern outlook, it is difficult to see how this intensive religious instruction, offered and accepted with so much enthusiasm and zeal, can bear fruit in the life of these young boys and girls after leaving school, when they have to facc the challenge of contemporary life and assume the rights and duties of Malay citizens. Much is expected of the Al-Azhar-trained young teachers, but, as has been stated earlier on, they seem to submit to the older generation of orthodox *'ulamā* who see no need for change or adjustment. Whatever the future may hold, it is certainly a knowledgeable generation of Muslims who will shape their lives and take their place in Malay society. How effective Islam will be must depend on a new generation of religious leaders and teachers, and their willingness to meet present-day needs and thus make it possible for their pupils to realise Islamic teachings in state and society. The value of traditional teaching is great and should not be belittled, but, even in an Islamic school with the emphasis on religious education, it is imperative that an integration should be attempted. As long as both streams, the religious and the secular, flow in isolation, instead of attempting to effect a junction where they can meet and merge, no young mind can realise the relevance of faith and morals to a life for which the other subjects are to prepare him. This has nothing to do with Islamic ideology, but simply with a rounded human personality. These religious schools offer a rare opportunity of showing how a mind, moulded by religious beliefs and teachings relative to individual and social behaviour, can apply them in his own life once he is trained for a vocation or profession, provided he is taught to see what topical significance attaches to Islam in moral and social behaviour, and what contribution its principles and moral precepts can make to the solution of national issues. Perhaps the Department of Islamic Studies in the national University of Malaya—or even a Faculty of Divinity established on a strictly scientific basis like any other university Faculty or modern academic institution, and independent of the existing institutions of traditional learning and teaching—can play a major part in this integration. Such an academic establishment, modern in outlook and teaching methods, may be of considerable help to the younger generation of religious teachers and scholars (among them those trained at Al-Azhar in Cairo) on whom so much hope is placed by the Western-educated and -oriented intellectuals, in gaining and maintaining their independence and in working for a more liberal interpretation and application of traditional Islamic law. This would not only be welcomed by the intellectuals in government, administration and the liberal professions, but may induce them to take an active interest in such a liberalisation which can only benefit Islam as a living faith, and indirectly Malay society.

There may be constitutional problems involved since religion is the responsibility of the rulers of the states. But since the constitution explicitly allows the federal government to support Islam financially, if necessary, such obstacles might be overcome. But one would like to see Malaya follow the example of other Muslim countries which look to a theological Faculty for that reinterpretation of the fundamentals of Islam which all Muslim believers desire. Such a course may not be advisable in Pakistan where Islam is such a controversial, political issue, since it might extend the conflict to the universities. But Tehran, Ankara, Tunis, Rabat and Fes are engaged in an educational experiment which may have far-reaching consequences.

CHAPTER 15

ISLAM AND NATIONAL ARABIC EDUCATION IN TUNISIA AND MOROCCO

In North Africa the situation is in some respects different.[1] Islam is not only the official religion, it is also part of the Arab heritage and closely linked to the vigorously pursued policy of Arabisation in Tunisia and Morocco. Arabisation underlines the Arab character of nationalism; it is not only a question of language in that Arabic should everywhere replace French, the legacy of foreign imperialism, as soon as possible. It is also an acknowledgement of spiritual roots, a determination to make the Arab-Islamic patrimony the dominant component of the national culture of a free people, always stressing naturally the composite Maghribī civilisation to which Tunisia and Morocco are conscious heirs. Arabisation is considered as the vehicle to national unity; it also means the absorption of the large Berber element in the Tunisian and Moroccan nations, the replacement of the Bedouin tent by the stone house in a village settlement and the integration of the Berbers in the urban civilisation of the cities.

Islam plays an important role in this Arabisation, for Arabic literature is, as far as it is classical, imbued with religious ideas stemming from Islam, and contains the Islamic cultural heritage of the Middle Ages, including the transmission of Hellenic and Hellenistic culture and civilisation. Both countries profess in their constitutions their attachment to Islamic teachings, and it may very well be that Islam will be the principal, or at least an important, element in the cultural nationalism which must replace the political nationalism which culminated and was fulfilled in the attainment of sovereign independence. This holds good, in particular, of Maghribī Islam and its contribution to Mediterranean culture and civilisation in the Middle Ages. Apart from French thought and institutions the reception of which is naturally today subject to searching criticism and evokes certain reservations, this medieval heritage constitutes the main source of inspiration. Especially, the Western-educated and -oriented intelligentsia understands Islam in this cultural sense in their stress on Islamic teachings as distinct from Islamic law and ritual.

TUNISIA

Islam did not play a conspicuous part in the nationalist struggle in Tunisia, and the *Neo-Destour* party adopted a neutral attitude compared with the *Istiqlal* in Morocco, a definitely religious and political nationalist party, as was stated earlier. But Islam now plays an important part in national education.

In Tunisia, Islam is an integral part of what is called "religious and civic instruction", and this connection is significant for it indicates that the political leadership in Tunisia intends to build Islam into the education for citizenship. The revolution in education in the wake of Tunisian liberation and independence is a natural and, indeed, essential accompaniment to the transfer of power and authority from the French to the Tunisians. Education is a nationalist government's surest means of influencing its future citizens and, in the first place, of safeguarding newly won freedom and creating and assuring national unity. The answer to diversified, unplanned education under the French with several types of education existing side by side (French, mixed French-Tunisian, and traditional Qur'an schools) was unified education controlled from the centre, the Ministry of National Education under M. Messadi. A plan was worked out broadly based on "the Arabic language, the cultural past and present of Tunisia, a country belonging to the Arab-Muslim civilisation, national history and geography and that of the Muslim world, especially of the Arab Maghrib".[2] Arabisation in the strict sense of making Arabic the sole vehicle of instruction must proceed gradually for lack of qualified teachers. Education is planned in three stages: primary, intermediate and secondary; and higher.

An important part of primary schooling is taken up with the teaching of Arabic and of subjects of national importance, that is, the formation of a national personality, over a period of six years. To this end, a new subject has been introduced: "civic and religious instruction" with which we are alone concerned here.

In secondary education, place of pride belongs to Arabic language and literature which were ousted under the Protectorate by French language and literature. These latter are now ancillary cultural subjects. French is used during this stage as the language of instruction to an extent dependent on the availability of Tunisian Arab-speaking teachers; the aim is complete Arabisation. In secondary education, too, a significant change is effected by the introduction of "Islamic Thought" in the sixth year of a two-phased instruction lasting three years each. This study of Islamic thought comprises theology (*Kalām*), Islamic philosophy (*Falsafa*) and law (*Fiqh*) and includes such thinkers as Al-Ghazālī, Ibn Khaldūn and Ibn Taymīya. It runs parallel with instruction in general philosophy.

"Civic and religious instruction" (*Tarbīya dīnīya wa-madanīya*) deserves a more detailed treatment on the basis of the syllabuses issued by the Ministry of Education. In the primary school it is called "Moral and Social Education" (*Tarbīya akhlāqīya wa-ijtimā'īya*), and the Qur'an, both whole *suras* and groups of or single verses, plays a major part in the programme. The children memorise them in the first two years, later selections from the Qur'an are chosen to teach morals (*akhlāq*) and religious duties (*'ibādāt*). History is taught, together with civics, in the last two years. The aim is to make the pupil a good Muslim (*muslim ṣāliḥ*) who takes his religion seriously, both in worship and in moral behaviour. History teaching is to instil in the child love of nation (*umma*) and of country (*waṭan*) and comprises the story of succeeding civilisations in Tunisia culminating in the story of the Arab-Muslim civilisation in all its stages, right down through the immediate past history to complete independence and the Tunisian Republic within the Greater Arab Maghrib. Civics teaching is to prepare the child for the exercise of his civic duties. The political order is to be explained in terms of the Tunisian Parliament, the government, the head of the Republic, the rule of law, elections, army, administration, social relations between citizens, international relations including the United Nations Organisation and the "International Charter of human rights" (*mīthāq 'ālamī liḥuqūq al-rajul*).[3]

It is a comprehensive education considering that it can only occupy a small proportion of the teaching time available. Its intention has been clearly formulated in these terms: "Tunisia is a country that is profoundly attached to Muslim tradition. Thanks to the reform [of education], this tradition will be maintained and renewed. From the very first years, the child will be placed within a spiritual climate which will make him conscious of the role and value of his religion; one will inculcate in him the desire to respect and follow its precepts." Stress is laid on explaining the sacred texts, not on just making him memorise them mechanically. The teacher is "to show him how to apply them in the daily life of the believer and citizen". The precepts of the Qur'an teach moral values for the individual as for the nation.

After the duties of a good Muslim, the child shall learn, through a natural link, the qualities and virtues of a good citizen. On this plane, he will be made to understand, by practical example, the notions and principles which govern the organisation of the state: Freedom, Labour, Right, Democracy, etc. The pupil must be given, through the study of History, a sense not only of the fatherland, but also of the common destiny of mankind.[4]

Primary education is compulsory and free for boys and girls. On the intermediate level, "religious and civic instruction" is more advanced, both in extent and in depth, and emotionally and intellectually suited to adolescents. Religious and civic education has to concentrate on those religious and human values which promote the emergence of good citizens and virtuous human beings. An increased consciousness of the meaning of religion, its doctrines and teachings must be transmitted in three years at a very impressionable and at the same time questioning age. It is important to teach social responsibility and concern for the good of the nation, to show the place of the individual in the nation and that of the nation in mankind.[5] The syllabus comprises the principal aspects of Islamic beliefs and convictions, the five basic religious duties and a selection of the *Sharī'a* relevant to a Muslim's life (personal status, *ribā*, etc.), and comments on Qur'an and *Ḥadīth* as they relate to right interhuman relations and transactions. The aim in religious and civic instruction on this level is to transmit a more intellectual approach and appeal, and to point to the harmony between the religious and civic realms and the complementary nature of their respective duties. Appropriate passages from Qur'an and *Ḥadīth* are suggested.

On the higher level of secondary education the appeal is to the personality of the pupil and its intellectual formation, in relation to the personality of the Tunisian nation whose religion is Islam.[6] The aim is to nurture the emotional and intellectual qualities making for good citizenship and character, common to all sound education. The intention of the government is to effect harmony between education and religious *milieu* (*taḥqīq al-insijām bayna tarbīyatihi wabayna wasaṭihi-l-dīnī*). In detail, the syllabus follows that for the intermediate education but is more specific and detailed. Both stress the place of Islam as the last and final of the revealed religions. Again, the plan follows the traditional division into *'ibādāt* and *mu'āmalāt* (duties to God and social duties). The teacher must show the connection between the questions treated in *Fiqh* and the practice obtaining in the Republic of Tunisia as evidenced in the measures adopted, e.g. the family laws.[7] Stress is to be laid on the social relevance of the Qur'an, and the *uṣūl al-fiqh* (Qur'an, Sunna, *ijmā'* and *qiyās*) are to be explained.

Higher education is in the hands of the University of Tunis—a creation of the government of President Bourguiba in 1958—a growing institution which had at the time of our visit a "Faculty of Letters Ibn Khaldūn", a Faculty of Laws and of Science, and also, since 1961, a Faculty of Theology. On the French model, there also exist several Institutes of Higher Studies and a Teachers' Training College under the dynamic direction of M. Mahjoub Ben Milad whose *Les Problèmes de l'Éducation*, as he translates the title of his Arabic book *Taḥrīk al-sawākin*,[8] gives an idea of the thinking that goes on in Tunisia about education and also about Islam and about a synthesis between Islamic ideas and modern, particularly French, philosophy.

Of particular interest for us is the transformation of the Muslim University (*madrasa*) *Zaituna* into the aforementioned Faculty of Theology. Its former rector, M. Ben Achour, is the dean of the new Faculty which is licensed to award a "Licence de Théologie et des Sciences Religieuses" after four years of general and special studies which though based on the old course are modernised through the inclusion of such subjects as "Introduction to the study of religion, of philosophy, of history and language, of orientation". The traditional Muslim sciences were taught in 1962 by the same professors in the same way as before. A modern language must also be studied. The special—Islamic—course includes "The principles of the political and social organisation in Islam"; "The social and economic doctrines" (of Islam). The Faculty also runs a three-year course leading to the Preacher's Certificate of the Zaituna; the students must study religious philosophy, social and economic doctrines, and the organisation of the Tunisian Republic in their third year.[9]

This is a most interesting experiment since the authorities hope and expect that the proximity of the other Faculties of the university will eventually achieve a real integration of a former stronghold of orthodoxy into the intellectual life of the young, but vigorous university as a modern scientific Faculty of strictly academic standing. It is further hoped that such a modern theological Faculty will be the consummation of the religious education at all levels of primary, intermediate and secondary education and will produce religious teachers and scholars of distinction who will inspire, especially in the Tunisian youth, a modern faith compatible with the highest cultural and social aspirations of the Republic. Religion in the schools is, as we have seen, on a par with secular subjects, but is intended to serve as a moral guide to citizenship and family life.

In discussing the syllabuses of the various stages of Tunisian education, we noted that Islamic teaching and law concerning family life played an important part in religious instruction. Of still greater significance, however, is the fact that by coupling religious with civic instruction religion is considered not only as the private affair of the citizen, but as a social force for good which, taught in the right way, should have a beneficial influence on the future citizens. The intention is good, but it remains to be seen in the course of the next few years after the full implementation of the educational reforms has become possible, whether the execution corresponds to the plan. This will depend on the right type of teacher and the right kind of text-books, but also on the right religious atmosphere in the home. This is not Tunisia's problem alone, it is universal wherever Muslims live, and it applies to the other world religions as well.

It would be tedious to repeat what has been stated before about the precondition of faith for any religious endeavour to succeed. But Tunisia offers—more than Turkey with its extreme attitude—

an example, or better an experiment, in officially instituting and encouraging religious education while at the same time excluding Islam from public life, confining the religious scholars and dignitaries to the mosque and the home and limiting their authority to cult and ritual.

If, however, faith is weak or absent, religious education in the service of the state will most likely lead to a secularisation of Islam, whose moral and cultural values and achievements may well inspire a modern humanism, but will hardly bring about a religious revival.

MOROCCO

Before independence, the situation in Morocco was similar to that prevailing in Tunisia. The schools were either French, mixed French-Moroccan or purely Moroccan of the traditional Qur'an school type. Among this diversity, which made for divisions and worked against Moroccan interests, there stands out the Mosque-university Qarawīyīn founded in 859, continually expanding in size and educational activity in spite of a succession of rulers with their dynasties. Considered the oldest university in the world the Qarawīyīn has maintained a high standard of traditional Muslim higher learning through eleven centuries and is only now undergoing changes which may prove significant. By its very stability it has been of immense benefit to Islam and its strength in Morocco, not to speak of its influence on Muslims from other countries who came to Fes to study at this Muslim university. Especially during the years of French paramountcy, the Qarawīyīn has been the symbol of the close link between the Alawi dynasty, especially King Mohammad V, the Moroccan people and Islam. The taint of collaboration certainly does not stick to the *'ulamā* as a group in Morocco as it does in Tunisia. Respect for the *'ulamā* of the Qarawīyīn reflected respect for Islam and Moroccan self-respect.

During the Protectorate only 10 per cent of Moroccan children had proper schooling, mainly the children of the traditionalist aristocracy. The French schools were naturally patterned on the lay schools in Metropolitan France, religious education was private in Qur'an schools before or after attending a French school. At the summit was the traditional education at the Qarawīyīn.

King Mohammed V appointed a Royal Commission on Education in 1947 whose work was, however, hindered by the French and proved largely abortive. A dramatic change set in after the attainment of independence with the appointment of a new Royal Commission in 1957 whose deliberations resulted in an entirely new system of a unified national education which aims at schooling the whole youth of the country in primary and secondary schools. In 1962 there still existed a few private schools. According to my information, there are in operation three different types of education: (1) independent schools on a European pattern and scale, but based on Arabic; (2) the Qarawīyīn still largely unchanged, but engaged in modernisation (as far as I know, this is the one institution which has never departed from all-Arabic instruction); (3) the modern school, completely Moroccanised and divided into a primary and a secondary stream. The first two years are largely devoted to the learning of Arabic, after which the languages of instruction, according to the subject, are Arabic and French. The aim is complete Arabisation. The secondary schools also have an Arabic base, with a reformed syllabus which leads to the Moroccan Baccalauréat. Religious education is in Morocco also linked with civics and is carried out in Islamic schools on a modern pattern, pedagogically speaking. Altogether this third type of education provides the basic instruction which is the same in all three kinds of schools covered by it. The only difference is the language of instruction. The Moroccan educationists are at one with their Tunisian counterparts in systematically and energetically striving for complete Arabisation of the entire school network. In Morocco, too, the aim of national education is the religious citizen, that is, a Muslim by faith who takes his civic responsibilities seriously.

In Morocco Islam is, to my mind, much more deeply rooted and practised than in Tunisia, judging from my observations in the towns. In the rural areas traditional Islam is very strong in both countries. Altogether, the two Maghribī nations share much of a common past culture and today also the problem of absorbing the Berbers fully into the national community. In Morocco this means a concerted effort at gradually eliminating customary law and replacing it by *Sharī'a* law in matters of personal status. In both countries, it principally means integration through national education.

My friendly contacts with educationists and educational administrators in the Ministry of National Education at the centre in

Rabat and on the provincial level at Fes—to whom I am indebted for my information—have confirmed me in my view that both Tunisia and Morocco have set their sights at the same aim and ultimate objective, but that Morocco can call on a larger fund of traditionalism in religion than can Tunisia which is more Europeanised and displays more drive and energy. This is not meant in any way as criticism: the national temper is not identical in both countries, and there are differences in size of territory and of population and in economic structure and enterprise as well as in social customs.

What the Tunisian educational authorities call "religious and civic instruction", the Moroccans term *'ulūm islāmīya wa-lugha 'arabīya* (Islamic sciences and Arabic language). The term "Islamic sciences" is used in much the same way as "Islamiat" in Pakistan. Islam and Arabisation are linked with nationalism in Morocco as in Tunisia, but there is this difference—already stressed—that in Morocco Islam played an important part in the nationalist movement from the start. There is thus perhaps less danger in Morocco than in Tunisia that the stress on Arabisation may lead to a growing secularisation of Islam. It is too early to say, and instead of speculation we would do better to wait and see. For we cannot isolate the terms "religious" and "political" in connection with Islam and the Arabs so easily as in a Western context. The classics of the Arabic language are largely religious, and Arab history is largely Islamic history after all. National consciousness—especially after a prolonged period of foreign rule—must be awakened and strengthened, and the national history is undoubtedly bound up with Islam. We need only think of the Fatimids, the Almoravids and the Almohads and their impact on North African history and culture and on Islam in this region.

A few details about religious instruction in Morocco, based on comprehensive syllabuses I was given, may round off this brief account. There is here a more varied programme comprising pre-Islamic and Islamic poetry, undoubtedly because the teaching of the Arabic language and of Islam are combined. Early Islamic history and the history of Islamic civilisation, including foreign influences such as Persian, Greek and Indian, are thoroughly studied. Qur'an and *Ḥadīth* are both treated from the religious and linguistic-literary angles.

In secondary schools, which are phased as in Tunisia, the religious duties (prayer, fasting, etc.) including their precise forms as laid down in the *Sharī'a* are fully explained, with appropriate passages from Qur'an and *Ḥadīth*. Social and moral behaviour is then illustrated in the same way. As in Tunisia, the passages are prescribed. Their relevance for the pupil growing up to be a good, useful citizen is emphasised. Material and explanations are increased from form to form.

Special attention is paid to the organisation of Islam from the prophet and the *khulafā rāshidūn* through the whole period of the caliphate. This covers political administration, society and literature. Social and moral lessons are drawn from history with a view to teaching the pupils to become good Muslims and good citizens. The teacher has to work through a detailed syllabus covering the history of the caliphate and the Ottoman empire, and leading to North African history and civilisation, under the aspect of *umma* and *waṭan* and of Arab nationalism and unity. This is followed by an introduction to constitutional theory and law and such concepts as authority and power in a parliamentary state. In the third year, selected topics from *Fiqh* relating to personal status law are taught, and the history of the Maghrib and Andalusia (Spain) is studied in great detail. In the sixth and last form, the principles of jurisprudence (*uṣūl al-fiqh*) and the four orthodox rites are explained, and the theories Islam entertains about life, especially on this earth, are expounded. Next "the Islamic order for an Islamic state" is discussed in terms of governmental power and authority and the rights and duties of a Muslim, including finance, administration of justice and *jihād*, with illustrations from the Qur'an and *Ḥadīth*.

It is clear that much thought and preparation have gone into this comprehensive plan of secondary education. It bears out what is claimed in an Arabic booklet on Fes on the occasion of the first Congress of the Committee for Arab Nationalism under the heading Religious Life: "The official religion in Morocco is Islam, and the Qur'an is the Moroccan North African authority in their religion and in their political and social affairs in all the varied matters that touch their life."[10]

However, the observer of the Moroccan scene cannot be sure that this statement covers all Moroccans, especially the younger and young generations. The future of Islam in Morocco as elsewhere largely depends on the success of religious education. But it can only be repeated that knowledge certainly aids faith, although it does not necessarily create it. The issue between Islam as a faith and a way of life and Islam as a cultural heritage is still to be decided. Much will also depend on the advanced teaching and research associated with a university. Outwardly similar to the incorporation of the Zaituna in the University of Tunis, the Faculty of Law of the University of Rabat is actually linked with the Qarawīyīn at Fes. The "Supreme Council of National Education" effected in 1960 the unification of all education by suggesting and implementing a modernisation of the Qarawīyīn by adding a Faculty of Law, another of Letters and yet another of Science.[11] The future will show whether these additions will harmoniously merge with the old-established traditional Islamic sciences and remodel these so as to bring them in line with contemporary ideas and needs. Unless all higher education is geared to the aspirations of a modern Muslim state and its people, Islam cannot gain the wholehearted allegiance of the academic youth: the leaders of tomorrow. A new look is not sufficient: what is needed is a new heart and a new mind to proclaim and practise the old truths afresh and to make them once more the signposts on the road to a just social order and to a rational faith and way of life.

EPILOGUE

We all, Muslims and non-Muslims, realise that the problem of the role of Islam in the modern national Muslim state demands an urgent solution. Its very complexity in the context of the contemporary political, economic and social situation favours the taking up of radical positions. Yet this can only increase confusion and contradictions, inevitable as this may be. Goodwill and mutual understanding are needed in order to create a public opinion which is well informed, rooted in the Islamic past and determined to support a truly national effort to establish a modern society on the pattern of the Good Society. It is essential that politically conscious and responsible citizens should—while recognizing the existence of extreme views and intentions—earnestly endeavour to bring about a reconciliation of attitudes and interests for the good of a united nation within the larger family of nations.

Co-operation cannot be confined within national boundaries. Newly won independence created internal problems which can only be solved within these boundaries. But the aftermath left by foreign domination and tutelage must and can only be cleared away and overcome by outside help limited only by human resources. For colonialism has left its mark both positively and negatively; yet at this early stage of national sovereignty, its benefits are inevitably dwarfed by the disadvantages caused by its negative features. The most important facet of these is the neglect of education and the consequent backwardness of the majority of the new citizens. This backwardness has widened the gulf between Western and traditional education.

A satisfactory and early solution presupposes that two essential nation-building factors are present: the one is the strength that flows from an Islamic consciousness based on knowledge and understanding of Islamic tenets, law, history and cultural achievement. The other, resulting from the former, is an open and positively critical attitude to the West.

As long as "the West" is identified with Christianity a peculiar theological argument clouds the discussion, prevents the necessary dialogue between East and West, blurs the burning issues of the day and, consequently, hampers a natural solution achieved in freedom and responsibility. Today, Christian missionary activity threatens Islam less than does an exaggerated nationalism which—though the natural result of colonialism and imperialism—has as little to do with Christianity as it is incompatible with Islamic teachings. If the Christian missions in the past presented a challenge, it derived less from the Christian message than from the secular European ideas embodied in the arts and sciences, especially their underlying principles of unhampered rational inquiry and literary and historical criticism. These challenge all historical world religions without exception. Many Muslims still identify "imperialism" with "Christianity" today. But this only confuses the issue, gets the real problem of religion in our age out of focus, and hinders us from coming to grips with modern life in its political, economic, social, cultural and, not least, religious aspects.

The scientific and technical achievements of our time are indispensable; without them, we would relapse into backwardness. But if we do not realise that they are only means to a truly human end—the Good Society—we would be left with nothing but a scientifically and technologically harnessed materialism and crude utilitarianism. If we want to meet and overcome this formidable challenge, if we want to build up a meaningful, dignified life individually, nationally and internationally, we have to pay a heavy price. This price—which is demanded of all of us irrespective of colour and creed—is a new attitude to Faith through a radical rethinking of our spiritual roots and values. It must lead us to a new evaluation of our heritage and must prompt us to implement in a radically different situation the old, newly understood values alongside with new insights and ideas. Believers, agnostics and humanists, we are all engaged in the same struggle: we are all seeking to discover a new meaning in life for us here on this earth and in space which we are in process of conquering, adding a new dimension to human life which insistently demands revolutionary changes and adjustments.

It would not help anybody to blame "the others" for our ills, failings and failures. Undoubtedly, in our inescapable self-examination we must uncover the reasons for our malaise. But we must do this not to absolve ourselves by accusing "imperialists" and "colonialists"; we should rather seek a practical solution to our common problem together by a concerted effort. Such a common effort will only be possible and successful if we tackle our specific problems on a national and individual level in a way best suited to our particular condition. Then, and then only, can we make a useful contribution to our collective human advance, on the basis of historical continuity and individual and collective responsibility.

The vital question, then, for Islam seems to be how its adherents can better concert their efforts towards an urgently needed Muslim *and* general solution: as a religious and moral force in a modern lay state, or through the implementation of its *Sharīʿa* in an Islamic state, howsoever the Muslims interpret and then preserve or modify it.

NOTES

CHAPTER 1

1 What follows is largely based upon: Şerif Mardin, *The Genesis of Young Ottoman Thought* (Princeton, 1962); Bernard Lewis, *The Emergence of Modern Turkey* (London, 1961); G. Jäschke, "Die Entwicklung des osmanischen Verfassungsstaates" in *WI*, v (1918), and "Der Islam in der neuen Türkei" in *ibid.* I (Leiden, 1951), 1–2; U. Heyd, *Foundations of Turkish Nationalism* (London, 1950); Ziya Gökalp, *Turkish Nationalism and Western Civilization*, trans. N. Berkes (London, 1959); in particular I. Süngü, "Tanzimat ve Yeni Osmanlilar" ("The Tanzimat and the New Ottomans") in *Tanzimat*, I (Istanbul, 1940), 777–857; and T. Z. Tunaya, "*Âmme Hukukumuz Bakimindan İkinci Meşrutiyetin Tefekküründe "İslâmcilik Cereyani*" ("The Islamist Movement in the political thought of the era of the Second Constitution...") in *Hukuk Fakültesi Mecmuasi*, XIX (Istanbul, 1953), 630–70, to which Professor B. Lewis kindly drew my attention and which Dr A. Mango kindly translated for me into English. Quotations from both Turkish studies later on are taken from these translations.

2 Cf. B. Lewis, *op. cit.*, especially pp. 75–175 and *passim*; also the literature cited there.

CHAPTER 2

1 '*Ulamā* has come to mean the Muslim religious scholars, both theologians and jurists (who are originally designated *fuqahā* = experts in *Fiqh*).

2 Cf. J. Schacht, *The Origins of Muhammadan Jurisprudence* (Oxford, 1950); his articles *Sharī'a* in *EI* and *Fiḳh* in *EI*[2], and the incisive study "Classicisme, Traditionalisme et Ankylose dans la loi religieuse de l'Islam" contributed to *Classicisme et Declin culturel dans l'histoire de l'Islam*, ed. R. Brunschvig et G. E. von Grunebaum (Paris, 1957). Cf. also Select Bibliography *s.v.* Schacht.

3 Cf. my *PTMI*, chapter "The Caliphate: Theory and Function", and the literature cited there.

4 Cf. Sami Shaukat, quoted by Sylvia G. Haim in her "Islam and the Theory of Arab Nationalism" in *WI*, n.s. IV (1956), 124–49, and Nicola Ziyada (Ziadeh), *ibid.* p. 140, and her anthology *Arab Nationalism* (Berkeley and Los Angeles, 1962), p. 175, "Abd al-Rahman al-Bazzaz" (also *WI*, n.s. vol. IV, 1954) and other Arab nationalists on the problem of Arabism and Islam.

5 Cf. my *PTMI* chapter "The Theory of the Power-State: Ibn Khaldūn's Study of Civilization", pp. 84–109. The *Muqaddima* is mostly quoted from the complete English translation by Franz

Rosenthal, *Ibn Khaldûn. The Muqaddimah* (London, 1958), vols. I–III. Cf. I, 92.

6 Cf. *PTMI*, pp. 94 f. My translation somewhat differs from Franz Rosenthal's, II, 138 f.

7 Quoted from *PTMI*, pp. 96 f.; cf. Franz Rosenthal, *op. cit.* I, 17 f.

8 Cf. *PTMI*, p. 98, and Franz Rosenthal, *op. cit.*, I, 449.

9 Cf. *PTMI*, pp. 365 f., n. 32.

10 Cf. *PTMI*, p. 100, and Franz Rosenthal, *op. cit.*, I, 386.

11 Cf. Franz Rosenthal, *op. cit.* I, pp. 386 ff., and my *Ibn Khaldûns Gedanken über den Staat* (München/Berlin, 1932), pp. 50–63 (*KGS*).

12 Cf. *PTMI*, pp. 230 ff., and Franz Rosenthal, *op. cit.*, I, 258 ff.; and for a full treatment my *KGS*, 68 ff. and *PTMI*, pp. 101 ff.

13 Cf. *PTMI*, p. 102, and Franz Rosenthal, *op. cit.*, I, 260.

14 Cf. Franz Rosenthal, *op. cit.*, III, 308 ff.

15 Cf. Franz Rosenthal, *op. cit.*, I, 458 ff.

16 Cf. *PTMI*, pp. 39 ff. and *passim.*

17 Cf. Franz Rosenthal, *op. cit.*, I, 459 f.

CHAPTER 3

1 What follows is based on Şerif Mardin, *op. cit.*; on I. Süngü; and B. Lewis, *op. cit.* pp. 126–70.

2 Sura iii, v. 153: "take counsel with them...."

3 E.g. by Şerif Mardin, B. Lewis, etc.

4 Cf. Şerif Mardin, *op. cit.* p. 282.

5 Quoted from I. Süngü.

6 Quoted in Şerif Mardin, *op. cit.* p. 18.

7 Cf. I. Süngü who quotes *Hürriyet*, nos. 15, 23 and 30.

8 Cf. *op. cit.* p. 20.

9 Cf. B. Lewis, *op. cit.* p. 121. He calls it "rather a digest than a code of *Şeriat* law of the Hanafi school" and acclaims it as "one of the great achievements of Turkish jurisprudence".

10 *Ibid.* pp. 327–31. Cf. also Şerif Mardin, *op. cit.* pp. 283–384 on Nāmik Kemāl's ideas, both Islamic and Western; on Ziya Paşa, Ali Suavi and Hayreddin Paşa.

11 *Op. cit.* p. 338.

12 Cf. G. Jäschke, *op. cit.* pp. 5 ff.

13 What follows is based on T. Tunaya, cf. p. 376, ch. I, n. I, above.

14 The sources of this summary are given in T. Tunaya, *op. cit.* Cf. also B. Lewis, *op. cit.* pp. 221, 229 ff.

15 Cf. on Turkism, B. Lewis, *op. cit.* pp. 337 ff., and U. Heyd, *op. cit.*; also Z. Gökalp, *op. cit.*

16 Cf. B. Lewis, *op. cit.* esp. pp. 225–33 (nationalist movement).

17 Cf. U. Heyd, *op. cit.* for an analysis.

18 What follows is based on N. Berkes's English translation of Gökalp's essays in selection (cf. p. 376, ch. I, n. I), chapter "Religion, Education and Family", pp. 184 ff.

19 *Ibid.* p. 185.
20 *Ibid.* pp. 192 f.
21 H. A. R. Gibb, *Modern Trends in Islam* (Chicago, 1947), p. 92, pointed this out. Cf. also U. Heyd, *op. cit.* pp. 68 ff.
22 Cf. below, Part II, pp. 292, 299 f., 303.
23 Quoted from Z. Gökalp, *op. cit.* p. 196.
24 *Ibid.* p. 195.
25 *Ibid.* pp. 198 f.
26 *Ibid.* pp. 200 f. and, much fuller, pp. 203 ff. and 208 ff. Cf. also U. Heyd, *op. cit.* p. 89.
27 Z. Gökalp, *op. cit.* pp. 202 ff. and p. 319, n. 6, where he expresses some doubt as to the genuineness of these articles, but in the light of a passage quoted by U. Heyd, *op. cit.* p. 89, it seems to me that these statements reflect Gökalp's thought.
28 *Ibid.* pp. 217 ff. Cf. also p. 220 on the incompatibility, in Gökalp's opinion, of Christianity with a modern state which has become completely laicised and in which religion is unofficial.
29 *Ibid.* p. 222.
30 *Ibid.* pp. 223 f.
31 *Ibid.* p. 226.
32 *Ibid.* p. 231.
33 *Ibid.* p. 233.
34 *Ibid.* pp. 235 f.
35 *Op. cit.* pp. 97 f.; cf. also Fr. Taeschner, "Der Islam im Banne des Nationalismus der Zwischenweltkriegszeit" in *BASI*, who quotes Gökalp as saying: "we belong to the Turkish nation, to the Islamic religious community and to Western civilisation" (p. 490).
36 *Ibid.* p. 103. Cf. also Howard A. Reed, "The Faculty of Divinity at Ankara" in *MW* (1956), pp. 295 ff. for the text of these recommendations.
37 Quoted from B. Lewis, *op. cit.* p. 262.

CHAPTER 4

1 Cf. C. C. Adams, *Islam and Modernism in Egypt* (London, 1933), and in particular M. Colombe, *L'évolution de l'Egypte 1924–1950* (Paris, 1951), pp. 124 ff.
2 Cf. C. H. Becker, *Islamstudien II* (Leipzig, 1932), pp. 231 ff.; R. Hartmann, *Islam und Nationalismus* (Berlin, 1948.), pp. 31 ff., 41 ff. and his *Die Krisis des Islam* (Leipzig, 1928), esp. pp. 30 ff. on pan-Islamism and pan-Arabism.
3 This is based on Albert Hourani, *Arabic Thought in the Liberal Age 1798–1939* (London, 1962), pp. 69 ff.
4 *Ibid.* p. 75.
5 Cf. my *PTMI*, pp. 217 f.
6 Translated into French with an important Introduction and notes by Henri Laoust under the title *Le Califat dans la doctrine de Rašīd Riḍā*

(Beyrouth, 1938). The first figure in the following quotations refers to the Arabic text and the second to the French translation. A fuller treatment than is here possible can be found in my "Some Reflections on the Separation of Religion and Politics in Modern Islam" in *Islamic Studies* (Karachi, vol. III, no. 3, September 1964) which deals in the main with Rashīd Riḍā, 'Ali 'Abd al-Rāziq and Muḥammad al-Ghazālī.

7 Cf. C. C. Adams, *op. cit.* pp. 45 ff., 109, 130 f., 175, 190 ff.

8 Cf. my *PTMI*, pp. 51 ff. for a brief treatment of the political ideas of Ibn Taymīya.

9 Cf. the French translation of Fr. Jomier, *Le commentaire coranique du Manâr* (Paris, 1954).

10 Cf. his *Islamic Law, its Scope and Equity* (London/Geneva, 1961), pp. 31 ff.

11 In his *The Principles of State and Government in Islam* (Berkeley and Los Angeles, 1961).

12 Cf. his *Islamic Government and Constitution*[2] (Lahore, 1960), and several of his numerous other writings (cf. Select Bibliography).

13 Both writers will be considered at length, below, pp. 125–36, 137–53.

14 Cf. *op. cit.* pp. 78/132.

15 Cf. his *La mission de l'Azhar au XXe siècle* quoted in Marcel Colombe, *op. cit.* p. 130.

16 Cf. *op. cit.* pp. 62 f./105 f.

17 *Ibid.* pp. 77/129, 137 ff./231 ff.

18 *Ibid.* pp. 83/138 f.

19 *Ibid.* pp. 32/55.

20 *Ibid.* pp. 93/156.

21 *Ibid.* pp. 84 f./142 f.

22 The Qur'anic passages are quoted from: A. J. Arberry, *The Koran Interpreted* (London, 1955), I, 60 and 105.

23 *Op. cit.* pp. 99/167 f.

24 *Ibid.* pp. 78 f./132 f.

25 *Ibid.* pp. 85/146.

26 *Ibid.* pp. 81/137.

27 *Ibid.* pp. 76/128 f.

28 *Ibid.* pp. 67/112, 70/117 f.

29 *Ibid.* pp. 123 f./209. Cf. also 'Abd al-Rāziq, below, p. 86.

30 *Ibid.* pp. 77/130.

31 *Ibid.* pp. 30 ff./151 ff.

32 *Ibid.* pp. 97/163.

33 Cf. my *PTMI*, p. 43.

34 Cf. p. 77, n. 29.

35 *Op. cit.* pp. 102/174.

36 *Ibid.* pp. 90/151.

37 *Ibid.* pp. 125 f./212 f.

38 *Ibid.* pp. 123/209.

39 *Ibib.* pp. 129/217.

40 *Ibid.* pp. 122/207 f.
41 *Ibid.* pp. 122/208.
42 Cf. *op. cit.* pp. 114 ff./194 ff. against Lloyd George and Lord Cromer.
43 *Ibid.* pp. 119/202. Against Lloyd George and Lord Cromer, pp. 120f., 203ff.
44 *Ibid.*
45 For the following cf. *ibid.* pp. 134–37/225–31, and also 94/159.
46 Cf. *ibid.* pp. 45 f./78 ff., and 129/217; a knowledge of Arabic is a religious duty (*ibid.* pp. 87 f./147).
47 Cf. *ibid.* pp. 94 ff./159 ff., and 43 ff./74–9; 136 f./229 ff.
48 Quoted from my article, *op. cit.* p. 264.
49 *Op. cit.* pp. 121/205.
50 *Ibid.* pp. 110/186.
51 *Ibid.* pp. 123/208.
52 *Ibid.* pp. 124/210.
53 *Op. cit.* pp. 185 f.
54 *Ibid.* p. 191.
55 *Ibid.* p. 193.
56 *Ibid.* p. 192.
57 Cf. below, Part II, ch. 8.
58 *Op. cit.* p. 133.
59 Cairo, 1925. The quotations are taken from the second edition. The second figure refers to the French translation by L. Bercher in *REI*, VII (1933), 357 ff. and (1934), 163 ff. Cf. also C. C. Adams, *op. cit.* pp. 259 ff.
60 What follows is largely taken from my article, *op. cit.* pp. 267–73.
61 Cf., for a similar view of Rashīd Riḍā, above, p. 77.
62 Cf. his *Aḥkām al-sulṭānīya*, ed. M. Enger (Bonn, 1853), p. 3 and my *PTMI*, esp. p. 28.
63 Cf. *Muqaddima*, ed. Boulaq, p. 191 and my treatment in *PTMI*, pp. 84 f.; also 'Ali 'Abd al-Rāziq, *op. cit.* pp. 13 ff./368 ff.
64 He quotes in support T. W. Arnold, *The Caliphate*, chapters II and III.
65 Cf. al-Ījī, *K. al-mawāqif fī 'ilm al-kalām* (Constantinople, 1292/1875).
66 Cf. *op. cit.* pp. 17 f./373 ff., 22 f./376 f.
67 *Ibid.* pp. 25/380.
68 *Ibid.* pp. 36/389; *Muqaddima*, p. 180.
69 *Op. cit.* pp. 29/383.
70 *Ibid.* pp. 38/391.
71 *Ibid.* pp. 35 f./389.
72 *Ibid.* pp. 27/382.
73 *Op. cit.* pp. 99/166 f., and H. Laoust's note 41 (p. 266).
74 *Op. cit.* pp. 15/370.
75 *Ibid.* pp. 90/209.
76 *Ibid.* pp. 91 f./211 f.
77 *Ibid.* pp. 95/214.
78 *Ibid.* pp. 66 ff./186 ff., a very important section of his treatise in which he extensively quotes from Qur'an and Sunna.

79 *Ibid.* pp. 68 f./189.
80 *Ibid.*, and also for what follows especially pp. 78–87/198–206.
81 *Ibid.* pp. 52 f./175.
82 *Ibid.* pp. 54 f./177.
83 *Ibid.* pp. 55–9/178–81.
84 *Ibid.* pp. 76/196 f.
85 *Ibid.* pp. 95 ff./214 ff. The whole chapter is instructive.
86 *Ibid.* pp. 58/180.
87 *Ibid.* pp. 98–102/217–22.
88 *Ibid.* pp. 59–62/180–4.
89 Pp. 91 ff. above.
90 *Op. cit.* pp. 69/199; cf. also pp. 52/174: "*Jihād* was only undertaken to affirm power (*salṭana*) and to aggrandize the kingdom (*mulk*)."
91 *Ibid.* pp. 85 f./204.
92 *Op. cit.* pp. 86/205; cf. Abu-l-Fidā, I, 142.
93 *Ibid.* pp. 103/221 f.
94 *Ibid.* pp. 83/202.
95 *Ibid.* pp. 77 f./197 f.
96 *Ibid.* pp. 88/206.
97 *Ibid.* pp. 82 f./203.
98 *Ibid.* pp. 102 f./220 f.
99 *Ibid.* pp. 22 f./377 ff.
100 *Ibid.* pp. 30/384; cf. also Kawākibi, quoted by H. Z. Nuseibeh, *The Ideas of Arab Nationalism* (Cornell University Press, 1956), p. 131, for an identical view.
101 Cf. my *PTMI*, pp. 146, 183 f.; and my "The Place of Politics in the Philosophy of Ibn Rushd" in *BSOAS*, xv/2 (1953), 258 ff.
102 *Op. cit.* pp. 69/190.
103 *Ibid.* pp. 101/220.
104 Cf. Nuseibeh's adverse criticism, *op. cit.* p. 155, which seems hardly justified.

CHAPTER 5

1 In *Der Islam*, xx (1932), 209 ff.
2 Cf. "The Search for an Islamic Democracy", being "Social Reform: Factor X" in *The Middle East in Transition*, ed. W. Z. Laqueur (London, 1958), p. 6.
3 Cf. Nuseibeh, *op. cit.* p. 155.
4 Cf. p. 70, above.
5 Cairo, 5th ed. English translation by I. R. el-Faruqi under the title *Our Beginning in Wisdom* (Washington, 1953). My translation is more literal.
6 Cairo, 1950. English translation by I. R. el-Faruqi under the title *From Here We Start* (Washington, 1953).
7 Cf. Preface to *op. cit.* p. xii.
8 Cf. Muḥammad al-Ghazālī, *op. cit.* p. 23.
9 E.g. Sa'id Ramaḍān, *op. cit.* pp. 23–6, also for a justification of *jizya*, *ibid.* ch. v; and the chapters on Pakistan in Parts I and II of this book.

10 Cf. *EI*[2], *s.vv. dār al-islām, dār al-ḥarb, dār al-ṣulḥ.*
11 Cf. my *PTMI*, pp. 97 ff., and my *KGS*, pp. 50–60.
12 Cf. *op. cit.* pp. 55 f.
13 *Ibid.* p. 68. In the same vein he remarks that nationalism "enabled Christian and then Zionist imperialism to rob us of our most sacred rights".
14 *Ibid.* pp. 120 ff., and Khālid Muḥammad Khālid, *op. cit.* pp. 156–9, 174.
15 Quoted in M. Colombe, *op. cit.* p. 146. Makram Ebeid Paşa, Minister of Finance, is also quoted as saying to a delegation which thanked him for generous financial support to build new mosques in 1936: "I am a Christian, it is true, through my religion, but through my fatherland, I am a Muslim."
16 *Ibid.* p. 201. My summary is based on the long section pp. 172–212. The English translation omits pp. 208–12 as well as the last two pages of the tract. Cf. also 'Allāl al-Fāsī's views on the position of women, below, pp. 168, 171, and those of Maudūdī and Parwez in Pakistan, especially as discussed below, p. 150 and in Part II, section 2, below, p. 208.
17 *Al-'Adāla al-ijtimā'īya fī-l-Islām* (Cairo, n.d.).
18 Cairo, 1953, translated by Sylvia G. Haim in *WI*, n.s. v (1958), 245 ff. My quotations are taken from this translation, as I was unable to obtain a copy of the Arabic original.
19 *Ibid.* pp. 247, 251 f.
20 *Ibid.* pp. 252 f.
21 Quoted from Z. I. Ansari, "Contemporary Islam and Nationalism: A Case Study of Egypt" in *WI*, n.s. VII, 1–4 (1961), 3 ff., a valuable, judicious analysis which I largely follow. Cf. also for their programme Franz Rosenthal, "The Muslim Brethren in Egypt" in *MW*, XXXVII (1947), 4, and especially J. Heyworth-Dunne, *Religious and Political Trends in Modern Egypt* (Washington, 1950).
22 Cf. Z. I. Ansari, *op. cit.* pp. 12 f.
23 *Ibid.* p. 22.
24 *Ibid.* p. 26.
25 Cf. Sylvia G. Haim, "Islam and the Theory of Arab Nationalism" in *WI*, n.s. IV (1956), 124 ff. For the terminology cf. B. Lewis, *A Handbook of Diplomatic Arabic* (London, 1947).
26 Cf. the full analysis of his thought by F. Steppat, entitled "Nationalismus und Islam bei Muṣṭāfā Kāmil" in *WI*, n.s. IV (1956), 241–341, on which my remarks are based.
27 Cf. *op. cit.* p. 278.
28 Cf. *ibid.* p. 328.
29 Cf. *op. cit.* p. 139.
30 Cf. R. Hartmann, *Islam und Nationalismus* (Berlin, 1948), p. 31.
31 In his *Al-Islām wa-l-qawmīya al-'arabīya* (Baghdad, 1952), trans. Sylvia G. Haim in *WI*, n.s. IV (1954), 201 ff., esp. 207, 214–18. I was unable to consult the Arabic original.

32 Quoted from H. Z. Nuseibeh, *op. cit.* p. 92, cf. also p. 53. I was unable to consult the Arabic original.

33 Quoted from S. G. Haim, *WI*, n.s. IV (1956), pp. 139 f. Did he perhaps mean nationalisms rather than nationalities?

34 Quoted from S. G. Haim, *ibid.* p. 145. Does *waṭanīya* actually mean territorial nationalism derived from a fatherland (*waṭan*)?

35 *Op. cit.* p. 28. This passage is also quoted in Nuseibeh, *op. cit.* p. 167, in a rather imprecise translation. The same definition of Islam is given by Muḥammad al-Ghazālī.

36 Quoted from Z. I. Ansari, *op. cit.* p. 23.

37 Cf. *ibid.* p. 28.

38 Quoted *ibid.* pp. 9 ff. Cf. also M. Colombe, *op. cit.* p. 277, for a judicious verdict on the utopian doctrines of the *Ikhwān*; also Franz Rosenthal, *op. cit.*

CHAPTER 6

1 Berkeley and Los Angeles, 1961. The long-drawn-out process of constitution-making in Pakistan will engage our close attention in Part II of this study, below.

2 *Op. cit.* p. 13.

3 *Ibid.* pp. 16 f. and cf. pp. 49 f., above.

4 *Ibid.* p. 30, and with missionary zeal, p. 33.

5 *Ibid.* pp. 38 f. In support he quotes Sura 33, *v.* 26, translating *mulk* by "sovereignty".

6 *Ibid.* p. 14, previously quoted.

7 *Ibid.* p. 51. Cf. also above pp. 24 f. (Ibn Khaldūn), pp. 43 f. (the Islamists in Turkey), and pp. 77 f. (Rashīd Riḍā) on the division of powers in an Islamic state.

8 *Ibid.* pp. 73 f.; cf. also, pp. 107 ff., above.

9 A detailed discussion follows in Part II. Cf. also L. Binder, *Religion and Politics in Pakistan* (Berkeley and Los Angeles, 1961), pp. 70 ff.

10 My summary is based on the 2nd ed. (Lahore, 1960); cf. also my review article "The Islamic Law and Constitution" in *International Affairs*, XXXVIII, 3 (1962), 365 ff.

11 We are here only concerned with his theory of the Islamic state and law and will discuss his part in the constitutional debate in Pakistan later in Part II.

12 This view is based on personal observation.

13 *Op. cit.* p. 107, spoken in 1948 at Lahore in the Law College. Cf. also the preamble to the 1956 Constitution, below, pp. 209 f.

14 *Op. cit.* p. 147, taken from his lecture on "Political Theory of Islam", 1939.

15 *Ibid.* p. 148.

16 Cf. *ibid.* pp. 53 and 57.

17 *Ibid.* pp. 77 ff., esp. 81 and 89 ff., a chapter based on his contribution to the Islamic Colloquium at Lahore in 1958. Cf. M. D. Rahbar, "Shāh Walī Ullāh and Ijtihād. A translation of selected passages..."

in *MW* (1955), 346 ff., for an authoritative exposition of what *ijtihād* actually is in classical Islamic jurisprudence.

18 Cf. *The Message of Jama'at-e-Islami* (Lahore, 1950), pp. 16 ff. This and other pamphlets (cf. Select Bibliography) are important, complementary witnesses to his determined advocacy of an Islamic revolution culminating in an Islamic state.

19 Cf. *The Islamic Law and Constitution*, p. 157.

20 Cf. *The Process of Islamic Revolution*[2] (Lahore, 1955), pp. 14 ff. (first delivered in 1947 at the Aligarh Muslim University).

21 *Ibid.* pp. 16 f.

22 *Ibid.* pp. 25 f.

23 Cf. *The Islamic Law and Constitution*, pp. 218 ff.

24 *Ibid.* p. 233.

25 Cf. pp. 145 f., above, with n. 19.

26 *The Islamic Law and Constitution*, p. 235; cf. p. 142, above.

27 *Ibid.* pp. 236 f.

28 *Ibid.* pp. 238 f.

29 *Ibid.* p. 241.

30 *Ibid.* pp. 242 f.

31 *Ibid.* p. 245.

32 *Ibid.* p. 265.

33 *Ibid.* p. 282. In this he agrees with Rashīd Riḍā (p. 72, above) and Muḥammad al-Ghazālī (pp. 112 f.).

34 *Ibid.* p. 346.

35 *Ibid.* p. 291. The two last quotations come from a chapter written in 1952 at the height of the debate on an Islamic constitution before the completion of the Report of the Basic Principles Committee (cf. below, pp. 214–17).

36 *Ibid.* p. 330. This chapter was published in 1955.

37 *Ibid.* pp. 316 f.

38 *Ibid.* p. 338. This is taken from proposals submitted to the First Constituent Assembly of Pakistan in 1952, and we shall come back to them below, pp. 221 ff.

CHAPTER 7

1 Cairo, 1952. His programmatic discourse delivered at the opening session of the Sixth Congress of the *Istiqlal* party in January 1962, published in book form under the title *Minhāj al-istiqlālīya*, can unfortunately not be discussed here.

2 Cf. Idrīs al-Kattānī, *Al-maghrib al-muslim ḍidd-al-lādīnīya* (*The Muslim Maghrib is anti-laic*) (Rabat, 1958).

3 Cf. *Al-naqd al-ḏātī*, p. 52.

4 On this point see I. Kattānī, *op. cit.* below, p. 327 with n. 6.

5 Cf. *Al-naqd al-ḏātī*, pp. 238 f.

6 *Ibid.* pp. 260 ff., esp. 263.

7 *Ibid.* pp. 280 f. and 283.

8 *Ibid.* p. 285. Cf. also, below, pp. 341 ff.
9 *Ibid.* pp. 332 ff. and below, pp. 368 ff.
10 *Ibid.* p. 430; cf. *Muqaddima*, ed. Quatrèmere, III, 434, English translation by Franz Rosenthal, III, 481.

CHAPTER 8

1 For the background cf. A. H. Albiruni, *Makers of Pakistan and Muslim India* (Lahore, 1950); I. H. Qureshi, *The Muslim Community of the Indo-Pakistan subcontinent* (S'Gravenhage, 1962); *The Evolution of India and Pakistan 1858–1947*, select documents, ed. C. H. Philips, N. L. Singh and B. H. Pandey (London, 1962), quoted as *EIP*.
2 Cf. especially Ian Stephens, *Pakistan*[2] (London, 1964), for a succinct and judicious account. Cf. also Select Bibliography.
3 According to Khalid bin Sayeed, "The Jama'at-i-Islami Movement" in *Pacific Affairs*, XXX, no. 1 (1957).
4 The following account is based on his *Ḥujjat Allāh al-bāligha* (Karachi, n.d.), the studies by M. D. Rahbar, cited previously, K. A. Nizami, "Shah Wali-Ullah Dehlavi and Indian Politics in the 18th Century" in *IC*, XXV, 1 (1951), 133–45, and A. Bausani, "Note su Shāh Walīullāh di Delhi" in *Annali dell'Istituto Universitario di Napoli*, n.s. X (1961), 93–147, the first important Western treatment of the doctrines and works of Shāh Walī Ullāh; and also on information received in Pakistan.
5 A. Bausani, *op. cit.* pp. 110 f.
6 M. D. Rahbar (*MW*, 1955) states that Shāh Walī Ullāh sought to temper authority with reason. The quotation comes from Aziz Ahmad, "Political and Religious Ideas of Shāh Walī Ullāh" in *MW* (1962), a study partly based on A. H. Albiruni.
7 *Op. cit.* p. 25.
8 Cf. *op. cit.* where parts are translated.
9 Information. Cf. also Khalid Bin Sayeed, *Pakistan: The Formative Phase* (Karachi, 1960), and G. W. Choudhury, *Constitutional Development in Pakistan* (London, 1959).
10 The following account is partly based on Albiruni, *op. cit.*, the work of a distinguished Pakistani historian who mainly writes in Urdu. Albiruni is a pseudonym.
11 *Op. cit.* pp. 34 f.
12 Quoted from *EIP*, p. 177.
13 *Ibid.* p. 180.
14 *Ibid.* pp. 183 f.
15 *Ibid.* p. 189.
16 Cf. A. H. Albiruni, *op. cit.* p. 55.
17 Cf. *ibid.* pp. 123–6.
18 *Ibid.* p. 128.
19 *Ibid.* p. 135. A crore is ten millions.
20 *Ibid.* p. 136.

21 Cf. his *India Wins Freedom* (Calcutta, 1959).
22 *Op. cit.* p. 147.
23 Cf. also Ian Stephens, *op. cit.* pp. 69 ff., I. H. Qureshi, *op. cit.* pp. 252 ff., 273 ff., and Khalid Bin Sayeed, *op. cit.* pp. 11–109.
24 Cf. *EIP*, pp. 239 f.
25 Quoted from Khalid Bin Sayeed, *op. cit.* pp. 112 f.
26 This is the title of his book, published London 1934. The passage against nationalism is on p. 178. Cf. also I. H. Qureshi, *op. cit.* pp. 262 ff.
27 *EIP*, p. 354.
28 *Ibid.* p. 353.
29 Quoted from Khalid Bin Sayeed, *op. cit.* p. 42.
30 *EIP*, p. 352.
31 *Report of the Court of Inquiry...to enquire into the Punjab Disturbances of 1953* (Lahore, 1954).
32 In the *Report of the Constitution Commission Pakistan 1961* (Karachi, 1962), and in *The Constitution of the Republic of Pakistan* (Karachi, 1962).
33 Cf. *op. cit.* pp. 164 ff. The views of G. A. Parwez were ascertained through interview and literature quoted below, pp. 252–6.
34 Cf. above, pp. 144 f.
35 *Op. cit.* pp. 169 f.
36 *Ibid.* pp. 159 f.
37 Quoted from *Debates of the Constituent Assembly of Pakistan*, vol. v, nr. 1, pp. 1 f.
38 *Ibid.*, vol. v, nr. 3, p. 44.
39 *Ibid.*, vol. I, nr. 2, pp. 19 f.
40 P. 69.
41 For convenience sake, quotations from the *Debates* are now quoted from Grace J. Calder, "Constitutional Debates in Pakistan" in *MW*, XLVI, no. 1, 1–3 (1956); this quotation comes from no. 1, p. 42.
42 Cf. L. Binder, *op. cit.* p. 156; he deals fully with this committee, its composition and deliberations and the attitude of the government and of the Constituent Assembly to their recommendations.
43 I.e. *amr bi-l-ma'rūf* and *nahy 'an al-munkar* (commanding what is seemly and forbidding what is displeasing (to Allah)).
44 Quoted from G. J. Calder, *op. cit.* no. 2, p. 146.
45 Cf. M. R. Feroze, "The Reform in Family Laws in the Muslim World" in *Islamic Studies*, Karachi, I, no. i (1962), 107 ff. The text of the Ordinance is to be found on p. 115.
46 Quoted from G. J. Calder, *op. cit.* no. 1, p. 58.
47 Cf. Sayyid Abul A'lā Maudūdī, *The Islamic Law and Constitution*², pp. 363 ff.
48 Cf. *The Constitution of the Islamic Republic of Pakistan* (Karachi, 1956), p. 8 and *The Constitution of the Republic of Pakistan* (Karachi, 1962), p. 12.
49 *Op. cit.* III, 28(*e*), (*f*), p. 9.
50 *Op. cit.* II, 2, articles 19 and 20, p. 15.
51 *Op. cit.* XII, 1, 197(1), p. 75; in the 1962 Constitution, p. 97 (X, 2, 207).
52 XII, 1, 198, pp. 75 f.

53 Maudūdī, *op. cit.* pp. 372 f., and pp. 215 f., above.
54 *The Constitution of the Islamic Republic of Pakistan 1956*, III, 25–29, pp. 8 f.
55 *Ibid.* pp. 98 ff.
56 Maudūdī, *op. cit.* p. 373.
57 Cf. his *Parliamentary Government in Pakistan* (Lahore, 1958), pp. 24, 29.
58 *Ibid.* p. 40.
59 Cf. his *Pakistan, An Islamic Democracy* (Karachi, n.d.), p. 21.
60 Cf. his "The Future Constitution of Pakistan" in *Islamic Review* (Woking, December 1950), p. 33.
61 The quotations are from an article by A. K. Brohi in *Dawn* (24 August 1952) and replies (7 and 21 September), and from K. B. Callard, *Pakistan* (London, 1957), pp. 213 ff. (His whole chapter "Islam and Politics" is very informative.)
62 Cf. pp. 209, 214 ff., above.
63 A good summary of the actual events can be read in K. B. Callard, *op. cit.* pp. 204 ff., cf. also pp. 203 f., above.
64 Cf. *The Civil and Military Gazette*, Lahore, 23 February.
65 Rabwah, 1959, pp. 9 ff.
66 Cf. Maulana Muhammad Ali, *Mirza Ghulam Ahmad of Qadian*[3] (Lahore, 1963), where the founder's denials are quoted on pp. 22 ff.
67 Cf. *Sir Muhammad Iqbal's Statement re The Qadianis* (Lahore, n.d.), p. 10.
68 Cf. *ibid.* p. 5.
69 *Op. cit.* p. 205.
70 *Ibid.* pp. 200–31.
71 *Ibid.* p. 200.
72 *Ibid.* pp. 231 f.
73 Cf. Ian Stephens, *op. cit.*, ch. 19, "Military Revolution", for a lively, authoritative assessment.
74 Cf. Khalid bin Sayeed, "Pakistan's Basic Democracy" in *MEJ*, XV (1961), 250, quoted from *Dawn* (20 December 1959).
75 *Op. cit.* p. 255.
76 Cf. the discussion of the Family Laws Ordinance, below, pp. 275 ff., 333 ff.
77 Cf. below, pp. 339 f.
78 Cf. below, p. 355.
79 Cf. his *I'lam al-muwaqqi'īn* (Delhi, 1313/14), III, 1.
80 Cf. e.g. *Nicomachean Ethics*, V, 7, 1135a.
81 Cf. below, pp. 268, 274, 351 ff.
82 Cf. his *Fatawa-i-Jahandari*, translated under the title *The Political Theory of the Delhi Sultanate* by Afsar Umar Salim Khan, with an Introduction, Notes and a critical study *Life and Thought of Ziauddin Barani* by Mohammad Habib (Delhi, n.d.).
83 Cf. the chapter on Education, below, pp. 344–61.
84 Cf. *Report of the Constitution Commission, Pakistan, 1961* (Karachi, 1962), p. 1.

85 *Ibid.* p. 114.
86 *Ibid.* p. 115.
87 *Answers to Constitution Commission Questionnaire* unanimously formulated in a meeting of nineteen 'Ulamā (1960), pp. 26–31.
88 *Answers...*, pp. 25 ff.; and cf. pp. 211 f., above, for M. A. Jinnah's contrary assertions.
89 *Report...*, p. 116.
90 P. 27.
91 P. 4.
92 *Basic Provisions...*, Article 7, p. 2; *Answers...*, p. 19, 2(i) and 3. Cf. also, Maudūdī, p. 152, above.
93 *Report...*, p. 120.
94 *Ibid.* p. 121.
95 *Ibid.* p. 123.
96 *Ibid.* p. 124. The quotation from Iqbal, *op. cit.*, comes from p. 163, not as stated in the *Report*, pp. 171–2.
97 *Ibid.* pp. 125 f.
98 Cf. the speeches of the law minister and members of the opposition reported in *Dawn*, 20 and 21 December 1963. I am indebted to Professor G. W. Choudhury for making this information available to me.
99 Cf. *The Constitution of the Republic of Pakistan* (Karachi, 1962), p. 4.
100 *Ibid.* p. 10.
101 *Ibid.* p. 12.
102 *Ibid.* p. 18; *1956 Constitution*, p. 9.
103 Cf. pp. 214, 221, above.
104 Articles 202–206, pp. 96 f.
105 Article 207, p. 97.
106 First Schedule, pp. 122 ff.
107 Cf. the report in *Dawn*, 31 July 1962, of his press conference. I am indebted to Professor G. W. Choudhury for the text. The amendments mentioned earlier were moved by the then law minister, Mr Khurshed (cf. p. 265 with n. 98, above).
108 Cf. Maudūdī, pp. 139 f., 145, 148 f., above.
109 Cf. its leading articles on 14 and 16 August 1962.
110 Cf. issue of 7 August 1962.
111 *Ibid.* 8 July 1962.
112 *Ibid.* 7 July 1962.
113 *Ibid.* 8 July 1962.
114 Cf. his "Pakistan Family Laws" in *Dawn*, 14 August 1962, and also Anis Mirza, "Family Laws Ordinance is not un-Islamic" in *Dawn*, 15 July 1962.
115 Cf. report in *Dawn*, 28 July 1962.
116 Cf. *ibid.* 29 July 1962.
117 Information received.
118 Information received.

CHAPTER 9

1 Malaya means the original "Federation of Malaya" without the other territories (North Borneo, i.e. Sabah and Sarawak) which today form together with it Malaysia. Cf. for what follows also my article "The Role of Islam in the Modern National State" in *The Yearbook oj World Affairs* (London, 1962), of which pp. 113–21 are devoted to Malaya.
2 Information.
3 Cf. Supplement to Federation of Malaya, *Government Gazette*, 11 December 1957, pp. 509 f.
4 *Op. cit.* pp. 522 f.; cf. also Third Schedule, Parts I and III, p. 604.
5 1962 Constitution, Article 13, pp. 17 f.
6 Fourth Schedule, p. 607.
7 Alor Star, 1959.
8 Cf. Al-Māwardī, *Aḥkām al-sulṭānīya*, ed. M. Enger (Bonn, 1853), pp. 8 ff., 12 ff., 19 ff., on election and designation of the caliph, and pp. 5 ff. on his qualifications. See also my *PTMI*, pp. 29–35.
9 *Enactment, Malacca*, Articles 1, 4, 10, 11, 34 and 35.
10 *Ibid.* Article 36.
11 *Ibid.* Article 37.
12 *Ibid.* Article 40(4).
13 *Ibid.* Articles 41 and 42.
14 *Ibid.* Article 62.
15 *Ibid.* Article 80.
16 *Ibid.* Article 88. *Zakāt* (alms) is the charity-tax obligatory on every Muslim; *fiṭra* (*fiṭr*) is a special tax payable at the end of the month of fasting (Ramaḍān) in rice or paddy or in money representing the value of the produce; and *Bayt al-māl* is normally the treasury, but in this case throughout Malaya a special Fund quite separate from the State Treasury and only to be applied to the specific purposes of the Department of Religious Affairs.
17 *Ibid.* Article 104.
18 *Ibid.* Articles 113–122, 131.
19 *Enactment, Negri Sembilan* (1960), Article 11(1).
20 *Ibid.* Article 35(1).
21 *Ibid.* Articles 142–144.
22 *Ibid.* Articles 149–151.
23 *Ibid.* Articles 159 and 160.
24 *Ibid.* Articles 160–169.
25 Cf. Supplement to the Federation of Malaya, *Government Gazette*, 21 October 1952, no. 25, vol. V, p. 473.
26 *Ibid.* Article 4(4).
27 Cf. *Enactment, Negri Sembilan* (1960), Articles 132 and 134.
28 Cf. Supplement..., *Government Gazette*, 6 March 1951, no. 4. vol. 10.
29 Cf. *Enactment, Trengganu* (1955), Articles 18, 19, 21.

30 *Ibid.* Articles 25, 26.
31 Cf. *ibid.* Article 57(1, *c*, 2), p. 23.

CHAPTER 10

1 Quoted from the French translation in J. E. Godchot, *Les Constitutions du Proche et du Moyen-Orient* (Paris, 1957), pp. 222 f.
2 *Ibid.* pp. 225 ff.
3 Cf. Godchot, *op. cit.* p. 408, and on the constitutional question in Turkey in general, G. Jäschke, "Dis Entwicklung des osmanischen Verfassungsstaates" in *WI*, v, 5 ff., esp. 38–50.
4 Cf. G. Jäschke, *Der Islam in der neuen Türkei* (*WI*, n.s. I, 1–2) (Leiden, 1951), p. 39.
5 *Ibid.* p. 34.
6 Cf. *MEJ*, XVI (1962), "The New Turkish Constitution", 215 ff., the official English translation.
7 Cf. the syllabus of this Faculty in *Ankara University. The Faculty of Divinity* (Ankara, 1959), which also contains an instructive Introduction.

CHAPTER 11

1 Cf. *Constitution of the Tunisian Republic*, Arabic and English (Sécrétariat d'État à l'Information); quotations follow, where possible, the English translation.
2 Or, Khayr-al-dīn, mentioned above whose treatise on government advocating constitutional reforms, based on *Sharī'a*, *qanūn* and *mashwara*, is analysed in A. Ḥourani, *op. cit.*, pp. 89–94.
3 Cf. Select Bibliography for his writings which are relevant to our problem.
4 *Op. cit.* Article 39.
5 Cf. the profound essay by Mohamed Talbi (University of Tunis), "L'Islam et le Monde Moderne" in *Politique Étrangère* (Paris, 1960), pp. 101 ff.
6 In his *op. cit.* p. 384, n. 2, above; cf. pp. 11, 13–17, 20–24 (his own programme). Although he pronounces against opening the *Istiqlal* party to Jews since it should be an Islamic party, he considers the people of Morocco—Muslim Arabs and Jews—one nation who share one fatherland, but profess different religions. Cf. also pp. 41–5 (Islam and Western Imperialism), 46–9 (Turkey), 60–73 (on the difference between Islam and Christianity), with the usual equation of Christianity with the West, thus the adoption of the Swiss Civil Code by Turkey is aping Christianity).
7 Cf. *Proclamation Royale* (*Dahīr*), dated 8 May 1958. I am indebted to M. Bahnini, the secretary-general of the royal government at the time of my visit, for a typescript copy of the French translation.
8 Quotations are from the official English translation (*The Constitution of the Kingdom of Morocco*) for which as well as for the Arabic text

(*Al-naṣṣ al-kāmil li-mashrūʿi-l-dustūr*) I am indebted to the Royal Moroccan Embassy in London. There are some discrepancies between the Arabic and English versions which are noted where necessary.

9 *Islāmīya* does obviously not mean "Islamic" in the strict sense of the term as I use it to distinguish it from a Muslim state.

10 Literally: "The one-party system is forbidden in Morocco."

11 Literally: "...the freedom to conduct their religious affairs."

12 The official translation has "accede to".

13 Literally: "It is incumbent on all citizens to take part in the defence of the fatherland."

14 The English translation has "guarantee".

15 Literally: "He is the Defender of the Faith."

CHAPTER 12

1 Cf. J. N. D. Anderson, *Islamic Law in the Modern World* (London, 1959), with an important Select Bibliography which includes a large number of his own studies. Of special importance is J. Schacht's "Islamic Law in Contemporary Islam" in *The American Journal of Comparative Law*, 8, 2 (spring 1959), 133–47.

2 A Ministry of Law publication in *The Gazette of Pakistan*, Karachi, 2 March 1961 (Ordinance no. VIII of 1961). Cf. also above, pp. 219 f., 275.

3 Quoted from M. R. Feroze, "The Reform in Family Laws in the Muslim World" in *Islamic Studies*, I, 1 (1962), 111, who cites *The Gazette of Pakistan* of 20 June 1956, p. 1206.

4 Cf. *ibid.* p. 112 (from *The Gazette of Pakistan* of 30 August 1955).

5 *Ibid.* pp. 113 f.; for further quotations see there.

6 Cf. above, pp. 275 f.

7 Cf. above, p. 277.

8 In his article "Family Laws Ordinance not un-Islamic" in *Dawn*, 15 July 1962.

9 Cf. M. T. Es-snoussi, *Code du Statut Personnel Annoté*², with a Preface by M. Ahmed Mestiri (Tunis, 1958).

10 Cf. *Mudawwanat al-aḥwāl al-shakhṣīya*³ (Rabat, 1958). My informant is a high legal authority.

11 Cf. G. Jäschke, *Der Islam in der neuen Türkei*, pp. 35 ff.

12 *Ibid.* p. 39.

CHAPTER 13

1 Cf. above, pp. 219 f., 237 f., 277.

2 Cf. Anis Mirza, "Women's Role in National Progress" in *Dawn*, 14 August 1962.

3 Cf. H. Z. Ülken, "Évolution de la Condition Féminine en Turquie" in *Sosyoloji Dergisi* sayi 15-1960 'dan (Istanbul, 1960), 140 ff., esp. 151 f.

CHAPTER 14

1 Cf. *Report of the Commission on National Education* (Ministry of Education, Karachi, 1960), Preface.
2 *Ibid.* pp. 10 f.
3 Cf. also the demand of the *'ulamā*, above, pp. 221 f.
4 Cf. *Report*, p. 22.
5 Cf. his *The Masters* (Lahore, 1957), p. 132, and *Higher Education Examined* (1956). Both are critical studies written when the author (to whom we are greatly indebted for befriending us during our long stay at Lahore) was vice-chancellor of the University of the Punjab, Lahore.
6 Karachi, 1960, p. 2.
7 This institute is directed by Professor M. M. Sharif to whom I am greatly indebted for his friendly assistance in my inquiries in Pakistan.
8 Cf. above, pp. 261, 263, 267 f.
9 Volume 1, General Introduction, Government of Pakistan, Ministry of Education, July–October 1960, pp. 38 f.
10 *Ibid.* pp. 75 f.
11 Cf. above, pp. 196 ff.
12 Cf. *Report*, pp. 76 f. The syllabus for the Islamic Studies Group is to be found on pp. 144 f.
13 *Ibid.* p. 81.
14 Information received.
15 Information received through my wife who visited the college.
16 Cf. Begum M. B. Siddiqi, "A College Grows up in a Wilderness" in *Dawn*, 14 August 1962.
17 Taken from a Report: *Jamia Millia Islamia. Review of Aims, History and Scope of Work, 1954–55*, p. 3.
18 Quoted from a speech made during the celebrations marking the fortieth anniversary of its foundation, p. 5. I am indebted to Professor M. Mujeeb for giving his permission to quote from the Report and the speech.

CHAPTER 15

1 Cf. above, ch. 11, pp. 316 ff.
2 Cf. *Nouvelle Conception de l'Enseignement en Tunisie* (Sécrétariat d'État à l'Éducation Nationale, Tunis 1958–59), pp. 21 ff., for this and the following quotations, and also Annexe II: *Loi No. 58-118 du 4 Novembre 1958 (21 rabia 2 1378) relative à l'enseignement*, pp. 77 ff. This official publication gives a comprehensive survey of the entire educational system.
3 Cf. *Programmes Officiels de l'Enseignement Primaire.* Fascicule VI. *Éducation morale et sociale* (Tunis, 1958) (in Arabic).
4 Cf. *Nouvelle Conception...*, p. 23.
5 Cf. *Programmes Officiels de l'Enseignement Moyen.* Fascicule VI. *Instruction civique et religieuse* (1959), pp. 3 ff. (in Arabic).

6 Cf. *Programmes Officiels de l'Enseignment Secondaire.* Fascicule VI. *Instruction civique et religieuse* (1959), pp. 6 ff. (in Arabic).

7 *Ibid.* p. 11.

8 Tunis, 1960. He is also the author of *Al-fikr al-islāmī bayna-l-ams wa-l-yawm* (*Islamic Thought between Yesterday and Today*).

9 Cf. *Decret* no. 61-357 of 27 Octobre 1961 (17 Joumada I, 1381).

10 Cf. *Fās. Al-mu'tamar al-awwal lil-lijāni-l-waṭanīyat al-arabīyat lil-UNESCO* (Fes, 1958), p. 22.

11 Cf. Abdel Hadi Tazi, *L'Université Qarawiyin* (French and Arabic), p. 42: *sharī'a, ādāb, 'ulūm* (which latter is translated by "culture scientifique").

SELECT BIBLIOGRAPHY

Only works relevant to this study are included. With the exception of Pakistan, texts and studies which appeared later than 1962 could not be considered. A *dagger* (†) in front of a title draws the reader's attention to an important bibliography contained in the work, and a *star* (*) to a work of later date than 1962 which should be consulted.

I. WORKS IN ARABIC

'Abd al-Rāziq, 'Alī. *Al-Islām wa-uṣūl al-ḥukm.* Cairo, 1925.

Afghānī, Jamāl al-Dīn al- and 'Abduh, Muḥammad. *Al-'urwa al-wuthqā.* Cairo, 1925.

Barnāmaj al-tarbiya al-akhlāqīya wa-l-ijtimā'īya (Primary Education). Tunis, 1958.

Barnāmaj al-tarbiya al-dīnīya wa-l-madanīya (Intermediate and Secondary Education). Tunis, 1959.

Barnāmaj al-'ulūm al-islāmīya wa-l-lugha al-'arabīya. Rabat, n.d.

Burqība, al-Ḥabīb (Bourguiba, Habib). *Al-islām laysa bi'arqalat fīwajhi-l-rūqī.* Published by the State Secretariat for Cultural Affairs and Information, Tunis, 1962. A sermon President Bourguiba preached on the occasion of the birthday of the prophet in the Mosque of 'Uqba b. Nāfi' at Qayruwān 1382/1962.

Dustūr al-Jumhūrīya al-Tūnisīya. Tunis, n.d.

Dustūr al-Mamlaka al-Maghribīya (*Al-naṣṣ al-kāmil li-mashru' al-Dustūr*). Rabat n.d.

Fās. Al-mu'tamar al-awwal lil-lijāni-l-waṭanīyat al-'arabiyāt lil-UNESCO. Fes, 1958.

Fāsī, 'Allāl al-. *Al-naqd al-d̲ātī.* Cairo, 1952.

Fāsī, 'Allāl al-. "Uṣūl al-ḥukm fī-l-islām" in *Al-Bayyina,* I, I. Rabat, 1962.

Fāsī, 'Allāl-al-. *Minhāj al-istiqlālīya.* Rabat, 1962.

Ghazālī, Muḥammad al-. *Min hunā na'lam*[5]. Cairo, 195–?.

Ibn Khaldūn. *Muqaddima.* Beirut, 1900; and E. Quatremère (ed.), Paris, 1858.

Ibn Mīlād, Maḥjūb (Ben Milad). *Al-fikr al-islāmī bayn al-ams wa-l-yawm*[2]. Tunis, 1961.

Ibn Mīlād, Maḥjūb (Ben Milad). *Taḥrīk al-sawākin.* I, Tunis, 1960; II, 1962.

Ibn Taymīya. *Kitāb al-siyāsa al-shar'īya fī iṣlāḥ al-rā'ī wa-l-ra'īya.* Cairo, 1951.

Kattānī, Idrīs al-. *Al-Maghrib al-muslim ḍidd al-lādīnīya.* Rabat, 1958.

Khālid, Khālid Muḥammad. *Min hunā nabda'.* Cairo, 1950.

Majallat al-aḥwāl al-shakhṣīya[3], with Commentary by Muḥammad al-Ṭāhir al-Sanūsī. Tunis, 1377/1958.

Manār, Al-, vols. I–VII, IX, XII, XVIII, XX, XXI, XXIV, XXXIII. Cairo.

Māwardī, Al-. *Al-aḥkām al-sulṭānīya*, ed. M. Enger. Bonn, 1853.

Mudawwanat al-aḥwāl al-shakhṣīya. Rabat, 1958.

Quṭb, Sayyid. *Al-'adāla al-ijtimā'īya fī al-Islām.* Cairo, n.d.

Riḍā, Muḥammad Rashīd. *Al-khilāfa aw al-imāma al-'uẓmā.* Cairo, 1341/1923.

Shaltūt, Maḥmūd. *Al-Islām, 'Aqīda wa-sharī'a.* Cairo, n.d.

Tāzī, 'Abd al-Hādī al-. *Jāmi' al-Qarawīyīn 859–1960.* Rabat, 1960.

Walī Ullāh, Shāh. *Ḥujjat Allāh al-bāligha.* Karachi, n.d.

2. WORKS IN EUROPEAN LANGUAGES

'Abd al-Rāziq, 'Alī. French translation of *Al-Islām wa-uṣūl al-ḥukm* by L. Bercher in *REI*, VII, 1933, 357 ff. and 1934, 163 ff.

Adams, C. C. *Islam and Modernism in Egypt.* London, 1933.

Ahmad, Aziz. "The Political and Religious Ideas of Shah Wali Ullah" in *MW*, 1962.

Ahmad, Khurshid. *An Analysis of the Munir Report.* Karachi, 1956.

Ahmad, Mirza Bashir-ud-Din Mahmud. *Ahmadiyyat or True Islam.* Rabwah, 1959.

Ahmad, Mirza Ghulam. *The Philosophy of The Teachings of Islam.* Rabwah, 1959.

*Ahmed, Manzooruddin. "Islamic Aspects of the New Constitution of Pakistan" in *Islamic Studies.* Karachi, 1963.

†Anderson, J. N. D. *Islamic Law in the Modern World.* London, 1959.

Anderson, J. N. D. "Recent Developments in *Sharī'a* Law" in *MW*, 1950–2.

Ansari, Z. I. "Contemporary Islam and Nationalism" in *WI*, n.s. VII, 1961.

Arberry, A. J. *The Koran Interpreted.* London, 1955.

Asad, Muhammad. *The Principles of State and Government in Islam.* Berkeley and Los Angeles, 1961.

Ayub Khan, Mohammad. *Pakistan Perspective.* Reproduced from *Foreign Affairs.* July 1960.

Ayub Khan, Mohammad. Press Conference in Mecca. Reported in *Civil and Military Gazette.* Lahore, 5 November 1960.

Ayub Khan, Mohammad. Address at Cairo University. Reported in *Dawn.* Karachi, 10 November 1960.

Ayub Khan, Mohammad. *Speeches and Statements by the President of Pakistan*, I–III. Karachi, n.d.
Azad, Abul Kalam. *India Wins Freedom*. Calcutta, 1959.
Baljon, J. M. S. *Modern Muslim Koran Interpretation*. Leiden, 1961.
Barani, Ziauddin. *The Political Theory of the Delhi Sultanate*, trans. Afsar Umar Salim Khan, with Introduction by Mohammad Habib. Delhi, n.d.
Bausani, A. "Note su Shāh Walīullāh di Delhi" in *Annali dell'Istituto Universitario di Napoli*, n.s. x, 1961, 93–147.
Bazzaz, 'Abd Ar-Rahman, Al-. "Islam and Arab Nationalism", trans. Sylvia G. Haim in *WI*, n.s. III, 1954, 201 ff.
Becker, C. H. *Islamstudien*, II. Leipzig, 1932.
Bel, A. *La religion musulmane en Berberie*. Paris, 1938.
Berque, J. *Les Arabes d'hier à demain*. Paris, 1960. (English translation: *The Arabs: Their History and Future*. London, 1964.)
Bowen, H. *See* Gibb, H. A. R.
Binder, L. *Religion and Politics in Pakistan*. Berkeley and Los Angeles, 1961.
Braune, W. "Die Entwicklung des Nationalismus bei den Arabern" in *BASI*. Leipzig, 1944.
Braune, W. *Der Islamische Orient zwischen Vergangenheit und Zukunft*. Bern und München, 1960.
Brohi, A. K. *Fundamental Law of Pakistan*. Lahore, 1958.
Calder, G. L. "Constitutional Debates in Pakistan" in *MW*, 1956.
Callard, K. *Pakistan. A Political Study*. London, 1957.
Caskel, W. "Western Impact and Islamic Civilization" in *Unity and Variety in Muslim Civilization*, ed. G. E. von Grunebaum. Chicago, 1955.
†Choudhury, G. W. *Constitutional Development in Pakistan*. London, 1959.
Choudhury, G. W. "Religious Minorities in Pakistan" in *MW*, 1956.
*Choudhury, G. W. *Democracy in Pakistan*. Vancouver, 1963.
Colombe, M. *L'évolution de l'Egypte 1924–1950*. Paris, 1951.
*†Coulson, N. J. *A History of Islamic Law*. Edinburgh, 1964.
Dawn. Karachi.
"Dustūr" in EI^2 (B. Lewis).
The Evolution of India and Pakistan 1858–1947. Select Documents, vol. IV, ed. C. H. Philips, H. L. Singh and B. N. Pandey. London, 1962.
Faruki, Kemal A. *Islamic Jurisprudence*. Karachi, 1962.
Feroze, M. R. "The Reform in Family Laws in the Muslim World" in *Islamic Studies*, I. Karachi, 1962.

*Fyzee, Asaf A. A. *A Modern Approach to Islam.* Bombay, 1963.
Gabrieli, F. *The Arab Revival.* New York, 1961.
Gardet, L. *La cité Musulmane.* Paris, 1954.
Ghazālī, Muḥammad al-. *Our Beginning in Wisdom*, trans. I. E. el-Faruqi. Washington, 1953.
Gibb, H. A. R. *Modern Trends in Islam.* Chicago, 1947.
Gibb, H. A. R. "The Search for an Islamic Democracy" in *The Middle East in Transition*, ed. W. Z. Laqueur. London, 1958, pp. 3 ff.
Gibb, H. A. R. "Social Change in the Near East" in *The Near East. Problems and Prospects.* Chicago, 1942.
Gibb, H. A. R. "The Future for Arab Unity" in *The Near East. Problems and Prospects.* Chicago, 1942.
Gibb, H. A. R. "Constitutional Organisation" in *Law in the Middle East*, I, ed. M. Khadduri and H. J. Liebesney. Washington, 1955.
Gibb, H. A. R. and Bowen, H. *Islamic Society and the West.* I. *Islamic Society in the Eighteenth Century.* Part I, London, 1950; part II, 1957.
Gibb, H. A. R. *Studies on the Civilization of Islam.* London, 1962.
Godchot, J. E. *Les Constitutions du Proche et du Moyen-Orient.* Paris, 1957.
Goldziher, I. *Die Richtungen der islamischen Koranauslegung* (1920). Leiden, 1961.
Gökalp, Zia. *Turkish Nationalism and Western Civilization.* Selected essays translated and edited with an Introduction by N. Berkes. London, 1959.
Grunebaum, G. E. von. *Islam.* London, 1955.
Grunebaum, G. E. von. *Modern Islam.* Berkeley and Los Angeles, 1962.
Haim, Sylvia G. "Islam and the Theory of Arab Nationalism" in *WI*, n.s. IV, 1956, 124 ff.
Haim, Sylvia G. *Arab Nationalism.* Berkeley and Los Angeles, 1962.
Hartmann, R. *Die Krisis des Islam.* Leipzig, 1928.
Hartmann, R. *Islam und Nationalismus.* Berlin, 1948.
Hartmann, R. and Scheel, H. *Beiträge zur Arabistik, Semitistik und Islamwissenschaft* [*BASI*]. Leipzig, 1944.
Heyd, U. *Foundations of Turkish Nationalism.* London, 1950.
†Heyworth-Dunne, J. *Religious and Political Trends in Modern Egypt.* Washington, 1950.
*Hottinger, A. *The Arabs.* Berkeley and Los Angeles, 1963.
Hourani, A. *Arabic Thought in the Liberal Age 1798–1939.* London, 1962.
Husain, Muhammad Afzal. *Higher Education Examined.* Lahore, 1956.
Husain, Muhammad Afzal. *The Masters.* Lahore, 1957.

Ibn Khaldûn. *The Muqaddima*, I–III, trans. Franz Rosenthal. London, 1958.

Inalcik, Halil. "Die Türkei und der Westen" in *Internationales Jahrbuch für den Geschichtsunterricht*, VII, 1959–60, 10 ff.

Iqbal, Muhammad. *The Reconstruction of Religious Thought in Islam*. London, 1934.

Jambu-Merlin, R. *Le Droit Privé en Tunisie*. Paris, 1960.

Jamia Millia Islamia. Report 1954–55. Delhi, 1955.

The Jamia Educational Quarterly, I. Karachi, 1960.

Jäschke, G. *Der Islam in der Neuen Türkei*. Leiden, 1951 (*WI*, n.s. I, 1–2).

Jäschke, G. "Das Osmanische Scheinkalifat von 1922" in *WI*, n.s., 1951.

Jäschke, G. "Zur Krisis des Islams in der Türkei" in *BASI*.

Jäschke, G. "Die Entwicklung des osmanischen Verfassungsstaates" in *WI*, V, 1918.

Jäschke, G. "Die weltliche Bedeutung des türkischen Staatsgrundgesetzes" in *WI*, V, 1918.

Jinnah, Mohamed Ali. *Speeches by Quaid-i-Azam Mohamed Ali Jinnah, Governor General of Pakistan*, 3 June 1947–14 August 1948. Karachi, n.d.

Jomier, J. *Le commentaire coranique du Manâr*. Paris, 1954.

Kemal, Rahimuddin. *The Concept of Constitutional Law in Islam*. Hyderabad, 1955.

Kerr, M. "Rashīd Riḍā and Islamic Legal Reform" in *MW*, 1960.

Khālid, Muḥammad Khālid. *From Here we Start*, trans. I. R. el-Faruqi. Washington, 1953.

Lahbabi, Mohamed Aziz. *Du Clos à L'Ouvert*. Casablanca, 1961.

Landau, Rom. *Islam and the Arabs*. London, 1958.

Laoust, H. *Doctrines Sociales et Politiques d'Ibn Taimīya*. Cairo, 1939.

Laoust, H. "Le Réformisme orthodoxe des 'Salafīya'" in *REI*, LI, 1932.

Le Tourneau, R. *Evolution Politique de L'Afrique du Nord Musulmane, 1920–1961*. Paris, 1962.

Le Tourneau, R. "North Africa. Rigorism and Bewilderment" in *Unity and Variety in Muslim Civilization*. Chicago, 1955.

Lewis, Bernard. *The Emergence of Modern Turkey*. London, 1961.

Lewis, Bernard. "The Impact of the French Revolution on Turkey" in *Journal of World History*, I, 1953, 105 ff.

Lewis, Bernard. "The Concept of an Islamic Republic" in *WI*, n.s. IV, 1956.

Lewis, Bernard. "Democratic Institutions in the Islamic Middle East" in *Democratic Institutions in the World Today*, ed. W. Burmeister. London, 1958.

Lewis, Bernard. *A Handbook of Diplomatic Arabic*. London, 1947.

Lewis, Bernard. "Turkey and Westernization" in *Unity and Variety in Muslim Civilization*. Chicago, 1955.

*Lewis, Bernard. *The Middle East and the West*. London, 1964.

Lewis, Geoffrey L. *Turkey*. London, 1955.

Lichtenstadter, Ilse. *Islam and the Modern Age*. London, 1959.

Lockhart, L. "The Constitutional Laws of Persia..." in *MEJ*, 1959, pp. 372 ff.

Malaya

The Constitution of the Federation of Malaya (Supplement to the *Federation of Malaya Government Gazette*, 11 December 1957).

The Laws of the Constitution of Perlis. Alor Star, 1959.

Federation of Malaya. The Civil Marriage Ordinance, 1952 (Supplement to the *Federation of Malaya Government Gazette*, 21 October 1952).

Federation of Malaya. The Civil Marriage Ordinance, 1952 (in Legislative Supplement (Subsidiary Legislation) to the *Federation of Malaya Government Gazette* of 23 December 1954).

The Civil Marriage (Amendment) Ordinance, 1955 (Supplement to the *Federation of Malaya Government Gazette*, 15 June 1955).

State of Negri Sembilan. The Council of Muslim Religion Enactment, 1957 (Supplement to the *Federation of Malaya Government Gazette*, 12 June 1957, Notification Negri Sembilan no. 325), superseded by *Muslim Law Enactment, 1960*.

State of Malacca. Administration of Muslim Law Enactment, 1959.

State of Perak. Majlis Ugama Islam dan 'Adat Melayu (Procedures) Rules, 1957 (*Federation of Malaya Government Gazette* 26 December 1957, Notification Perak, no. 1831).

State of Pahang. Administration of the Law of the Religion of Islam Enactment, 1956 (Supplement to the *Federation of Malaya Government Gazette*, 6 March 1957, Notification Pahang no. 124).

State of Trengganu. Administration of Islamic Law Enactment, 1955 (1375) (Supplement to the *Federation of Malaya Government Gazette*, 29 March 1956, Notification Trengganu no. 176).

Mardin, Şerif. *The Genesis of Young Ottoman Thought*. Princeton, 1962.

Maudūdī, Sayyid Abul A'lā. *The Islamic Law and Constitution*[2]. Lahore, 1960.

Maudūdī, Sayyid Abul A'lā. *The Political Theory of Islam* (1939). Lahore, n.d.

Maudūdī, Sayyid Abul A'lā. *The Ethical View-Point of Islam*[2]. Lahore, 1953.

Maudūdī, Sayyid Abul A'lā. *Economic Problem of man and its Islamic Solution*. Lahore, 1955.

Maudūdī, Sayyid Abul A'lā. *The Islamic Way of Life*[2]. Lahore, 1955.

Maudūdī, Sayyid Abul A'lā. *The Message of Jama'at-e-Islami*[2]. Lahore, 1955.

Maudūdī, Sayyid Abul A'lā. *The Process of Islamic Revolution*[2]. Lahore, 1955.

Montesquieu, C. de S. *De L'Esprit Des Lois* (Œuvres Complètes II). Paris, 1951.

Morocco

The Constitution of the Kingdom of Morocco (English translation issued by the Royal Moroccan Embassy). London, 1962.

Muhammad Ali. *Mirza Ghulam Ahmad of Qadian*[3]. Lahore, 1963.

Muhammad Ali. *Sir Muhammad Iqbal's Statement re the Qadianis*. Lahore, n.d.

Nizami, K. A. "Shah Wali Ullah Dehlavi and Indian Politics in the 18th Century" in *Islamic Culture*, XXV, I, 1951.

Nolte, R. "The Rule of Law in the Arab Middle East" in *MW*, 1958.

Nuseibeh, Hazem Zaki. *The Ideas of Arab Nationalism*. Cornell, 1956.

Pakistan

Report of the Court of Inquiry...Punjab Disturbances of 1953. Lahore, 1954. (*Munir Report*.)

The Constitution of the Islamic Republic of Pakistan 1956. Karachi, 1956.

Report of the Commission on National Education. Karachi, 1960.

Government Resolution on the Report of the Commission on National Education. Karachi, 1960.

Report of the Curriculum Committee for Secondary Education, I. Karachi, 1960.

Constituent Assembly Debates. I and V. *Karachi*. Karachi, 1947–56.

Report of the Constitution Commission, Pakistan, 1961. Karachi, 1962.

Answers to the Questionnaire of the Constitution Commission by Prominent Ulama (together with *Basic Principles of an Islamic State*). Lahore, 1960.

Answers to the Questionnaire of the Constitution Commission, Pakistan, issued by Idara-e-Tolu-e-Islam. Lahore, n.d. (G. A. Parwez's followers.)

Basic Provisions of an Islamic Constitution for Pakistan. (By the same group.)

The Muslim Family Laws Ordinance, 1961 (*The Gazette of Pakistan Extraordinary*, 2 March 1961).

The Constitution of the Republic of Pakistan. Karachi, 1962.

Paret, R. "Islam und Nationalismus im Vorderen Orient" in *Die Welt des Islam und die Gegenwart*, ed. R. Paret. Stuttgart, 1961.

Parwez, G. A. *Fundamental Rights in Islam*. Lahore, n.d. (This is a reply to an article by Mr Justice M. Munir entitled *Fundamental Rights in Islamic Law* reprinted in this pamphlet.)

Pritsch, E. "Das Tunesische Personenstandsgesetz" in *WI*, n.s. v, 1958, 188 ff.

Qureshi, I. H. *Pakistan, An Islamic Democracy*. Karachi, n.d.

Qureshi, I. H. *The Muslim Community of the Indo-Pakistan Subcontinent*. 's-Gravenhage, 1962.

Qureshi, I. H. "The Future Constitution of Pakistan" in *Islamic Review*. Woking, December 1950.

Rahbar, Muḥammad Daūd. "Shāh Walī Ullāh and Ijtihād" in *MW*, 1955, 346 ff.

Rahman, F. "Muslim Modernism in the Indo-Pakistan Sub-continent" in *BSOAS*, XXI, 1958, 82 ff.

Ramadan, Said. *Islamic Law. Its Scope and Equity*. London, 1961.

Rashid, Rifat. *Social Welfare Needs and Field Work Practices*. Lahore, 1960.

Reed, H. A. "The Faculty of Divinity at Ankara" in *MW*, 1956, 1957.

Reed, H. A. "Turkey's New Imam-Hatip Schools" in *WI*, n.s. IV, 1956.

Riḍā, Rashīd. *Le Califat dans la doctrine de Rašīd Riḍā*, trans. H. Laoust. Beyrouth, 1938.

Rondot, P. *L'Islam et les Musulmans d'aujourd'hui*. Paris, 1958 (I); 1960 (II).

Rosenthal, Erwin I. J. *Political Thought in Medieval Islam* (1958). Cambridge, 1962.

Rosenthal, Erwin I. J. *Ibn Khaldûns Gedanken über den Staat*. Munich and Berlin, 1932.

Rosenthal, Erwin I. J. "The Place of Politics in the Philosophy of Ibn Rushd" in *BSOAS*, XV, 2, 1953.

Rosenthal, Erwin I. J. "The Role of Islam in the Modern National State" in *The Year Book of World Affairs 1962*. London, 1962.

Rosenthal, Erwin I. J. "Some Reflections on the Separation of Religion and Politics in Modern Islam" in *Islamic Studies*, III, 3. Karachi, 1964.

Rosenthal, Franz. "The Muslim Brethren in Egypt" in *MW*, 1947.

Rousseau, J.-J. *Du Contrat Social* (Oeuvres Complètes, IV). Paris, 1859.

Sammān, Muḥammad ʻAbdullah As-. *The Principles of Islamic Government*, trans. Sylvia G. Haim in *WI*, n.s. v, 1958.
Sayeed, Khalid Bin. *Pakistan: The Formative Phase*. Karachi, 1960.
Sayeed, Khalid Bin. "The Jama'at-i-Islami Movement" in *Pacific Affairs*, xxx, 1, 1951.
Sayeed, Khalid Bin. "Pakistan's Basic Democracy" in *MEJ*, 1961.
Schacht, J. "Šarīʻa und Qānūn im modernen Ägypten" in *Der Islam*, xx, 1932.
Schacht, J. *The Origins of Muhammadan Jurisprudence* (1950). Oxford, 1959.
Schacht, J. "The Law" in *Unity and Variety in Muslim Civilization*, ed. G. E. von Grunebaum. Chicago, 1955.
Schacht, J. "Pre-Islamic Background and Early Development of Jurisprudence" in *Law in the Middle East*, I, ed. M. Khadduri and H. J. Liebesney. Washington, 1955.
Schacht, J. "The Schools of Law and Later Developments of Jurisprudence" in *Law in the Middle East*, I, ed. M. Khadduri and H. J. Liebesney. Washington, 1955.
Schacht, J. "Classicisme, Traditionalisme et Ankylose dans la Loi religieuse de l'Islam" in *Classicisme et Declin Culturel dans l'Histoire de l'Islam*, ed. R. Brunschwig and G. E. von Grunebaum. Paris, 1957.
Schacht, J. "Islamic Law in Contemporary States" in *The American Journal of Comparative Law*, VIII, 2, 1959.
Schacht, J. Articles "Sharīʻa" in *EI* and "Fiḳh" in *EI*[2].
*Schacht, J. *Introduction to Islamic Law*. Oxford, 1964.
Smith, W. Cantwell. *Islam in India*. London, 1946.
Smith, W. Cantwell. *Islam in Modern History*. Princeton, 1957.
†Stephens, Ian. *Pakistan*[2]. London, 1964. (Also as a Pelican Book.)
Steppat, F. "Nationalismus und Islam bei Mustafa Kamil" in *WI*, n.s. IV, 1956, 241–341.
Süngü, Ihsan. "Tanzimat ve Yeni Osmanlilar" in *Tanzimat*, I. Istanbul, 1940, 777–857.
Taeschner, F. "Der Islam im Banne des Nationalismus der Zwischenweltkriegszeit" in *BASI*.
Talbi, Mohamed. "L'Islam et le Monde Moderne" in *Politique Étrangère*, XXV, 2, 1960.
Tunaya, Tarik. "Âmme Hukukumuz Bakimindan İkinci Meşrutiyetin Tefekküründe 'İslâmcilik' Cereyani" in *Hukuk Fakültesi Mecmuasi*, XIX. Istanbul, 1953, 630–70.
Tunisia
Code du Statut Personnel. Annoté de M. T. Es-snousi (French version). Tunis, 1958.

Constitution of the Tunisian Republic (official English version). Tunis, n.d.

Nouvelle Conception de l'Enseignement en Tunisie. Tunis, 1958. (Secretariat d'Etat à l'Education Nationale.)

Turkey

"Constitution of the Turkish Republic [1961]" in *MEJ*, 1962. Translated for the Committee of National Unity.

Ankara University. The Faculty of Divinity (*Organisation and Regulations*). Ankara, 1959.

Ülken, Hilmi Ziya. "Evolution de la Condition Féminine en Turquie" in *Sosjoloji Dergisi*, Sayi: 15–1960 'dan. Istanbul, 1960.

Ülken, Hilmi Ziya. "L'Occidentalisme en Turquie" in *Ankara Üniversitesi İlâhiyat Fakültesi Dergisi*, Cilt: VIII, Yil: 1960 'dan. Ankara, 1961.

Zakaria, Nasim. *Parliamentary Government in Pakistan.* Lahore, 1958.

INDEX

Abbasid dynasty, 13, 21, 23, 36, 58, 75, 81, 90, 248; absolutism of, 16
'Abd-al-Rāziq, 'Ali, 17, 59, 65, 79, 103, 104, 106, 108, 136, 233, 379 n. 6; views of, 85–102; answered, 105
'Abduh, Muḥammad, 13, 15, 17, 65, 70, 82, 106, 154, 155, 165, 191; modernism of, 48, 103, 119; periodical of, 66
Abdülaziz, Sultan, 35
Abdülhamid, Sultan, supports Islamists, 39; deposition of, 44
Abdullah, S. M., 277, 335
Abu Bakr, first caliph (d. 634), 92; as first temporal ruler, 86; opposition to, 90; religious behaviour of, 95; political wars and conflicts of, 96
Abu-l-Fidā, 98
Abu Yūsuf, 53
Adam Smith, George, 176
Adams, Charles, 82, 380 nn. 53–6
Advisory Council of Islamic Research (Pakistan), 261, 267–79 *passim*, 353; functions of, 270–3, 275
Afghānī, Jamāl al-Dīn al-, 44, 65, 66, 70, 86, 106, 119, 154; modernism of, 48, 121
Africa, 5, 121
  North, 67, 110; Islam in, 316, 362
Africans, 167
aḥkām (ordinances), contrasted with *din*, 24
ahl al-'aqd wa-l-ḥāll (spiritual leaders), 69, 72, 78, 90, 148, 149, 161, 214; Ankara deputies as, 71; training of, 74
ahl al-kitāb, 213, 266, 336
Ahmad, Aziz, 187
Ahmad, Mirza Bashir-ud-Din Mahmud, 231–2
Ahmad, Mirza Ghulam, claims of, 231–2
Ahmad Khan, Sayyid, 182, 187, 193, 201, 208; founds Aligarh, 189; education work of, 190–1; commentary on Qur'an, 191, 345
Aḥmad, Shaykh (of Sirhind), 187
Aḥmadīya sect, 231–3; agitation against, 213, 230–1
Ahmadiyyat (Mirza Bashir-ud-Din Mahmud Ahmad), 231
Ahrar, the, 231
'A'isha (wife of Muḥammad), 113
Al-i'tisām (Shāṭibī), 142
Al-naqd al-ḏātī ('Allāl al-Fāsī), 154, 175–6, 178
Alawi dynasty, 368
Albiruni, A. H., 189, 191, 192, 193, 385 nn. 1, 10, 16–20
Algeria, 162, 316
'Ali, fourth caliph (d. 661), 19
Ali Khan, Liaqat, 209, 250
Aligarh, 191, 283, 284, 356; founding of college at, 189
Allahabad, 196
Almohads, 23, 316, 370
Almoravids, 23, 316, 370
America, North, 110, 161; treatment of negroes in, 150; universities in, 348; *see also* United States
Amīn, Aḥmad, 123
amīr, 132, 146; see also *sulṭān*
amīr al-mu'minīn, 325, 331
Andalusia, 371
Anderson, J. N. D., 333
Ankara, University of, 313, 314, 361
Ansari, Z. I., 117–18, 382 nn. 21–4
Answers to Constitution Commission's Questionnaire, 251–8 *passim*
'aqīda (doctrine), 106
Arab League, 115, 117
Arabia, 4, 110, 168, 188, 248, 354; conditions in seventh century, 128
Arabic (language), 173, 362, 380 n. 46; importance of, 145; neglect of, 147, 314, 317; in Morocco, 329, 369, 370; in Malaya, 359, 360; in Tunisia, 363, 364
Arabism, 5, 69, 76, 81
Arabs, 167; as spearhead of Islam, 121; as merciful conquerors, 121; as teachers, 359

Aristotle, 36, 43, 100, 115, 217, 240; dictum of, 15
'asabīya (corporate loyalty), 21, 23, 25, 26, 66, 90, 161; concept of, 18, 80–1
Asad, Muhammad, 68, 146, 148, 170, 208, 227, 248, 257; political theories of, 125–36
Ash'arī, Al-, 167
Asia, 121; South-East, 5
Assembly, Constituent (Pakistan), 138, 144, 202, 209, 214–30 *passim*, 250, 256; (Iran), 307, 308; (Turkey), 311
  Grand National (Turkey), 33, 58, 71, 311
  National (Pakistan), 237, 249, 290; women members of, 276, 340; (Tunisia), 317, 318, 319; (Morocco), 328
  National Consultative (Turkey), 36, 43
Atatürk, *see* Kemal Atatürk
Auqaf Ordinance (Pakistan, 1959), 278
Aurangzeb, 248
Ayub Khan, Mohammad, 220, 248, 263, 278, 279, 333; seizes power, 235–6; statements of, 274–5
Āzād, Abul Kalām, 70, 191, 201, 282; revivalism of, 192–4, 345
Azhar, Al-, 325; *'ulamā* of, 64, 70, 104, 113; Grand Council of, 85; *muftis* and *qāḍīs* trained at, 302; teachers trained at, 360, 361

Balkan War, 46
Baluchistan, 196
Bannā, Ḥasan al-, views of, 116–18
Barani, Ziauddin, 248, 283
Bari, Mian Abdul, 265
Basic Principles Committee (Pakistan), 214, 219, 220; Report of, 217, 251
Basic Provisions of an Islamic Constitution, 252, 253, 256
Bausani, A., 185
bay'a (oath of allegiance), 29, 90
Bayt-al-māl, 297; defined, 389 n. 16
Bazzāz, 'Abdu-l-Raḥmān al-, 121
Becker, C. H., 378 n. 2
Ben Achour, M., 321, 366
Ben Milad, Mahjoub, 321, 366
Benares, 283; controversy at, 189
Bengal, 190; partition of, 195
Bengali (language), 348–9
Berbers, 167, 316, 320, 362, 369; polygamy of, 169
Berkes, N., 33
Bible, the, 74
Binder, L., 383 n. 9, 386 n. 42
Bourguiba, Habib, 317, 322, 323, 340–1, 366; presidential system suited to, 318
Britain, in occupation of Egypt, 119, 173; in occupation of India, 143–4, 188–94 *passim*, 199, 247, 272; democracy in, 160–2; education in, 262; in occupation of Malaya, 288, 304, 306
Brohi, A. K., 220–1, 229, 274
Buddhists, in Malaya, 287
Butler Act (1944), 172

Cairo, 302, 361
Calder, G. J., 386 nn. 42, 44, 46
caliphate, 38, 55–6, 57, 76, 201; abolition of, 3, 59, 195; power of threatened, 13–14; decline of, 14; as a divine injunction, 43; Rashīd Riḍā's inconsistent views on, 77; necessity of denied by 'Ali 'Abd al-Rāziq, 79, 87–8; see also *khilāfa*
caliph, 8, 38, 69, 77, 166; status of, 12, 14–15, 43–4; as symbol of unity of *ummet*, 57–8; four types of, 58–9; compared with Pope, 78; as temporal ruler, 88; accused by 'Ali 'Abd al-Rāziq, 99; believers as, 145–6; see also *khalīfa*
Callard, K. B., 387 nn. 61, 63
capitalism, 161, 165
Cevdet Paşa, 30
Ceylon, 287
Chakravarty, R. K., 219
China, 110
Chinese, in Malaya, 287; in Singapore, 287–8
Choudhury, G.W., 212, 388 nn. 98, 107
Christianity, 34, 41, 42, 56, 65, 111, 119, 165, 313, 327, 374; identified with West, 5, 43, 44, 67, 373; re-orientation of, 11; political irrelevance of, 43; irreconcilable with modern state, 57; in social

Christianity (*cont.*)
ethics, 84; challenged equally with Islam, 105; in India, 199
Christians, 119, 151, 322; rights of, 30, 36; hostility to Islam of, 40; treatment of by Islam, 107–8; in Pakistan, 204–5, 212; in Malaya, 287
civics, 348, 358, 363–4, 369
civilisation, as touchstone of contemporary life, 48; distinguished from culture, 57, 60; faulty principles of modern, 145; Phoenician, Roman and Byzantine in North Africa, 316
'Code Civil et Commercial Tunisien' (1899), 319
Collège Sadiqi, 319, 323
Colombe, M., 85, 378 n. 1, 379 n. 15
colonialism, ending of, 3; mark left by, 373
Commission on National Education (Pakistan), 346; *Report* of, 346, 348
communalism, in India, 182, 193, 194–6, 196–7, 202, 219, 282, 286; in Singapore, 287; in Malaya, 288
Communism, 112, 130, 149, 165, 314, 343; Islam as barrier to, 305, 306
Congress, Indian National, 183, 189, 193, 194, 197, 202
Constitutions
Belgium (1831), 39
Egypt (1923), 65, 102, 104; (1956), 102
Iran (1906), 307
Malaya (1957), 288–92
Morocco (1962), 329
Ottoman Empire (1908), 46
Pakistan (1956), 204, 209, 221–42 *passim*, 264–7, 347; (1962), 182, 204, 222, 237, 242, 249, 263–81, 290
Tunisia (1957), 321
Turkey (1876), 39; (1923 and 1961), 310–12
Constitution Commission (Pakistan), activities of, 250–63; *Report* of, 257, 262–3, 266
Contrat Social, Du (Rousseau), 111, 160
Copts, the, 112, 119
Corsica, 328
Cottage Industries (APWA), 339, 342
Cromer, Lord, 68, 81–2
Crusaders, the, 105, 134
culture, distinguished from civilisation, 51; as basis of nation, 57; a definition of, 60; French, 157
Curriculum Committee (Pakistan), Report of, 353–4, 358

Dacca, 194, 249, 352
dār-al-ḥarb (realm of war), 45, 108, 283
dār-al-islām (realm of Islam), 45, 58, 108, 184, 283
Datta, B. K., 210, 217–18
da'wa (call to religion), 18, 117; as complement to *'aṣabīya*, 23, 81
Dawn (newspaper), 236, 266, 274, 276, 387 n. 61, 388 n. 98
Dawwānī, Al-, 66
Decree of Reforms (1856), 30–1
Delhi, 283, 356
democracy, 218; 'Allāl al-Fāsī's option of, 161; English, 177; for Pakistan, 208, 210, 213, 235–7, 250, 252; for Tunisia, 317; for Morocco, 328–9
Denmark, 174
Deoband, 187, 191, 210, 345; foundation of, 188; its suspicion of Aligarh, 189
Descartes, René, 6
dictatorship, 161; in Pakistan, 236
Diderot, Denis, 167
ḏimmīs (second-class citizens), 205, 283; status of, 107–8; Muhammad Asad on, 129–30, 131–3; Maudūdī on, 150, 152
dīn (religion), 111, 171; contrasted with *aḥkām*, 24; remote from *siyāsa*, 100–1
divorce, 169–70, 219–20, 237, 245, 275, 297, 306, 332, 333–5, 336; see also *ṭalāq*
Dostoevski, Feodor, 154
Durkheim, Emile, 51
Dustūr, the, 33

Ebeid Paşa, Makram, 382 n. 15
education, 133, 152, 190–1, 306, 324, 339; Islamic, 59; under Atatürk,

education (*cont.*)
61; as key to patriotism, 66; of women, 113, 171, 233, 348; as key to progress, 144, 174, 189, 241, 305; in Morocco, 171–4; in Pakistan, 221, 237–8, 243, 262; in Iran, 307, 310; Islam in, 344–58, 359–61, 363–8, 368–71; neglect of, 373
Royal Commissions on (Morocco), 368–9
Supreme Council of National (Morocco), 372
Egypt, 102, 173, 174, 218, 354; modernism in, 64–6; liberation of, 110, 119; as source of teachers, 302, 326, 359
Ehya Sherif Institution, 359–60
Encyclopedists, the, 6
Ethics, teaching of, 359, 360
Europe, 29, 35, 57, 105, 173, 176, 348; criticised by Islamists, 41; as replica of Islam, 45; in conflict with Islam, 60, 103, 134; Islamic rule in, 164; Iqbal's judgement of, 206–7

Faiza (journal), 341
falāsifa (philosophers), 17, 50, 100, 321
falsafa (philosophy), 364
family, 171; importance of, 167
family planning, 278, 340, 355
Family Laws Ordinance, Muslim, 257, 333, 338; opposition to, 275–6, 277
Fārābī, Al-, 100
Fascism, 130, 149, 161
Fashoda, 119
Fāsī, 'Allāl al-, 322, 325, 326, 327; views of, 154–78
Fatimids, the, 370
fatwā (legal decisions), 25, 26, 56, 72, 164, 295, 299, 302
Feroze, M. R., 385 n. 45
Fes, 324, 326, 361, 368–72 *passim*
Fichte, J. G., 146
fikr (thinking), types of, 156
Fiqh (jurisprudence), 15, 71, 145, 164, 240, 248, 257, 283, 309, 319; defined, 12; sources of, 53, 135; excluded from *Sharī'a*, 125, 269; Maududi's approach to, 139; Walī Ullāh's attitude to, 187; teaching of, 359, 360, 364, 371
fiṭra (religious dues), 297; defined, 389 n. 16
France, 154, 160, 164, 173, 319; as colonial power, 3, 110, 157, 159; democracy in, 160–2; in occupation of Morocco, 171, 175, 316, 325; in occupation of Tunisia, 316
French Revolution, the, 62, 79, 105, 146, 160, 172; impact of on Muslim mind, 6, 9, 29

Gandhi, Mahatma, 193, 198, 282, 356
Ghaus, G., 275–6, 277
Ghazālī, Al- (b. 1058), 15, 77, 108, 217, 359, 364, 379 n. 6; views of, 104–6, 109–14; significance of, 114; on divorce, 169
Gibb, H. A. R., xii, 103, 381 n. 2
Gide, André, 177
girls, aspirations of, 326; education of, 341
God, belief in, 8, 107, 114, 145, 157
Goethe, J. W. von, 146
Gökalp, Ziya, 51, 85, 86, 98, 378 nn. 28 and 35; views of, 51–61
Goldziher, I., 13
Good Society, the, 373, 374
Government of India Act (1935), 203
Greek tradition, 106, 362
Gülhane, Rescript of, 7, 35
Gunong Semanggol, 359

Ḥadīth (tradition), 73, 111, 126, 145, 147, 187, 240, 260, 365; fabricators of, 208; Parwez's rejection of, 228, 238; teaching of, 359, 360, 370–1
Haim, Sylvia G., 121, 382 nn. 18–20, 25, 31, 383 nn. 33f.
Halakhah (Rabbinic law), 49, 128
Ḥalīm, Muḥammad Sa'īd, 40, 47; opposition of to French ideas, 46
Hanafi (sect), tenets, 296; law, 302, 336; rite, 336
Hanbali (sect), tenets, 296; law, 302
Haqq, Iḥtishām al-, 333–5
Hartmann, R., 382 n. 30
Hassan II, king of Morocco, 160, 329
Ḥayreddin, 39, *see also* Khereddine

Hegel, G. W. F., 146
Heyd, U., 51, 60, 119, 377 nn. 15, 17, 378 nn. 21, 26f.
Heyworth-Dunne, J., 382 n. 21
Hijāz, the, 69, 185
Hilāl, Al-, 192–3
Hindi (language), 285
Hinduism, 182, 195, 199, 247, 282; as a social order, 198, 255
Hindus, 151, 190, 194–6, 198–9, 255, 282; partnership with Muslims, 182–3, 189, 194, 201–2; in Pakistan, 204–5, 210, 212, 286
Hitler, Adolf, 146, 175
Hobbes, Thomas, 6, 100
Hong Kong, 287
Hourani, A., 66, 378 nn. 3f.
Hudaifa, 90
ḥudūd (penalties), 68, 80, 83, 105, 136, 141; for theft and adultery, 140
Ḥujjat Allāh al-bālighah (Shāh Walī Ullāh), 185
Hukum Shara', 293, 300
Human Rights, Bill of, 109, 132, 205
Hunter, Sir William, 190
ḥurriya, hürriyet (freedom), 30, 157, 167
Husain (seventh century), murder of, 91
Husain, Mahmud, 219, 355
Husain, Muhammad Afzal, 347
Husain, Zakir, 201, 282, 356
Hyderabad, 283, 355; University of, 284
Ḥusain, Taha, 17

'ibādāt (religious duties), 8, 105
Ibn Ḥazm, 90, 126
Ibn Jamā'a, 15
Ibn Khaldūn (1332–1406), 16–17, 50, 66, 80–1, 87, 90, 93–5, 109, 119, 120, 230, 321, 364; on *khilāfa* and *mulk*, 17–27; political realism of, 28; influence of on 'Ali 'Abd al-Rāziq, 85, 90, 92, 99; as creator of social science, 176–7; birthplace of in Tunis, 318; influence of on 'Allāl al-Fāsī, 165; Muslim state of, 245, 320
Ibn Qayyim al-Jawzīya, 15, 67, 239
Ibn Rushd (1126–98), 100
Ibn Sīnā (980–1037), 100, 309
Ibn Taymīya (1263–1328), 13, 67, 77, 88, 185, 364; as source of modern reformers, 15
Iftikharuddin, Mian, 219
ijmā' (consensus), 15, 90, 141, 236, 366; as a source of *Fiqh*, 12, 33, 72; Iqbal on, 205
ijtihād (independent judgement), 15, 24, 67–83 *passim*, 131, 139, 142–3, 205–6, 219, 236–43 *passim*, 260, 301, 302, 308–9, 327, 334; difficulties of application, 16, 49; the proper place of, 126; woman's right to, 170; Shāh Walī Ullāh's view of, 186–7; in Tunisia, 319; as a general right, 335
Ikhwān-al-Muslimūn, *see* Muslim Brotherhood
Ikramullah, Begum, 219
imāma of necessity, 69; see also *khilāfa*
Imams, 263, 279
imperialism, influence of, 3, 175, 177, 198; in relation to education, 345; identified with Christianity, 374
India, 4, 67, 110, 143, 287; bondage of Muslims in, 76; contemporary problems in, 182–4; post-Mutiny period in, 188–94; communalism in, 194–6; as a Muslim country, 197; dream of unity in, 193, 201; Muslim states in, 248; outlook of Muslims in, 282–6
Indian Civil Service, 202, 203; exclusion of Muslims from, 190
Indian Mutiny, 182, 247
Indians in Malaya, 287
Indonesia, 124
inheritance, 303, 327, 332
integrity, public, 348
Ipoh, 359
Iqbal, Muḥammad, 193, 232, 236, 260, 354; stresses dynamism of Islam, 137, 165, 187, 208; on Muslim India, 196–8; on Pakistan, 205–7
Iran, 5, 117, 315, 354; Islam in, 307–10, 311
Iraq, 326, 359
Irwin, Lord, 197
Isfahan, 310

ishrāq (mystical illumination), philosophy of, 309
ishtirā', 78, 80–1
Islam, nature of crisis of, 4, 10, 50; three attitudes towards, 5; defined, 7; re-orientation of, 11, 235; religious or secular, 12; in relation to Turkish nationalism, 28–63; Young Ottomans love of, 37; N. Kemāl's concept of, 38; equality and liberty in, 44, 91; place of in education (Gökalp), 59; in present-day Turkey, 61–2, 310–15; belief in perfection of, 67; as solvent of modern problems, 82; in social ethics, 84, 91; as exclusively religious, 86–7, 101, 121; as universal religion, 99, 109; in relation to Arab nationalism, 103–24; as unity of creed and law, 105, 110, 155, 186; essence of formulated, 123; as natural law of God, 128–9; comprehensiveness of, 133–4, 156–7, 303; as 'movement', 158, 322; rule of in Europe, 164; peculiar character of in India, 182; in Indian sub-continent, 199–200; as an ideology, 227, 248–9, 345; obstacles to synthesis of with West, 227–8; Pakistani attitudes to, 237–9; in Pakistan's constitution, 263–81; in present-day India, 282–6; as state religion in Malaya, 288–306; in Iran, 307–10; not mentioned in Turkish constitution, 311; in Tunisia, 316–24; in Morocco, 324–31; dangers to, 343; in secondary education (Pakistan), 353–4; as final revealed religion, 366
Islam wa'-usūl al-ḥukm, Al- ('Ali 'Abd al-Rāziq), 85
Islamic Culture (periodical), 284
Islamic Culture, Institute of, 352
Islamic history, teaching of, 353–4, 359
Islamic Law and Constitution, The (Maudūdī), 137
Islamic League, proposed, 115
Islamic Research, Central Institute of, 241, 244, 258, 261, 270, 279, 350–1; comment on objectives of, 352–3
Islamic Studies (journal), 352
Islamic way of life, basis of defined, 346
Islamist movement, 86, 104; nature of, 39–47
Isma'īl, Khedive, 70, 102, 104
Israel, 105
Istanbul University, Theological Faculty of, 61
istiḥsān, 140
Istiqlāl (party), 154, 162, 323, 363, 390 n. 6; supported by King, 327
Ithna 'asharī, 307, 308

jāhilīya, 110, 121
Jām'iat al-'ulamā-i-Hind, foundation of, 193
Jamā'at-i-Islāmī (party), 137, 257, 274–9 *passim*, 283; purposefulness of, 247; demands universal suffrage, 269
Jamāl, Abbās al-, Sheikh, 70, 104
Jamia Educational Quarterly, 356
Jamia Islamia (Bahawalpur), 355
Jamia Millia Islamia (Delhi), 283, 356–7
Jamia Talim-i-Milli (Malir), 355, 357
Jamiatul Ulema-i-Islam, 277
Jamiyatul Falah, 243
Jäschke, G., 376 ch. 1, n. 1, 377 n. 12, 390 ch. 10, nn. 3–5
Jews, 119, 167, 205, 322, 336–7; treatment of by Islam, 107–8; in Morocco, 390 n. 6
jihād (holy war), 45, 58, 70, 99, 105, 234, 371, 381 n. 90; Muḥammad engaged in, 7, 94; interpreted as defensive, 108, 133
Jinnah, Mohammad Ali, 183, 211, 217, 256; as leader of Muslim League, 195; on Hindu–Muslim problems, 198–9, 201–2; quoted, 212, 255
jizya (poll-tax), 108, 133, 208
Judaism, 11, 84, 105, 111, 165
Juin, Marshal, 328
juz'īyāt, 42, 43–4

Kabir, Humayun, 282
Kairouwan, 317
Kajars, the, 309
kalām (theology), 74, 364

Kāmil, Mustafa, 118–20
Karachi, 243, 244, 350, 352, 355; University of, 355
Kathi Besar, 296, 297
Kattānī, Idrīs al-, 327, 390 n. 6
Kawākibi, 'Abd al-Raḥmān al-, 121, 381 n. 100
Kayani, Mr Justice M. R., 230
Kāzim Effendi, Musa, 43
Kedah, 303
Kelantan, 301, 306
Kemal Atatürk, 52, 71, 310, 312; suspends *Sharī'a*, 33, 54; reforms of, 39, 61; abolishes caliphate, 3, 56, 195
Kemāl, Nāmik, 48; views of, 29–39
Khālid (seventh century), 96
Khālid, Khālid Muḥammad, 104, 106, 110, 113–14, 136; some views of, 111
khalīfa, 22, 69, 146, 318; as spiritual and temporal ruler, 8; duties of, 14–15
  khalīfa of Aḥmadīs, 231–2; spiritual authority of, 233
  khalīfat-Allāh, 325
Khatibs, 278, 279
Khayal, Taj Muhammad, 354
Khereddine, 319, 390 ch. 11, n. 2
khilāfa, 55, 214, 221; concept of, 12–17, 42; in relation to *mulk*, 17–27, 34, 120; religious and political unity of, 22–3; advocated by Rashīd Riḍā, 66–85; regarded as unnecessary, 86; dependence on force, 90, 99; dissociated from Islam, 98; two-pronged, 186, 187; *see also* Caliphate
Khilāfat movement, 193, 195, 198
Khuda Bukhsh Library, 283
khulafā rāshidūn, 13, 16, 58, 77, 81, 86, 128, 148, 198, 340, 371; guided by God, 105; social insurance derived from, 133; Conventions of the, 146–7, 149
Khurshed, Mr, 273, 388 n. 107
khutbah (Friday sermon), 78, 135
Kings, divine right of, 147
Klang, Muslim College of, 302, 359
Kuala Kangsar, 359
Kuala Lumpur, 292, 302
kulliyāt, 42, 43–4
labour, dignity of, 166
Lahore, 243, 244–5, 276, 339, 352, 355; disturbances at, 230
Lahore Resolution, 198, 250
Lahoris, 231–2
lambaga, 303
Laoud, H., 378 n. 6
law, origin and nature of, 10 *et passim*; Natural and Divine, 11, 16, 33, 35; rule of, 21–2; static and dynamic, 23–4; French, 33; secularisation of, 54; Islamic attitudes to, 84–5; evolution of Islamic, 141; proposed academy of, 144; content of Islamic, 145; practice of in Morocco, 163–5; changes in, 332–7
lay state, 34, 84, 101, 103; Turkish, 5, 51, 61, 88; French, 9; essence of, 9–10, 107; advocated in Pakistan, 241, 250, 280; in Tunisia, 319
Lebon, Gustave, 110, 121
Lenin, 146, 175
Lewis, Bernard, xvi, 39, 377 nn. 1, 3, 9, 10, 14–16, 37
Locke, John, 6, 100
Lucknow, 191, 218, 345; hostility to Aligarh, 192
Lucknow Pact, 195, 202
Luther, Martin, 6
Lytton, Lord, 190

Maghrib, 21, 23, 156, 363, 371; al-Fasi on, 158–60; Greater, 317, 327, 329, 364
Mahdī, the, 307; Ahmad as, 231–2
Majlis, in Malayan states, 295–7; in Iran, 307, 308
majlis ash-shūrā, 136; Muhammad Asad's proposals for, 131–2
Malacca, 288, 289, 303; Council of Religion, 295–7
Malay (language), 287, 293, 297
Malaya, 4, 52, 124, 260, 310, 311, 314, 318, 336; composition of, 287–8, 389 n. 1; constitution of, 289–92; state constitutions of, 293–300; social evolution in, 305; religious education in, 359–61
Malaysia, 288, 389 n. 1
Malik (seventh century), 96, 168
malik (temporal ruler), 19, 92

Mālikī, rite, 163, 167, 169, 296; decisions, 165, 166; law, 168, 302, 318, 325, 336; jurists, 169

Mameluks, 58, 59, 90

Manār, Al- (journal), 66, 68, 72, 82, 119, 191

Maraboutism, 316, 321

Mardin, Şerif, 376 ch. 1, n. 1, 377 nn. 1, 3, 4, 10

marriages, child, 168, 334, 335–6

Marx, Karl, 146, 175

Marxism, 44, 165

maṣlaḥa (public welfare), 15, 54, 77–8, 97, 131, 139, 159, 268

Massignon, L., 163

Maudūdī, Sayyid Abul A'lā, 112, 192, 193–4, 201, 202, 221–72 *passim*, 327, 384 n. 18; on *Sharī'a*, 68–9, 170; political theories of, 137–53; imprisoned, 153; party of, 184, 194; projected law college of, 206; clear objective of, 247, 264

Mawaqif, Al-, 90

Māwardī, Al- (tenth century), 13, 24, 55; defines *imāma*, 15, 20; on necessity of *khilāfa*, 42–3, 89

Mecca, 185, 302

Mecelle, the, 33, 377 n. 9 (III)

Medina, Statute of, 94

Messadi, M., 363

milla, millet (religious community), 19, 21, 38, 44, 119

Min hunā nabda' (Khālid), 104

Min hunā na'lam (al-Ghazālī), 104

Ministry of Pious Affairs, proposed, 55

Mirza, Anis, 335

modernists
- in Egypt, 64, 103, 119, 185
- in India, 188–9
- in Pakistan, 186, 201
- in Turkey, 48–9; views of on caliphate, 59

Mohammed V, king of Morocco, 160, 327, 368; banishment of, 328; declarations of, 328–9

Mohammedan Educational Conference, 189

Molière, 167

Montesquieu, C. L. de S., 7, 29, 35, 39, 146, 154, 161, 167, 176; translated by al-Tahtawi, 66

Morocco, 314, 316, 322, 333, 337; independence of, 154; religious question in, 157; political parties in, 162; legal practice in, 163–5; economics in, 165–7; social thinking in, 167; status of women in, 167–71; education in, 171–4, 368–72; Islam in, 324–31; emancipation of women in, 341–2

Mossul, 69

Mu'āwiya (d. 680), 81, 115; traditional bias against, 14, 19; establishes a *mulk*, 16, 87; said to have murdered Husain, 91

mufti (judge), 25, 54, 56, 98; in Malayan states, 295–6, 300, 302, 303, 304

Mughuls, 183, 185, 247

Muḥammad (prophet), 146, 231, 334, 371; source of authority of, 7; as religious leader, 87, 91–4, 95–6; engages in *jihād*, 94, 97, 108; simplicity as keynote of, 96–7; abstains from politics, 99; as a source of legislation, 115, 144; two kinds of successors of, 186; improves status of women, 228; birthday of celebrated, 274

Muhammad Ali (Maulana), 201, 232, 387 n. 66

Mujeeb, M., 356

mujtahid (independent decisor), 69, 74, 143, 240, 301, 309, 318; of Qum, 308–9

mulk (temporal rule), 16, 87, 230; in relation to *khilāfa*, 17–27, 34, 120; natural to man, 18; modern significance of, 20–1, 26–7; stages in development of, 21

mullah, 147, 243, 258, 263, 279

Munir, Mr Justice M., 230; pronouncements of, 269–73

Munir Report, 203, 230, 233–5, 238, 240, 252, 263

Muqaddima (Ibn Khaldūn), 17, 177, 178

Musa, Salāma, 111–12

Muslim Brotherhood, 47, 85, 104, 112, 114, 122, 137, 185, 257, 327; ideology of, 116–17, 124

Muslim League, 189, 194–204 *passim*, 242, 257; Lahore Resolution of, 198, 250
Muslim state, contrasted with strictly Islamic, 26
Mussolini, Benito, 175

Nadwa, Al- (journal), 192
Nadwat-al-'Ulamā, 191, 192, 218
Nadwi, Sayyid Sulaiman, 191, 218, 212
naṣṣ (Qur'anic text), 68, 273; in relation to *'urf*, 52–4
nationalism, primary objective of, 3, 103, 201; relation of to Islam, 4–5, 316; Arab, 5, 29, 38, 103–24, 316, 371; changing character of, 11; Turkish, 28–63; Balkan, 38; as a spiritual value, 59; distinguished from patriotism, 65; as enemy of Islam, 104, 111, 129, 145, 374; as return to tribalism, 110; attitude of Ḥasan al-Bannā to, 116; as a Western conception, 118; political and spiritual, 118–21; Zuraiq on, 121; Indian, 193; in relation to internationalism, 243; Moroccan, 328, 370
Negri Sembilan, 297–8, 299, 300, 303, 306
Neguib, General, 218
Nehru, Jawaharlal, 282
Neo-Destour party, 317, 321, 323, 327, 341, 363
Nietzsche, F. W., 146, 198
Nizami, K. A., 187
North-West Frontier Province, 196
Nuseibeh, H. Z., 381 nn. 100, 104, 383 n. 32
nuṣūṣ, 140; as general principles, 126; codification of, 135–6

Objectives Resolution (Pakistan, 1949), 209, 214–29 *passim*, 250, 345
Omar (second caliph, d. 644), 133, 228
Osmania University (Hyderabad), 283
Ottoman dynasty, 58, 164
Ottoman state, 29–30, 36–7; backwardness of, 35

Padang Rengas, 359
Pahang, 299, 300
Pahlavi dynasty (Iran), 307
Pakistan, 4, 17, 34, 67, 117, 124, 182, 192, 311, 322, 323, 361; M. Asad's plans for, 125–36; Maudūdī's plans for, 137–53; creation of, 183–4, 193; minority problem in, 196; political and religious problems of, 200–9; constitutional debates in, 209–35; 'Islamic Republic of', 216, 225, 229, 265; end of Islamic Republic in, 235–7; views and attitudes in, 237–50; constitution commission in, 250–63; new constitution in, 263–81; emancipation of women in, 338–40; education in, 344–58
Pakistan, Constitutional Development in (G. W. Choudhury), 212
Pakistan: The Formative Phase (Khalid bin Sayeed), 194
pan-Arabism, 44, 117, 118, 121
pan-Islamism, 45, 59, 65, 117–23 *passim*, 288; logical basis of, 44; Abul Kalām Āzād on, 192–3
Paris, 319
Parliament, demanded by Mustafa Kāmil, 120; in Pakistan, 204, 208, 242–3, 268; in Malaya, 291; in Iran, 308; in Morocco, 330
Parsis, 212
Parwez, Ghulam A., 74, 205, 238, 244, 248, 257, 286; views of, 208–9, 227–8, 236; report of followers of, 252–8 *passim*
Patna, 283
Patriarchate, the, 30
Penang, 288, 289, 295, 303, 306
people, sovereignty of the, 6, 10, 57, 79, 115, 138, 160, 217; equated with *bay'a*, 29; Kāmil's concept of, 119–20; Asad on, 129
Perak, 303, 359
Perlis, 303, 311; constitution of, 293–4
Persia, 111
Persian (language), Qur'an translated into, 185
Persians, 60, 81
Peshawar, 244; University of, 246, 340
Plato, 20, 36, 43, 66, 100, 115, 217
political science, 217; neglected by Muslims, 100; contested, 147

politics, human and divine, 28; in relation to ethics, 43; Muslim divisions in, 188–94; Zafrullah Khan on, 211
Politics (Aristotle), 100
polygamy, 168–9, 219, 237, 245, 306; legislation on, 220, 275, 333–7
Pope, the, 78; authority of, 147
Principles of State and Government in Islam (Muhammad Asad), 125
prophecy, Ibn Khaldūn on, 18; Muḥammad al-Ghazālī on, 110
Protestantism, as alleged imitation of Islam, 57
Punjab, 196, 340; report on disturbances in, 203, 230; University of, 244
purdah, 355; in Swat, 246
Pushto (language), 348

qāḍī (judge), 170, 321; growing importance of, 24–5; in relation to *mufti*, 54, 56, 98; court system, 277; in Malaya, 292, 296–7, 300, 302, 303; in Iran, 308
Qadian, 231
Qadianis, 231–2
Qaid-i-Azam, the, 212, 250, 255
Qaid-i-Millat, the, 250
Qānūn, *qawīnīn* (political ordinances), 28, 313, 329; defined, 16; mixed with *Sharī'a*, 103; *qawānīn siyāsīya*, 29, 230; Ibn Khaldūn on, 22, 24, 26
Qaraites, 49, 128
Qarawīyīn (Fes), 174, 324, 326, 369, 372; antiquity of, 368
qiyās (analogy), 12–13, 140
Quraish, the, 69, 157
Qur'an, 73, 93, 95, 99, 166, 205, 334–5; as principle of jurisprudence, 12; as basis of *Sharī'a*, 13, 42, 47, 83–4, 125–7, 142; as basis of government, 15, 146, 208; N. Kemal's view of, 33; superiority of to science of morals, 36; commentary on, 68; on women's rights, 72; without relation to politics, 89; fundamental nature of, 111, 124, 184; translated into Persian and Urdu, 185; compatibility with modern science, 191; application in Pakistan, 209, 215, 217, 221–9 *passim*, 238–41, 252, 257; reinterpretation of, 244; misuse of, 299; teaching of, 349, 359, 360, 364–5, 370–1; social relevance of, 366
Qureshi, I. H., 227–8, 236, 240, 352
Quṭb, Sayyid, 112, 113, 123, 166

Rabat, 370; University of, 326, 361, 372
Rabwah, community at, 231–3
Radhakrishnan, S., 282
Rahbar, M. D., 186
Ramaḍān, Sa'id, 68, 123
Ramadhan, 261, 298; a novel interpretation of, 320
rasūl (apostle), authority of, 92
reason, 155; law of, 6, 11; conflict with revelation, 11
Reed, H. A., 378 n. 36
Reformation, the, 6
religion, 75, 109, 151, 247; political relevance of, 21–3, 26; separation of from politics, 28, 38, 79, 85–102, 211, 245, 280, 301, 305, 309; unity of with politics, 42, 211; in primitive and organic societies, 52; as character-building element, 55; as diminished social factor, 61; significance in modern Turkey, 62; use of for political ends, 95; linked with patriotism, 118, 156–7; in schools, 172–3; Muslim divisions in, 188–94; as ideology, 200–1; free exercise of, 213, 219, 229, 266, 280, 289, 312, 317, 329; views on in Pakistan, 240, 243, 245, 274–5; in opposition to secularism, 258; vitality of in Malaya, 304; equated with reaction, 314; as civilising force, 349, 367
Religious Affairs, Departments of (Malaya), 291, 295–305 *passim*, 359; Office of (Turkey), 312
Renaissance, the, 6
Republic (Plato), 20, 100
Repugnancy Clause (Pakistan), 215, 220–30 *passim*, 259, 265, 273
Reşīd Paşa, 30
Resolution on National Education (Pakistan), 347–50

Revolution
Egyptian (1952), 102; French, 104 (*see also* French Revolution), Russian, 104, 146
ribā (interest), 68, 136, 220, 365; Qur'anic prohibition of, 165; proposed elimination of, 214, 225, 230; interpretation of as usury, 267; in Malaya, 301, 304, 306
Riḍā, Muḥammad Rashīd, 13, 15, 17, 48, 59, 65, 86, 87, 103, 104, 106, 131, 191, 379 n. 6; views of, 66–85; on socialism, 91, 112
Roman tradition, 106
Rosenthal, E. I. J., 376 n. 5, 377, 381 n. 101
Rosenthal, F., 382 n. 21, 383 n. 38
Rousseau, J-J., 7, 29, 35, 66, 111, 146, 160
Russia, 112, 160, 161; universities in, 348

Sacy, Silvestre de, 66
Safavid dynasty, 309
Salaf, the, 14, 65, 122
Salafīya, the, 68, 75, 154, 169; *Neo-salafīya*, 154, 325
Sammān, Muḥammad 'Abdullah As-, 120, 129; views of, 115–16
Santillana, D., 319
Saudi Arabia, 359
Sayeed, Khalid bin, 194, 236
Sayyid, Aḥmad Lutfi al-, 122
Schacht, Joseph, xvi, 13, 103, 333, 391 ch. 12, n. 1
Selangor, 302–3
Selim I, sultan of Turkey (1465–1521), 58
Seljuks, 58, 59
Şeyh-ül-Islam, 34, 43, 44, 46, 98; wrong authority of over *qāḍīs*, 56
Shafi, Muhammad (Mufti), 218
Shāfi'ī, tenets, 296; rite, 296, 300; law, 302, 303
Shah Nawaz (Begum), 219; alleged suggestion of, 277
Shahabuddin, Mr Justice Muhammad, 250
Shahinshah, the, 307–8, 311
shar' dīnī, distinguished from *Sharī'a*, 101
Sharī'a, Şeriat, 19, 21–2, 45, 46, 48–9 66–85 *passim*, 97–8, 137, 143, 214, 240, 243, 261, 269, 283, 294, 301, 332, 336, 375; authority of, 8, 12, 15, 26; obstacles to acceptance of, 8–10; as ideal constitution, 13; Young Ottomans' respect for, 30–8; suspended by Atatürk, 33; political principles in, 41–2; as supreme law of Ottoman state, 47; traditional and social, 52–4; irrelevance to al-Rāziq, 89, 101; its fate vitally significant, 103, 106; real basis of, 125–6; Maudūdī's conception of, 139, 144; as basis of Moroccan law, 163–4, 170–1, 176; universal sufficiency of, 168; reconciled with *maṣlaḥa*, 186; adaptability of, 239, 308
Sharī'a-courts, 32, 65, 164, 277, 296–7, 308, 318, 337; abolished in Turkey, 311, 337
Sharī'a law, 120, 163, 237, 238, 292, 313, 336, 337
Shāṭibī, 142
Shaw, G. B., 110
Shawkat, Sami, 122, 383 n. 33
Shī'a (sect), 8, 307, 308
Shiblī (Maulana), 191–2, 195, 345
Shiraz, 310
Shirāzī, 309
shūrā (consultation), 43, 70, 72, 77, 101, 130–1, 149, 158, 208, 214, 253, 301; (Council of advisers), 236, 245
Sicily, 164
Sind, 196
Sindhi (language), 348
Singapore, 287–8, 306
siyāsa 'aqlīya, 17, 19–20, 120–1
siyāsa dīnīya, 17, 19–20
siyāsa mandanīya, 20
siyāsa shar'īya, 77, 88
social conscience, divine nature of, 53
Social Justice in Islam (Quṭb), 113, 123, 166
socialism, 284; Islamic, 91; Russian, 112; National (Germany), 146, 183; Christian, 165–6
society, four estates of, 66

Sorbonne, 319
sovereignty, views of Maudūdī on, 138, 144, 147; distinguished from authority, 210; *see also under* people
Spain, 164, 354; in occupation of Morocco, 171
Stalin, 175
state, new concept of, 6; classical concept of, 12–27; distinguished from nation, 51; Maudūdī's definition of, 146; Usmani on the Islamic, 211
statehood, emergence of, 3
Stephens, I., 385 n. 2, 386 n. 23, 387 n. 73
Steppat, F., 119, 120, 382 nn. 26–8
Suavi, Ali, 39
Sublime Porte, the, 30, 31
suffrage, in Pakistan, 243, 254, 269, 279, 355
suffragettes' movement, 73
Sufism, 121, 309, 322, 324; teaching of, 359
Suhrawardy, 309
sulṭān, 35, 92; threat of to caliphate, 13–14; governmental system of, 19; in Malayan states, 298
sultanate, the, 55–6
Süngü, I., 376 n. 1, 377 nn. 1, 5, 7
Sunna, 15, 33, 46, 73–4, 93, 95, 111, 146, 205, 334–5, 347; as basis of *Sharī'a*, 13, 83–4, 125–7, 142; as principle of jurisprudence, 12; without relation to politics, 89; on *ribā*, 165; Parwez on, 208; application in Pakistan, 215, 217, 221–8 *passim*, 238–41, 252, 257, 259
Sunnī, 107, 293
Supreme Court (Pakistan), 215, 220, 223, 224, 254, 270
Swat, Muslim state in, 245–6
Swiss Civil Code, adopted in Turkey, 54, 337, 390 n. 6
Switzerland, 338
Syria, 110, 112, 326

Taeschner, Fr., 378 n. 35
Tahtawi, Rifa'a Badawi Rafi' al-, 65
ṭalāq (divorce), 169, 170, 333, 335
Ta'līmat-i-Islamīa, Board of, 214, 215
Tanzimat (1839), 7, 55, 60; reaction to, 28–9, 30; incompatibility with *Şeriat*, 31–2
taqlīd (accepted legal authority), 24, 49, 67, 186–7
Tarjuman al-Quran (periodical), 153
ta'wīl (interpretation), 140
teachers, Hindu, 190; lay state advocated by, 241; girls trained to be, 246; lay teachers of religion, 312; supply of, 351, 363; trained at Al-Azhar, 360, 361
Tehran, 309; University of, 310, 361
theft, the penalty for, 273; inapplicability of, 209, 228; defended, 239
Theological Faculty, desirability of, 361
Tonnies, F., 51
Tolstoi, Leo, 154
Torah (Hebrew scriptures), 49, 74
treatises, constitutional, practical character of, 13–14
Trengganu, 298, 299, 300, 301
Trotsky, 146
True Islam (journal), 208
Tunaya, T., 39, 42, 46, 376 ch. 1, n. 1, 377 ch. 2, nn. 13f.
Tunis, 317, 341, 372; University of, 321, 361, 366
Tunisia, 89, 162, 333, 362, 369, 370, 371; Islam in, 316–24; code of 1956 in, 336; emancipation of women in, 340–1; education in, 363–8; Mufti of, 321
Turkey, 5, 101–2, 194, 317, 344, 367; modernisation of, 7; as Islamic state, 34; nationalism in, 28–63; Rashīd Riḍā on, 75–6; warned by Lord Cromer, 82; 'Allāl al-Fāsī on, 162, 173; as example for Pakistan, 240, 241; Islam in contemporary, 310–15; alleged failure of laicism in, 327; emancipation of women in, 340
Turkists, 44–5

'Udah, 'Abd al-Qādir, 124
'ulamā (Muslim scholars), 12, 13, 31, 66, 82, 103–4, 143, 205, 208, 335; rigidity of, 3, 284, 337; restricted function of, 25–6; lack of independence of, 70; as *mujtahids*, 77;

'*ulamā* (Muslim scholars) (*cont.*)
of Pakistan, 137, 214, 217–40 *passim*, 251, 257, 258, 274–9 *passim*; of Deoband, 187, 210; in Malaya, 301, 360; in Iran, 307, 308; in Tunisia, 319, 321, 368; in Morocco, 324, 325, 368; modern meaning of, 376 ch. 2, n. 1
Ulken, H. Z., 391 ch. 13, n. 3
'Umar, 133; *see* Omar
Umayyad dynasty, 14, 21, 23, 58, 75, 81, 90, 248
Umm al-banīn, Lycée, 326
umma (community of believers), 3, 7, 12, 118, 171; unity of the, 8, 13, 44, 327; in relation to *waṭan*, 38–9, 364, 371; in Gökalp's philosophy, 51, 57; co-existence with *waṭan*, 65; as creation of Muḥammad, 86; a definition of, 121; as nation, 123, 162, 236; identified with Legislature, 208
'*umrān* (civilisation), 24, 97
Union and Progress, Committee for, 55, 76
United Nations, 109, 132, 205, 234, 243, 244, 270, 364
United States of America, 240, 318; *see also* America
Universities, supplemented in Pakistan, 347; assisted, 350
Untouchability, outlawed in Pakistan, 216
Urdu (language), 189, 195, 285, 348–9; Qur'an translated into, 185
'*urf* (custom), 8, 16, 169; in relation to *naṣṣ*, 52–4
Usmani, Shabbir Ahmad, 201, 210, 211
Usūs al-ḥukm fī-l-Islām (As-Sammān), 115

Voice of Islam (journal), 243
Voltaire, F. M. A. de, 7, 146, 154, 155, 167

Wafd, the, 64, 70
Wahhabism, 13
Walī Ullāh, Shāh, 248, 283, 385 n. 6; views of, 185–8; letters of, 187; Qur'an translation of, 185, 186, 187; quoted, 260; Academy, 355
waqf (religious endowments), 64, 186, 215, 225, 291–2
wasaṭ (equilibrium), Ibn Taymīya on, 71, 76
waṭan (fatherland), 30, 65, 156, 158, 371; Nāmik Kemāl's concept of, 37–9; love of, 66, 119, 123, 171, 364
waṭanīya (nationalism), 123, 383 n. 34
Western influence, 3, 5–6, 9, 29, 104, 121, 332; danger of, 41; in religion, 62–3
Westernisers, 39, 45, 70, 80, 103–4, 210
Westernism, 47, 127, 155, 314; in relation to Islam, 48–63
women, 136, 305; position of, 64, 69, 72–3, 112–13, 163, 167–71, 208, 220, 243, 277, 323, 326; rights of, 71, 72, 150, 161, 207, 213, 237, 277, 330, 355; education of, 113, 171, 233, 348; status of improved by Muḥammad, 228; demonstrations by, 276, 338–9; emancipation of, 338–43; colleges for, 355
Union of Tunisian, work of, 340–1
Women, International Council of, 341
Women's Association, All Pakistan (APWA), 220, 248, 277, 342, 355, 358; activity of, 237–8, 339
Workers' Educational Association, 174

Yang di-Pertuan Agong, 288–96 *passim*
Young Ottomans, 28; aims of, 29, 37; accused of resisting progress, 35
Young Turks, 28, 39, 45, 75, 86; Revolution of (1908), 50

Zafrullah Khan, Mohammed, 211, 232
Zaghlūl Pasha, 70
Zaituna, the, 317, 321, 366–7, 372
Zakaria, N., 225–6
zakāt (alms), 108, 181, 209; as answer to social ills, 91, 140, 166; organisation of, 215, 225; in Malaya, 291–2, 297, 301, 306; defined, 389 n. 16
Zeb, Major-General Miangul Jahan, Wali of Swat, 245–6
Ziya Paşa, 29, 38; views of, 30–1, 36–7, 39
Zoroastrians, 205
Zuraiq, Qustantin, 121–2